Cunningham THE COMMANDER

Other books by S.W.C. Pack:

Anson's Voyage
Weather Forecasting
Admiral Lord Anson
The Battle of Matapan
Windward of the Caribbean
The 'Wager' Mutiny
'Britannia' at Dartmouth
Sea Power in the Mediterranean
Night Action off Cape Matapan
The Battle for Crete

1 (frontispiece) Commander-in-Chief, Mediterranean at Algiers, February 1943

Cunningham

THE COMMANDER

S.W.C. Pack
Captain RN, CBE, US Legion of Merit

SINK, BURN, DESTROY. Let nothing pass

B.T. BATSFORD LTD, *London*

I dedicate this book
to the memory of Admiral of the Fleet
Viscount Cunningham of Hyndhope,
KT, GCB, OM, DSO, LL.D,
and to the mutual trust between Allies
which that Great Sailor
did so much to inspire.

First published 1974
© S.W.C. Pack 1974

ISBN 0 7134 2788 4

Printed in Great Britain
by Cox & Wyman Ltd, Fakenham, Norfolk
for the publishers B. T. Batsford Ltd
4 Fitzhardinge Street, London W1H 0AH

Contents

List of Illustrations

List of Maps

Preface and Acknowledgments

This book is not a glorification of war, but a reminder of a great sailor whose brilliance and devotion to duty came to our aid in the nick of time. Let us never forget him: Admiral of the Fleet Viscount Cunningham of Hyndhope, KT, GCB, OM, DSO**, LL.D: a second Nelson. It requires no stretch of the imagination to say that without him this country could have lost the Hitler war; for it was because of Cunningham's resolute attitude that Britain determined to hold the Mediterranean, even when Malta was close to collapse and the Mediterranean Fleet had been badly battered though not beaten.

Admiral Sir Andrew Cunningham was appointed to the command of the Mediterranean Fleet in June 1939, and during the next four years built up an imperishable reputation. Defiant in adversity, and magnanimous in victory, he endeared himself not only to his own Fleet but to the Italians as well. His selection as Allied Naval Commander Expeditionary Force owed much to the high regard of the Americans, who admired his skill and resolution, and valued his integrity and optimism.

I was privileged to serve under Cunningham, first in the Mediterranean in 1941, and again in 1942 when Cunningham was a member of the Combined Chiefs of Staff Committee in Washington. I am most grateful for the numerous personal contributions and eye-witness accounts that have been sent to me. The enthusiasm shown in these has been encouraging, and they form a valuable collection. I regret that it has not been possible to include them all, owing to space restriction, but they have all nevertheless served their purpose in conveying a consistent and overall description. Those extracts which have been quoted are acknowledged in the Chapter References at the end of the book.

I particularly wish to thank the Viscountess Cunningham of Hyndhope for her kind help in permitting me to read and quote from her collection of letters, and also for permission readily given by her and by Messrs. Hutchinson & Co. for me to quote from *A Sailor's Odyssey*.

I am also grateful for access to, with permission to quote extracts where relevant, the unreserved sections of the Cunningham Add. MS at the British Museum, and the Cunningham Papers at Churchill College, Cambridge. I wish to add my thanks to Stephen Roskill and Oliver Warner for hospitality, help, and encouragement given: all much appreciated.

In addition to using my own notes and the contributions which were

sent to me, I have consulted the books listed under Bibliography at the
end of the book, and wish to thank authors, publishers, and copyright
holders for the privilege of quoting brief extracts. Also at the end of the
book are appendixes giving (I) a summary of Cunningham's life, (II)
code names of conferences and operations, and (III) common
abbreviations.

Rear-Admiral Royer Dick who was in turn Staff Officer (Plans),
Deputy Chief of Staff, and Chief of Staff to Cunningham, and served
him over a long term of years, has very kindly read my manuscript and
helped immeasurably with valuable suggestions and contributions. This
kindness has added greatly to the authority and value of the book, and I
much appreciate it.

I am very grateful for the considerable help provided by Messrs.
Brennan, Hine, and Squires in the selection of photographs appropriate
for reproduction, and wish to thank the Imperial War Museum for
permission to reproduce them. In order to convey acknowledgment, I
should be glad to trace the source of the picture of H.M.S. *Rodney*,
kindly lent by Mr. Carter of the National Maritime Museum, to whom
I owe my thanks. I am also indebted to Colonel E. P. J. Ryan for the
picture of the high power group at Teheran.

I am greatly indebted to Britannia Royal Naval College for information
concerning Cunningham's training time in the *Britannia*, and also for
help generally from the College library.

Once again I wish to express my thanks to Miss Freda Busby for her
splendid typing and great ability in deciphering my hand-writing, and
for making useful suggestions. Above all I owe the greatest gratitude to
my wife for her endless encouragement and help.

Blossom's Pasture,   S. W. C. Pack
Devon

'Remember then, that your life's vocation, deliberately chosen, is WAR – WAR, as I have said, as the means of peace: but still WAR: and in singleness of purpose, for England's fame, prepare for the time when the welfare and honour of the Service may come to be in your keeping'.

Extract from Alsons's *Seamanship Manual*, 1865

Mr Winston Churchill, as First Lord of the Admiralty, while on passage to Boulogne in H.M.S. *Codrington* of the Dover Patrol, 4 April 1940, asked the captain, Casper Swinley, to read this to him.

A Glimpse of Cunningham

It is appropriate that in a series which includes such names as Nelson, Napoleon, Hitler, Rommel, Eisenhower, Alexander, and Montgomery, the name Admiral of the Fleet Viscount Cunningham of Hyndhope, KT, GCB, OM, DSO**, LLD, should also appear. Without the benefit of Anglo-American supremacy at sea, and the availability of vast allied naval forces of which by common consent Cunningham became commander (under Eisenhower as supreme commander), neither Alexander nor Montgomery could have landed in Sicily and Italy in 1943, finally penetrating the Fortress of Europe after four years of occupation by the Axis powers.

Nor is it likely that Rommel would have been stopped at the gates of Egypt had there been no Cunningham to dominate the central and eastern Mediterranean in those grim days when Britain was alone, and a miraculous success such as the TIGER convoy, fought right through to Alexandria in May 1941 in spite of German air superiority, enabled 238 desperately needed tanks and 43 Hurricane aircraft to reach, by the shortest route, the British Command in the Middle East.

Just as Nelson had become a major obstacle for Napoleon, so had Cunningham for Hitler and Mussolini, nearly a century and a half later. In both instances, sea power was the crucial factor, exploited to the full by both Nelson and Cunningham, sometimes against great odds. Names such as Calabria, Taranto, Tripoli, Matapan, and TIGER convoy are reminders of Cunningham's continually aggressive policy at a time when his fleet suffered material and numerical inferiority compared with the powerful new ships of Italy, and he himself was determined to miss no opportunity to reduce the balance. His one aim was to retain British control of the Mediterranean in spite of the absence of allies and the desperate shortage of air power and military equipment.

Never to be forgotten is Cunningham's famous signal to his fleet during the supreme test in the battle for Crete: 'Stick it out. Navy must not let Army down', and his insistence on a principle summed up in his equally famous aphorism: 'It takes the Navy three years to build a ship. It would take three hundred to rebuild a tradition.' There is little doubt that without the stubborn if hopeless British and Imperial resistance to the German occupation of Greece and Crete, Hitler's carefully planned blitzkrieg into Russia June 1941 would have been successful; Hitler regarded the subjugation of Britain as the immediately next step to follow what he intended to be the lightning conquest of Russia.

Cunningham of Hyndhope, known more affectionately by his initials ABC, is widely regarded as the greatest seaman of modern times, respected not only in his own country but abroad as well. The US Navy's Chief of Naval Operations, 1941–45, Fleet Admiral Ernest J. King, admired Cunningham's fighting qualities, and saw in him a spiritual successor to Admiral of the Fleet the Earl of St. Vincent (1735–1823). General Eisenhower had the utmost confidence in Cunningham's appointment as Allied Naval Commander in 1942. In spite of numerous differences of strategical opinion during the difficult planning stages for the combined Anglo-American landings on the North African coast, allied plans were agreed, and executed with mutual co-operation and success, all the naval and maritime forces being under Cunningham's command. Eisenhower's confidence in Cunningham grew in the following months, and he is recorded as saying that he thought him 'the finest gentleman he had ever met' and of the North African Campaign, that he made no major decision without first asking ABC's opinion.[1] A successor to Eisenhower, in his later role as Supreme Allied Commander in Europe, was General Alfred M. Gruenther who wrote:

'We all loved Admiral Cunningham very much. He had a delightful flair which attracted people to him. He was brilliant; he was interested in others; and he had an unchallengeable integrity. The world is a much better place because of his stay here.'

Flair, brilliance, interest, integrity: four essential characteristics for a successful commander. A fifth should be mentioned at this stage: voice. Cunningham seldom used a loud voice, but he spoke with deliberation and assurance. Admiral Sir Sidney Meyrick writes of him as a junior Rear-Admiral attending tactical courses in 1933: 'His opinion was always listened to and valued . . . he was looked upon as treading that narrow road towards the top.' Another, who particularly remembers his voice from the early destroyer days says: 'It was a friendly voice even in anger. It did not matter what words he used to a defaulter, or in giving orders. The voice had a charm which endeared him to everyone, even if they did not realise it.'

By most, Cunningham will for ever be remembered for his courageous command in the Mediterranean 1940–42, and his resolute and relentless determination to overcome the enemy, whatever the difficulties and shortages his fleet suffered. He will be remembered not only for victories such as Matapan and Taranto, but also for the gallant struggle to defend Crete against overwhelming enemy air superiority and his policy that the army must be looked after by the navy, whatever the cost.

To lend conviction and verisimilitude to what might otherwise appear as general statements about ABC in this first chapter, which is virtually an introduction, it is appropriate to quote particular extracts of letters from those who served with him or knew him, many of whom themselves became distinguished and brilliant leaders. Some of the letters refer to his infectious optimism or to his sense of humour, others to his humanity in spite of a frequently forced appearance of ruthlessness. There is an exhilaration in others, expressing pride at having been associated with ABC's 'band of brothers'. One may at first look askance at some of the superlatives, but there can be no denying the greatness of a man who is the subject of so much spontaneous veneration and whose qualities of leadership are extolled repeatedly and with deep affection.

And what about the debit side? Few adverse remarks were received by the author, and those appeared to stem mainly from an inability on the informant's part to accept justifiable rebuke. They have, of course, been included here. Cunningham was not one to suffer fools gladly, and he was not slow to reproach any serving officer or man who was irresolute or was lacking in effort to achieve the highest standard. Cunningham's aim was perfection, and with that goal in mind he drove himself and those serving under him. He was not a big man in stature, but his steely blue eyes revealed an iron determination that was not to be thwarted.

'He exuded confidence and inspiration,' writes Ravenhill,[2] ... 'he understood the stresses which his officers and men were subjected to in war, and he frequently overlooked misdemeanours, provided he was satisfied that the culprit was normally loyal and conscientious. ... As a leader Cunningham was quite unequalled.'

Admiral Glennie[3] had 'abounding affection and admiration for ABC', and says, 'No other officer could have driven the Fleet as he did and got the results which he achieved, often under almost impossible pressure from London and misunderstanding by his fellow Commanders-in-Chief. There were those who could not stand him, considering him a bully and careless of other people's opinions and feelings. I will not go along with this at any price.'

Admiral Lord Tovey, who was not one to make exaggerated statements, referred to Cunningham as the greatest sailor Britain had had since Nelson.[4] Admiral Sir Bernard Rawlings, himself very highly thought of by Cunningham and the navy generally, especially in view of his gallantry at Crete, considered ABC *'the greatest sailor of all time'*.[5]

Referring again to the qualities of confidence and inspiration, it is apparent from the many reports of those who served in his fleet that Cunningham's presence during a sortie had such a stimulating effect as to extract the utmost endeavour from all concerned. 'If the "old man" was in the *Warspite*,' writes Rear-Admiral R. L. Fisher,[6] 'they knew everything would be all right. What is more, the Italians knew that it wouldn't be all right for them.'

This supreme confidence in ABC's ability to succeed is revealed in a number of reports, and dates back long before the Second World War. His messenger, when Cunningham was captain of H.M.S. *Rodney* in 1930, was Ordinary Seaman Amos West[7] who describes a sailing race at Palma in which he was crewing for ABC in the gig, an attractive, fast carvel-built boat with two dipping lugsails. At a moment when all seemed to be going well and ABC had a comfortable lead, the tiller broke. They were at least a mile from the ship, and *there was no spare tiller*. West refers to his own unbounded confidence that his captain would nevertheless be able to sail them back without a tiller. 'But there was Hell to pay when we returned,' he concludes, 'because there was no spare tiller in the gig.'

Cunningham's assistant secretary,[8] when he was commanding the Battle Cruiser Squadron, describes his great sense of justice. He illustrates with an incident in which a steel wire parted when the mighty *Hood* was being berthed alongside a jetty in 1937, and a number of young seamen were severely injured. Vice-Admiral Andrew Cunningham had only recently taken over the command of the Battle Cruiser Squadron from Vice-Admiral Sir Geoffrey Blake who was ill. A Board of Inquiry had already found the Lieutenant-Commander of the quarter-deck to blame for the incident, and he had been disciplined accordingly. Cunningham however looked afresh at the circumstances, and when it was found that the accident was due to the action of those on the bridge, he had the decision reversed and the officer of the quarter-deck cleared of all blame. Cunningham himself had a great reputation for ship handling, picked up during his long service in destroyers, and although he experienced some qualms at first in handling the 34,000-ton *Rodney* he found little difficulty in applying this aptitude in the narrowest of waters as soon as he had got used to what he called 'her majestic dilatoriness' in answering helm and propellers.

As Captain (D) he encouraged all destroyers to manoeuvre at the highest practicable speed consistent with safety and local considerations, especially when getting under way to leave harbour, or securing upon arrival. The same outlook applied when he became Rear-Admiral (D) in the Mediterranean in 1934.

'You could bet your bottom dollar,' writes McCall,[9] 'that if *Coventry* his flagship was in harbour, and that if you had to pass her to take up your berth, that he would be on deck to see what sort of a job you made of it ... going up Sliema Creek stern first with the maximum speed and the minimum of orders to take up Head and Stern buoys, an evolution on which ABC set much store.'

A further instance of Cunningham's love of justice is illustrated in a story by Commander Isaac,[10] his secretary 1934–36:

'When destroyers were engaged in night exercises off Alexandria, a collision occurred in pitch darkness between two of them proceeding at 25 knots, and both were seriously damaged. Having studied the report from the Captain (D) concerned, ABC recommended that no disciplinary action should be taken. The Commander-in-Chief agreed with him that a collision in such circumstances was always a possibility, and provided it was not due to negligence or carelessness, which would result in a court-martial, any disciplinary action would tend to stifle the initiative of commanding officers.'

On the other hand, when Regulations were disregarded or disobeyed, ABC did not hesitate to take a stern line.

There is frequent reference by officers who were on his staff to his being 'a hard taskmaster' and that they were 'driven hard', but this is covered by such statements as 'he was thoroughly fair and human'. Having been addressed on the bridge as a B.F. one of them found solace when later offered a glass of sherry by ABC in his sea cabin. Right from very early days Cunningham possessed an outstanding air of authority and confidence, derived not only from a continuous command of torpedo craft for 11 years from the age of 25, of which seven were spent in the famous *Scorpion*, but stemming also from his own self-reliance developed through hard work and application, together with speed of thought and clarity of mind. It is fashionable today to condemn authoritativeness as tyrannical arrogance, and to show a preference for conciliation or appeasement. It is a matter of controversy as to which quality produces better results, but there can be little doubt that taut discipline and the rule of law led to a maintenance of high standard and a happy sense of achievement in his ships' companies. For Cunningham, nothing below perfection seemed to be acceptable, and his methods may at times have appeared to be brutal, but they worked. It is a measure of his greatness that he was able to instil in others the drive and initiative which he himself possessed in such large measure. And, with few exceptions, his officers and men admired and liked him all the more for his drive and strength of will. Referring to the ABC of 1943 Harold Macmillan[11] wrote: 'Everyone loved him, even if many were rather frightened of him.'

Brutality, bullying, belligerence, fighting, aggression: all are harsh words somewhat loosely used at times to denote a quality of being resolute in the preservation of order. Methods used in the navies have varied over the years, and although for example flogging was regarded by many as inhuman, the conditions of the times required it, when decent seamen might have to share the mess-deck with rogues from the gaols who would stop at nothing, but for the existence of traditional deterrents. It is interesting to read a sentence of Cunningham's in which he accepts the need for 'sticking a pin into people', a favourite expression of his, as a necessary process towards the preservation of excellence. In *A Sailor's Odyssey*, p. 54, he refers to 'our new Captain (D) ... was a man of strong character who demanded, and obtained, a very high standard. We liked him, particularly as he allowed no one to bully us but himself.'

There will be many who remember nostalgically the joyous singing of hymns by ships' companies assembled every Sunday on the quarter-deck before the abolition of compulsory church. Judging by the enthusiasm with which they sang such hymns as 'Onward Christian soldiers', and 'Soldiers of Christ arise', they seemed to enjoy every minute of this compulsory devotion which was so brutally forced upon them by existing regulations. Himself devout, how ABC would smile at the prospect now of each man trying to muster moral courage to attend something he likes but which is almost barred by being voluntary. Except for the individual-ist, the cynical service expression 'never volunteer for anything' still very largely applies.

Like Admiral Lord Anson two centuries earlier, Cunningham was resolute. There was little that would deter him from his purpose even when hardships, shortages, and disasters befell him. At a time when his fleet was near breaking point during the evacuation of the army from Crete, and in spite of disastrous losses of men and ships, and his own diminished supplies of ammunition, he brought in a note of optimism in a signal which said 'STICK IT OUT'. There are indications that enemy resources are stretched to the limit. We can and must outlast them.' It proved to be a close-run thing. Crete was lost; nevertheless Cunningham's fleet, in spite of near exhaustion and disastrous losses, took off 17,000 British and Imperial troops, and preserved a long-held tradition.

Cunningham was an admirer of Anson, and must have had in mind the latter's instructions prior to departure for the South Seas[12] 'to annoy and distress the Spaniards . . . by sinking, burning, or otherwise destroying all their ships' when he issued his famous signal from Tunis 8 May 1943: 'Sink, burn, destroy; let nothing pass.'

Cunningham also resembled Anson in his insistence on training and preparedness. On 3 May 1747 Anson surprised and captured all nine French warships of a fleet escorting a valuable convoy off Finisterre. Cunningham never missed an opportunity of getting to sea for exercises, and 'was always the first to sight the attacking destroyers', writes Commander Wilkinson.[13] 'It amused me as officer of the watch to see the Admiral's staff searching for the enemy with their super night glasses, and yet being seen off by ABC. I cannot remember his ever using binoculars at night. His vast experience enabled him to know exactly what to look for, no matter what the visibility.' His inistence on night exercises in peacetime certainly paid off at the battle of Matapan.

There is a further similarity between Anson and Cunningham, and this applies to humanity generally, and in particular towards prisoners of war. Anson's reputation for fair treatment of Spanish prisoners spread quickly in the South Seas, and led to an alleviation of conditions and a slackening of the deprivations at first suffered by some of his men who were captured after the shipwreck of H.M.S. *Wager*. Admiral Iachino,[14] the 1941–42 Italian fleet commander-in-chief, praises Cunningham for his recognition of the gallantry of Italian naval officers who damaged Cunningham's battleships H.M.S. *Queen Elizabeth* and H.M.S. *Valiant* in Alexandria harbour on the night of 19 December 1941. He also extols Cunningham's behaviour when he 'demonstrated his noble and generous character by communicating to Rome on the morning of 29 March 1941 the positions of the wrecks of the Cattaneo Division'. Cunningham had sunk five of Iachino's ships in a night attack off Cape Matapan, and was picking up Italian survivors when his fleet was spotted by reconnaissance aircraft. In spite of the risk of divulging his own position and probable movement, he was determined that the positions of survivors should be known to Italian authorities; many of them were later picked up by an Italian hospital ship. In reprisal German Stukas attacked Cunningham's fleet heavily later that day.

With his typical brevity, Cunningham comments on Anson:[15] 'He was a great organiser and a fine seaman – Dudley Pound was to some extent like him, more of the former than the latter.' Cunningham's own resemblance had more of the latter than the former. In matters of administration he was effectual by decentralisation, with an overriding supervision, but he placed great reliance on his staff. He was not fond of paper work. In matters of seamanship, he was unsurpassable, and this included strategical and tactical warfare.

In matters of ceremony, dress, and the customs of the Service, Cunningham was a stickler. He took great pride in the traditions of the Royal Navy, and was insistent on smartness, punctuality, and marks of respect, though prepared to waive such matters if it was in the interest of the Service to do so. His practical attitude was 'Let's get on with it': what his messenger Amos West described as being 'always on a split yarn'.

An incident which occurred at Alexandria in 1941 is worth telling. A motor-boat belonging to an Australian destroyer was leaving the shore jetty when a man in plain clothes asked the coxswain if he could put him on board *Warspite* as he passed. The coxswain agreed, but he told the man, whom he believed to be the *Warspite*'s canteen manager, that he would have to jump for the ladder as they passed *Warspite*'s gangway; clutch trouble prevented the boat from going astern. The passenger duly jumped as the boat swept past the flagship's middle gangway. On arrival at his own ship the coxswain was shown a signal from the Commander-in-Chief to the commanding officer thanking him for a lift. Only then did he realise the identity of the passenger he had ordered to jump.

The main mood in the fleet at that time was a reflection of Cunningham's determination to get to grips with the enemy. Barnard[16] writes:

'Whenever enemy forces were reported at sea in a position which gave us a possible chance of interception before they could get back home, ABC's burning desire to get at them and utterly destroy them would at once become evident to those of the staff who knew the form. He would pace one side of the Admiral's bridge, always the side nearest the enemy; the speed of advance of the battleship was never fast enough for him and every second was grudged when a turn from the main line of advance was required for operating aircraft. This mood was known colloquially among the staff as the "caged tiger act". . . . It was always, for all beholders, an inspiring example of single-minded concentration on the one object of getting to close grips with the enemy.'

With his desire to 'get moving' ABC had more regard for the personal side of things than the material, and attached tremendous importance to morale, persuasion, inspiration, method, and example. His messenger in the *Rodney* describes a small but penetrating incident when the ship was lying at the detached mole at Gibraltar after the combined fleet exercises in 1930. Captain Cunningham was at work at his desk in his vast day cabin. Ordinary Seaman Moss was within call in the lobby, improving the shining hour by reading the Seamanship Manual (as recommended by ABC). Suddenly there was a dull thud and a short sound of scraping as the great ship rubbed against the mole. The quarter-deck hands were renewing a wire hawser, an evolution which could be done noiselessly and without unwanted movement of the ship, provided the eye of the new cable was first slipped through that of the old cable. The jarring sound indicated that this precaution had been omitted, probably because of slack supervision. ABC at once sent Moss away to get a spare lanyard, and asked him to demonstrate the evolution using a model bollard with two lanyards to represent the old and new cables. Only when he was assured that his own messenger knew how, did he send for the officer of the quarter-deck to raise the matter. 'There was hell to pay,' concluded Moss, who himself was frequently being asked during a round of the ship, 'What's that for?' 'I don't know' was not an acceptable answer. 'I will find out' was the right answer, and ABC would ensure that he did.

The following incident reveals a rare mishap for Cunningham. As a Commander in command of H.M.S. *Termagant*, he took part in Keyes's raid on the German submarine base at Zeebrugge in April 1918. Although this was a celebrated episode in naval history, he makes little of it in *A Sailor's Odyssey*. The *Termagant*'s Engineer Officer describes how Cunningham was ordered to tow out of the harbour an ex-Mersey ferry-boat which had been in close action and had suffered heavy casualties. With his usual impetuosity he wanted 15 knots by the engines *at once*. A 6-inch wire might cope with a 500-ton ship at a steady speed, but not when subjected to sudden acceleration. 'The tow parted,' writes his engineer. Nevertheless the necessary acceleration was achieved at the next attempt, and she was got clear. There were 75 dead lying about the decks when the tow finally began.

There is a story which reveals Cunningham's constant concern about expenditure, a feature which appears to have been remembered by a number of people who point out that it sometimes lacked judgment and proved to be a false economy. His Fleet Gunnery Officer[17] who joined him in the Mediterranean Fleet late in 1941 writes:

'One of the first things I wanted to do as FGO was to get the ammunition of the fleet ashore, instead of having it in an ammunition supply ship in harbour, and wrote a paper proposing this. Not knowing ABC well at that time I included among my reasons the fact that the ammunition would be safer from bombing and its issue to the fleet would be easier, and thus efficiency would increase. It would cost about £6,000.

'In due course ABC sent for me and said, "I don't pay £6,000 to increase the efficiency of departments. I stick pins into them'." He then threw the papers at me and I withdrew.

'I think it was within a week that the Master of the ammunition supply ship accidentally blew his scuttling charges; his ship with all the 15-inch ammunition for the fleet sank. I at once returned with my proposal to put the ammunition ashore, and ABC with a twinkle in his eye said: "If only you had done what I told you to do a week ago this would not have happened".'

Cunningham was not one to grovel. Such behaviour might undermine authority. The twinkle in the eye was sufficient admission that there could have been an error of judgment; one liked him all the more for it. Admiral Glennie describes how one felt 'the great strength of the man', and how one never failed to leave his presence with 'a sense of uplift', and yet 'he was kindness itself' especially in difficult circumstances.

In similar vein Admiral Dalrymple-Hamilton[18] says that his 'presence was most stimulating and one never came away from an interview with him without the feeling that one was treading on air and that all problems and worries would soon fade out. He was thoroughly imbued with Nelson's principles.'

General O'Connor[19] who did so brilliantly in the Western Desert December 1940–January 1941, advancing 500 miles to Benghazi in two months, supported by the guns of the Royal Navy and the ships of the Inshore Squadron, writes:

'I was tremendously impressed by Admiral Cunningham and could well understand the admiration and affection in which he was held. . . . He was at his best commanding the fleet in the Mediterranean. He was the greatest sailor since Nelson.'

Admiral Sir William James[20] is also much of the same mind and writes: 'His Mediterranean Campaign was one of the greatest episodes in our history.'

Perhaps Cunningham's proudest moment was the occasion of the submission of the Italian fleet when he made a signal to the Admiralty 11 September 1943: 'Be pleased to inform Their Lordships that the Italian Battle Fleet now lies at anchor beneath the guns of the fortress of Malta.' The American General Bradley (*A Soldier's Story*, 1951) says 'Cunningham had a right to be proud. For three desperate years he had held the Mediterranean Sea lanes open to Malta and Suez, even though Axis air attacks had cost the lives of hundreds of British seamen.' ABC, who was a master of words, would have disagreed with the use of the word 'desperate' which literally means 'without hope'. With unfailing optimism and resolution he never gave up hope.

During his life (see summary in Appendix I) which spanned 80 years (1883–1963), he exercised command in every rank in the Royal Navy from midshipman to Admiral of the Fleet, serving in three wars. It was in destroyers that he first made his name as an outstanding commander, but it is with the Mediterranean that his imperishable memory will always be associated, first in the years of peril 1940 to 1942 as Commander-in-Chief, and again as Commander of the Allied Fleets in 1942–43 before his final appointment as First Sea Lord at the Admiralty. Less well known but quite as important is the time spent in Washington in 1942 with the Combined Chiefs of Staffs Committee, when so many important command decisions and strategic plans had to be agreed.

Mahan once said that Nelson was the embodiment of the sea power of Britain. Of Cunningham it could well be said that he typified all that was best in the Royal Navy's tradition of the offensive spirit.

A description of Cunningham by Captain Smith, his assistant secretary for so many years, ends with a fervent prayer:

'God grant that such a commander comes when the Royal Navy needs him again.'

Fight You on Sunday:
Formative Years (1883–98)

Andrew Cunningham was born in Dublin of Scottish parents on 7 January 1883, and joined the Royal Navy 14 years later, entering the cadet training ship H.M.S. *Britannia* at Dartmouth on 15 January 1897, eight days after his fourteenth birthday. None of his forebears had served at sea, but he himself had always been interested in boats and the sea, and during his service career he became a dedicated boat sailer, taking more interest in that sport than in any other game. He professes to have been mediocre at games, and it is evident that while in the *Britannia* he preferred to spend most of his spare time becoming proficient in sail and seamanship. Although the race between navies to supersede sailing ships by steam-propelled ironclads had already begun, there was still much sail in use in the Royal Navy in the nineties. H.M.S. *Wave*, a barque-rigged sailing and steam-driven vessel of 300 tons, and the barque-rigged sloop H.M.S. *Racer* of 970 tons, were tenders to the *Britannia*, borne for the purpose of instruction in sail, steam, and the use of chart and compass. The aim was to cruise under sail, perhaps for a week, in summer months only, and to use steam for entering and leaving harbour. Steam was one of the subjects in the training curriculum which comprised (in addition to seamanship, the most popular subject), mathematics, physics, navigation, naval history, English, French, and drawing. The standard was high, and mathematics, for example, extended to spherical trigonometry for the solution of problems in nautical astronomy. Entry was keenly competitive, and acceptance rightly regarded as an indication of high ability.

Religious knowledge was yet another important subject, in which instruction was provided every day in the *Britannia*.[1] This subject was so highly regarded at one cramming establishment for naval entry, that the principal was seen by his wife to 'take up a Bible and hit a little boy very hard on the head, saying, "Damn you, you little devil, I'll teach you not to know who Jesus was".'[2] Cunningham had spent his three cramming years at Stubbington, where the teaching of scripture to the laggards was assisted by the stimulating use of a switch. He refers to the 'driving' of knowledge into the 'heads of the unintelligent', and remarks approvingly on the fact that he remembered much of what he learnt there.

Cadet Cunningham was fourteenth in order of merit among the 65 cadets of his term entering the *Britannia*, and tenth on passing out in April 1898. He refers to himself as being lazy and not having to work really hard, but this presumably is as he saw it from his own standard of what hard work should really entail. On passing out he was awarded a First Class Pass in Mathematics and in Seamanship, and a Second Class Pass in other subjects.

In reply to a particular question as to whether Cunningham showed any gift of leadership while in the training ship, one of his term-mates[3] writes:

'We were very young in the *Britannia* of our day, 13 or 14 years, and were hustled through our time in the ship due to the expanding Fleets. I believe we were the second term to stay only 15 months against the previous two years. I would say that Cunningham showed no interest in leadership in the ship but was very much above the average all round. He will be principally remembered at Dartmouth for his offensive spirit and could be seen paying off old scores up at the field on Sunday afternoons. "Fight you on Sunday" was the cadet way of clinching an argument. He was called "Meat Phaz" because of his propensity for fighting and a bloody face.'

The list of punishments issued to Cadet Cunningham is of interest. For the best part of a year in the *Britannia* he received only two minor punishments. In the final four months, however, from 4 December 1897 to 28 March 1898, his recorded transgressions increased to an average of more than two a month, and the punishments were more severe: e.g. '2 days' No. 7' involved being segregated from the remainder of the cadets throughout two days and two nights, and being taken for a walk on the side of the river opposite to the normal landing place. A white band would be worn round the left arm, and the punishment might start with a public caning of six or 12 strokes carried out by the Chief Petty Officer in the presence of all cadets assembled on deck and standing to attention to witness punishment.[4] And all this for 'laughing in study'. One might think that such treatment would act as a deterrent, but it seems instead to have acted as a spur to Cunningham to see how far he could misbehave and make fun, and how much punishment he could take. Here was resilience in the making.

His conduct was assessed as Very Good, despite the following misdemeanours:

3 Mar. '97	Bringing sweets on board	2 weeks' pocket money stopped
18 May '97	Talking at Muster after being cautioned	1 day's No. 4
4 Dec. '97	Laughing in study after being punished with a Mod. (one hour's drill)	2 days' No. 7
11 Dec. '97	Improperly dressed at Muster	1 day's No. 4
21 Jan. '98	Talking in study after being cautioned	1 day's No. 4
26 Jan. '98	Skylarking at Muster	1 day's No. 3
24 Feb. '98	Slack in dressing and leaving sleeping deck	1 day's No. 4
11 Mar. '98	Talking in study after being cautioned	1 day's No. 3
12 Mar. '98	Improperly marching to study	1 day's No. 4
24 Mar. '98	Misbehaviour in the Mess Room	7 day's No. 5
28 Mar. '98	Disobeying Cadet Captain's orders	1 day's No. 3

It is a moot point whether heredity or environment is the predominant factor in the making of character, and it is reasonable to assume that each plays its part. There are some individuals, however, who are not greatly influenced by environment. Others may be deeply affected by this factor, perhaps because of the very existence of some hereditary quality. Be that as it may, there seem to have been few cadets on whom the *Britannia* training left little impression, and there were many who later praised its high value. It was tough, effectual, and practical; and discipline was good. Deserved punishment was taken with a pride. At one period (in 1891), six years before Cunningham joined, bullying was reputed to be rife, but this was stamped out. Part of the training was to imbue each of the young gentlemen with the sense of being an officer; they had their servants, were addressed as 'Mr.', and were required to have tidy hair, and caps fitting correctly. Among many celebrated names of cadets who had entered the *Britannia* (dates in brackets), and reached the highest rank, were John Jellicoe (1872), David Beatty (1884), Ernle Chatfield (1886), and Dudley Pound (1890), each of whom in due course became First Sea Lord. Andrew Cunningham (1897) was destined to succeed Dudley Pound in 1939 as Commander-in-Chief Mediterranean, and in 1943 as First Sea Lord.

Another celebrity, who entered the *Britannia* a decade before Andrew Cunningham, was 'Ginger' Boyle, later Admiral of the Fleet the Earl of Cork and Orrery, GCB, GCVO, who has given a picture of 'a very happy existence',[5] indicating that fighting was all part of the happiness, and did not apply only in Cunningham's day. He describes an inter-term fight:

'About 120 boys took part on a Sunday afternoon, the opposing forces being ranged up in two lines facing each other on the football field, and the battle was started by the dropping of a handkerchief by, of all people, the Chief Cadet Captain, who was subsequently disrated for this lapse on his part.

'When the flag fell the two lines charged and went for each other with their fists. A somewhat desultory engagement ensued and lasted until the lieutenant of the day was sighted approaching at the double, when the combatants scattered and fled in all directions.

'Not much harm resulted, a few broken fingers and black eyes being the chief injuries.'

Andrew Cunningham's term were described as a fine lot, with the superb record of two of them (A. B. Cunningham and J. Somerville) becoming Admirals of the Fleet, one of them (C. J. C. Little) becoming a full Admiral, and two (B. J. D. Guy and E. G. Robinson) gaining the Victoria Cross. The record speaks well for the forward-looking attitude of 'Fight you on Sunday'. It probably owes much also to the fine character of the Term Lieutenant George Trewby who later rose to Flag rank, the Commander Christopher Cradock who died gallantly against great odds at the battle of Coronel in 1914, and the Captain the Hon. A. G. Curzon-Howe who was renowned for his punctilious manner, a quality certainly imbued in Cunningham. Mention should also be made of the Naval Instructor the Reverend N. B. Lodge whom Cunningham regarded as the best teacher he ever had. The Director of Studies was J. C. P. Aldous, known to the cadets as 'Jeremy Yap Yap'; he had been appointed Chief Naval Instructor as long ago as 1875 and remained in charge of studies for 23 years.

From the hereditary angle Cunningham was well endowed, for both his paternal grandfather and his father were gold medallists, and of a scholarly nature. The grandfather had a determined character, and, though a little unorthodox, had advanced views. He was an influential member of the Church of Scotland and became a DD of the University of St. Andrews, a LLD of Glasgow University, and a LLD of Trinity College, Dublin. He possessed a keen sense of humour and loved a fight. Although he died when ABC was only ten, he left a keen impression upon the latter, especially in the matter of prompting the Sunday recital of psalms which was customary in the presence of grandmother, who was rather a disciplinarian and sometimes filled the grandchildren with awe.

ABC's father was popular with most people with whom he came into contact. He was a hard worker; a 1st Class graduate in Medicine; later an MD; and a Professor of Anatomy, first in Dublin, later in Edinburgh. He was the author of a standard book on Anatomy. He possessed the family characteristics of determination and self-confidence in a marked degree; qualities which helped to restore stability after the loss of savings due to the failure of a Glasgow bank, at a time soon after his marriage. Because of the loss, the early part of the marriage was not easy and must have led to a stringent attitude towards spending which may have left its mark on ABC, who was always careful over the spending of public money, especially when he held senior appointments. The father had a bold and distinguished handwriting, as had also ABC. His life was very fully occupied, and he continued working until his death in 1909 at the age of 59, while in the Chair of Anatomy at Edinburgh University. In addition to being elected a Fellow of the Royal Society he received the honorary degrees of MD and DSC from the University of Dublin, DCL from Oxford, and LLD from the Universities of St. Andrews and Glasgow. Because of his many activities and strenuous work his children saw little of him except in the summer holidays, but it seems likely that so many of the fine qualities of this accomplished and dedicated scholar must have been passed on to ABC and to ABC's brother Alan who became a General and was High Commissioner of Palestine in its most controversial years. He was obviously a disciplinarian, not only in his own life, but in the upbringing of his children who found him intimidating, even though they admired him: but this was a feature of life in general long before the present era of appeasement and permissiveness.

ABC was the third child, preceded by sister Elizabeth and brother John, and followed by brother Alan and sister Cecil.

Fear of father was more than offset by an adoration for a mother who though sometimes stern had a 'very sweet temperament'. The mother's father had been a minister of the church.

It can be seen therefore that Andrew Cunningham's forebears were closely related to professionalism: scholarship, research, medicine, and the church; careers which may at first appear to be far removed from military and naval glory; until we remember Nelson. Many times has Cunningham been called the Nelson of this century. Certainly in his continual urge and preparation for the destruction of the opposing fleet he favoured the maxim of that great sailor, 'No captain can do very wrong if he places his ship alongside that of an enemy'.

3

A Taste for Action
(1898–1917)

Having stated a preference for service on the Cape station upon passing out from the *Britannia*, Midshipman Cunningham was serving there in H.M.S. *Doris* when the Boer war broke out on 12 October 1899, and by February 1900 had winkled his way into the Naval Brigade. By June 1900 he was in the front line advancing towards Pretoria, developing a taste for action, experiencing the hardships of long marches and journeys by train and horseback, and seeing the use to which mobile naval guns (12-pounders and 4·7-inch) could be put. Some influence was exercised by Lord Roberts, a friend of Cunningham's father, in getting the young Cunningham to the front, an act which was contrary to the wishes of Captain Bearcroft who commanded the Naval Brigade. The latter seems to have taken this affront very much to heart, for in due course Cunningham's name was the only one omitted from the list of those midshipmen of the *Doris* who had been to the front and accordingly 'noted for early promotion'.

This setback upset him but he took it philosophically, and remarked on the benefits accruing to a boy of 17 in the matter of improvisation and self-reliance, together with the valuable experience of seeing action and facing hardship. Above all it helped him to realise the cheerfulness and endurance of the British sailor under difficult conditions.

It is worth recording Cunningham's first meeting, while at the front, with Lieutenant Walter Cowan who was naval ADC to Lord Kitchener, and already famous in the navy. ABC was much impressed with the fact that, although only 29, Cowan had seen more active service and collected more medals than many admirals. By this time ABC himself had won his first campaign medal.

Following his active service at the Cape, Cunningham spent the year 1901 as a midshipman in three different ships: the battleship *Hannibal* in the Channel Squadron; the sail training brig *Martin* at Portsmouth;

and the cruiser *Diadem* in the Channel Squadron. He took the qualifying examination in seamanship for the rank of acting sub-lieutenant on his nineteenth birthday (7 January 1902) prior to beginning his 'sub's' courses at Greenwich and at Portsmouth. To distinguish oneself in 'sub's' courses required an acting sub-lieutenant to gain a first-class pass in each examination which took place at the end of each of the five courses: Seamanship, Greenwich, Navigation, Gunnery, Torpedo. There were few who achieved this. The two or three who did, gained seniority over those who did not; but what is more important, the distinction of 'five firsts' was recorded in the Navy List for all to see, and implied outstanding ability and promise. These results often had far-reaching effects on an officer's subsequent career. Cunningham remarks that he had been unfortunate during his midshipman's time in not being in a ship in which a Naval Instructor was borne. Nevertheless he did pretty well to collect a first in Seamanship and Torpedo, and a second in each of the Gunnery, Navigation, and Greenwich courses.

A contemporary who got off to a flying start with five firsts, and enjoyed early promotion at every stage to the rank of admiral, was Charles Little. Modestly he describes himself as lucky, and explains that the 'five firsts' were due to his being three years in one ship as a midshipman, with good officers. It is interesting to speculate about the relative advantages of serving in different types of ships. In small ships there are more duties per officer, and therefore greater chances of showing initiative. In large ships, on the other hand, a junior will become known to a wider range of officers, some of whom may already be on the road to the top, where in due course they will show preference for those they know to be competent or outstanding. Assessing the relative merits of exceptional officers who show great promise has never been an easy matter, although the greatest of care is exercised to ensure not only regular and full reports by commanding officers, but that the personal factor of the reporting officer is taken into account by promotion boards. How can a selection committee compare one report written by a naturally eulogistic captain with another written in stringent terms by an officer who expects nothing but the best, and applies an analysis in the strictest and severest sense? What chance is there for the officer who may have questioned the decision or opinion of his superior who may vindictively report 'not recommended for promotion'? It depends upon a knowledge of both the subject and the reporting officer. There are many subjects who have survived an adverse report: there are others, well known to have shown great promise, who fall foul of a difficult commanding officer at a crucial stage and promptly wreck a

2 H.M. *ships* Britannia *and* Hindustan *at Dartmouth 1897*

3 Cunningham's term 'splicing the mainbrace', Diamond Jubilee 1897.
Cunningham is absent. The tall cadet, glass in hand, is Charles Little. The small
cadet, next but one to Little, on his right in the front, is James Somerville.
See Plate 4

promising career. To reach the top requires not only ability and stamina but good fortune.

In the present study of Cunningham it is irresistible to select three cadets from his *Britannia* term, who, although showing no exceptional promise there, nevertheless reached the highest rank of Admiral of the Fleet in the case of two of them (Andrew Cunningham and James Somerville), and nearly so in the case of Charles Little. Their relative progress over the years can be seen in the table below.

Comparative Promotions of Three Cadets who entered
H.M.S. Britannia in January 1897

Promoted	Charles Little	Andrew Cunningham	James Somerville
Lieutenant	January 1903	March 1904	March 1904
Commander	January 1913	June 1915	December 1915
Captain	June 1917	December 1919	December 1921
Rear-Admiral	February 1929	September 1932	October 1933
Vice-Admiral	September 1933	July 1936	September 1937
Admiral	June 1937	June 1939 (acting); January 1941 (confirmed)	February 1942
Admiral of the Fleet	—	January 1943	May 1945

In due course all three were to reach the distinction of commanding a fleet; but in the words of Charles Little:[1] 'We joined on the crest of the wave, and enjoyed the advantage of the expansion for the first war, and accelerated promotion in two wars!' ABC regarded his own success as due to long service in destroyers, and the exercise of command from early days. Little describes his own promotions as 'fortuitous', helped by service in submarines; 'a new branch in its infancy, much frowned on by the Service in general, which later turned up trumps'. He also refers to service as a lieutenant in two battleships where he met 'prominent officers'. In the case of Somerville, it was an odd twist of fate that caused him, at a stage when heading for high places, first to be placed on the retired list in peacetime as a Vice-Admiral, unfit for further active service, and then to be recalled to active service a few months later to assume command of Force H in war. He went on to command the Eastern Fleet, and in 1945 reached the highest rank of Admiral of the Fleet, only two years after Cunningham had been promoted to that august rank. On the other hand Little, who raced ahead through all the stages to Admiral, becoming Commander-in-Chief China Station in January 1936, and Second Sea Lord in September 1938, unluckily missed a sea-going command in war, and subsequently retired without being promoted to Admiral of the Fleet.

Following 'sub's' courses, ABC spent six months of 1903 in the battleship *Implacable* in the Mediterranean, but his most rewarding time as a sub-lieutenant took place when he transferred to the destroyer *Locust* in September of that year, and served as second-in-command under a young commanding officer Lieutenant Dutton. The latter had been given command because of his ability and efficiency, and was renowned for getting rid of sub-lieutenants who failed to come up to his requirements. The *Locust* was a coal-burning 30-knot destroyer of 300 tons with a complement of 58, armed with a 12-pounder and five 6-pounders as well as two 18-inch torpedo-tubes. Decks were kept spotless by constant scrubbing, not helped by cinders from the four funnels. ABC lived up to the trust placed in him by his commanding officer however, and when Dutton left the ship received a certificate that gladdened his heart. The fact that he had asked for the job, in spite of Dutton's fearsome reputation, indicates that even at this stage he was not afraid of work or responsibility or a harsh tongue: his one aim was that his destroyer should be better than the others. The results did not pass unnoticed by the Captain (D) who lived in the depot ship *Egmont* at Malta: he was John de Robeck, later to make a name for himself at the Dardanelles and in 1919 to become Commander-in-Chief Mediterranean. Thus began Cunningham's long period in destroyers.

His first four years as a lieutenant however were spent in other vessels, beginning with the old barque-rigged two-funnel cruiser *Northampton*, and followed by the more modern *Hawke*; both were used for ratings' training in home waters. ABC found the training service an essential and satisfying duty, and remarks that 'to teach, one has to learn how'. One can well imagine that he would never be without a copy of the Seamanship Manual.

From the *Hawke* Lieutenant Cunningham was appointed to the cruiser *Scylla* in the summer of 1906, and it is interesting to note that in that year one of the first 'trade' exercises was held, in which merchant ships were involved as well as warships, in the western approaches. In this same year Cunningham was appointed for a two-year commission to the new county class cruiser *Suffolk* of 9,800 tons, 22 knots, armed with 14 6-inch guns. As part of the Mediterranean Fleet she took part in fleet manoeuvres and carried out numerous gunnery and torpedo

4 *Cunningham's term reunion 1948: 50 years after leaving* Britannia.
Standing, left to right: *Capt N. M. C. Thurston DSO; Capt L. A. Smythes; Capt A. A. Lovett-Cameron; Capt R. E. Eyre-Huddleston; Admiral Sir Charles Little GCB, GBE; Rear-Admiral Sir Cloudsley Varyll Robinson KCB; Admiral of the Fleet Sir James F. Somerville GCB, GBE, DSO; Admiral of the Fleet Viscount Cunningham of Hyndehope KT, GCB, OM, DSO (two bars), LLD; Capt E. A. B. Stanley DSO, MVO; Capt E. G. de S. Jukes-Hughes CBE; Vice-Admiral R. S. Wykes-Sneyd DSO; Capt J. D. Campbell OBE, DSC; Cdr J. S. Tyndall; Engineer Capt H. H. Gordon; Lt-Cdr Sir Henry A. Colt, Bart, DSO, MC; Cdr C. C. Swift OBE; Cdr B. J. D. Guy VC, DSO.*

Sitting: *Capt J. P. Champion CBE, DSO; Cdr G. L. Brown; Rear-Admiral J. S. C. Salmond; Rear-Admiral H. G. Thursfield; Vice-Admiral G. Trewby CMG, DSO (Officer of Term); Capt R. T. Amedroz; Rear-Admiral E. G. Robinson VC, OBE; Capt R. B. England DSO*

5 Beagle-*class destroyer (similar to* HMS Scorpion*) carrying troops to the* Dardanelles *in 1915*

6 *Sailing regatta race for galleys, March 1930.* Left to right: London, Tiger, Rodney, Queen Elizabeth

practices, in addition to the routine cruises showing the White Ensign in the Aegean, Adriatic, and Mediterranean generally. Cunningham was detailed during one firing to a gunnery control position where he had to work a complicated instrument. He was intrigued to read subsequently in an official report: 'The extreme ingenuity of this instrument rather blinds one to its absolute uselessness.' Among his real detestations was Whale Island, the home of naval gunnery, where, perhaps as a result of initiative displayed in returning equipment to a locked hut, requiring the breaking of a window, he had been issued with a certificate stating that his general conduct was not satisfactory: a smudge quite unjustly bestowed, he says. The certificate became one of his proudest possessions.

This attitude towards gunnery remained entrenched in his mind throughout his service life, and it may help to understand him a good deal better, to read a piece written by Vice-Admiral Sir Geoffrey Barnard.[2]

'ABC had a healthy respect for the gun as a weapon *if properly used*,' says Barnard, 'and an almost boyish delight in the sound of guns going off in a good cause; but he must have suffered much from earnest gunnery officers in the course of his Service career. As a result anything savouring of long-range gun actions with "black magic" about curvature of the earth, and canted trunnions and all that, was anathema to him.'

H.M.S. *Suffolk* paid off in the spring of 1908, and to his great joy, and as a result of persistent requests, Cunningham then found himself appointed in command of Torpedo-Boat No. 14. He was not only back to his beloved 'boats', but now in sole command at the early age of 25, with the determination to get the most out of himself and his crew in making her the best. She was brand new, oil-fired, fitted with steam turbines to give her 26 knots, and mounted two 12-pounders and three torpedo-tubes.

There were at that time two types of above-water vessels armed with torpedoes: torpedo-boats and torpedo-boat-destroyers. The former type were originally designed for a purely defensive role in the 1870s, to be used against enemy ships which might lie off-shore with intent to blockade or bombard. The other type was designed in the 1880s and 1890s, when it began to be realised that long-range guns on shore had neutralised the possibility of close blockade by the enemy, and something fast and more offensive was required. It was increasing competition for higher speed that led to the development of the Parsons steam turbine, giving the torpedo-boat-destroyers speeds up to 36 knots. And it was the arrival of Admiral Sir John ('Jacky') Arbuthnot Fisher as First Sea Lord at the Admiralty in 1904 that, among many other innovations, led to a boost in the design and development of the destroyer as a combined defensive and offensive warship.

Though trained in sail, Fisher was alive to the importance of new techniques and was particularly aware of the torpedo as a factor which would permit new tactics. He was also one of the first to realise that the biggest threat to Britain's supremacy at sea lay no longer with France but with Germany. The great race to build modern ships had begun, and in naval circles it was already clear that war with Germany was inevitable.

The exact role of the destroyer in war had not yet evolved, but its offensive potentiality was realised as it grew in size and power. By 1910 there were 40 British ocean-going destroyers on the stocks.

The advent of war, added to his own ceaseless importuning, and the increasing number of vessels becoming available, were factors responsible for keeping Cunningham in destroyers. From *T.B.14* he was temporarily relieved in June 1909, when his father died. On returning to duty, he assumed command of the *Vulture*, a 30-knot coal-burning destroyer. Though she was regarded as a more important command, he thought her inferior to *T.B.14*, and complained to his Captain (D), Reginald Tyrwhitt, that he had been given an 'Irishman's rise'. Tyrwhitt was rather annoyed. Nevertheless ABC seems to have won his point, for he was given command of the destroyer *Roebuck*, which he described as 'a beautiful little ship (although a coal-burner); fast, handy, economical on fuel, and with palatial captain's quarters'. Unfortunately she developed boiler trouble after only three months and was paid off in December 1910. With more than two and a half years of destroyer service behind him, he believed that he might be due to go back to a big ship in accordance with a reputed policy that lieutenants should get a wide experience of as many warship types as possible. Cunningham was not the man to accept such a possibility lightly, having become by that time dedicated to his 'boats' and a life that continually offered opportunity for hard work and enterprise. A word to his new Captain (D), Mortimer Silver, was followed by some anxious weeks of waiting and doubt. But his luck held, for within a month of paying off *Roebuck*, to his amazement and great delight he received an appointment to the destroyer *Scorpion*, in command. She was one of the new 900-ton ocean-going 'Beagle' class (combined TB and TBD), turbine-driven to give a speed of 27 knots, and armed with a 4-inch gun in addition to three 12-pounders and two 21-inch torpedo-tubes.

There were two snags, however. The first was that she was coal-fired. This condition resulted from a prevailing desire that Britain should be self-sufficient at a time when war seemed likely with Germany, and all oil had to come from abroad. In addition to being dirty and less economical, coal-firing imposed a delay compared with oil-firing, when speed increases were urgently required.

The second snag was the fearsome reputation of the Commodore of the Home Fleet Flotillas, Sir Robert Arbuthnot. ABC fell foul of him almost as soon as he joined the *Scorpion* at Harwich, being ordered to repair on board the leader, the light cruiser *Boadicea*, to explain why there was mud on the *Scorpion*'s port anchor. But this was the first and last time that he was in trouble with Sir Robert, an officer from whom he learnt a lot about discipline, and one whom he came to respect and admire. It is certain that although he was aware of the harshness imposed by Sir Robert, especially in matters of appearance and dress when returning from a gruelling exercise, he acquired some of these characteristics, despite the fact that they, as he himself has said, 'would not answer in these enlightened days'.[3]

Destroyer life was hard, with constant exercising in all weathers, and small protection from rough and breaking seas. Arbuthnot believed in hard work and much sea time, and few faults escaped his eagle eye. A submarine officer of those days writes: 'The Harwich destroyer captains . . . were all a pretty hard-bitten lot in the early days.'[4]

Soon after taking over the *Scorpion*, Cunningham was shown an Admiralty order that all officers in command of destroyers must take and pass an examination in navigation, gunnery, torpedo, and signals. Sir Robert Arbuthnot told him that he had better try. 'But it doesn't matter if you pass or not,' he added. 'You won't leave the *Scorpion*.' The order was conveniently forgotten or ignored. ABC was destined to remain with the *Scorpion* for a further seven years, four of which were to be spent in Mediterranean waters, whither the *Scorpion* was transferred in the autumn of 1913.

Although Britain had not become involved, the Balkan wars from March 1912 to August 1913 had ended in the partitioning of most of Turkey-in-Europe, leaving her with only a small area enclosing the straits into the Black Sea, and giving Greece much greater influence in the Aegean Sea. (See map 5 of Mediterranean.)

Those four years in the Mediterranean were at the time considered unrewarding by Cunningham, who together with many others felt that the Mediterranean was regarded as a backwater. More honour would be found in Home waters. The allied sea campaign during the war, which broke out on 4 August 1914, never seemed to get properly co-ordinated in the Mediterranean, and was a story of missed opportunities. It began with the escape of the German battle cruiser *Goeben* and light cruiser *Breslau* into the Black Sea (see map p. 24), a 'shameful episode' (in the

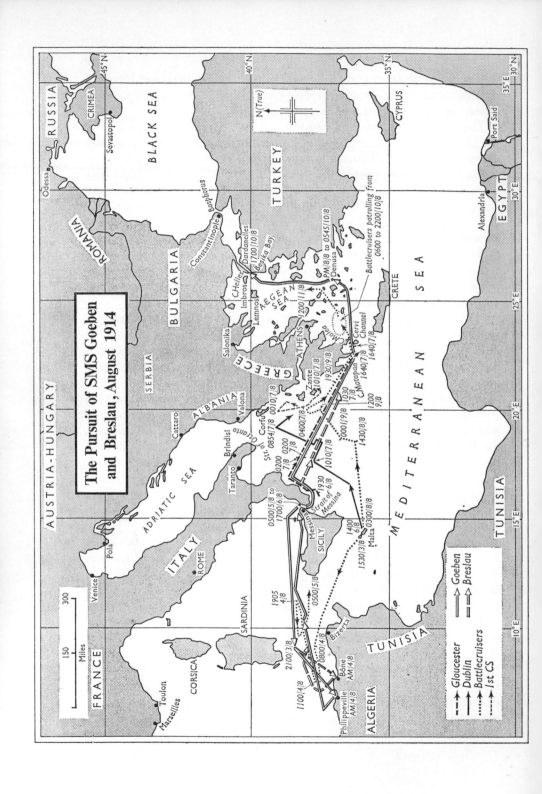

The Pursuit of SMS Goeben and Breslau, August 1914

words of the First Sea Lord, Prince Louis of Battenberg),[5] as a result of misinterpretation of an Admiralty signal which stressed the need to aid the French, and ended with the words 'Do NOT at this stage be brought to action against *superior* forces'. By 30 October Turkey had entered the war on the side of Germany, and the *Goeben* was bombarding the Russian port of Sevastopol.

With Italy still neutral and the Austrian fleet shut in the Adriatic, the Mediterranean was safe for allied shipping, though in due course German U-boats would gain an entry; but at the eastern end Russia was cut off from her allies by the Turkish Straits.

Now came the opportunity for Britain to exercise the use of sea power and to take the Gallipoli Peninsula in a combined operation, thus putting Turkey out of the war, and opening communications with hard-pressed Russia and the Black Sea. Such an operation would reinforce the encirclement of the Central Powers.

The opportunity was seen and taken, but not initially as a combined operation or with whole-hearted co-operation. It developed into a tragedy of errors caused by fundamental differences of opinion, delays, and lack of preparation. Its failure contributed largely to the Russian collapse in 1917 and almost certainly lengthened the war. Unfortunately it began as a naval expedition, unsupported by troops, 'To bombard and take the Gallipoli Peninsula, with Constantinople as its objective'. Completely disregarded by Churchill and the War Staff was the historical lesson reiterated by Mahan in 1911: 'Ships are unequally matched against forts.' Add to this the new risk of submarines and minefields, and the difficulties are at once apparent (see map p. 27). Fisher had been brought back as First Sea Lord in October 1914 by Churchill who was then First Lord of the Admiralty, and was quite opposed to a scheme that failed to use troops to support naval bombardment.

The destroyers were employed in a tight patrol off the entrance to the Dardanelles, boarding and inspecting all merchant ships entering or leaving. There was no sheltered anchorage at first, and Cunningham refers to a dreary life, with heavy seas and north-easterly blizzards, with sleet and snow. It was as bitterly cold as anything he had experienced in the North Sea where he so longed to be.

On 3 November 1914 the outer forts of the Dardanelles were bombarded by the two British battle cruisers *Indefatigable* and *Indomitable* assisted by two French battleships. First reports were favourable. Much damage was claimed and the Turk was said to be demoralised. After-events proved these claims to be optimistic, said Cunningham. One of the adverse results was the German resolve to strengthen all the Turkish defences against any future assault, both in gun emplacements ashore and minefields in the straits.

An allied naval expedition to force the narrows began on 19 February 1915, the new 15-inch battleship *Queen Elizabeth* being employed, together with the *Inflexible* and 16 pre-Dreadnought battleships. Cunningham was thrilled at the appearance of the *Queen Elizabeth*, later to distinguish herself as the flagship of so many Commanders-in-Chief Mediterranean. Most modern ships were at that time required at home, to be with the Grand Fleet in preparation for the expected confrontation with the German High Seas fleet. The idea behind the Dardanelles expedition was a step-by-step advance by the big ships, while the straits were being swept by the destroyers. The battleships would advance and silence each fort.

'Few of us in the destroyers had all that touching faith in naval gunnery,' wrote Cunningham with memories of his experiences at Whale Island.

Initially the scheme was successful, but it was apparent that the forts could not be permanently silenced unless troops were landed to complete the job: and while the forts remained, mine-sweeping became hazardous and ineffectual. Periodically the weather deteriorated, and operations would be stopped by north-easterly gales, heavy rain, and poor visibility. The dreary routine of the patrol boats would have to continue. Later, destroyers landed parties of seamen and marines who completed the destruction of many guns at Sedd-el-Bahr near Cape Helles, and two forts near Kum Kale on the Asiatic shore, before getting back to their ships. It was obvious however that real progress could be made only by troops of occupation. The purely naval expedition ended with a disastrous big push on 18 March 1915, after strenuous assaults from the fleet both by night and by day. Four capital ships were sunk or damaged. Progress into the straits had been made as far as Chanak (see map 2), and valuable information of conditions ashore obtained by landing parties that had advanced as far as Krithia, a village at the foot of the steep hill Achi Baba. It was only learnt later that the Turks were very near to collapse through a shortage of ammunition.

The combined allied attack of naval bombardment and landing of troops did not take place until 25 April 1915, by which time the Turks, supported and reinforced by the Germans, were more than ready. Neither then nor in the eight fruitless months which followed did allied troops gain much more than a foothold on the beaches, in spite of grim determination and gallantry. Casualties were heavy on both sides. Three more old battleships were sunk, one torpedoed by a Turkish destroyer, the other two by a German U-boat.

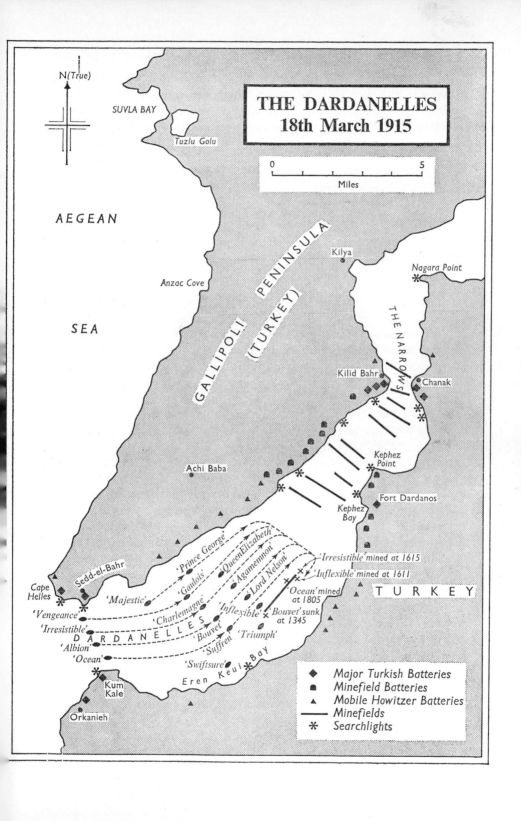

N(True)

SUVLA BAY

Tuzlu Golu

THE DARDANELLES
18th March 1915

0   5

Miles

AEGEAN

Kilya

Nagara Point

Anzac Cove

GALLIPOLI PENINSULA (TURKEY)

THE NARROWS

SEA

Kilid Bahr

Chanak

Kephez
Point

Achi Baba

Fort Dardanos

Kephez
Bay

'Prince George'

'Irresistible' mined at 1615

'QueenElizabeth'

'Inflexible' mined at 1611

'Gaulois'

'Agamemnon'

'Majestic'

'Lord Nelson'

'Ocean' mined
at 1805

TURKEY

'Charlemagne'

'Inflexible'

'Bouvet' sunk
at 1345

Cape
Helles

Sedd-el-Bahr

'Vengeance'

'Bouvet'

'Suffren' 'Triumph'

'Irresistible'

DARDANELLES

'Albion'

'Ocean'

'Swiftsure'

Eren Keui Bay

Kum
Kale

Orkanieh

◆   Major Turkish Batteries
■   Minefield Batteries
▲   Mobile Howitzer Batteries
—   Minefields
✳   Searchlights

This abortive expedition ended with the complete evacuation from Gallipoli at the beginning of January 1916, the only gain having been to bring Italy into the war on the side of the Allies in May 1915. Perhaps another beneficial effect was the lasting impression made on a number of young naval officers, of the detrimental effect that could be brought about by delays and indecision; and for one in particular, who was to play such a vital role in those waters in the Second World War, it served as an indispensable apprenticeship. The role of the destroyer as an all-purpose and essential fighting element was now evident, and the potential danger from torpedo and submarine had been clearly established, as forecast by Fisher. It was inevitable that attention should soon turn to the anti-submarine possibilities of a fast destroyer, thus adding yet further demand for these vessels that had become 'maids of all work'.

A letter from a writer who was serving in the destroyer depot ship *Blenheim* gives us a glimpse of ABC during those arduous days:[6]

'Occasionally he came over to see the Fleet Paymaster. On one occasion he requested the Assistant Paymaster to kick the nether regions of his sub-lieutenant [in the *Scorpion*], upon learning that both were playing rugger ashore [at Mudros] in the afternoon. "He [the sub] needed them well waking up." Anyone who could exist in a state of near somnambulation in the *Scorpion* would, I think, have been of a race apart.

'One has only to record the names of such officers as Cdr. England (*Harpy*); Lt.-Cdr. Sworder (*Arno*); Lt.-Cdr. Pridham-Wippell (*Comet*); Lt.-Cdr. Bonham-Carter (*Shark*); Lt.-Cdr. Victor Crutchley (*Sikh*); Cdr. Poe (*Acheron*); and Cdr. Corlett (*Badger*), to name but a few of the officers of the 5th Flotilla which was then operating in the Eastern Mediterranean, to realise what effect such training had on their later achievements . . . [four became Admirals]. One is reminded too of the sterling quality of the crews.' Gravenhall then describes the presentation of the Conspicuous Gallantry medal and a gold watch to A. B. Small of H.M.S. *Bulldog*, who saved an officer's life when she hit a mine. 'He was doing 14 days, No. 10 on the following Tuesday.'

'Our mess (writers) was immediately beneath the Ward Room of the *Blenheim*,' continues Gravenhall, 'and one can imagine, following the return of one or two boats from patrol, a dinner in the Mess and the inevitable hurling of a matchbox into the air with the resultant scrum, and the din that followed.'

What of ABC himself at this time? We see him as a tough, relentless, courageous captain of a destroyer, always on the offensive, always prepared, and with an instinct for correct decision, instilling with supreme self-confidence, zest in his ship's company, leaving no doubt as to what had to be done, and insisting above all that it should be done speedily and in a seamanlike manner. The award of the DSO and promotion to Commander (30 June 1915), advancing him 250 places in the Navy List, was an indication of Their Lordships' recognition of exceptional performance. It is evident that he was well thought of by officers who were already distinguished and whom he very much admired: de Robeck, Keyes, and Tyrwhitt.

Life in destroyers continued to be very strenuous during 1916 and 1917, and a major role for the *Scorpion* was escorting convoys of merchant ships. Cunningham gave the task much thought. Believing that exact station-keeping was the secret of success, he rigidly insisted that it should be carried out by all ships of the convoy. His suggestions were embodied in Fleet Orders; another indication of official confidence in his judgment. He lost no ships in convoy, but on reflection was inclined to put this down to sheer luck. It is of interest that in later years, when the Mountbatten Station Keeping instrument was produced, he became sceptical as to whether it was really necessary, considering that the answer lay in the careful observation and good judgment of the officer of the watch.

In the flotilla the *Scorpion* had a reputation for having a swift succession of First Lieutenants, presumably because of failure to meet requirements. A well-publicised turn in fleet theatricals at Mudros was reputed to begin with a loud splash and a 'Good God, what was that?'; to which the reply was 'Only another First Lieutenant being flung out of the *Scorpion*'.[7] The story is substantiated by Admiral Sir Richard Symonds-Tayler who claims that he was ABC's thirteenth First Lieutenant. He loved the man, and was ever grateful for the advice, experience, and training he received during a year's service in the *Scorpion*. Cunningham's view was that although he himself had no high opinion of a particular officer, the latter might do better under the command of some other perhaps more tolerant or understanding captain. The fair thing was to arrange a change as soon as possible.[8] His own reputation for competence was so high, however, that there were those who were more than willing to fill a vacancy. One young officer, Flynn, who admired the dash and precision with which the smart and efficient *Scorpion* was handled by ABC and his ship's company, applied for transfer to that destroyer, anxious to improve his own standards. He writes:

'I believe the foundations of ABC's subsequent fame were laid in those seven years in *Scorpion*. Sir Robert Arbuthnot was probably the great influence which fanned the sparks of South African and first commands into a glowing fire in *Scorpion*. By 1918 he had a big reputation both as a destroyer commander and a man of action in the Mediterranean and he was determined to strive for excellence.'

'Excellence' and 'a glowing fire' just about summarise the general impression of those days.

Cunningham writes:[9] 'I have often reflected how curiously history repeats itself. When I left the Mediterranean as a young commander in 1917 I knew it very well. Malta, the Adriatic, Greece, Crete, and a multitude of lovely islands in the Aegean were all old friends. I served in the Mediterranean again between the wars. Little did I imagine how the accumulated knowledge was to be of service to me years later in a position of far greater anxiety and responsibility.'

4

Impressionable Days with Keyes and Cowan(1918–19)

During the summer of 1917 Cunningham was offered an appointment as Commander (D) of all the destroyers based upon Malta, at a time when coal-fired destroyers such as the *Scorpion* were gradually being withdrawn from the Mediterranean and replaced by smaller, oil-fired destroyers from home. Assured in his own mind that really active periods of sea service in the Mediterranean had ended, he asked instead for a ship under Commodore Tyrwhitt in the Harwich Force, or for one with Vice-Admiral Roger Keyes at Dover. This led to his return to Plymouth in the *Scorpion*, and her paying off 21 January 1918. He had been in command of her for seven years, and spoke of his ship's company as 'quite wonderful officers and men'. The *Scorpion* had certainly had a high reputation.

There followed temporary command of the destroyer *Ophelia* in the Grand Fleet, which was not at all to his liking, for a state of deadlock had set in after the battle of Jutland, and there seemed to be little chance of action. He had not long to wait however, for on 28 March he was appointed to the *Termagant* of the Dover Patrol; a 32-knot destroyer armed with five 4-inch guns. She was refitting at Hull, but because of extreme secrecy Cunningham was not told of this until he visited Admiralty. This caused unnecessary delay in his joining *Termagant*, which infuriated him. From various moves of officers and unexpected detachment of ships, he knew that something was brewing and was anxious to be in it. He had arranged for stores, torpedoes, and ammunition to be ready in advance at Sheerness, so as to avoid any further delay, and upon completion of *Termagant*'s refit at Hull, proceeded there at 30 knots through the swept channel. In spite of a hurried embarkation and early departure for Dover, he arrived too late to take any principal part in the operation that was pending. This was Keyes's raid on the German submarine base at Zeebrugge, in which blockships were to be sunk at a strategic point 23 April 1918. Cunningham's *Termagant* was however detailed, together with two other destroyers, to escort 15-inch monitors to their bombarding position off the entrance of the Scheldt on the evening before the raid. They soon ran into thick fog; nevertheless the monitors were able to anchor accurately in the previously selected bombarding positions marked by a buoy, a feat of navigation which ABC did not fail to note, and they carried out deliberate fire during the night.

In his *Sailor's Odyssey* Cunningham says practically nothing of what followed during the raid, but the engineer officer of the *Termagant*[1] gives the story, already described in Chapter 1, of the parting of the tow of the ferry-boat (littered with dead bodies). He implies that this was due to ABC's impetuosity and for once bad judgment, and because he valued good seamanship it was an event he would prefer to forget.

The Dover Patrol proved to be a lively task mainly because of the proximity and enterprise of German destroyers. Cunningham's arrival did not pass unnoticed. A young officer, who in later years became a great friend and admirer, remarks:[2] 'After brilliant service in the destroyer *Scorpion* during the Dardanelles campaign he came at his own request to the Dover Patrol in the destroyer *Termagant*. At that time I was in command of the destroyer *Murray* also at Dover. We, of course, knew of his reputation and the younger C.O.'s wondered, with some apprehension, as to whether our shortcomings would be too obvious to one who had seen so much active service for so long. In fact we expected a good "shake-up". This in my case was not long in coming, as the next time the patrol put to sea I was hailed from the *Termagant* and told "IF YOU DON'T KEEP OUT OF MY WAY I'LL SINK YOU". It was not very easy to keep out of anybody's way in Dover harbour.'

The fact that a young commander with less than three years seniority could not only behave in this forceful manner but do so with such assurance, and without fear of retaliation, is in itself evidence of his acceptance as a rising star. To many influential senior officers such as de Robeck, Keyes, and Tyrwhitt, he was already known as an effectual leader, aggressive fighter, and competent seaman. And beneath the display there still lay that sense of fun which in *Britannia* days had led to records of 'Laughing in study', 'Skylarking at Muster', 'Misbehaviour in the Mess', 'Fight you on Sunday'. (Perhaps he had even found some zest in being the star in the awesome ceremony of a public caning, with all cadets assembled on deck at attention to witness punishment.)

Cunningham found that there was more chance of action when the *Termagant* was stationed at Dunkirk, and preferred this to the monotony of escorting troop transports from Dover to Calais. He was promised a 'front seat' for the *Termagant* at the next blocking operation against Ostend but, because of postponement, the date clashed with *Termagant*'s programme for boiler cleaning. Shortly afterwards however, while in charge of four destroyers operating from Dunkirk, in company with the 15-inch monitor *Terror*, he detached his four destroyers and chased four German destroyers to the north-eastward at full speed, and informed the *Terror* of his intention to engage. He received no reply, and since they were by now closing the enemy fast, he ignored the considerable flashing from the *Terror* which his yeoman of signals thought might be the recall, but could not be certain because of the flying spray due to steaming at full speed in a rough sea head on to a fresh north-easterly wind.

It was a case of the 'blind eye'; but the sequel was tame. The Germans were reinforced by five more destroyers from the north-east, at which time Cunningham opened fire at 9,000 yards. A further four appeared from the same direction soon afterwards. By this time radio signals were coming through from Dover and Dunkirk, and as one of his destroyers had fired practically all her ammunition, and it was now 13 against four, Cunningham broke off the action. Torpedoes were fired at the enemy line during the turn away, but without results. What was even more exasperating to Cunningham was the fact that the German destroyers had received no damage of note. He attributed this to the fact that all destroyers were so hardworked that there was little time for exercising and for gunnery practice. He himself had experienced 18 consecutive nights at sea, while his men had been at action stations most of the time. Nevertheless, from then on, his division came in for much fire control and gunlayer practice.

The second blocking operation at Ostend had been ruined by thick weather. Admiral Keyes considered that poor ship-handling had also been responsible for the failure, and asked Cunningham if he would take on a third attempt. It was realised that after two abortive operations, a third attempt would be hazardous in the extreme. Cunningham was, however, to choose his own officers, and Chatham would supply ratings from a list of volunteers: 'a wild lot ready for anything' as he described them. The old battleship *Swiftsure* was to enter between the break-waters, put her helm hard over so as to ram the western arm, and then swing across channel. An old cruiser was to follow close, so as to ram the *Swiftsure* and push her across the entrance: demolition charges in their bottoms would do the rest. All that was then necessary was the withdrawal of survivors by means of smaller craft: a formidable proposition. Preparations such as sandbagging, machine-gun mountings, and double-bottom explosives, were well advanced after three weeks, and sea trials then took place.

Three days before the date planned for the blocking, the operation was suddenly cancelled. Ostend was no longer being used by the Germans, and a large minefield in the approaches made it in any case extremely unlikely that *Swiftsure* could penetrate. Cunningham speaks of 'bitter disappointment'. The end of the war could not be long delayed, and opportunities for gallantry, honour, and glory were becoming scarce.

It is amusing to hear that the ship's company of the *Termagant*, who of course knew nothing of the proposed Ostend venture, spread the rumour that Commander Cunningham had been removed from *Termagant* because he had been too severe with the sailors. It must have been fun for him to see their faces when he returned to the destroyer, bent on introducing 'some of the Mediterranean discipline, cleanliness, and efficiency in a ship in which they were sorely needed'. From this time on, all the trips to sea by Vice-Admiral Roger Keyes were made in the *Termagant*, though he lived on board the *Douglas* at Dunkirk. The latter was a new flotilla leader, but orders had been issued that she was not to be unduly risked. These trips brought Cunningham very much under the eye of Keyes who had already formed a high opinion of him. Both were supporters of the maxim 'live dangerously'. Cunningham wrote: 'I shall always count myself fortunate in having served in the Dover Patrol, and under the command of Sir Roger Keyes. A great fighter and fearing nothing, he had outstanding qualities as a leader; above all, that asset which counts so much in war – the burning desire to get at the enemy at all times and by any means.'

By September 1918 hopes of victory for the Allies were high. The long retreat in France had come to an end, and it was the Germans who were pulling out. By October there were signs of evacuation from strategic points along the Belgian coast, but there was no sudden collapse; heavy German coastal batteries continued to operate from Zeebrugge, and minefields were extensive in waters where few allied ships had hitherto operated. Nevertheless it was Keyes's intention, doubtless with the enthusiastic support of Cunningham, to investigate the changing position at close hand, little concerned at the various hazards. With two destroyers in company, *Termagant* proceeded to Ostend, but was stopped two miles short of the breakwater when warned of mines by a fishing-boat. Keyes and Cunningham then transferred to the *Termagant*'s motor-boat, which immediately broke down. Undeterred they then took to the whaler. Landing ashore they were given a great welcome by the Belgian authorities, who informed them that the Germans had not quite completed their evacuation. This was the information they sought. While returning to the *Termagant* they received confirmation when swamped by a near miss from a shell fired by a German shore battery farther up the coast.

Termagant returned to Dunkirk, and within hours had the honour of embarking the King and Queen of the Belgians together with Sir Roger Keyes, and of carrying them to Ostend. All went well, but evidence of continuing hazards was shown when a monitor fouled a mine and blew up. Further trips of exploration with Keyes were thereupon carried out in a coastal motor-boat, so as not to hazard the *Termagant*.

The armistice came on 11 November 1918. For his service with the Dover Patrol Cunningham was awarded a bar to the DSO won in 1915. *Termagant* had the distinction of bringing back from Boulogne to Dover the British Naval Representative who had signed the document. This was Admiral Sir Rosslyn Wemyss, then First Sea Lord, who had been captain of the *Suffolk*, a crack ship, in which ABC had served 1906–08. ABC had also met Wemyss in 1915 when serving at the Dardanelles. The selection of a ship for the distinction of carrying celebrities must obviously be fortuitous, but provided all goes well, can do the 'owner' no harm. As a rising star, already well known to this distinguished and influential passenger, Cunningham would have been under observation upon such an occasion, and his ability to conduct affairs and his acknowledged skill in handling the ship would be very much in evidence. *Termagant* continued her duties as a cross-Channel ferry for the great ones, embarking at different times the Duke of York, the Duke of Connaught, Admiral Lord Beatty, and (in a real snorter of a south-easterly gale) the Prime Minister, Mr. Lloyd George.

As his time in the *Termagant* was drawing to an end, Cunningham applied for a destroyer abroad, and on 1 March 1919 was appointed in command of *Seafire*, one of a new class of destroyer, faster than the *Termagant*, and initially intended for China.

Although the armistice of November 1918 had brought about an end to hostilities, there were many international and political problems that remained to be solved, and vast regions in the Baltic Sea, Black Sea, and the Aegean Sea, where it was necessary for the Royal Navy to preserve stability. Nevertheless the show of naval strength had to be tempered with economy. Not only was there a large reduction in the number of active service ships, but also a rapid demobilisation which added to difficulties in complementing ships for foreign service. For the time being therefore, there was to be no destroyer flotilla for the Far East. The *Seafire*, with only three-quarters of her proper complement, instead sailed early in March for the Baltic, as part of a force of light cruisers and destroyers under the command of Rear-Admiral Walter

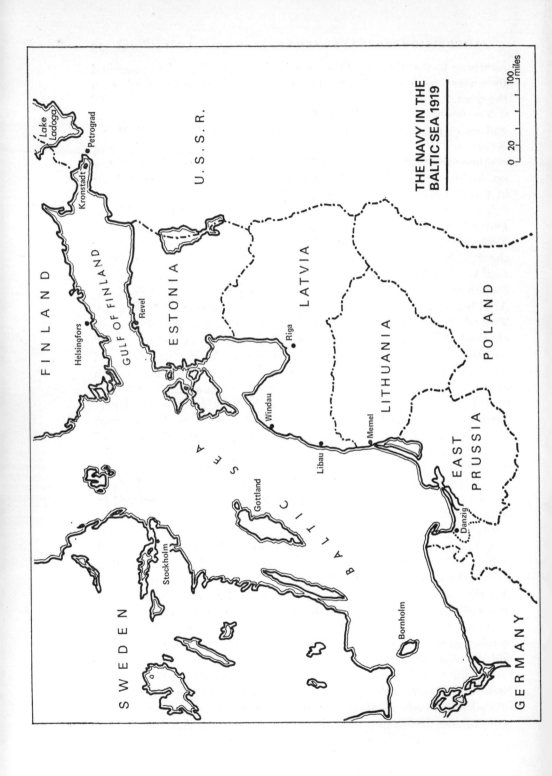

THE NAVY IN THE
BALTIC SEA 1919

0 20   100
          miles

Lake Ladoga

Petrograd

Kronstadt

FINLAND

U.S.S.R.

Helsingfors

GULF OF FINLAND

Revel

ESTONIA

LATVIA

Riga

Windau

LITHUANIA

Libau

Memel

POLAND

SWEDEN

Gottland

BALTIC SEA

EAST PRUSSIA

Stockholm

Bornholm

Danzig

GERMANY

Cowan, whose particular task at this moment was the support of Latvia (see Map 3). That Baltic State, together with Estonia and Lithuania, was still struggling to maintain independence from the encroaching Bolsheviks and also from those irregular German troops under General von der Goltz who had been in occupation of Latvia at the time of the armistice. Von der Goltz, contrary to the terms of the armistice, was endeavouring to incorporate Latvia and Lithuania with East Prussia as a German protectorate, at the same time as the Bolsheviks were pushing southward from Estonia.

Cowan's mission was not an unusual one for the Royal Navy, especially as Britain was providing Latvia with arms and munitions. For Cunningham however it provided yet another view of the use of sea power, and the opportunity to show initiative under the watchful eye of Cowan. He had met this much decorated officer in unusual circumstances 19 years earlier, when Cowan had been naval ADC to Kitchener. Cunningham wrote of Walter Cowan that he divided men into three classes: (*a*) the man who did well, (*b*) the man who did badly, and (*c*) (much the worst) the man who failed to do his utmost. 'A harsh judgment perhaps,' he continues, 'but in my opinion a very right one.'[3]

Cowan was forthright, deplored conceit, and would soon cut a man down to size. It was a few years later when, as Commander-in-Chief West Indies, watching his ships enter the basin at Montreal, he saw the *Capetown* ram the wall hard and fracture her stem: she was commanded by a distinguished ex-navigating officer who liked to be seen manoeuvring smartly. 'There you are, Cunningham,' said Cowan to his flag captain. 'When you get an ex-gunnery officer as a captain, his ship never hits the target; an ex-torpedo officer loses all his torpedoes; and an ex-navigator always hits the wall.'[4] To a salt horse like Cunningham such words were heard with relish.

Also with Cowan's Latvia force was Charles Little, Cunningham's class mate in the *Britannia*, and at this time captain of the light cruiser *Cleopatra*. He writes:[5] 'In 1919 we found ourselves in the Baltic; Cunningham's episode with the Germans in the river at Libau was typical. . . . Here he came under the notice of Cowan. Cowan's reports would have been very useful in bringing Cunningham's name forward.' Cowan's bold and forthright qualities also came under the eye of Cunningham, and there is no doubt that he was much impressed and full of admiration. There was however an early difference of opinion after Cunningham had been ordered to take the *Seafire* to Windau, a small port on the west Latvian coast, and had delayed rejoining Cowan at Libau 60 miles to the southward, because of the thick fog which covered the tortuous swept channel between the two ports. Long experience with destroyers in minefields in narrow waters had produced a caution against hazarding H.M. ships unnecessarily. Though courageous, Cunningham was certainly not reckless.

'We arrived at Libau next day,' says ABC,[6] 'and on reporting myself on board the *Curacoa* I found the delay was not at all to the taste of Walter Cowan. He did not consider that fog should deter destroyers, while I could only insist that I had taken a reasonable and seamanlike precaution in unfamiliar waters. We parted in some disagreement.'

Even in his very early days Cunningham could never have been accused of possessing what Admiral John Godfrey used to call V.S.O.V. (Very Senior Officer Veneration). The first lieutenant of the *Seafire*[7] describes how incensed was Cunningham on returning from his interview with Cowan, but considers he was even more incensed on the occasion when 'going alongside a British cruiser in a narrow basin in Hamburg, her Post Captain was unwise enough to offer some advice to ABC about the throw-off which *Seafire*'s wash, when going astern, might cause in so confined a space. It took a bowl or two of strawberries and cream in an open-air restaurant on the Alster for my master ship-handler Captain to recover.'

At Windau Cunningham had been close to the front line where the Bolsheviks were being held, and had found a practically starving population. His sailors improvised soup kitchens, and then parted with most of their own rations. It was because Cowan was anxious to hear details of the situation that he had been piqued at the delay in Cunningham's return to Libau.

The port at Libau consisted of a large outer harbour sheltered by breakwaters; it was here that the cruisers lay. Leading from the outer harbour were two minor harbours: a naval harbour which could be entered through a narrow canal spanned by a swing bridge; and a commercial harbour which lay some distance up a river, and itself consisted of a narrow stretch of water with wharves on the town side.

In the naval harbour was a cargo ship laden with arms for the Latvian army. Unfortunately her engines had broken down, and as she lay alongside a jetty, close to German barracks, there was a danger of her being seized by German soldiers. Cowan ordered Cunningham to take the *Seafire* into the naval harbour, make the necessary repairs to the arms ship, and bring her out to the outer harbour where she would be under his eye. All went well with the *Seafire* as she entered the narrow canal and gave four blasts for the swing bridge to open and allow her to pass. Cunningham secured her astern of the arms ship and sent on board his engineer officer, who reported that the necessary repairs would take 24 hours.

Captain Charles Little, of the *Cleopatra*, visited him during the following forenoon, having sailed up from the outer harbour in his galley; but his visit was suddenly interrupted by the appearance of a black-bearded, wild-eyed Latvian who was ushered into the cabin by the officer of the watch. In broken English and with much gesticulation the Latvian conveyed the news that the Latvian GHQ, a mile away in the forest, had been captured by the Germans. This was obviously no time for a ship laden with arms to be lying alongside, and Cunningham was determined to move her to the outer harbour, even if it meant towing her. Charles Little set off at once in his galley to return to the outer harbour, and report to Cowan. Cunningham accompanied the bearded Latvian ashore to see for himself, and to confirm the news of the assault. He saw much evidence of looting by German soldiers, and the burning of headquarters, and also heard rumours of the capture and manhandling of senior Latvian officers.

On returning to the *Seafire*, Cunningham to his great joy found the arms ship all ready to proceed, and was able to lead her out through the canal to the safety of the outer harbour. But his task was not yet complete, for he now received a signal from Cowan to proceed with the *Seafire* and the *Scotsman* (Lieutenant-Commander D. J. D. Noble) into the commercial harbour to embark fleeing members of the Latvian government.

Cunningham ordered the manning of the guns, and took the *Seafire* and *Scotsman* stern first up the river into the narrow commercial harbour which lay to the southward of the naval harbour. The two destroyers were thus pointing the right way if a hurried exit should become necessary. As they secured at a wharf alongside the Customs House, there was evidence of great activity among the Germans at the machine-gun posts on the jetty. This however hurriedly ceased as soon as the destroyer's gun crews were sighted, and in response to a polite message which Cunningham sent ashore the machine-guns were taken away.

The situation remained tense all that day and well into the night. Two deposed Latvian ministers managed to find their way to the *Seafire* and brought the news that the Latvian Prime Minister and other ministers had taken refuge with the British Mission. Soon after dark two Latvian trawlers also sought refuge close under *Seafire*'s bows, with intent to remount guns which had been removed under the terms of the armistice. Cunningham forbade this, but found little peace, for shortly afterwards he was visited by a German officer, armed to the teeth, who truculently said he had been ordered to search the Customs House, presumably for Latvian arms and refugees. Permission was granted subject to there being no fighting, and the officer was to be accompanied by Noble, the captain of the *Scotsman*, and a petty officer with a loaded revolver. It so happened that at one tense moment during the search of a vast dark cellar, the revolver went off accidentally, which only served to increase the excitement. But after two hours, Noble had still not returned, and Cunningham, now quite anxious, decided to go ashore to the Customs House himself.

German sentries made half-hearted attempts to stop him, but he made his determination clear, doubtless using that well-known naval password 'Bugger off!', and pushed his way past them to enter the great building. In an upstairs room he found that Noble had discovered an interrogation of five men and one old woman taking place, the interrogator emboldened by the presence of two loaded pistols on the table before him, but quite frustrated by Noble's intrusion. As might be expected with the sudden arrival of Cunningham at such a spectacle, the intimidation and interrogation ceased and developed into loud laughter and the liberation of the Latvian prisoners. It is particularly apt to read Cunningham's description of Cowan at this time in words which could so well be applied to Cunningham himself: 'Admiral Cowan was well in charge of the situation. . . . All his messages to the Germans were frigidly polite, always firm, and sometimes acrimonious. Von der Goltz did not appear to realise that we were dictating terms, not discussing them.'

Although unable to do much about the presence of British destroyers in the commercial harbour, the Germans endeavoured to prevent the local inhabitants from approaching the ships; this they did by having a line of sentries on the wharf. This led to some cruelty by angry sentries towards children who had slipped through the line only to be given slices of bread and jam by British sailors; and it could have resulted in ugly scenes if allowed to develop. But the German solution was to build a high wooden barricade with a door in which a sentry would be posted. Cunningham was assured that this would ensure privacy for his sailors who had been troubled by the local populace. Patiently he waited during the two days it took for the construction. On being assured at last that it was complete, and that there would be no further disturbance, he ordered the *Seafire* and *Scotsman* to shift berth along the wharf so as to be beyond the confines of the German barricade. The populace arrived in flocks, and it was not long before the Germans exploded.

'An enormous red staff car drove at full speed on to the jetty,' writes Cunningham. 'It contained a general, I believe von der Goltz himself, who stood up in the car berserk with rage, and started shouting and waving his arms in the air. He addressed no remarks to us. What he roared to his staff was anybody's guess.'

In due course the excitement died down and the Latvian government resumed office, permitting Cowan to take his force to other likely trouble spots in the Baltic, there to exert his firmness and tact, and always ready if occasion demanded, to have a go at the Kronstadt fleet, whatever its size and potential. But changes were imminent. The over-worked and reduced crews of the 33-knot *Seafires* were now to be relieved by the new Vs and Ws with full crews.

Towards the end of April 1919, Cunningham, in company with the *Curacoa* which had hit a mine and damaged her steering gear, took the *Seafire* back to England. Having paid her off in the following November, he was able to take some well-earned leave before receiving promotion to the rank of captain on 31 December 1919. Although his promotion was two and a half years behind that of his classmate Charles Little, who had achieved exceptional selection, Cunningham's own promotion was unusually early; he was not yet 37, and had served only four and a half years in the rank of commander, whereas the normal for those fortunate enough to be promoted at this 'run-down' period was five and a half to six years. He was in the promising position of being bottom of the list of those promoted captain, in other words the junior promotion of the batch. Because of the run-down of ships, promotions were fewer; only 16 commanders were promoted to captain on this occasion, whereas a year earlier the number had been 30. For his services in the Baltic Cunningham was awarded a second bar to his DSO, giving this young captain the equivalent of three DSO's. Doubtless his outstanding ability and exceptional leadership while serving under such influential admirals as Keyes and Cowan had been fully reported. It is obvious that he shared many of their characteristics, in particular single-mindedness of purpose backed by immense courage.

5

Post Captain (1920–31)

One great advantage experienced by Cunningham so far, was that for 11 years, and much of that in wartime, he had had his own command, and had been able to develop powers of leadership, and demonstrate his self-assurance. He had scarcely put a foot wrong. With the advent of nominal peace, the navy was now to suffer huge reductions both in men and in ships. Future prospects for service personnel looked grim, in spite of the immediate and continuing need for the stabilising presence of naval and military forces in the Baltic and Mediterranean seas. Two decades would elapse before Britain was again at war and in particular need of experienced leaders. During much of that time there would be false reliance on a peace based on the principles of collective security sponsored by an impotent League of Nations, and a continuing edict that there would be no major war for at least ten years. There were many lessons to be learnt from the 'Great War' both militarily and politically, but the real wish was to forget.

For Cunningham they were to be important years wherein he would gain experience wider than that to be obtained in his beloved destroyers. The post-war navy was to consist of two main fleets; one in the Mediterranean, and the other, based on home ports, the Atlantic Fleet later called Home Fleet. Each was composed of capital ships, cruisers, destroyers, submarines, and auxiliaries. In addition to the main fleets there were cruiser squadrons abroad at the stations then known as East Indies, China, America and West Indies, Africa. There were also small ships in the Yangtse, West River, and Persian Gulf.

After a year attached to the Naval Inter-Allied Commission of Control in Germany to superintend the destruction of Heligoland, Cunningham attended the Senior Officers Technical Course at Portsmouth, which consisted of lectures at the various technical schools in gunnery, torpedo, signals, and anti-submarine developments brought about during the war. Regrettably, although there were many younger officers, and a sprinkling of older men too, who considered that battleships would soon be outdated by the innovation of aircraft carriers and the rapid development of aviation, there were still a great many who put their faith in the heavily gunned and armoured battleship.

Under the pioneering lead provided by the Royal Naval Air Service in 1911, aviation generally had made good strides during the 1914–18 war, and seaplane carriers were gradually being developed into aircraft carriers that could accompany the fleet at sea, with wheeled aircraft that could fly on and fly off, providing not only extensive local reconnaissance but a swiftly mobile striking force. A great set-back to naval aviation was suffered however in 1918 when the Royal Naval Air Service was merged with the Royal Flying Corps which then became the Royal Air Force, and control of naval flying was removed from the Admiralty to the Air Ministry, a situation which remained in force until 1937 when control of the Fleet Air Arm was assumed by the Admiralty. Cunningham's attitude towards 'air' in the Second World War is well known, for, as we shall see below, he was repeatedly calling for more air support which would be directly under the control of the Commander-in-Chief of the Fleet, not only in the matter of offence and defence, but particularly in the role of ordered reconnaissance. There have been suggestions that his views of early days concerning flying changed considerably, implying that he was not a strong supporter. His own writings and some following remarks should dispel any such illusion. It is likely that any contemptuous attitude that he may have shown was in accordance with his critical and questioning examination of most things, and his belief that it could be done better.

A letter from an officer who served as his secretary says:[1]

'Regarding your reference to Air Power, I got the impression that ABC was not very fond of the Air Service which may have been due to the fact that he considered the standard of efficiency and discipline of the personnel was not up to his standard. ABC was a "Salt Horse" and he judged officers mainly on their ability as seamen.

'Later, he spent some time at the Admiralty [DCNS 1938] and it may have been there that he was persuaded to realise the importance of Air Power, and no doubt he realised it more than ever during the war in the Mediterranean.'

His observer[2] in the *Warspite* in 1941 writes in April 1972: 'If Cunningham had lived I don't think we would have lost the carriers,' referring presumably to political decisions of the Labour government of 1967. In a later letter October 1972 he says, 'ABC was the greatest of the protagonists for the FAA.'

A naval pilot[3] who served with him first in 1935 and again in 1939 says: 'My next service in his command was as Commander (F) in *Eagle*

(1939–41)' [ABC was then Commander-in-Chief Mediterranean] 'and I found that his attitude towards the AIR had undergone quite a "volte face" since the days of RAD Med (1935).' The inference from the context was that his conversion in favour was quite sudden and occurred soon after the combined fleets exercises in the spring of 1935.

Cunningham certainly realised the potential of naval aviation in early days, but was apprehensive of a reduction of traditional navy standards which might accompany the hiving off to a new service. 'From start to finish,' he writes,[4] 'the control of the Naval Air Arm by the Air Ministry was a ghastly failure which militated against the vital air efficiency of the navy. As the Air Estimates were ruthlessly shorn, the Naval Air Arm became a sort of Cinderella, starved, neglected and nearly forgotten. It was not until 1937, after a severe and protracted struggle on the part of the Admiralty when Admiral of the Fleet Lord Chatfield was First Sea Lord, that ship-borne aircraft again came under the full operational and administrative control of the Royal Navy with whom they would work in war. It was only just in time.'

From the Senior Officers Technical Course ABC was appointed once again to his beloved destroyers, this time (April 1922) to the flotilla leader *Shakespeare* at Portsmouth, as Captain (D) of the 6th Destroyer Flotilla in reserve. Not content to be in reserve, he importuned for ratings at the three manning ports, and by a temporary rearrangement of complements was able to be present with some of his destroyers at the Atlantic Fleet exercises based on Invergordon. The Commander-in-Chief was Admiral Sir John de Robeck, his old acquaintance of 1915 at the Dardanelles, and it was now that he first met Robeck's Chief of Staff, W. W. Fisher, a senior captain, widely regarded as a rising star. ABC was greatly impressed, as were most people, and referred to him as 'tall, good-looking, imposing, and rather intimidating'. He was certainly all of these, and was commonly known as 'The Great Agrippa'. He was an enthusiast and a hard worker. A great future was forecast for him, but he died at a relatively early age in 1937 while serving as Commander-in-Chief Portsmouth.

Cunningham's appointment as D 6 ended in December 1922 when he was appointed to the flotilla leader *Wallace* as D 1. The 1st Flotilla belonged to the Atlantic Fleet, but had been temporarily detached to the Mediterranean, to support British ships based on Istanbul. Britain was almost on the point of war with Turkey who under Kemal Ataturk had practically annihilated the Greek Army, and had in defiance of the Treaty of Sèvres of 1920, re-occupied all those territories which were not already under Allied occupation. The reinforced British Mediterranean Fleet held authority in the Straits from the Black Sea to Gallipoli, and in particular at Istanbul and Chanak. A crisis was reached when Turkish transports assembled with a view to transferring troops across the Bosphorus. This was averted when Cunningham was ordered to steam with his eight destroyers up and down at 30 knots, so as to wreck the transports should the Turkish Army embark.

His stay in this area was of short duration, for the 1st Flotilla was ordered home in March 1923 to rejoin the Atlantic Fleet.

In spite of the drastic cuts which accompanied the Geddes Axe and the Washington Disarmament Conference, and caused gloom and dismay among naval personnel, the navy continued to work hard, stimulated by leaders such as Cunningham who spared no pains to maintain a high standard and to admonish and exemplify where necessary. Drastic fuel economy imposed economical speed as a normal procedure, nevertheless strenuous training continued, spurred by the competitive aspect of Admiral's inspections and tactical and strategical exercises. The role of the destroyer was becoming of increasing interest, not only for its offensive potential with torpedoes in a mass attack against heavy ships, day or night, but also as a protective screen for the battle fleet by virtue of under-water detection and destruction of submarines.

It is clear that Cunningham gave considerable thought to exercises which involved destroyers in an offensive role. In later years, when in command at the battle of Matapan, he was described as handling the battle fleet as if it were a division of destroyers. Instead of the generally accepted turn-away of battleships on sighting the enemy at night, the signal for the turn-towards was made: an inspired decision as it happened.

A glimpse of Cunningham in 1923 is provided by two old shipmates. A letter from a signalman in the *Wallace* says:[5] 'He was a bit of a terror. . . . *Wallace* had a bumpy trip across the Bay of Biscay; several destroyers lost their topmasts, etc., etc. As we entered Arosa Bay he made "During this last passage communications were much to be desired and semaphore seems to be a thing of the past". I admired him as a signalman, he could read semaphore and morse with the best. . . . I reminded him of this signal [nearly 20 years later in the *Warspite*] . . . and he quoted every detail of the trip. He also remembered all the commanding officers' names. I adored him. . . . I could never understand why he was not more popular with the lower deck . . . he thought a lot of them.'

Perhaps it was this trip to which ABC referred when describing[6] 'the cynical contempt which the small ship sailor had for his contemporary in a battle-wagon'. Even the battleships were rolling heavily, and he heard one of his own sailors say that he reckoned the battle-wagons might have to postpone the final of the petty officers' billiards handicap.

ABC was seldom stumped for an admonitory rebuke for errors committed. His Staff Torpedo Officer writes:[7]

'I was in the *Wallace*, 1922–23. As you are no doubt aware, Cunningham commanded the destroyer *Scorpion* for something like seven years; assuming command while still a "two striper", and a commander by the time he relinquished command. He seems to have acquired the reputation while in the *Scorpion* of being a very taut hand, so we were something apprehensive when we heard he was to come to us [from the *Shakespeare*]. . . . For about a month after he took over, the 1st Flotilla wondered what had hit it. . . .

'Ordinarily ABC would make signals: "*Wallace* to so-and-so." Upon occasion, when things were "hotting up a bit", he would start to make signals "*Shakespeare* to so-and-so", and we pricked our ears. But when his signals commenced: "*Scorpion* to so-and-so" such members of the Flotilla Staff as could contrive to do so "lost themselves" with all convenient speed . . . he had a knack of getting rid of officers of whom he entertained no very high opinion.'

By September 1923 the number of fully commissioned flotillas under Rear-Admiral (D), Atlantic Fleet, had been increased to five, but this did little to alleviate the shortage of sea jobs for commanders and captains. It is understandable that there would be keen competition between the flotillas for smartness in appearance and competence in exercises, and it is certain that Cunningham's 1st Flotilla had a high reputation. He refers with obvious relish to a passage up the Manchester Ship Canal where there were nine bridges. Every destroyer of his flotilla had to lower her topmast on passing beneath each bridge, and re-hoist it *immediately* afterwards. Doubtless a record would be kept of the speed and competence of each performer of these operations.

At this time, apart from a large number of ships of all classes in reserve, the navy maintained in full commission its seagoing fleets and squadrons all over the world: 13 battleships; 2 battle cruisers; 31 light cruisers; and 63 destroyers. It was still a force to inspire authority and stability. Nevertheless it was difficult to provide all captains with adequate sea time.

Cunningham's time as captain of a destroyer flotilla ended in May 1924, and was followed in October 1924 by a shore job. This was at Port Edgar, a destroyer base on the South Queensferry side of the Firth of Forth, as Captain in Charge, so he was not yet to be parted altogether from destroyers. A young lieutenant[8] appointed there in 1925 writes of the splendid work done in the training of Boys for the Fleet and the glowing reports received from sea. 'ABCs house,' he writes, 'was in the middle of the establishment, just a tin hut with windows on all sides and he missed nothing. It is said that no grass has ever grown at Port Edgar since as the speed at which we all moved got the place down to bedrock. I myself was married then (anathema to ABC) and I got away with it for two years by telling my wife she was never to appear in public, so ABC never met her.' It is interesting to be reminded of the attitude towards marriage of those days, when foreign commissions lasted two and a half years. This was long before marriage allowance was approved for naval officers in 1938.

By a stroke of luck the Commanding Officer, Coast of Scotland, was an officer whom he knew well, Rear-Admiral Sir Reginald Tyrwhitt, who was relieved in June 1925 by another old and distinguished friend, Vice-Admiral Sir Walter Cowan. In the following year this led inevitably to an appointment which would gladden any captain's heart: Flag Captain and Chief Staff Officer to the Commander-in-Chief, North America and West Indies station. The Commander-in-Chief from June 1926 was to be Cowan himself, and it was he who had asked for Cunningham. There were on the station four 'C' class light cruisers of 4,000 tons, each mounting 6-inch guns; there were also two sloops, one of which was the ill-fated *Valerian* of 1,250 tons.

Cunningham commissioned the *Calcutta* in May 1926, took her out to the Fleet base at Bermuda, and was joined a few weeks later by Sir Walter Cowan who would live and work ashore at Admiralty House, Bermuda, when not cruising in his flagship. The station covered both the east and west coasts of North America and the whole of the Caribbean. The duties consisted of liaison with the Royal Canadian Navy and showing the white ensign. This involved considerable steaming over vast areas, and calls at numerous ports. Occasionally there would be calls for help at times of insurrection and disaster. At convenient times of the year, the squadron would assemble at Bermuda for competitive shoots, tactical exercises, recreational activities, and annual inspection.

Cunningham speaks of meeting Lieutenant-Commander Alan Kirk, USN, who acted as liaison officer while the flagship was on a visit to Philadelphia. He liked him and found him most able, and subsequently corresponded with him every year at Christmas. It seems fitting therefore that Kirk should have become one of the naval assault force commanders for the invasion of Sicily in 1943.

Cunningham's appointment as Chief Staff Officer was his first introduction to what he called the 'mysteries' of staff work. Throughout his career he was fond of alluding to the fact that he never did a staff course, and would superficially offer a contemptuous attitude towards paper work and red tape, implying that much of it was unnecessary. As Flag Captain he commanded and 'drove' the flagship, with a splendid executive officer Commander H. B. Maltby, as second in command; but as CSO he had to involve himself in the administration of the fleet, together with the Admiral's Secretary, the Staff Officer (Operations), and the various 'Fleet' officers for each specialisation. He was more at home in handling the squadron of light cruisers when together, with the Admiral closely watching and 'galloping' every move. Cowan would allow no signal, not even 'Anchor instantly', to remain at the mast-head more than a second or two. Immediately a signal was hoisted 'close up', it had to be hauled down.

Cunningham was very pleased with the *Calcutta*'s performance in harbour drills, sea manoeuvres, and squadron competition. Thirty of her ship's company were boys who had served under him at Port Edgar for special training, and on whom he had so obviously left his stamp in matters of smartness and seamanship. As a result the ship was well in the lead in all activities. The executive officer Commander Maltby had a way with ratings, most of whom liked and respected him. Cunningham exerted a mesmeric effect on them too.

'It was on the North America and West Indies station,' writes J. A. G. Troup,[9] captain of the *Cairo*, 'that I began to learn his stature. The Flag Captain had an intense will to win. . . . Many a time and oft in the last war [World War II] did I long for what could not be: ABC and Walter Cowan racing into action, with myself tailing on at utmost speed in some lesser command. After his West Indies service it became clear, from the appointments he held, that ABC was destined for the highest commands.'

But the omniscient Cunningham admits to an error of judgment concerning a hurricane which was reported approaching Bermuda on 21 October 1926. The cruisers normally lay alongside the dockyard when in port, but Station Orders instructed that all ships should leave port at the approach of a hurricane, and either go to sea or anchor in the Great Sound. On this occasion he allowed himself to be persuaded by two experienced navigating officers who held the view that the centre of the hurricane would pass 300 miles to the north of Bermuda. In the ensuing storm the *Calcutta* received damage when rolling against the solid masonry of the jetty, and later when the anemometer had recorded 138 miles per hour, sailed across the basin, having parted bow and stern wire hawsers and extracted some of the bollards from the jetty. She was only halted in her passage to destruction by an anchor which brought her head to wind, and both engines going full speed ahead. In spite of this near disaster ABC was able to see the humour of the moment when a signalman rushed to the Commander with a message which read 'There will be no tennis at Admiralty House to-day'.

Ironically, tragedy had struck elsewhere with the loss of the sloop *Valerian* at sea only a few miles south of Bermuda. Cunningham believed her to have capsized near an outlying reef. By good fortune the *Capetown* found the spot and was able to pick up a Carley float with 29 survivors.

Admiralty reproach might have been expected over the damage sustained by the *Calcutta*, particularly as she had not been taken to sea as instructed in Station Orders, but Cunningham appears to have been exonerated when taking the sensible line that a dockyard port that could not be used in any weather was scarcely worthy of the name. Various improvements in the matters of hawsers, bollards, and fenders were then put in hand. It could have been after this event that Troup began to visualise the great future destined for ABC. 'His comments, verbal and written,' he says, 'on people of all ranks were candid, witty, generous, and could be delightfully pungent.'

An important experience for Cunningham, still a bachelor, occurred when *Calcutta* called at Trinidad early in 1927, and he and Admiral Cowan stayed at Government House with the Governor Sir Horace Byatt. It was then that he met Miss Nona Byatt, the Governor's sister, whom he was to marry in December 1929. Following week after week of steaming great distances, calls, sight-seeing, dancing, lavish entertainment, and speech-making, which tended to be wearying, and 'ruinous to the digestion', he found the relaxed atmosphere and the surf-riding and bathing at Trinidad a great joy.

The 'C' class cruisers were to be gradually relieved by the larger and newer 'D' class cruisers. By the end of 1927 the *Despatch* had arrived at Bermuda to assume the duties of flagship on a station to which the whole of the South America coast had just been added. There followed a three months' cruise by the Commander-in-Chief to the Caribbean, Panama, Ecuador, Peru, Chile, Venezuela, and back to Bermuda by way of Trinidad, Barbados, and Antigua: obviously an exhausting trip, particularly for the Admiral, but also a most instructive one the details of which Cunningham has amply recorded.[10] Always in his mind when meeting a President and other national leaders, was the importance to be attached to international relationships. 'British sailors are among our best ambassadors,' he wrote. In particular, his visits to American cities such as Boston and Washington must have developed a fair understanding which was to serve him well in the Second World War.

With the advent of 1928 Cunningham's time on the America and West Indies station was nearing an end, as was that of the Admiral.

They were both relieved in August 1928, and it is interesting to read the former's opinion of the latter whom he so much resembled in many qualities, and who must have greatly moulded him during their two years of close association showing the flag over such a large area of the world.

'He taught me a lot,' writes Cunningham[11] of Cowan. 'His ideals of duty and honour were of the highest, and never sparing himself he expected others to do the same. ... Nothing ever daunted him. ... I have spent no happier years at sea than when serving with Sir Walter in the *Calcutta* and the *Despatch*.'

ABC was to spend the latter part of 1928 at an Army School for Senior Officers at Sheerness, before being appointed to a course at the Imperial Defence College for most of 1929. He learnt much about the problems facing all three Services, and a good deal about foreign affairs and economics. His *Britannia* shipmate, James Somerville, also a captain, was a member of the instructional staff.

Perhaps the most important event for Cunningham at this time was his engagement in October 1929 to Miss Nona Byatt; his marriage was to be a very happy one. At about the same time, or shortly afterwards, he was informed that he was to take command of the 34,000-ton battle-ship *Rodney*, 'showing', as Charles Little has written, 'how well he was thought of', and presumably being a final test of suitability for promotion to flag rank when his turn came to be considered. Charles Little was already a rear-admiral, having been promoted to flag rank in February 1929.

As a consequence of the fuel economy of those days, and the limitations imposed on the Royal Navy by disarmament, there were relatively few ships in commission. 'I was in *Rodney*,' writes a young lieutenant[12] of the time, 'from July 1929 to December 1930, during which we had three captains, as they were rationed to a year or less of sea-time. ... When ABC was appointed we were all rather apprehensive as he had a reputation as a tiger from the destroyer command. ... In fact we found him much less frightening and put this down to the fact that he had recently married. ... We had a strong team of officers many of whom reached flag rank and included Bob Burnett (Commander), George Creasy, G. N. Oliver, P. B. R. W. William-Powlett, Rupert Sherbrooke, and George Collett. I was 2nd Torpedo Officer and ABC chased the Torpedo Party quite a bit because we were seen too often in overall suits maintaining our torpedoes and the ship's electrical system which he didn't think right for seamen; this put us on our metal and we entered a crew for the Crash Cutter competition which won the ship competition and subsequently the fleet competition, and no one could have cheered louder than ABC. . . . We heard less about not being seamen from then on.'

The *Nelson* and *Rodney* were two handsome floating fortresses completed and commissioned in 1926–27, bearing an armament of nine 16-inch, twelve 6-inch, and six 4·7-inch guns; at 23 knots designed full speed however they were relatively slow. They were also difficult ships to manoeuvre. Cunningham, who had never commanded anything larger than a light cruiser, found the *Rodney* difficult to handle at first, but stated in due course that she was little different from the smaller ships to which he was accustomed.

Cunningham inspired all with the sense of competition so as to bring out the best in them. G. N. Oliver[13] writes:

'In January 1930 I joined *Rodney* as (G) [the gunnery officer]. We spent much time in company with our one and only sister ship, *Nelson*, the flagship [of the Atlantic Fleet, soon to become the Home Fleet]. As we were generally doing the same things at the same time, rivalry was pretty hot and ABC would certainly not accept second place for *Rodney*. The year before, *Rodney* had been soundly beaten in the annual Fleet Sailing Regatta. ABC, a dedicated boat-sailor, was determined to avenge this. After the official part of the summer cruise, each ship could choose one port to visit. There was some astonishment when ABC asked to take *Rodney* to the Scillies in July 1930. There, we squeezed ourselves into the anchorage off St. Mary's, and, for the next four days, every boat, already tuned up and manned with picked crews and helmsmen, was away under sail from morning till evening with none but the local seagulls to spot our form. Then, we rejoined the Fleet at Falmouth for the Regatta. This lasted several days and it blew hard all the time. *Rodney*'s boats swept the board.'

There is an interesting annex to this which reveals a characteristic that was not unusual in ABC as well as other great men; that of being vehemently against some precautionary measure when it applied to himself, and yet full of authoritarian reproach for anyone else who omitted such precaution. It didn't matter whether it applied to the wearing of a 'tin hat' in action, or the carrying of spare equipment in a sailing race as described by his messenger in the *Rodney* in Chapter 1.

'ABC had a disappointment,' continues Oliver, referring to the Fleet Sailing Regatta, 'carrying away one of his masts when lying well up in the race for galleys. As he stubbornly refused to carry a spare, he had to finish under a single mast and, though placed, could not win.' It was the Commander who had urged him to take a spare. 'The Commander's face on my return was a picture,' comments ABC.

As so often follows with a taut ship, she was a happy and successful one also. Bob Burnett the Commander had an excellent way with the men, and it was a sad day when he and ABC left at the same time.

'I have sometimes wondered,' continues Oliver, 'whether things would not have gone differently in the ship in 1931 at Invergordon had they been there. Bob Burnett was a ball of fire and a great extrovert. He wrote and produced comic operas for us to put on at Pollensa Bay during the spring cruises. There is a tale which *may* be apocryphal, though I believe it. ABC was giving a lunch party when we were at Gib. Bob dressed up as a female guest, in place of someone who had fallen out, and was duly "received" in the cuddy and got away with it.' Those who remember the podgy Bob Burnett, a P.T. specialist, with his eternal red-faced grin, may also believe it.

There is a story (also perhaps apocryphal) about Oliver himself, given to me by a midshipman[14] then serving in the *Rodney*, which describes Oliver explaining to Cunningham the reason for some gunnery failure. 'In what capacity are you appointed here?' asked ABC. 'Your gunnery officer, sir,' responded Oliver. 'Go away then,' said ABC. 'Make your toys work. And don't waste my time with excuses.' Such bombast was not untypical, yet ABC himself refers to Oliver's 'outstanding ability and personality', and in the Second World War found him 'a tower of strength': praise indeed by Cunningham's standards.

Although Cunningham's time in *Rodney* had to be limited to a year because of the rationing of sea-time for senior captains, it was a strenuous period especially when ships were at sea and every opportunity for exercising had to be seized. The Commander-in-Chief Atlantic Fleet was Admiral Sir Ernle Chatfield with his flag in the *Nelson*. Ten years older than Cunningham, and one of the best all-rounders of his day, he had had close association with Beatty especially during the First World War when he was his Flag Captain in the *Lion*. He had been Controller of the Navy, and after his present appointment was to become Commander-in-Chief Mediterranean Fleet, and then First Sea Lord. He was an advocate of a fleet action at night, strongly supported by the Rear-Admiral, 1st Battle Squadron, the Hon. R. A. R. Plunkett-Ernle-Erle-Drax, with his flag in the *Barham* also of the Atlantic Fleet, at a time when controversy raged on this subject, there being a strong body of opinion from many senior officers that a powerful fleet should not risk the hazards of night, and especially the possibility of a concerted torpedo attack by destroyers. It was hoped to explore various problems during the large combined exercises with the Mediterranean Fleet, but in the event the two fleets did not make contact, as the Flag Officer commanding the opposing side was flatly against night action. Interest was however to quicken during the early 'thirties'.

7 *Mediterranean Fleet at Gibraltar, March 1934. In centre, beyond the hospital ship* Maine, *is Cunningham's flagship* Coventry *when he was* RAD *(Med)*

8 *C-in-C's staff in* HMS Warspite, *December 1940. Seated, left to right:* Barnard (FGO), *Dick* (SOP), *Greeson* (FMO), *Shaw* (SEC), *Willis* (COS), *ABC (C-in-C), Fisher (Capt), Shelley* (COF), *Carne* (FTO), *Hampton* (ASOP), *Penfold* (FRMO)

9 HMS Hood, *Cunningham's flagship when in command of* BCS, *1937–8*

Cunningham left the *Rodney* in December 1930. Knowing that he would be near the top of the captains' list in a little over a year, it was pleasing to be told that his next appointment was to be as Commodore of the Royal Naval Barracks at Chatham, generally regarded at that time as a job leading to promotion to flag rank. He had however been unwell for some months suffering from internal trouble, and now took the opportunity of some leave to 'have the necessary operation'. The last time he had been in hospital was in 1926 prior to going out to the West Indies, to see if they could 'sort out' his inside which had been troubling him for a year or so. After following a false scent the surgeons had removed his appendix. He left in such a hurry that he had joined the *Calcutta* swathed in bandages.

6

Flag Rank (1932-36)

At the time of Cunningham's appointment to the Royal Naval Barracks, Chatham, in July 1931, he was a captain with a seniority of 11½ years, and there were still a few months to go before selection from his batch of captains would reveal who was to be promoted to flag rank on the active list, and who was to retire. The title Commodore Second Class was not a substantive rank; nor was Commodore First Class. But it was generally regarded that holders of appointments bearing such titles were almost certain to be promoted when they reached the top of the captains list. Cunningham was a marked man already, and it was in the spring of 1932 that he was informed by Their Lordships that he was to be promoted in due course to the rank of Rear-Admiral and would be retained on the active list. Promotion took place 24 September 1932, but after 12 years and nine months as a captain, a relatively long period to serve in this rank, caused by the blockage which became cumulative with increasing disarmament. His *Britannia* classmate, Charles Little, had acquired flag rank after only 11 years and eight months, and was now three years and seven months senior to him.

Cunningham's spell in the barracks brought him closely in touch with advancement and welfare problems of sailors, and left him of the firm opinion that the manning of a warship should not be restricted to a particular port such as Portsmouth, Devonport, or Chatham, but should be done by a central drafting authority. There was much opposition to this 'newfangled' idea, and the proposal had to be dropped. It was to be several years before it was adopted and shown to be practicable.

It was less than three months after Cunningham had taken over command of the barracks at Chatham that he was to learn of the mutiny of units of the Atlantic Fleet at Invergordon, caused directly by an Admiralty Fleet Order delineating cuts in pay which were to come into force on 1 October 1931. Though mutiny was inexcusable, it was soon realised that the forecast cuts, had they been implemented, would have brought about extreme hardship especially among married ratings with families living on the border-line of poverty.

'We were all to blame,' writes Cunningham.[1] 'No officers in command of ships, least of all those in command of shore establishments with large bodies of men, could acquit themselves of blame for being unacquainted with the subject and their failure to make representations to higher authority.'

There was little indication of mutinous intention at Chatham, since the battle cruiser *Repulse* had just recommissioned there, taking over 1,000 ratings from the barracks, and had given no trouble at Invergordon. Nevertheless Cunningham issued an open invitation for any rating to see him to reveal hardship or state a complaint. He saw about 500 men this way, and learnt of many hard-luck cases where pay was insufficient to allow a margin for illness and emergency or even the cheapest of amusement. He greatly admired his old friend, formerly Commodore of the Harwich Force, now Admiral Sir Reginald Tyrwhitt, Commander-in-Chief, the Nore, whom the sailors trusted for his firmness and understanding.

In view of Cunningham's well-known disapproval of any overbearing of complement, either of ratings or of officers, it is pertinent to read the following comment written by Captain R. D. Butt, RN, of an occasion when he was Commander of RN Barracks, Devonport: 'I saw ABC about ten days before he died when he came to H.M.S. *Drake* for the memorial unveiling of the Wee McGrigor's tablet in the church. He was exactly as I remembered him in *Queen Elizabeth* in 1942, and his mind was crystal clear and memory faultless. I had a long chat with him in the mess afterwards, including about Walter Starkie [killed at Crete] who was his flag lieutenant and had been my Dartmouth House Officer. He then asked me "Commander, how many men have you got in the barracks guard?", and when I said 20, he replied "Not enough; I had 100 when I was Commodore at Chatham at the time of the Invergordon mutiny, and needed every one".'

With the mutiny over, and part of the pay cuts rescinded, Cunningham concluded that the navy had been paying too much attention to the material side of the Service, and far too little to the human side. The mutiny did lead to a strengthening of the divisional system and greater attention being devoted by officers to the welfare of ratings in their divisions.

Though now assured of further service on the active list Cunningham had to wait several months before receiving a flag appointment, but was retained in command at Chatham Barracks until February 1933, although that appointment rated a captain. He was then appointed to Portsmouth for courses: first the Senior Officers Technical Course to acquaint himself with the latest technical developments in the navy; and then to the Senior Officers Tactical Course where fleets and squadrons could be handled (a little unrealistically), in war games played with models on large charts set out on the floor.

A letter from a qualified naval observer,[2] a young naval lieutenant at that time, and instructor at the RAF 'School of Naval Co-operation', reveals that he had been 'borrowed to teach other naval officers to be naval observers, a practice which followed the nightmare policies thrashed out by such supermen as Trenchard and Roger Keyes (hard to believe, isn't it?). I was told off,' he continues, 'to lecture the SOTC about Naval Observers, a species that had hardly appeared as a possible part of Fleet activities even then, a decade or two after they had been invented.'

'One of the uses of this strange animal was that it took photographs out of the open cockpits of that era (using believe it or not, an enormous camera with glass plates . . .!). Enthralled with an hour of this stuff, the Senior Officers found the call of the bar was too strong and they trooped off to whet their whistles: all except Andrew B, who beckoned me.'

ABC then asked the naval observer if he could fly over and photograph the house where ABC lived, during the next day or two. In foul weather, with the observer nearly falling out of the plane to get a decent shot, the job was done. But it was ABC alone among those Senior Officers who had had the conception of a practical use for naval observing.

'I never heard another word,' writes Gowlland. 'Most senior officers in mid-30s were very sceptical about the FAA generally, and thought of observers as a form of ballast, if at all.'

It is sad but right to record this attitude. It is fair also to recall that the Herculean task of getting the Fleet Air Arm again under the control of the Admiralty had already begun with the arrival of Admiral Sir Ernle Chatfield at the Admiralty as First Sea Lord in June 1932. It was to be a matter of only eight years or so before the widely held sceptical attitude towards naval aviation was rudely shattered at Taranto and at Matapan, ABC himself then being the naval Commander-in-Chief Mediterranean.

An old friend, J. A. G. Troup (in the term below him in the *Britannia*), then a senior captain, and earlier in command of the Navigation School, directed the Tactical Course. Also on the course was Captain F. Dalrymple-Hamilton[3] who, as a newly promoted captain, in charge of destroyers laid up in the Medway, had met and admired ABC when he was Commander of Chatham Barracks.

'I soon realised Andrew Cunningham and I had quite a few tastes in common,' he writes: 'love of service in destroyers being one of them and fishing another; golf and gardening also had a part when time permitted. . . . Andrew was the greatest fun at any time whether at play or on real naval business.

'What I did not know at that time was that Andrew had been selected to be Rear-Admiral (Destroyers) in the Mediterranean Fleet of which the Commander-in-Chief was Sir William Wordsworth Fisher; three flotillas [the 1st, 3rd, and 4th] comprised the Destroyer Command.'

'The tactical course ended,' continues Dalrymple-Hamilton, 'I received a note from the Naval Secretary to say I had been selected as Captain (D) of the 4th Flotilla in H.M.S. *Keith*. For a young captain there was no better command to be had, especially under such a brilliant leader.' Dalrymple-Hamilton also referred to 'Nelsonic principles' and the fact that Cunningham knew he could rely on his subordinates, both officers and ratings, to do their utmost to serve him in whatever capacity they were called to do so: the 'Band of Brothers'.

Cunningham says of his appointment as RA (D) Mediterranean (1 January 1934) that it was the one appointment he would have chosen above all others. His Commander-in-Chief was eight years older than he, and Cunningham found him a great inspiration and considered himself fortunate to serve with such a leader. Success in the Services frequently depends not only on ability but on being in the right place at the right time with the right boss. There have been many officers of outstanding merit who were unlucky in this respect. Fisher made his mark early in his career. Competent as well as accomplished, and imposing in appearance, he had been selected and groomed for a succession of responsible appointments, and was regarded as a certainty for the highest post in due course. He would be greatly needed in the war which to many now seemed inevitable. Yet his name is hardly remembered now, for he died at the age of 62, two years before the outbreak of the Second World War. It is only admirals who win battles who become immortalised. Cunningham in due course paid tribute when he himself was Commander-in-Chief Mediterranean, and Britain was at war with Italy.[4] 'How right Sir William Fisher was in 1935–36 during the Abyssinian time. When confronted with a difficult situation I cast my mind back and ask myself what he would have done, and the answer always comes the same – to take the bold and direct course – and it pays.'

But on 1 January 1934 when ABC hoisted his flag in the light cruiser *Coventry* as RA (D) he 'found him very difficult to get on with'. This initial relationship between two such strong characters is understandable, but it did not take many weeks for the development of a great mutual regard, and Cunningham particularly liked Fisher's fresh approach to problems. On this day of hoisting his flag for the first time, with a little over a year's seniority as a rear-admiral, he became a Companion of the Order of the Bath.

The Mediterranean Fleet at this time consisted of:

> First Battle Squadron: Queen Elizabeth (fleet flagship), Revenge, Resolution, Royal Sovereign
> First Cruiser Squadron: London (flag), Sussex, Devonshire, Shropshire
> Third Cruiser Squadron: Delhi (flag), Despatch, Dauntless, Durban
> Aircraft Carrier: Furious
> Destroyer Group: Cruiser Coventry (flag), 1st, 3rd, 4th destroyer flotillas (8 destroyers and a flotilla leader in each), and destroyer depot ship Sandhurst

The Coventry was an old and slow light cruiser, and though adequate as a 'private' ship was hard pressed to accommodate an admiral and his personal staff, secretary Paymaster Lieutenant-Commander A. P. Shaw and flag lieutenant Lieutenant-Commander D. O. Doble. In addition there were the squadron torpedo officer (Commander Charles Lambe, later First Sea Lord), and the staff officer operations (Lieutenant-Commander Anthony Buzzard, later Rear-Admiral Sir Anthony Buzzard, Bart., CB, DSO, OBE, and Director of Naval Intelligence).

Destroyer training and tactics were still much influenced by memories of the First World War. But both the Commander-in-Chief Home Fleet (Admiral Sir William Boyle who became Earl of Cork and Orrery during 1934) and the Commander-in-Chief Mediterranean (Admiral Sir William Fisher) were now seized with the importance of training a fleet for night action, so as to prevent an enemy escaping as the Germans had done at Jutland because of Jellicoe's apprehension of possible disaster from destroyer attack; and this had been policy since the early 'thirties. The annual combined fleet exercise seldom attracted public attention, but that of March 1934 was outstanding because of Fisher's great 'victory' over the Home Fleet, a matter in which 'RA (D) and the ships of his command had no small part in bringing about with precision the situation designed by Fisher'.[5]

The object of the Home Fleet was to escort a mythical expeditionary force from the Azores to some port on the 400-mile Atlantic seaboard of Spain and Portugal. The Mediterranean Fleet, who knew of this intention, was to sail westward from Gibraltar, with the object of destroying both convoy and escort before arrival. They could only surmise however that the destination would be Lisbon or, alternatively, Arosa Bay 250 miles farther to the northward. It requires a glance at the vastness of the ocean, and a knowledge of the prevailing dirty weather, to realise the difficulty of interception (see map p. 60).

Fisher's flag officers all considered that the enemy convoy and battle-fleet escort would use the most southerly and shortest route, that to Lisbon. But Fisher's opinion was that they would steer the more northerly course for Arosa Bay.

Except in destroyers and aircraft, the Home Fleet, with the battle-ships *Nelson* (flag), *Rodney, Malaya, Valiant, Barham*, and the battle cruisers *Hood* and *Renown*, were superior to the Mediterranean Fleet. The weather off Cape St. Vincent, as the Mediterranean Fleet cruisers and destroyers steamed northward to enter the search area, was a full north-westerly gale with a very heavy sea. Air reconnaissance was out of the question, and for 24 hours the destroyers, taking green seas, were practically hove to. Fisher's aim was to hold back his battleships, with a small force of destroyers as an anti-submarine screen, and to send on all cruisers and remaining destroyers to search a large area in the western approaches to Arosa Bay. Ships would be in line abreast, 12 miles apart, steaming westward during the day, and retiring eastward during the night.

At daylight on 13 March, the two Home Fleet battle cruisers *Hood* and *Renown* were reported by a Mediterranean Fleet submarine on the direct route to Lisbon from the Azores, and at the southern boundary of the Mediterranean Fleet search area. Fisher made no alteration in his plans, but sent four of his destroyers to shadow the battle cruisers. Later in the day however one of his cruisers at the northern boundary of the search area reported the four Home Fleet battleships, with convoy, on the direct route to Arosa Bay from the Azores. The battle cruisers, 250 miles to the southward, were obviously intended to lure the Mediter-ranean Fleet towards them, while permitting the convoy to make safely for Arosa Bay. With their high speed the battle cruisers could withdraw at will from the slower Mediterranean Fleet battleships.

But Fisher was already in a suitable position to press on northward with his own battleships, and in spite of high seas, estimated that he could make contact and bring the Home Fleet to action at midnight long before the battle cruisers could rejoin. The element of surprise would more than make up for any disadvantage in numbers. Cunning-ham with a flotilla of destroyers was already in touch with the Home Fleet battleships, and shortly before 1.0 a.m. on 14 March he was ordered by Fisher to attack from astern. This he did, and the glare of his searchlights and star-shells gave Fisher a chance for his 'darkened' ships to adjust their final position. It was to be almost exactly seven years before Cunningham as Commander-in-Chief Mediterranean, this

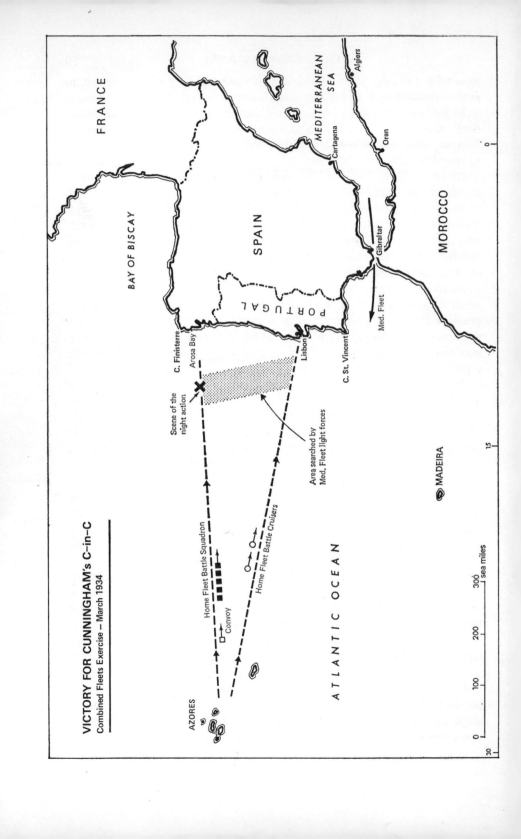

VICTORY FOR CUNNINGHAM's C–in–C
Combined Fleets Exercise – March 1934

FRANCE

BAY OF BISCAY

SPAIN

PORTUGAL

MEDITERRANEAN SEA

Algiers

Oran

Cartagena

Gibraltar

Med. Fleet

MOROCCO

C. Finisterre

Arosa Bay

Lisbon

C. St. Vincent

Scene of the night action

Area searched by Med. Fleet light forces

Home Fleet Battle Squadron

Convoy

Home Fleet Battle Cruisers

ATLANTIC OCEAN

AZORES

MADEIRA

0   100   200   300
sea miles

0

15

30

time with the benefit of radar, bore down on the enemy in the dark, with his battleships off Cape Matapan. Fisher, with his battleships steaming at 16 knots on a suitable line of bearing, now brought them into action simultaneously at a range of 6,000 yards (three miles).

'These bold and masterly tactics not only put an end to the exercise,' writes Cunningham, 'but settled once and for all the much-debated question as to whether or not British heavy ships could and should engage in night action.'

It was almost as if this culmination of the 1934 exercise were a rehearsal for Matapan, and it is certain that all the tactical details were absorbed and remembered by ABC whose tactics were equally bold and masterly. Fisher was hailed by the press as the greatest naval genius of modern times. He himself referred to his understudy ABC as a 'Great Trump'.

Private descriptions of Cunningham as RA (D) are more numerous than those for other periods of his career, and it is valuable to record them in this chapter to reflect the spirit that existed in destroyers. Hero-worship obviously shines through, but generally the accounts adhere to a pattern: the pattern reveals an exceptional character that would not be held back.

His squadron torpedo officer[6] considered ABC a quick and active-minded man who made decisions instantly, but one who 'will always listen to what you have to say first'. The amazing five days in the Atlantic during the 1934 exercise was about the worst sea he had ever seen, but the *Coventry* did not suffer so badly as the battleships and destroyers.

Commander G. N. Oliver,[7] in the destroyer *Veteran*, found life stimulating. 'As Surtees said of fox-hunting,' he writes, 'it was "the image of war without its guilt, and only five-and-twenty per cent of the danger". There was intense *esprit de corps* as COs were made to discover that they could manoeuvre and handle their ships by day and (especially) by night with something approaching the dash that ABC expected. It was sometimes scarifying and there may have been some near misses, but I can't remember any bumps. In harbour, we could (sometimes) relax at Casa Pietà, where the Cunninghams kept open house for the Destroyer Command.' Incidentally this house was an excellent viewing point from which to observe the manner in which destroyers might enter and secure in Sliema Creek.

'A very junior Destroyer CO,'[8] writes that in 1934 he 'had the good fortune to come under the sway of his great leadership which was so compelling. What struck me at the time was that he was so very much more human and kindly than his rather tough reputation could have led me to believe.

'During the Abyssinian war in an exercise night torpedo attack (we were kept pretty busy at these), I contrived a pretty devastating collision when retiring at very high speed after firing. When it was all over I went in due course with my Captain (D) to see the great man. I felt, at once, that I was not being "carpeted" but that I was receiving very genuine sympathy.' On such occasions ABC used the phrase about being unable to make an omelette without breaking eggs.

Cunningham had been fortunate, when Commodore of Chatham Barracks, in having A. P. Shaw as his secretary. They got on well together, Shaw being mature, imperturbable, competent, and sound; and a good listener. He was to be with Cunningham afloat and ashore from 1932 to 1946. Admirals lean heavily on their secretaries, and in ABC's case he was prepared to leave details and paper work very largely to his secretary and staff. As he himself was an indefatigable worker, it follows that his staff had to work hard too; and often much harder. Shaw was devoted to ABC who refers to him as 'my trusted and experienced secretary'. Nevertheless, after less than a year in the *Coventry*, during which he received promotion to Paymaster Commander, Shaw was compelled through overwork to be temporarily relieved by Paymaster Lieutenant-Commander H. T. Isaac, and to go home for a long rest. Isaac was somewhat apprehensive as he had heard that this admiral was 'rather difficult to please'. However he joined Cunningham as his secretary in November 1934 and remained with him until April 1936, when the admiral struck his flag as RA (D), to await his next appointment: and a period of unemployment.

Isaac[9] writes:

'ABC was a person of tremendous energy. . . . He had a wonderful memory and he knew practically all the Commanding Officers and First Lieutenants [a constantly changing number up to 90] of the vessels under his command. He was a shrewd judge of character, detested laziness and inefficiency, and dealt firmly with those who disobeyed or disregarded his orders and the Regulations.' ABC frequently regarded himself as immune from such restrictive matters.

'He did at one time report his disappointment at the number of promotions in the destroyer command to the Commander-in-Chief, emphasising his opinion that the responsibility of COs of modern destroyers exceeded those of officers of similar seniority in battleships and cruisers, and that they should be recognised by a higher number of promotions.'

Isaac, as a temporary substitute for Shaw and junior to him, could afford to take a more relaxed view of ABC, and reveals two instances where not everything went right.

'It was an experience,' he continues, 'to be present on the bridge of the flagship during exercises conducted by ABC, particularly those in which massed attacks by destroyers with dummy torpedoes were carried out on battleships and cruisers. During one of these exercises off Gibraltar, when the Governor and Senior Military Officer were invited on board *Coventry*, the destroyer flotillas having delivered their attacks, retreated out of the way to enable the *Coventry* to fire her torpedoes. The order to fire torpedoes from one side was given. Nothing happened. The ship then turned to fire the salvo from the other side. Again nothing happened. There was much disappointment among the visitors. A very angry ABC dispatched his Squadron Torpedo Officer to investigate the failures . . . found to be due to a faulty batch of impulse cartridges. The Gunner (T) was most unpopular.'

Supported by his charming wife, ABC was most hospitable in entertaining destroyer officers and their wives at Casa Pietà. Isaac describes a dinner-party there one Christmas night, and the firing of the Christmas pudding. Unfortunately, instead of brandy, paraffin had been poured. 'The Chief Cook was not at all popular,' writes Isaac.

In view of ABC's reputed coolness towards aviation, it is worth recording a note by Keighly-Peach,[10] who describes joining the *Coventry* in February 1935, and being 'wheeled along the quarter-deck to the after end, where a rather red-faced little man was standing gazing across Sliema harbour. It was ABC and he turned to greet me as his new SOO but his eyes immediately alighted on the flying badge on my sleeve. "Do you intend to keep that thing on your sleeve whilst on my staff?" he said. Somewhat abashed at this opening gambit, I said yes I did, as it was part of the recognised uniform for the FAA. No reply to that. However, later on during the subsequent spring cruise, we were approaching Gibraltar with a view to intercepting the Home Fleet which had the aircraft carriers *Furious* and *Courageous* on their side. Suddenly out of the sky appeared a great many torpedo-carrying aircraft (Rippons I think) which attacked us from all angles. ABC was *furious* – and outwardly expressed the view that they would "all have been shot down, and NO hits on our side". I always think that his views on aircraft at sea underwent a great change that afternoon, and as we all know, he couldn't have been more air-minded as Commander-in-Chief Mediterranean, and was continually badgering the First Sea Lord for more fighters (in particular) in the early days of the war.' Cunningham, referring to those 1935 exercises, says they provided plenty of opportunities for initiative on the part of junior officers, and as if to add credence to the thought expressed above by Keighly-Peach, adds that 'certain old lessons, which we had been apt to forget, we re-learnt'.

The year 1935 was to be somewhat different from the halcyon days of previous years, and the Mediterranean Fleet routine was never to be quite the same again. In 1934 Cunningham had enjoyed a January cruise with his flotillas to French and Italian ports in North Africa; a foretaste perhaps of later visits under very different circumstances. After spending February in Malta, the fleet had departed for the exercise against the Home Fleet in March, to be followed by the spring cruise, which in RA (D)'s case involved a visit to the French Riviera and Italy. No opportunity was missed, while on passage, for exercise, drills, and manoeuvres. May and June were spent at Malta, the loveliest time of the year before it gets too hot, and gunnery and other practices would be interspersed with normal recreation and sport. The first summer cruise took them in July to the Greek islands, the Adriatic, and Crete, culminating in the Fleet Assembly at Navarin for the always keenly competed Fleet Regatta. August was spent back in Malta for storing and docking prior to the second summer cruise, which took RA (D) in September to those frequently (before 1935) visited ports of Yugoslavia where the White Ensign was always enthusiastically welcomed: Dubrovnik, Split, and Cattaro (Kotor). Such visits were not only stimulating and instructive for the ships' companies, but fruitful in bringing about good international relationships. ABC himself was much impressed by the reputation that still survived on the Dalmatian coast concerning the skill and bravery of Captain Sir William Hoste (a great admirer of Lord Nelson) who, with two ships only, forced the capitulation of the French when they occupied Cattaro in 1814. November found most ships of the Fleet back at Malta, where docking, storing, and base activities would continue until the next year cruises began all over again in January 1935.

To ensure that no ship was idle during the short stay at Malta, Fisher arranged for Cunningham to organise spontaneous activities which would require ingenuity among the ships at any time of the day or night without special warning. Contrary to this being found a tiresome procedure, the scheme led to intense competition between ships when ordered to carry out such tasks as mounting guns or searchlights ashore, or setting up radio stations and electricity generators. ABC of course took this scheme very much to heart. It was in this year, 1935, that the Fleets were to assemble at Spithead for the Jubilee Review by King George V in July. A substantial part of the Mediterranean Fleet sailed home to be present. Cunningham was there and flew his flag in the *Coventry*, but transferred his flag soon afterwards to the slightly younger and larger cruiser *Despatch*, in which he had served as Flag Captain and Chief Staff Officer to Admiral Sir Walter Cowan in the West Indies in 1928.

Concern was already growing over Mussolini's designs on Abyssinia, and the feeble efforts of the League of Nations to deter him. Drastic measures such as the closing of the Suez Canal might well have led to war, an eventuality for which Admiral Fisher was prepared. But the general feeling at home was that the Mediterranean Fleet was not powerful enough to meet the Italians. Reinforcements began to arrive in the Mediterranean from all over the world, and included the aircraft carrier *Courageous*, three cruisers, and two more destroyer flotillas. Alexandria now became the Fleet base for stores and ammunition, and war plans were drawn up. At the western end of the Mediterranean Gibraltar was strengthened by the arrival of the Battle Cruiser Squadron, a squadron of cruisers, and a destroyer flotilla. Cruisers and destroyers also gathered at Aden.

Cunningham now had five destroyer flotillas under his command: the 3rd, 4th, and 5th at Alexandria; the 1st and 19th at Malta. The 19th was under the immediate command of Captain Philip Vian, and consisted of old destroyers called up from the Reserve, and recently worked up especially in the task of submarine detection. Among his commanding officers were Commander Lord Louis Mountbatten, Commander B. A. Warburton-Lee (who won the Victoria Cross at Narvik in 1940), and a considerable number of officers who were to distinguish themselves in various ways during the Second World War. All the flotillas were constantly at sea exercising, particularly in torpedo attacks against *fast* targets, which was a problem to which ABC directed considerable study at that time in addition to that concerning submarine detection. If war were to come, the Mediterranean Fleet was to take the offensive immediately, in accordance with Fisher's detailed plans. ABC was more than ready to see that his 45 destroyers and the *Despatch* would effectively do their job.

Cunningham's new Squadron Torpedo Officer[11] who had joined him after the Jubilee Review writes:

'I very soon became aware of RA (D)'s ruthless attitude to the Italian aggression and he was constantly making plans against their naval forces and territory. He set a high standard of training for the numerous ships now under his command, special attention being given to day and night firings and exercises at high speed, anti-aircraft firings, look-out organisation, and other matters connected with small ship actions. . . . Numerous intriguing night encounter exercises were hatched up. These were most realistic and provided splendid training for the major war not so far distant.

'Every important exercise had to be analysed by ABC's staff and then demonstrated with minimum of delay to those who had taken part so that lessons learnt and mistakes made could be dealt with before they had become forgotten. These were strenuous occasions for the staff but ABC is alleged to have said that he had never heard of any of his Staff Officers *dying from overwork*.

'Exercises at sea showed that ABC's flagship the elderly *Despatch* was unable to maintain the high speeds necessary when operating destroyer flotillas, so that when the new cruiser *Galatea* [5,220 tons, 32¼ knots] arrived in the late autumn of 1935 she was at once seized by ABC and became an excellent substitute. A splendid example of peacetime piracy!'

ABC squared this with the Commander-in-Chief by pointing out that to retain the slower *Despatch* would place him in an unenviable position.

Commander Casper Swinley[12] of the *Express* gives a picture of the scene during a 'Club Run' at sea: 'When for some 36 hours one had to keep a pretty good look out for signals from RA (D) in *Galatea*. Tom Halsey got one of these: "What are you idling for? Come and take me in tow." Then to *Express*: "Go and bombard. . . ."'

'Another day my No. 2 Wyatt Larken broke his leg, and in the channel leading to the Great Pass Beacon, I made a signal to RA (D) requesting permission to pass ahead owing to my No. 2 having broken his leg. "Approved" from RA (D) in *Galatea*: and at the same time ABC leant over his bridge, took off his cap and waved me on.'

Swinley goes on to describe an occasion when the 5th Destroyer Flotilla was detailed to shadow and attack at night three cruisers (posing as Italians) under Rear-Admiral Max Horton. Advancing at 28 knots in the dark, followed by sharp turns after firing torpedoes, destroyers met some congestion, and *Echo* and *Encounter* suddenly found themselves alongside each other at 28 knots. Much bumping and scraping took place before they were able to part. This necessitated three months in dockyard hands at Malta, but RA (D) who was pleased at the demonstration of resolute spirits merely referred to his 'omelette' simile.

It was about this time that the *Ausonia* incident occurred, involving a large ship of the Italian Lloyd Triestino line, lying in Alexandria harbour not far from the Fleet flagship *Queen Elizabeth*. The harbour was crowded with ships. Early in the forenoon of 18 October 1935, flames and smoke were seen to emanate from her, and the thought arose that she might be loaded with explosives which could cause a disastrous explosion similar to that which had shaken Halifax harbour in 1915. This was just one of the kinds of emergency for which the fleet was ready, and in a short time passengers and crew had been rescued, and the *Ausonia*, doused with water, had been towed away to a mud bank.

ABC was of the opinion that the fire was accidental, but admired the prompt and energetic action which was displayed.

The *Galatea* was equipped with a 2-seater Osprey which could be catapulted into flight and recovered by crane. The observer for this float-plane was Lieutenant-Commander J. H. Wilkinson,[13] appointed to the ship also for general duties, who remarks that ABC treated the aircraft as somewhat of an encumbrance, and was not sure at that time how best to use it.

A further opinion about ABC's attitude to the 'air' at this time comes from Lieutenant-Commander Salter,[14] who was his Squadron Navigating Officer from September 1935 until April 1936. He remarks on the fact that when the *Galatea* arrived on the Station she had an armour-plate bullet-proof roof over the bridge, presumably as a defence against machine-gun attack from fighters. ABC liked an open bridge, and soon arranged for the roof to be removed, as it obstructed his view. 'I think that this is an earnest of ABC's opinion about danger from the air,' writes Salter. '*When* he changed his mind I don't know.'

It would be wrong to infer from this that ABC failed to appreciate the danger from the air at that time. To the contrary, and Admiral Salter as an experienced navigator would be the first to agree, it was a flagrant gesture of disapproval of high policy. ABC was only too well aware of the potential of naval aviation, as shown by Keighly-Peach in his description earlier in this chapter of his reaction to an attack by torpedo-carrying aircraft. It is certain that Cunningham at that time, as did Chatfield, much deplored the fact that naval aviation was not yet under the control of the Admiralty, but under a Ministry barely familiar with naval requirements of search and reconnaissance as well as defence, and with limited interest in the biggest promise of all, the weapon of the torpedo-carrying aircraft as an integral part of the Fleet, giving inestimable advantages of mobility, flexibility, and surprise. There was however no shortage of enthusiasm, or skill among those naval officers and men who were being trained to become pilots, observers, and air gunners.

When in fact German dive-bombing attacks began to be experienced by ships of the fleets less than five years later, it became essential for the officer conning the ship to have an unobscured view of the attacking aircraft, so that the necessary helm could be applied at the appropriate moment. This, together with a concentrated AA fire from all ships in company, did much to frustrate such attacks, as ABC was one of the first to realise.

Cunningham's two years as RA (D) would end in January 1936, and his relief was to be Rear-Admiral James Somerville, his old class-mate of *Britannia* days. No immediate appointment was available for him, and he was told by the Naval Secretary that he could expect to remain unemployed until 1938. Severance from the destroyer service, with which he had been so closely connected during the past 28 years, was itself a blow which the news of half-pay ahead did nothing to diminish. He hauled down his flag in March 1936, and although there was as yet no job in sight, was promoted Vice-Admiral July 1936. He was always an optimist, and his good fortune was to continue.

Although Admiral Sir W. W. Fisher's relief as Commander-in-Chief had been announced as Admiral Sir Dudley Pound, to take place in the autumn of 1935, the international situation was considered too uncertain to permit an immediate change. Pound however volunteered to serve as Chief of Staff to Fisher, and assumed that appointment in October 1935. Expectation of war with Italy gradually receded as the British Mediterranean Fleet reached imposing dimensions, and in March 1936 Pound hoisted his flag in the *Queen Elizabeth* as Commander-in-Chief Mediterranean. Admiral Sir William Fisher later in that year went to Portsmouth to hoist his flag in the *Victory* as Commander-in-Chief Portsmouth, it being generally considered that it would be only a matter of two years or so before he would relieve Chatfield as First Sea Lord. He died however on 24 June 1937 while holding the Portsmouth command. Sickness and mortality have often upset the plan for appointments among senior officers. It was shortly after Fisher's death that Cunningham learnt of the illness of Vice-Admiral Sir Geoffrey Blake commanding the Battle Cruiser Squadron, and was offered that command as a temporary appointment. He leapt at the opportunity. More than 15 months had elapsed since he hauled down his flag as RA (D) Mediterranean. During this time he had not been left unemployed but had presided over a distinguished committee investigating problems of habitability and ventilation in His Majesty's ships. Great events had also taken place: King George V had died in January 1936, being succeeded by his son King Edward VIII who abdicated later in the same year. Edward's brother had then acceded to the throne as King George VI, and had been crowned in May 1937. The coronation had been followed in the same month by a great Naval Review at Spithead. According to the Press there was little to worry about, as far as war was concerned.

But from the naval point of view there was the continued possibility of war with Italy, and a growing aggressiveness by Germany encouraged by the general leaning towards appeasement shown by both France and Britain. The outbreak of the Spanish Civil War in July 1936 had done nothing to relieve the gloom, but added to the Royal Navy's tasks of coastal patrol and preparedness for sudden attack, not only on the sea and below, but also from the air. Incidents were occurring, and though becoming more frequent were given little notice in the Press. The author was serving in the battleship H.M.S. *Royal Oak*, and remembers well the conditions of dwindling peace. There were[15] 'many weeks of patrol duty in the spring of 1937 off Valencia, Majorca, and Bilbao . . . dawn action stations, constant vigilance, shadowing of warships, darkened ships at night, and uncomfortable proximity to the stealthy work of German and Italian ships, who were believed to bombard Spanish ports at night. While anchored off Valencia one night in February 1937, *Royal Oak* was hit by a stray shell during the bombardment of Valencia by an unknown ship: four British officers were wounded.'

Perhaps the most important event of 1937 occurred when the Admiralty at last retrieved control of the Fleet Air Arm which it had lost in 1918. The necessity for such control had been emphasised by Cunningham on many occasions, and he praises Chatfield, the First Sea Lord for his relentless efforts to secure it during his term of office. In his book[16] Cunningham quotes an important note on the subject of naval aviation by Fleet Admiral Chester W. Nimitz upon relinquishing his appointment as Chief of Naval Operations of the United States Navy:

'The development between World Wars I and II of naval aviation provided naval forces with a striking weapon of vastly increased flexibility, range, and power. . . . It spearheaded our Pacific attack. First it swept the sea of all naval opposition. . . . In all these operations the employment of air-sea power demonstrated the ability of the Navy to concentrate aircraft strength at any desired point in such numbers as to overwhelm the defence at the point of contact. These operations demonstrate the capability of naval carrier-based aviation to make use of the principles of mobility and concentration to a degree possessed by no other force. . . .'

Cunningham's return to active service and the Admiralty's resumption of control of naval aviation were not a moment too soon.

Command of the Battle Cruisers and an Unexpected Spell At Admiralty (1937-39)

It was soon apparent that Admiral Sir Geoffrey Blake would be unable to resume his command of the battle cruisers and would be sent home from Malta as soon as his condition might improve sufficiently for him to travel.

When Cunningham assumed command of the squadron in July 1937 it consisted of the battle-cruisers *Hood* and *Repulse*. But also within the Admiral's administration were the aircraft carrier *Glorious* and the fleet repair ship *Resource*. His appointment was also as Second-in-Command Mediterranean Fleet. ABC found it most encouraging to be well received by Admiral Sir Dudley Pound, the Commander-in-Chief, who favoured a free exchange of views and was glad to have as deputy an officer of such stature and wide experience.

Cunningham hoisted his flag in the *Hood*: the 'mighty' *Hood* as she was affectionately known throughout the navy; 42,000 tons, eight 15-inch guns, 144,000 shaft-horsepower, and capable of 32 knots. As his appointment was temporary, he took over Blake's staff, but in due course was joined by his former secretary Paymaster Commander A. P. Shaw. It is interesting to catch a glimpse of ABC at this critical stage as deputy commander of the whole fleet.

'He arrived quietly and without style,' writes J. S. S. Smith, who was his assistant secretary in 1937.[1]

'His arrival at short notice was viewed with some interested surmise and even with some awe by the older and better informed. I remember his Staff Officer Operations (later Vice-Admiral Sir Gordon Hubback) talking of the Admiral's habit of testing any proposal – and the officer who made it – by an attitude of vigorous and thrusting opposition which was sustained to see if the individual stood his ground and justified his case. If he could and did, there was quiet ungrudging approval. No "Yes man" could get by here.'

His Squadron Torpedo Officer[2] writes:

'I particularly remember the exceptional way he handled the battle-cruisers during fleet exercises. . . . We were always in the right place at the right time and if only the Italian fleet had come to sea we should have had another Trafalgar.'

The direct menace from the Italian fleet gradually subsided, thus permitting much freer use of Malta by British ships, and the maintenance facilities which were so much superior to those available at Alexandria. The Spanish Civil War had broken out in July 1936 and had been raging for a year, bringing new problems: problems which were all the more difficult to solve because of sinister casualties among British ships, especially near the Spanish coast. It was fairly certain that the ships were sunk by Italian submarines, numerous in the Mediterranean at that time, but circumstances were rigged by the Italians to make it look as if Spain were the culprit. This led to the Nyon Conference of September 1937, at which Germany and Italy declined to assist in a solution. Britain and France however quickly agreed that their merchant ships in the Mediterranean should keep to predetermined routes patrolled by destroyers and aircraft ready to counter-attack unauthorised submarines.

Cunningham accompanied Sir Dudley Pound in the Commander-in-Chief's flagship, temporarily the *Barham*, to Oran, to meet the Mediterranean French Admiral Esteva and to discuss detailed arrangements for the Nyon patrols. It is of interest that the hitherto regular flagship the *Queen Elizabeth*, and her sister battleships the *Warspite, Valiant*, and (to a lesser extent) the *Malaya*, were all to be reconstructed, re-engined, and modernised. With the addition of armour and anti-aircraft armament, they would provide a timely augmentation of Britain's capital ship strength at a critical period in the early 'forties, and were also to play their part in the war in the Mediterranean. With the imminence of war in 1938 it was not found practicable to re-engine the *Barham*; this was regrettable, for with her top speed of only 22 knots there were to be many occasions when she became more of a liability than an asset.

Admiral Esteva appears on the scene again at a later stage, but under vitally different circumstances. At this moment Cunningham and Pound found him alert, co-operative, and effectual. Pound now proceeded in the *Barham* to initiate the patrol off the Spanish coast, with his fleet reinforced by Home Fleet destroyers and supported by RAF flying-boats based near Oran and maintained by the submarine depot ship

Cyclops. Submarine sinkings of merchant ships ceased. Cunningham, who had returned to the *Hood*, speaks of Mussolini's piratical and puny efforts to assist the Spanish Nationalists as being effectually scotched.

Nevertheless the Spanish Nationalist movement, started by insurgents in Spanish Morocco and supported by Italian and German Fascists, was slowly gaining momentum in Spain under the leadership of General Franco. It was this faction which attempted to dispute the right of British merchant ships to enter Government-held ports such as Valencia, Barcelona, and Palma.

In October 1937 Cunningham sailed from Malta in the *Hood* to relieve Pound in his vigil over the patrol. This required visits to Oran, Gibraltar, Tangier, Palma, Valencia, and Barcelona, and many interviews with local commanders concerning the newly-established Nyon patrols. It was not always easy to ascertain who was on which side, and he was glad to return to Malta in November for a two-months spell of normal activities, until taking on a further turn of duty in January 1938. By this time there was a recrudescence of submarine sinkings, and flagrant work by Spanish warships all of whom had to be shadowed by British forces. There were also indiscriminate bombing raids by Italian S 79s (three-engine monoplanes) during which British merchant ships were occasionally hit, and there was confrontation at critical times between British warships of both the Mediterranean and Home Fleets, and those of the insurgents.

There are many naval officers who will remember those uncertain days when Britain, nominally at peace, had many warships undertaking the task of trade protection around the coast of Spain, prepared for instant action, if necessary, against ships such as the *Almirante Cervera*, the *Canarias*, or the *Baleares*. The British destroyers *Kempenfelt* and *Boreas* rescued 400 Spanish sailors when the Insurgent cruiser *Baleares* was torpedoed by a Spanish Government destroyer.

In February 1938 Cunningham was informed that he would be appointed to the Admiralty in the autumn to succeed Vice-Admiral Sir William James as Deputy Chief of Naval Staff. Here was clear proof of the regard in which he was held, not only by Chatfield the First Sea Lord, but by Admiral Sir Roger Backhouse who was himself to become First Sea Lord in September 1938. Backhouse was at that moment Commander-in-Chief Home Fleet flying his flag in H.M.S. *Nelson*, which was paying a short visit to Malta. ABC's attitude towards the DCNS appointment was one of reluctance, because of his lack of staff experience. He told Backhouse that he was no good at paper work, and would be quite unsuitable. Sir Roger merely replied with a smile.

The year 1938 was unsettled, not only because of the Spanish Civil

War and Italy's uncertain attitude, but because of Hitler's bellicose moves. Although to many in Britain war seemed inevitable, the influential press adopted a conciliatory attitude, and appeasement was in the air, with an unwarranted faith in the policy of 'collective security'. Hitler took advantage of this to acquire without bloodshed first Austria, and then the Südetenland of Czecho-Slovakia. The annual combined exercises of the Mediterranean and Home Fleets took place in March 1938, this time as a series of exercises covering a night encounter, a day approach, a massed destroyer attack (which had to be repeated the following night because of failure), and a convoy passage involving aircraft and destroyers. There was also a strategical exercise in which Cunningham commanded one side, and his old class-mate James Somerville [then RA (D) Med] the other side. Cunningham was impressed with the importance of not permitting 'one's aircraft carrier to operate apart from the fleet'. The exercise concluded with the usual 'wash-up' conference at Gibraltar which was attended by Admiral of the Fleet Sir Ernle Chatfield, paying his farewell visit to the Fleets. The Home Fleet departed shortly afterwards for home waters, ending the cruise with a steam-past H.M.S. *Nelson* of three destroyer flotillas, the 2nd Cruiser Squadron, and the battleships *Royal Oak*, *Revenge*, and *Ramillies* in farewell to Admiral Sir Roger Backhouse, the Commander-in-Chief.

The Mediterranean Fleet resumed its uncertain role in the Nyon patrol, interspersed with visits to some of the more frequented ports, but with the notable exception of those along the Dalmatian coast. Ironically, it was the Dalmatian ports that had in the past shown the greatest regard for the White Ensign, but who now found that visits by British warships would not be welcome for fear of unfavourable reactions by the Axis partners Italy and Germany. The peak of irony was reached when an Italian squadron of two battleships, the *Conte di Cavour* and *Giulio Cesare*, with four destroyers, were to be entertained (by instruction of the British Government) during a visit to Malta in late June. Entertainment on both sides went on unceasingly, and was especially lavish on the part of the Italian Admiral Riccardi. He took some pride in showing Cunningham his palatial apartments, and in particular *The Life of Nelson*, a book that always lay at his bedside. 'His subsequent actions during the war rather showed that he had not greatly profited by his nightly reading,' wrote Cunningham.[3]

ABC particularly noted the fine work done by the Italians in modernising their two old battleships, and furnishing them with a good armament of ten 12-inch guns, a few anti-aircraft guns, and new machinery which would give them a speed of 26 or 27 knots. Their high speed (for a battleship) would give them great scope for eluding pursuit.

The summer cruise saw the battle cruisers on a visit to Corfu early in July 1938, followed by the whole Mediterranean Fleet assembly at Navarin for the annual sailing regatta. Cunningham's flagship the *Hood* swept the board. Perhaps as a pointer to the future, Cunningham was given command of the fleet during three days of the passage back to Malta; there was scarcely time for relaxation as he tried out several of his own ideas in various exercises. He had seen a good deal of the Commander-in-Chief, and found Pound frank in expressing views about the future. After a further turn of duty on the Spanish patrol in August, Cunningham returned in the *Hood* to Malta, and turned over to his successor Vice-Admiral Geoffrey Layton, DSO (later Admiral Sir Geoffrey), before returning to England for leave.

It seems certain that Cunningham by that time was sufficiently well thought of to be considered a possibility for the highest appointments; nevertheless it must be realised that he was still a Vice-Admiral with but two years seniority, and junior to a score or so of Admirals and Vice-Admirals, of whom many were also particularly outstanding. The DCNS appointment was propitious and could not have been better timed had ABC been in the process of being groomed for the most responsible post in the Royal Navy.

Charles Little, his term-mate in the *Britannia*, by this time Admiral Sir Charles, and also Commander-in-Chief, China Station, had already been DCNS from 1933 to 1935, and was to become Second Sea Lord and Chief of Naval Personnel on 30 September 1938. Sir Roger Backhouse, already a sick man, took up his appointment as First Sea Lord on 10 August 1938. Cunningham's appointment as DCNS was for 17 October 1938, but because of the Südetenland crisis he was instructed to join the Admiralty 24 September, and to study the war plans. Charles Little[4] writes:

'I met Cunningham briefly [in 1929 when ABC had the *Rodney*], and not again till 1938 when he was DCNS and I was Second Sea Lord. We were thrown much together when Roger Backhouse was ill. C of course was a made man by then and his appointment to relieve Pound when Backhouse died was obvious.'

As DCNS, Cunningham worked immediately under the First Sea Lord. Backhouse was a prodigious worker who preferred to deal with most matters himself, even to the smallest detail, and was reluctant to delegate. Nevertheless he unloaded all matters concerning the Spanish Civil War on to Cunningham, and also turned over to him the destroyer building programme which had tended to lag behind other naval requirements. The principal task facing the Admiralty at this time was that of rearmament.

It may not be amiss to remind the reader of the naval constitution of the Board of Admiralty late in 1938, and briefly their duties, under the Presidency of the First Lord of the Admiralty, Lord Stanhope:

Admiral Sir Roger Backhouse: First Sea Lord and Chief of the Naval Staff; supported by a Deputy (Cunningham) and three Assistants, and responsible for maritime operations all over the world, and the disposition of ships. (The title DCNS was in April 1940 changed to VCNS).

Admiral Sir Charles Little: Second Sea Lord and Chief of Naval Personnel; personnel, recruiting, and welfare.

Admiral Sir Reginald Henderson: Third Sea Lord and Controller; technical matters.

Rear-Admiral G. S. Arbuthnot: Fourth Sea Lord; supplies.

Vice-Admiral the Hon. Sir Alexander Ramsay: Fifth Sea Lord; naval aviation.

In general the more immediate tasks were the rapid modernisation of obsolescent capital ships, anti-submarine techniques, the arming of merchant vessels, the defence of ports and dockyards, the extension of anti-aircraft armament, and the development of RDF (radio direction-finding, later to be called radar) in warships. There was a woeful shortage of almost everything except ideas. A further worry for the Admiralty stemmed from the belief firmly held by both the RAF and the Army, that Malta was not worth the expenditure of time and money in equipping with modern armament, as this fleet base would be unable to withstand the scale of attack to be expected if Britain were to go to war against Italy. 'The surprising thing is that Malta was able to hold out as it did,' wrote Cunningham.[5] 'If at the outset the Army and RAF had seen eye to eye with the Navy as regards the defence of our principal naval base in the Mediterranean, its ordeal would have been lighter.'

Although Italy had much enhanced her status in the Mediterranean by her intervention on behalf of Franco, in a war which was to end in Franco's favour and with the rapid collapse of Spanish government forces by March 1939, it was still not clear whether or not Mussolini would join forces with Hitler in the coming war. They had both benefited in experience of war, the Germans in the technique of dive-bombing, the Italians in their high-level bombing.

March 1938 saw the German 'Anschluss' on Austria, and by late September it was clear that Hitler intended to occupy the Südetenland. The imminence of war led to orders for naval mobilisation, which were cancelled after the Munich settlement of 29 September 1938. It became apparent in Britain that the settlement meant merely a brief respite, and for Hitler the 'scrap of paper' agreement permitted him to gain yet another strategic advantage of crucial importance without material loss. Cunningham's attitude was to deplore further appeasement, but to make the maximum use of the respite now offered. At the time of the Munich crisis the Mediterranean Fleet had assembled at Alexandria, and as soon as tension was relieved, Pound had made recommendations concerning the naval strength he thought necessary, and the amount of stores and ammunition required. He deplored the weakness of Malta from the defence point of view, and drew attention to the insufficiency and inflexibility of RAF squadrons and bases, and the fact that the fleet would have to make do with but one aircraft-carrier. He also asked for more destroyers and submarines (of which the fleet possessed only seven).

Britain no longer needed to concentrate most of her sea power in the North Sea as at the outbreak of the First World War, for Germany, except in submarines and commerce raiders, had not yet progressed sufficiently to cause immediate concern in the war at sea. The Home Fleet should be adequate for its role, and the Mediterranean Fleet should suffice while France stood by Britain. There was an understanding that France would be allocated control of the western half, thus safeguarding her sea route to Africa, while Britain would control the eastern half and sea communications to the Suez Canal, Syria, Iraq, and Persia. Turkey's attitude was neutral, and it was unlikely that Greece would take sides until Italy had shown her hand. Spain was too exhausted after the Civil War to show attachment to any cause. America seemed to be more concerned about Japan's aims and the war between China and Japan which had begun in July 1937.

Early in December 1938 Germany informed Britain that she intended to invoke a clause of the Anglo-German Naval Agreement of 1935 which permitted her, in exceptional circumstances, to have the same submarine strength as Britain's. Cunningham headed a naval mission to Berlin to protest, and especially warned Admiral Raeder of the adverse effect which further submarine building would have on British public opinion. Hitler was informed of this warning but refused to change his plan to build more submarines, arguing that Britain was rearming at an increasing rate. ABC's reaction was to press on with rearmament in every possible way, since appeasement merely gave Hitler more confidence and greater truculence. As is now known, Germany had in any case been building submarines to the limit of her capacity. It was already realised that Germany would use submarines as in the First World War for unrestricted warfare against shipping; this would require Britain to have more escort vessels. The solution lay in Cunningham's suggestion to build a large quantity of destroyers of the small escort type which were moderately cheap and rapidly built. This would to some extent meet the First Sea Lord's concern over the shortage of destroyers generally, and was the genesis of the 40 small 1,000-ton 'Hunt' class, 33-knot destroyers that were to give such splendid service. It is pertinent to read ABC's remark that:[6] 'To avoid hurting the susceptibilities of Parliament the first 20 were originally included in the Navy Estimates as "fast escort vessels".'

Though the German Navy was small her ships were new and fast. The ships of the Royal Navy were in general old and slow, but a modernisation programme for which Chatfield at the Admiralty had been pressing for several years, had been introduced in 1936, when it was realised that Italy was modernising her ships. In the matter of new British warships there were 200 building in 1939, including the first of the six armoured deck aircraft carriers of the 'Illustrious' class (soon to be followed by the *Formidable* and the *Victorious*), and the battleships *King George V* and *Prince of Wales* of the new 35,000-ton 29-knot class. New cruisers were also being built. The time was not far distant when every ship would be pressingly needed, including those in reserve and those yet to be built.

On 14 February 1939 Cunningham was summoned to an investiture at Buckingham Palace, where King George VI conferred the honour of knighthood upon him, and he was invested with the insignia of a Knight Commander of the Most Honourable Order of the Bath.

Sir Andrew Cunningham now began to find life at the Admiralty increasingly arduous, and matters were not helped by the deteriorating health of the First Sea Lord. By 14 March 1939, on the day that German troops marched into Czecho-Slovakia, Sir Roger Backhouse was on the point of collapse, and on the follwing day made his last public appearance. As his deputy, Sir Andrew now found that an immense amount of the First Sea Lord's work fell to him to deal with, and although he was greatly helped by Little, the Second Sea Lord (himself DCNS 1933 to 1935), it was generally accepted that Sir Roger would never be able to resume at the Admiralty and a successor must be appointed; Sir Roger Backhouse died on 15 July 1939.

In the meantime, Italy had astonished the world by invading Albania on Good Friday, 7 April 1939, presumably as a reply to Germany's invasion of Czecho-Slovakia, at a moment when British warships were visiting various Italian ports in conformity with a British Government gesture of friendship. The ships were recalled as soon as the news filtered through, and were dispersed to Malta for victualling and fuelling, and then to Alexandria.

An obvious successor to Sir Roger Backhouse as First Sea Lord was

Admiral Sir Dudley Pound, an administrator of wide and varied experience. At the Admiralty he had been Director of Plans, Assistant Chief of Naval Staff, and Second Sea Lord. At sea he had served as Chief of Staff both Admiral Sir Roger Keyes and Admiral Sir William Fisher in the Mediterranean, had held command of the battle-cruisers in the Home Fleet, and was now completing three years as Commander-in-Chief Mediterranean, then traditionally regarded as the most responsible sea command in the Royal Navy. ABC, who refers to Pound as an officer of untiring energy and forcefulness, was himself offered the Mediterranean command on 9 May 1939, with acting rank of Admiral, and 'accepted with alacrity'. Command of a fleet (and what a fleet) was much more to his taste than difficult administrative problems and paper work. A relief was appointed, Rear-Admiral Tom Phillips, who took over from ABC as DCNS 23 May 1939, to allow Sir Andrew to pack and travel to Alexandria to relieve Sir Dudley as soon as practicable.

A commentary by a very senior admiral[7] who in his time served Chatfield as COS in both the Home Fleet and the Mediterranean Fleet, and at the Admiralty as DCNS, and but for the Munich crisis would himself have relieved Pound in the Mediterranean Fleet in 1938, is valuable as a record of opinions prevailing in 1939, especially concerning the appropriateness of Cunningham's appointment to the fleet to relieve Pound.

'I have always thought that ABC was the right man for that appointment. He had all the gifts for dealing with the complicated problems. I think his whole career in destroyers had fitted him for the tasks that faced him. I had been a gunnery lieutenant and served all my time in the big fleets and had learnt a lot from Chatfield about handling a big fleet but I had very little experience of "small ship" life. The days of the big majestic fleets, deploying for battle and engaging in a long range duel, were over. What was required now of a C-in-C was that he should have the same qualities as the good destroyer officer, capable of making quick decisions when faced with some new and unexpected situations, knowing intimately the capabilities of all the smaller types and what he could demand from them. It always seemed to me that ABC was a gift from the Gods to us at that moment in history. . . .

'Roger Backhouse was a very sad case. He was such an able and such a charming man but he was the arch centraliser. I was still DCNS when he succeeded Chatfield.

'W. W. Fisher would have succeeded if he had not died at Portsmouth. He was a great man and in every way a much more talented officer than Pound. . . .

'Pound was too fond of Courts of Enquiry and finding scapegoats when anything went wrong. He had not the gift for command. He was a driver not a leader.'

Having asked for Paymaster Captain A. P. Shaw to become his secretary, and chosen Lieutenant Walter Starkie to be his flag lieutenant, Sir Andrew Cunningham travelled across France to join the cruiser *Penelope* at Marseilles for passage to Alexandria. He experienced great joy in being in a ship again, steaming in perfect weather in the sea where he had already spent $10\frac{1}{2}$ years in eight different ships. That apprenticeship had now reached fulfilment. An Axis war which might well become another world war was imminent, and Britain was fortunate in having at the right time and in the right place an officer who was to be her greatest sailor since Nelson.

On arrival of the *Penelope* at Alexandria, Sir Dudley and Sir Andrew exchanged official calls. At sunset 5 June 1939, Sir Dudley hauled down his flag in the *Warspite*. Sir Andrew hoisted his flag in the *Warspite* the following morning, by which time Sir Dudley was well on his way to Britain in a flying-boat.

In Command in the Mediterranean (1939-40)

A magnificent fleet of ships had been gradually assembled at Alexandria after the Albania crisis, in preparation for what was expected to be an Axis war. By the summer of 1939 a floating dock capable of accommodating battleships had been towed from Portsmouth to Alexandria, stores were accumulating in Egyptian warehouses, and arrangements were in hand to improve the defences of Alexandria.

Inter-Allied war plans for the Mediterranean were practically non-existent other than those roughly agreed at Command level: that is, the western end to be under French influence, while the eastern end would be protected by the British. It was by no means certain that Italy would join Germany if the latter were at war. Cunningham sensed a fallacious belief in political circles at home that Italy could be knocked out at the outset of any war by naval bombardment, and was quick to point out that she could be defeated only if and when her armies were defeated. His own first priority was the destruction of the enemy fleet. His policy was to destroy Italy's supply lines to the forces in Libya, until such time as Allied forces in the shape of troops and aircraft could be provided to conquer Libya and the Italian colonies in East Africa. He would carry out a relentless offensive against the mainland, bombarding ports in the hope of enticing the Italian fleet to action. He was not unduly worried about the risk of air attack on his capital ships, and maintained that ships moving at high speed and with full freedom of manoeuvre were not easy targets. Moreover in the face of anti-aircraft fire from a concentration of warships, aircraft would find it hard to attack.

His fleet at this time consisted of four old 15-inch battleships, the *Warspite* (fleet flagship), *Barham*, *Malaya*, and *Ramillies*; together with an old aircraft carrier the *Glorious*, the 1st and 3rd Cruiser Squadrons, three destroyer flotillas, a few submarines, the depot ships *Woolwich* and *Maidstone*, and many small auxiliaries. As befitted an important

Command, the Admiral's operational staff was composed of carefully selected first-class officers, all of whom were to distinguish themselves, and many of whom were to continue with him for several years (unlike the rapid succession of first lieutenants of the *Scorpion* of long ago). His Chief of Staff was Commodore A. U. Willis (later Admiral of the Fleet Sir Algernon Willis, GCB, KBE, DSO). Commander R. M. Dick (later Rear-Admiral, CB, CBE, DSC) was Staff Officer Plans and Deputy Chief of Staff. Commander M. L. Power (later Admiral Sir Manley, KCB, CBE, DSO*) was Staff Officer Operations. Commander G. Barnard (later Vice-Admiral Sir Geoffrey, KCB, CBE, DSO*) was Fleet Gunnery Officer. Commander W. P. Carne (later Captain, CBE) was Fleet Torpedo Officer. Commander T. M. Brownrigg (later Captain, CBE, DSO) was Fleet Navigating Officer and Master of the Fleet. (See Appendix III for abbreviations adopted below.)

Poland was attacked by Germany at dawn 1 September 1939, and that same day a British and French ultimatum was delivered to Hitler. War would be declared unless he withdrew his troops from Poland. It was on Sunday, 3 September, that both Britain and France declared war on Germany. Cunningham says that he received news of the declaration of war during the squadron regatta in Alexandria harbour. Commander E. L. Pemberton was actually talking to the C-in-C in his day cabin in the *Warspite*, having been taken in to see him by Brownrigg in connection with tentative plans for an attack on Tobruk. 'During this discussion,' writes Pemberton, 'someone came in with a signal for the C-in-C. He read it carefully and then said "Not Italy?"

'"No, sir."

'"You're sure?"

'"Yes, sir."

'He then went across to the pigeon-holes in his desk on the port side and picked out some from a batch of signals which had obviously been already drafted, handing them after checking to the bearer of the message. Admiral Cunningham then carried on our discussion in the presence of Commander Brownrigg for a minute or two. I couldn't help feeling that this was pretty cool, as I guessed the purport of the incoming signal. I then waited outside the cabin door for a moment while the C-in-C spoke alone with Commander Brownrigg.

'As we walked along the passageway between decks Commander Brownrigg made me a remark which I have always privately classified with Stanley's famous one on meeting Livingstone. "If it's of any interest to you," he said calmly, "you're at war with Germany".'

As Cunningham himself said, there was little to be achieved. He had been doubtful about Mussolini entering the war until it was clear which

THE ENGLISH CHANNEL AND THE MEDITERRANEAN

North Sea

EIRE

GREAT BRITAIN

DENMARK

SWEDEN

Dover

Ostend

HOLLAND

GERMANY

ENGLISH CHANNEL

Cherbourg

Boulogne

Dunkirk

BELGIUM

LUX.

Brest

Bay of Biscay

FRANCE

SWITZ.

AUSTRIA

ITALY

Rimini

Bordeaux

Marseilles

Pisa

Leghorn

PORTUGAL

SPAIN

CORSICA

La Maddalena

Naples

BALEARIC ISLANDS

SARDINIA

Decimomannu

Cagliari

Tyrrhenian Sea

Gibraltar

MEDITERRANEAN   SEA

Bizerta

Trapani

SICILY

Palermo

Catania

TANGIER

SP. MOROCCO

Skerki Bank

The

Comisa

Syracuse

Casablanca

Oran

Algiers

Bône

Tunis

PANTELLERIA

Narrows

MALTA

MOROCCO

ALGERIA

TUNISIA

LAMPEDUSA

Sfax

KERKENAH IS.

Tripoli

0   500
            Miles

TRIPOLITANIA

~ARTHUR BANKS~

LITHUANIA

ltic Sea

EAST PRUSSIA

U.S.S.R.

P O L A N D

ECHOSLOVAKIA

HUNGARY

RUMANIA

YUGOSLAVIA

BULGARIA

Black Sea

Bosporus

RIATIC SEA

ALBANIA

G R E E C E

Valona

Dardanelles

TURKEY

Taranto

Aegean Sea

Ionian Sea

Athens
Piraeus

Aleppo

ggio Calabria

Navarino

SYRIA

na

C.Matapan

Maleme

RHODES

CYPRUS

CRETE

DODECANESE Is.

Haifa

MEDITERRANEAN   SEA

PALESTINE

TRANS-
JORDAN

Derna

Port
Said

Gazala

Bomba   Tobruk

Sidi Barrani

Mersa Matruh

Alexandria

Suez
Canal

Benghazi

Bardia

Suez

Gulf of
Sirté

Sollum

El Alamein

Cairo

rat

CYRENAICA

E G Y P T

ARABIA

BYA

El Agheila

way it would develop. There was not much that Italy could do while Britain and France held the Mediterranean. In the evening the Admiralty signalled 'Winston is back', and this gave considerable satisfaction. Churchill had been First Lord of the Admiralty previously from 24 October 1911 to 26 May 1915.

In the next few weeks after the outbreak of war against Germany, Cunningham's magnificent and highly efficient fleet began to disperse. By the end of the year 1939 there were but three light cruisers and a handful of destroyers left in the Mediterranean, and naval activities had to be restricted to the enforcement of contraband control. At the departure of the *Warspite* for duties in home waters in October 1939, the Commander-in-Chief was directed by the Admiralty to establish his headquarters in Malta, where he could best keep touch with the French Admiral Esteva, and at the same time the Army and Royal Air Force Cs-in-C whose headquarters were at Cairo. With the knowledge that the Mediterranean Fleet might have to be re-assembled at very short notice, dependent on Mussolini's whims, ABC retained his complete staff. He never lost faith that the war would come back to the Mediterranean. There was a strong opinion, held especially by the French, that Germany would break through the Balkans into the Mediterranean in the spring of 1940. Conferences were therefore held with Turkey, with a view to holding Allied command of the Dardanelles and the Bosphorus if occasion should demand. Turkey, though wary, appeared to welcome a friendly approach by Britain and France, but was keen to remain neutral. In due course, following ABC's recommendation that a senior naval officer should be appointed to Turkey as a liaison officer, Admiral Sir Howard Kelly was appointed. The author can vouch for the imposing presence and competence of this charming officer who as Commander-in-Chief China in 1932 took the initiative in successfully subduing a potentially explosive international situation. He was well received in Turkey, and did much in preventing that country from siding with Germany.

Such incidents as Commodore Harwood's success at the battle of the River Plate in December 1939, and Captain Philip Vian's dramatic rescue of British prisoners in the *Altmark* at Trondheim in February 1940, did much to boost British morale; but these were more than offset by failure in April 1940 to frustrate Germany's swift and successful occupation of Denmark and Norway despite the strength of the Home Fleet which had been blockading Germany in the North Sea for several months. This setback was only slightly relieved by Captain Warburton-Lee's gallantry at Narvik and the *Warspite*'s success there. The Germans had shown audacity and scored great gains. In anticipation of a more belligerent attitude from an encouraged Mussolini, the Admiralty now realised that Cunningham's Mediterranean Fleet must again be strengthened and assembled in the eastern Mediterranean. To achieve this it would require the withdrawal of heterogeneous units from home waters and from various parts of the world. By mid-May 1940 there was no longer any doubt that Italy would enter the war: the only question was when. Germany had overrun Belgium and Holland (10 May) and subsequently made a breakthrough into France, imperilling both the British and the French armies. On that same day Neville Chamberlain had been virtually compelled to resign as Prime Minister, and the King had sent for Winston Churchill to form a National Government. In addition to becoming Prime Minister, Churchill also assumed the role of Minister of Defence. He was succeeded as First Lord of the Admiralty by Mr. A. V. Alexander.

By the end of May the allied armies in France had collapsed, but by superb organisation, suitable weather, and local command of sea and air, 338,000 soldiers were miraculously transferred from Dunkirk to England in the course of nine days, and 192,000 more were taken off from various French ports.

France capitulated and asked for an armistice (17 June 1940). For the next four years France was to be nominally administered by a Government at Vichy, while Paris remained under German occupation. German occupation was to expand into Vichy France in November 1942, by which time there had been growing collaboration with Hitler; a situation which was to complicate relationships at the time of the North Africa landings in which Cunningham was to play such a prominent part.

Italy had declared war on 10 June 1940. By then, the Mediterranean Fleet at Alexandria had grown to quite an imposing one again. It consisted of the battleships *Warspite, Malaya, Royal Sovereign*, and *Ramillies*, together with the 7th Cruiser Squadron, the 3rd Cruiser Squadron, 25 destroyers, and a dozen submarines returned from China waters. The 20-year-old carrier *Eagle* provided the only naval aircraft present: with 3 Gladiator fighters and 17 Swordfish, TSR. The already acute shortage of naval 'air' had been sadly cut still further by the loss of the old carrier *Glorious* sunk off Norway by the German battle cruisers *Scharnhorst* and *Gneisenau* two days earlier (8 June). Also at Alexandria under the immediate command of the French Vice-Admiral Godfroy was the battleship *Lorraine* with four cruisers and three destroyers: all under Cunningham's overall command. The combination produced a fleet strong in battleships, but very weak in destroyers, some of which were veterans of the last war, slow and of low endurance. A lack of destroyers and fast craft in the Royal Navy was traditional. Jellicoe claimed that the operations of the Grand Fleet had been hindered by a lack of destroyers. Nelson repeatedly complained of a lack of frigates. The shortage of destroyers had become more acute after serious losses sustained during the evacuation from Dunkirk. Most of Cunningham's ships were old, but the 25-year-old *Warspite* had been re-engined and modernised, and her 15-inch guns could now compete with modern guns in elevation, range, and rate of fire. The British battle squadron of four old 15-inch battleships did not then compare unfavourably with the Italian strength of four less ancient battleships armed with 12·6-inch guns; but two new Italian battleships with 15-inch guns, the *Littorio* and the *Vittorio Veneto*, were soon to be in commission, and would be greatly superior.

As soon as the Commander-in-Chief had news of the Italian declaration his fleet raised steam, and later proceeded on a sweep. The battleships and carrier steamed to the north-west in the region of Matapan and Crete; the cruisers swept westward and then southward to an area off Benghazi and Tobruk; Admiral Godfroy, complying with Cunningham's overall plan, steamed to the Aegean and the Dodecanese. Such combined operations gave the French a sense of comradeship which was to prove helpful in later negotiations. Cunningham was much in favour of a British occupation of Crete which would provide a good harbour at Suda Bay and a storing and fuelling base for his ships operating in the central Mediterranean and the Aegean. He had however been warned in a message from the First Sea Lord that no such operation should be carried out unless Italy first attacked Greece.

In a message to the First Sea Lord 6 June 1940 Cunningham had said:
'You may be sure that all in the fleet are imbued with a burning desire to get at the Italian fleet, but you will appreciate that a policy of seeking and destroying his naval forces requires good and continuous air reconnaissance.'

Cunningham said he intended to take a strong force westward, including battleships, ready to counter any Italian action against Malta. He was even prepared to make an attack on Augusta as a diversionary relief for Malta if she were attacked, as seemed most likely, but was anxious first to gain some idea of the enemy's air and submarine strength before committing his capital ships close to enemy shores. Italy's central position in the Mediterranean could prove a liability to her, but would also serve her as a strategic advantage, particularly as Cunningham's fleet base was now so far to the East, Alexandria being 800 miles eastward of Malta. Not only Malta, but the sea route through the Sicilian narrows off Tunis, and the narrow stretch between Crete and Cyrenaica, soon to be known as 'Bomb Alley', were all within easy bombing distance of

Italian airfields based either on Sardinia, Sicily, or Cyrenaica. So far the influence of air power in restricting local fleet movements was unknown. While the French fleet existed in the western Mediterranean, the Italians must be prepared for attacks from both directions at once.

Cunningham's sweep after Italy's declaration of war was disappointing. The cruisers found a few minesweepers at work off Tobruk, and discovered the position of some of the Italian minefields. Incongruously the Regia Aeronautica failed to put in an appearance, though it was shortly to prove a serious factor; whereas an Italian submarine made a skilful attack and sank the British light cruiser *Calypso*, an episode which was not at all typical of the following three weeks during which ten Italian submarines were destroyed.

The Fleet Torpedo Officer[1] gives us a picture of the return to Alexandria.

'While we were at sea enemy submarines had been active off Alexandria sinking a merchant ship and laying mines. They sprang a surprise on us by laying their mines in deeper water than we had thought possible. But by the time the fleet returned, our sweepers had cleared a channel and the Australian destroyers who had been left behind had chivvied the submarines to good purpose and there was strong reason to believe that the *Voyager* had sunk one.'

ABC says that two were destroyed and others damaged and frightened.

Soon after return to harbour the Commander-in-Chief sent three cruisers and the French battleship *Lorraine* to bombard Bardia, and upon receiving an air reconnaissance report that Italian cruisers and destroyers might be in Tobruk harbour, sailed three British destroyers and the French cruisers *Suffren* and *Duguay Trouin* as a reinforcement. The bombardment produced good results. This was the last operation in which the French participated. Although there had been no sign of the Italian main fleet, Malta was being repeatedly bombed, the beginning of the ordeal which it was to suffer for the next two years.

At the fall of France, the Admiralty quickly assembled a squadron of warships at Gibraltar, to offset the loss of the French fleet in the western Mediterranean. This had been made possible by virtue of the heavy damage inflicted on German warships during the Norwegian campaign. The squadron came to be known as Force H, comprising in the beginning the battle cruiser *Hood* (flag), the battleships *Valiant* and *Resolution*, the carrier *Ark Royal*, the cruisers *Arethusa* and *Enterprise*, and a dozen destroyers, all under the command of Vice-Admiral Sir James Somerville, Cunningham's *Britannia* class-mate, flying his flag in the *Hood*. The selection of Gibraltar as a base for Force H was highly valuable strategically. Reinforcements could be sent into the Atlantic to support the Home Fleet when required, or cover the trade route to Freetown. More important from Cunningham's point of view, it was only 1,000 miles west of Malta, and could provide escort for eastbound convoys in the Mediterranean, and additional strength in central Mediterranean waters in time of need. Conditions would be hazardous for any British ship in 'Bomb Alley' during daylight. The largest possible concentration of anti-aircraft fire must therefore be available when required.

'I am afraid you are terribly short of "air",' the First Sea Lord had written to Cunningham, 'but I do not see what can be done because, as you realise, every available aircraft is wanted in home waters. The one lesson we have learnt here is that it is essential to have fighter protection over the fleet whenever they are within range of enemy bombers. You will be without such protection. . . .'[2]

Following the entry of Italy, and faced with the collapse of France, the Admiralty had been concerned about the maintenance of Cunningham's fleet in the eastern Mediterranean. The number of Italian troops in Libya so greatly outnumbered the British Army of the Nile that the safe retention of Alexandria as a supply and repair base was in question. In a message on 17 June, the day on which France asked for an armistice, and before the establishment of Force H, the First Sea Lord suggested to Cunningham that it might be necessary to withdraw from the eastern Mediterranean and transfer his fleet to Gibraltar for the protection of the vital trade routes in the Atlantic. Withdrawal would entail blocking the Suez Canal if the army were unable to continue to hold on to Egypt. In either case, the army would be supplied via the Cape of Good Hope. It was made clear that no decision had yet been taken, but it was necessary to have plans ready, pending a decision.

Cunningham replied the same day outlining the arrangements that would have to be made. He also added that the possibility had already been considered by General Wavell, who believed that without the fleet Egypt could not be held for long.

It was not long before Cunningham sent a further message, perhaps stirred by thoughts of Britain's withdrawal from the Mediterranean in 1796, and the resulting loss of influence and flexibility of manoeuvre suffered by Britain until such time as Admiral the Earl St. Vincent sent Nelson into the Mediterranean in 1798. Having already stressed the vital importance of keeping Malta, and the fact that it must fall if the Mediterranean Fleet were to be withdrawn, he stated that in his opinion such withdrawal would result in a landslide not only of territory but of prestige. It was his 'earnest hope that such a decision would never have to be taken'. With the departure of the fleet, he said, Egypt would be untenable, and even the Italians might be stirred into activity. It would be regarded as surrender, and the probable loss of Malta, Cyprus, and Palestine would endanger Turkey's potential loyalty. Cunningham also expressed his belief that he had sufficient force to contain the Italian heavy ships and keep the route to Malta open when required. A recommendation to continue to maintain a fleet in the eastern Mediterranean was made by the British Chiefs of Staff soon afterwards, and the decision was also taken, in spite of pressing needs at home and elsewhere, to increase Malta's fighter strength.

'I do not know how near we came to abandoning the eastern Mediterranean,' Cunningham wrote; 'but if it had come to pass it would have been a major disaster, nothing less.'[3]

Upon the collapse of France, Marshal Pétain and Admiral Darlan had repeatedly declared that no French warships would be allowed to fall into Axis hands. It soon became evident that they were not in a position to enforce this. Hitler's armistice terms were intentionally not harsh, as he still hoped that Britain too would seek an armistice; and no attempts were made by him to gain French bases in North Africa, in spite of Mussolini's insistence that Italy should occupy Tunisia. Nevertheless little belief was placed in his solemn declaration that Germany did not intend to use the French warships, especially when it became clear that the Germans were issuing instructions to the French fleet in Admiral Darlan's name.

Cunningham was informed by signal on 29 June 1940 that it was under consideration to seize the French ships at Alexandria, to prevent their escape. He writes[4] of his utter repugnance at the prospect, and describes at great length every move in the almost insoluble problem with which he was faced, and which might easily have ended in great bloodshed, but which in the end was amicably settled.

'The next few days,' writes Carne,[5] 'were very difficult and anxious ones. At first the attitude of the French officers appeared to be favourable to our cause, but as more and more news came from France of the failure of their government and of the armistice with Germany and of the threat to their families by the Germans if any French officers joined the British forces, their attitude gradually changed. It was clear that we should get no help from them and if we tried to coerce them we might meet resistance. Admiral Cunningham was a personal friend of the French Commander, Admiral Godfroy, and did his best to persuade the French to adopt a friendly attitude. But by this time Admiral Godfroy was receiving direct orders that he was not to co-operate with the British in any way and was to take his ships away from Alexandria. At this Admiral Cunningham was forced to give orders that if any French ship was seen to be making preparations for sea she was immediately to be sunk at her moorings, and an ultimatum was issued to the French giving them a time limit in which to make up their minds.'

Meanwhile the Commander-in-Chief arranged for each French ship to be visited by the captain of the British ship responsible for her, and to reason, not coerce, and especially to point out the helplessness of their situation, and the deep reluctance to opening fire when the time expired. Although many of the French officers spoke English, Dick, who had just been promoted captain, was fluent in French, and was able to compose a telling note which was communicated and broadcast in every possible manner.

'During the morning, as we watched,' wrote Cunningham,[6] 'it was interesting to see the leaven gradually working among the French sailors. ... The morning passed in suspense. Then after luncheon we saw all the French captains go on board Godfroy's flagship. About an hour later he signalled his desire to come on board to see me. During his visit he conducted himself with great dignity, and the upshot of our meeting was that he yielded to overwhelming force.'

An immediate agreement was concluded at 1530 on 4 July 1940, and the Admiralty was informed by signal about the following items:

(a) All oil fuel to be discharged from the French ships forthwith.
(b) All French ships to hand in to the custody of the French Consulate-General, with right of British inspection, obturating pads of large guns and firing mechanism of small guns, together with all war-head pistols.
(c) Reduction of ships' companies.

Cunningham says that he had never experienced such a whole-hearted feeling of thankful relief as on the conclusion of this agreement. Prodding signals received from Admiralty had been exasperating and had shown little comprehension of the uncertain and quickly changing atmosphere which could so easily have exploded into unnecessary and deplorable slaughter. One of the signals received late 3 July urged drastic action and ended: ... 'before dark to-night. Do not, repeat NOT, fail'. Cunningham to his everlasting credit ignored it. Having assembled his Flag Officers on board the *Warspite* that evening, he informed them that it was not his intention to take action in accordance with the Admiralty signal. That same day, 3 July, Somerville at Mers-el-Kebir near Oran had been forced to open fire on French capital ships, though with utter repugnance, after the failure of negotiations; 1,297 Frenchmen, allies until recently, had been killed.

The Commander-in-Chief sensed the quality of integrity in Godfroy whom he liked, and who in the long and weary months that were to follow remained with his demilitarised ships at Alexandria, and seldom went ashore. Each success of the British fleet was the occasion for a letter of congratulations to Cunningham. With the problem of the French ships now settled, Cunningham felt quite free to take the fleet to sea to continue operations against the enemy.

Dick writes: 'ABC's moral courage and width of view over this period is the moment when one first realised his qualities of greatness. Of course we knew him as a fine dashing leader, but his handling of the French problem was masterly and one wonders how many others would have had the breadth of mind let alone the moral "guts" to disregard his instructions. That was truly Nelsonic.'

It is interesting to get a glimpse of Cunningham at this time from his assistant secretary John Smith,[7] who had been with him in the *Hood* in 1937, and had rejoined him in the *Warspite* at Alexandria in May 1940.

'It was typical of the Admiral that he told me on arrival that I was to see that his Secretary Paymaster Captain A. P. Shaw, my old boss, did not overwork.

'My abiding and predominant memory of the next two years when the fleet was operating from Alexandria with its single, long swept channel approach, with no alternative base, initially with virtually no aircraft and many other urgent needs, was of ABC's unequivocal and unflinching personal leadership often in circumstances which daunted others but never rattled him. No thought of compromise anywhere to ease the strain or reduce the many tasks, no minimising the operational risks or pruning the commitment appeared to enter his head. In fact, of course, with casualties and losses as they were, these thoughts must have occurred to him, but I do not believe he confided them to anyone beyond, perhaps, his Chief of Staff. For he knew that even bare consideration could weaken resolve. He bore the load himself, but to those around him he seemed to bear no load at all.

'The Fleet Medical Officer ventured to see the C-in-C personally to mention symptoms of nervous strain and exhaustion in the fleet. He made a rapid exit with, it is said, a couple of volumes of the Navy List flying after him and something to the effect that if he wasn't careful he'd get a dose of nervous exhaustion himself.

'Always he became more serene and more genial when we got to sea and whenever there was the possibility of contact with enemy units he became positively elated.'

Italy's communication with the Dodecanese had already been effectually stopped, and her route to Libya was seriously threatened. Italian submarines were more cautious and there was yet no sign of the Italian battle fleet proceeding to sea. Cunningham praised the morale of the men in his own fleet, and their keenness to get at the Italians. His ships were old, he was short of aircraft, destroyers, and minesweepers, and both Malta and Alexandria were poorly defended. Improvisation seemed to be necessary in all questions of refits, repairs, stores, and ammunition.

'Looking back on those early days of the war against Italy,' writes Cunningham,[8] 'no less than upon the strenuous months that were to follow, I again realise how much we owed to the magnificent spirit of our officers and men. . . . It was their outstanding spirit of invincibility in any emergency that enabled them to rise over all our difficulties.'

Few would question the fact that it was from the C-in-C himself that the spirit of invincibility issued. 'If the old man's with us we shall be all right' was the general feeling throughout the fleet.

Seek Out and Destroy (1940)

There was no doubt concerning Cunningham's intentions to reduce the enemy fleet as soon as possible. Nevertheless, despite Mussolini's extravagant pronouncements, it soon became apparent that the Italian fleet would adopt a defensive strategy with the aim of maintaining a 'fleet in being'. The main role of the fleet would be to cover convoy work to Libya, and such tasks could be undertaken only when the way was clear. Cunningham suffered severely from lack of air reconnaissance, whereas the Italians were well off in this respect, and could adjust their movements so as to wait until British ships were well away from the central Mediterranean.

The Italian High Command turned down a suggestion that an Italian naval expedition should be launched to take Malta, and preferred to rely on the belief that this weakly defended base would succumb from bombing by the Italian Air Force. Unfortunately for Mussolini, as recorded by his son-in-law Count Ciano, there was no love lost between their navy and the air force: 'The usual air force boasts were inspired by their hatred and distrust of the navy.'[1] The lack of any aircraft carrier and the misunderstanding of the navy's aviation requirements by the Italian Air Force was to cost Italy dearly.

Having immobilised the French ships at Alexandria, Cunningham felt free once more to take his own ships to sea (7 July 1940) in quest of the Italians, a supplementary reason being the covering of two important convoys carrying essential needs for Alexandria from Malta, together with the evacuated families of British servicemen. By chance, though Cunningham was unaware of it, an Italian convoy of five merchant ships had put to sea the evening before from Naples (on 6 July 1940) with the battleships *Cesare* and *Cavour*, and 16 cruisers, all under Admiral Campioni.

Cunningham's fleet was in three groups: five cruisers in the lead, *Orion* (flag of Vice-Admiral J. C. Tovey), *Neptune*, *Sydney*, *Gloucester*, and *Liverpool*; next, the *Warspite* (fleet flag) with a screen of seven

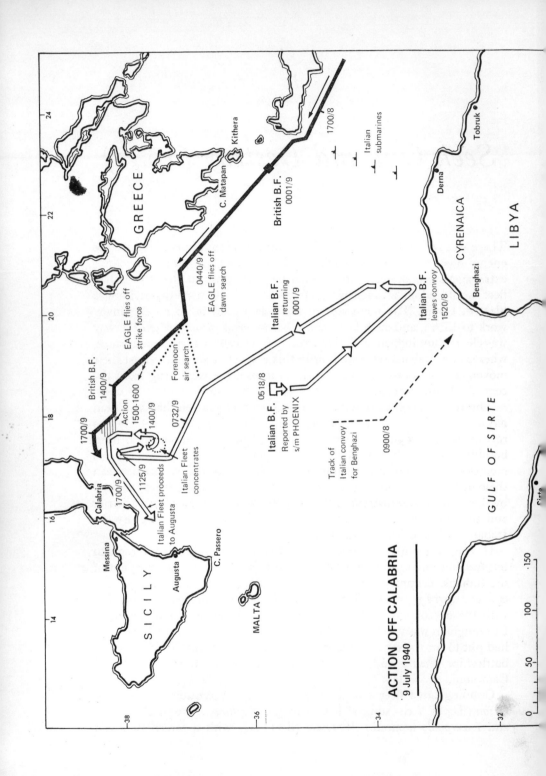

ACTION OFF CALABRIA
9 July 1940

GREECE

C. Matapan

Kithera

1700/8

Italian
submarines

Tobruk

Derna

CYRENAICA

LIBYA

Benghazi

EAGLE flies off
strike force

EAGLE flies off
dawn search

0440/9

British B.F.
0001/9

British B.F.
1400/9

Forenoon
air search

Action
1500-1600
1400/9

0732/9

1700/9

1125/9

Italian Fleet
concentrates

Italian Fleet proceeds
to Augusta

1700/9

Calabria

Messina

SICILY

Augusta

C. Passero

MALTA

Italian B.F.
returning
0001/9

Italian B.F.
Reported by
s/m PHOENIX

0518/8

Italian B.F.
leaves convoy
1520/8

Track of
Italian convoy
for Benghazi

0900/8

GULF OF SIRTE

Sirte

0   50   100   150

24   22   20   18   16   14

38   36   34   32

destroyers; finally, the aircraft carrier *Eagle* with the old unmodernised battleships *Malaya* and *Royal Sovereign*, and two destroyers in the rear. This distribution clearly indicates Cunningham's wish to have his only fast and modernised battleship, the *Warspite*, independent of the movements of the *Eagle* when flying on or flying off, and unhampered by the slowness and poor range of the *Malaya* and the *Royal Sovereign*. The merits and liabilities of the *Eagle* in a fleet action were still unknown, more especially with regard to the effectiveness of air reconnaissance, torpedo strikes, and local air defence. The *Eagle* normally carried no fighter pilots or fighters, but had two squadrons, 813 and 824, of TSR aircraft, with 17 Swordfish in all, and enthusiastic though inexperienced air crews. Keighly-Peach the Commander (Flying) was however an old fighter pilot.

'I succeeded,' he writes,[2] 'in unearthing some four Gladiators (in reserve at RAF maintenance depot Abu-Sumr for *Glorious*) and finally got them aboard *Eagle*. I think that made him happier.' What really made ABC happy was to see Keighly-Peach and another pilot take up the Gladiators, and between them, despite a thigh wound incurred by Keighly-Peach, shoot down a shadower and two bombers.

The cruisers (all 6-inch gun ships, comparing unfavourably with the numerous Italian fast 8-inch gun cruisers) were to carry out their traditional role, spread ahead of the fleet on a line of bearing to locate and report the position of the enemy's battle fleet when sighted: a slow and old-fashioned task compared with air reconnaissance, but more dependable when flying conditions were poor.

Early in the forenoon of 8 July (see map p. 94), while steaming north-westward at 20 knots in a position south of Crete, Cunningham received a report from the submarine *Phoenix* that she had sighted two enemy battleships steaming to the southward in a position roughly 200 miles to the eastward of Malta. He at once signalled Vice-Admiral, Malta, to send a flying-boat to shadow and report, convinced that the Italian fleet must be covering an Italian convoy to Benghazi. He remarks upon the high standard and persistence of the Italian high-level bombers from the Dodecanese, with attacks pressed home all that day, from about 12,000 feet, in the face of heavy anti-aircraft fire from the British fleet. Although hundreds of bombs fell close to his ships, only one scored a hit, this tragically upon the *Gloucester*'s bridge, killing Captain F. R. Garside and 17 others. The *Gloucester* thereafter had to be steered and fought from the after control position.

On the following day 9 July, signals from a British flying-boat, and later the *Eagle*'s reconnaissance aircraft, revealed two battleships, a large number of cruisers, and numerous destroyers, spread out over a wide area. At noon they were some 50 miles eastward of Cape Spartivento at the southern tip of the Calabrian coast, about 75 miles to the westward of Cunningham, and appeared to be concentrating, with the intention of moving northwards on a course for Taranto. Cunningham, now well served in reconnaissance by *Eagle*'s aircraft, continued to steam in a north-westerly direction so that even with his slow battleships he could not fail to cut off the Italians from Taranto. The weather was fine, and a light breeze from the north-west enabled the carrier to fly off and fly on without large alterations of course. Apart from the carrier and the modernised *Warspite*, Cunningham's fleet was greatly inferior to Campioni's. The battleships *Malaya* and *Royal Sovereign* with a range of 23,400 yards for their 15-inch guns were outclassed by Campioni's modernised battleships *Cesare* and *Cavour*, both of whom could steam at 26 knots compared with *Malaya*'s 23 knots and *Royal Sovereign*'s 20 knots. Perhaps more serious was the disproportion in cruisers of which he had four undamaged 6-inch compared with Campioni's six 8-inch and ten 6-inch. Campioni's preponderance of destroyers, about twice Cunningham's strength, was also a serious factor. Ironically, in spite of the great advantage of shore-based air strength close at hand, Campioni was not aware of Cunningham's proximity until an aircraft was cata- pulted at noon from his flagship and reported the British fleet. It was still the hope of the Italian high command that shore-based bombers could seriously reduce Cunningham's fleet before Campioni would be obliged to engage. It is equally ironical that Cunningham, though with- out shore-based air support, had at his disposal the great asset of torpedo strike aircraft in the *Eagle*, but with as yet inexperienced air crews consequent upon the long period between the wars, when the Admiralty had been denied control of its own air arm. Although he commended their skill and gallantry, they failed to hit either of the enemy battleships. They had other successes however, and ABC particularly welcomed the constant reconnaissance which they provided.

At 1508/9 the *Neptune*, Captain Rory O'Conor, reported 'Enemy battle fleet in sight'; the first warship to do so in the Mediterranean since Nelson sighted Brueys at the Nile in 1798. Six minutes later the cruisers came within range of Italian cruisers who opened fire. 'Mean- while,' says Cunningham,[3] 'we had sighted the enemy advanced forces from the *Warspite* [then 12 miles ahead of the *Royal Sovereign* and the *Malaya*] and had opened fire at a range of 26,400 yards on one of the ships engaging the British cruisers.

At 1530 the enemy turned away under a smoke screen, and the *Warspite* at 24½ knots turned a complete circle of about two miles in diameter to allow the *Malaya* to catch up, and then fired a few salvoes at two cruisers attempting to get at the *Eagle* away to the east.'

'The great moment came,' continues Cunningham, 'when at 1553 the *Warspite* opened fire on the leading enemy battleship at a range of 26,000 yards. The Italians shot well and straddled us at this great range.' But the culminating point of the engagement soon came. Cunningham, watching the *Warspite*'s great splashes straddling the target, suddenly saw a bright orange flash. It was immediately followed by a large volume of smoke. Campioni's *Cesare* had received a direct hit at 13 miles, and he without more ado, aware of the big reduction in speed suffered, ordered a turn to the west and smoke screens by all ships of the fleet. From then on the whole western horizon was obscured by smoke, and except for 6-inch salvoes from both sides during destroyer attacks, the general action had ceased. Suspecting a submarine trap, Cunningham decided against steaming into the enemy's smoke screen, and continued on his course with the intention of working round to windward and northward of the retiring enemy now reported by *Warspite*'s aircraft as heading at high speed for the Straits of Messina and Augusta. Campioni had at least been successful in drawing Cunningham close to shore-based bombers who made a series of heavy attacks in large formations between 1640 and 1925. 'It was most frightening,' writes Cunningham,[4] not a man to be frightened normally. 'At times a ship would completely disappear behind the great splashes. . . . I was seriously alarmed for the old ships *Royal Sovereign* and *Eagle*, which were not well protected. A clutch of those eggs hitting either must have sent her to the bottom.' He had the satisfaction however of learning from the *Warspite*'s observing aircraft that the Italians had not sorted themselves out until about 1800, and meanwhile, to Campioni's intense rage, had been heavily attacked by their own bombers.

Having approached to within 25 miles of the Calabrian coast by 1735 and realising that there was no hope of again engaging the enemy before they reached the confined waters near Messina, Cunningham took his fleet to a position south of Malta, and the next morning 10 July sent in the *Royal Sovereign* and destroyers to fuel. Both the fast and slow convoys, and the fleet eventually arrived safely at Alexandria. Nevertheless the intensity of the high-level bombing indicated a continuing hazard to all ships in the future until such time as fighter defence could be provided. What little defence was provided by the Royal Air Force for the fleet was achieved by adapting some of their Blenheim bombers for long-range work.

The action off Calabria is called by the Italians the encounter off Punta Stilo, and is objectively considered by them as a draw,[5] on the basis that no ships were sunk, and each side got convoys safely to destination. Materially this is fair enough, but it is important to consider the British achievement in the light of the fears which had prevailed only five years before, at a time moreover when the French fleet was in being. Cunningham's audacity in closing the Italian coast with three old battleships and an old and vulnerable carrier, in the presence of a powerful enemy fleet and an experienced hostile air force, established a moral victory which set the pattern for the next 18 months in times both of triumph and of adversity. The daring attitude of 'Fight you on Sunday' shown by a small *Britannia* cadet more than 40 years before was now revealed to the world. His fleet was already imbued with this spirit.

A few days later, the light cruiser *Sydney*, manned by the RAN, confronted the two Italian light cruisers *Bartolomeo Colleoni* and *Bande Nere* off Cape Spada in north-west Crete (19 July) and scored what the Italians called 'an exceedingly lucky hit'[6] on the former, which stopped her after a long running fight. The *Sydney*, commanded by Captain J. A. Collins, RAN, continued to chase the latter, while the destroyers *Hyperion* and *Ilex* closed to finish off the *Colleoni* with torpedoes. When running short of ammunition the *Sydney* had to give up the chase, and the *Bande Nere* escaped to Benghazi. Collins was immediately awarded the CB. 'A well deserved honour,' commented the C-in-C.

In spite of the very limited number of bombers in Egypt available for offensive operations in the Western Desert, the RAF had made repeated attacks on Italian shipping in Tobruk harbour and on the neighbouring airfield at El Adem since Italy had entered the war. Benghazi was out of range: see map 5. It was now the turn of the Fleet Air Arm, who with torpedo-carrying Swordfish disembarked from the *Eagle* and operating from an advanced airfield at Sidi Barrani dropped torpedoes in the harbour at Tobruk with successful results. The transport and maintenance difficulties can be appreciated when it is realised that Sidi Barrani was 200 miles west of the naval air base at Dekheila near Alexandria. Cunningham in his dispatch paid tribute to the co-operation provided by the RAF in patrols and photographic reconnaissance.

'Much time and money had been spent before the war,' writes the Fleet Torpedo Officer,[7] 'developing the torpedo aircraft. The results of this attack on Tobruk did much to reassure us as to the potency of this weapon and encouraged us to use it again in the future.' The Commander-in-Chief intended to carry torpedo attacks further into enemy territory where they could have decisive results. This would be particularly applicable if the enemy continued the policy of 'keeping a fleet in being' and seldom allowed her ships to go to sea.

After Calabria, Cunningham ordered the *Eagle* to send her Swordfish into Augusta for a dusk torpedo strike on three Italian cruisers which the RAF had reported to be there. The FAA aircraft were to return to Malta after the attack, since night landing on a carrier was not at that time feasible, and would re-embark in the *Eagle* in the morning when she sailed for Alexandria. Regrettably the harbour was found almost empty. It was this sort of fiasco which caused Cunningham to complain so much in the future at not having an air reconnaissance group directly under his own control. Most of the reconnaissance was carried out by a few RAF flying-boats working from Malta and Alexandria. These behaved with great gallantry in the face of Italian fighters, but results were fitful and limited.

Cunningham had quite enough of administrative worries besides the annoyance of finding the Italian fleet elusive and the Italian Air Force almost always present overhead. There were times of great irritability and frustrated belligerence. During the return to Alexandria from Calabria, when in an afternoon watch 171 bombs were dropped near the *Warspite*, one sees a picture in an inconsequential but graphically described story by the FTO who was in attendance on the Admiral's bridge, and had already been 'badly bitten' for not wearing his tin hat, and had also been reproved for failing to fall on his face at the sound of an approaching bomb. Realism is added to the story when it is appreciated that FTO was affectionately known in the Royal Navy as 'William the Silent'.

'The Admiral slept in his chair between each attack,' writes the FTO; 'at least he sat still with his eyes closed, and if he did not sleep he was a very good actor. When other men were frankly frightened as they heard the whistle of the bombs, the Admiral's reaction was to become quite furious at his inability to hit back. These attacks only lasted a few seconds but at the time it was just as well to keep clear of him. Just before 4.0 p.m. we were attacked by 12 planes from the port quarter. We saw them a long way off and put up a good barrage, but they came steadily on. I obediently fell on my face as the first 12 bombs fell close. As I was getting up the Admiral turned to me and said in a furious voice: "That was a very determined attack."

'This seemed to me to be a very obvious remark, not calling for a reply, and as I once more heard the whistle of bombs I again fell on my face. These straddled us: three to port, nine to starboard. As I again got to my feet a red face was thrust into mine and a voice thick with rage said:

'"I said that was a very determined attack!"'

'Thinking that there was enough war going on outside the ship without starting a new one on the Admiral's bridge, I hastily gave a soft answer, saying: "Yes it was a determined attack."

'Just then I heard the third lot of bombs arriving and once more took up a recumbent position. These fell close alongside. The resulting noise, smoke, spray, and chaos were such as to make it difficult to believe that I was still alive. As I got up I found two closed fists being shaken in my face. From a face purple with rage, through clenched teeth came the strangled words:

'"Why the hell didn't you say so the first time?"'

Though trifling, this story reveals a picture of those frustrating conditions so often experienced by ships in the central and eastern Mediterranean from July 1940 to November 1942. In alleviation of this discordant spectacle, FTO describes the human side of ABC who was concerned about the FTO's damaged hand sustained when he was blown over backwards by a blast from B turret. 'I shall always remember,' he continues, 'how in the next few days, when he was beset by every form of anxiety and trouble, he always found time to enquire after my welfare.'

Based on his experiences in the action off Calabria, Cunningham asked for another battleship like the modernised *Warspite*, with a good firing range and a reasonable speed. Both the *Malaya* and *Royal Sovereign* were becoming liabilities. He also asked for one of the new armoured carriers. Meanwhile, in agreement with a plan evolved with his fellow Commanders-in-Chief, General Sir Archibald Wavell and Air Chief Marshal Sir Arthur Longmore, his old battleships, with RAF fighter cover, knocked out Italian strongholds at Bardia and Sollum.

On hearing of forthcoming reinforcements for his Mediterranean Fleet, the C-in-C wrote to the First Sea Lord on 3 August 1940 saying:

'Our principal trouble is that we cannot move without our movements being known. . . . They send planes over Alexandria every day, and no force in the last three weeks has been at sea without being discovered and bombed, in some cases very heavily. . . . I shall be glad when the reinforcements arrive to strengthen our AA.'

Malta received a valuable accretion of anti-aircraft strength on 12 August when 12 Hurricanes were flown off the old carrier *Argus* from a position south-west of Sardinia. Though essential, this was a hazardous and expensive operation, since it required their carriage all the way from the United Kingdom and through the western Mediterranean.

At the end of August 1940, all Cunningham's available ships sailed from Alexandria for operation HATS, to meet the fleet reinforcements in a position north-west of Malta whither they were to be escorted by

Somerville's Force H. The risk from the air and minefields and submarines was considerable but the operation was completely successful,
and Cunningham was joined by the old but modernised battleship
Valiant, the new 23,000-ton armoured deck carrier *Illustrious*, and two
old but specially adapted anti-aircraft light cruisers, *Calcutta* and
Coventry. Apart from the added strength, the two large ships were fitted
with an early form of radar. This was to prove a considerable asset
which could give warning of attacking aircraft 50 miles away or of surface vessels visually obscured by fog or darkness. The arrival also of the
carrier's two squadrons of Swordfish (TSR) and a squadron of Fulmar
fighters gave great encouragement to Cunningham's schemes, though
unfortunately it was not to be long before it would be realised that the
accession provided only a temporary alleviation of the enemy's 'air'
superiority in the central Mediterranean and Libya. A handful of naval
aircraft in the hands of enthusiastic and gallant young naval airmen
was to do wonders, but only at great cost: and the price for the next
two years was very nearly beyond redemption. Meanwhile the passage
of convoys, British east-west, Italian north-south (see map 16), was
becoming more difficult and costly, and neither side was able completely
to stop the other. In general, with the Italian battleships now confined
to the 'safe' harbour of Taranto, Cunningham could be said to rule the
sea, though with reservations depending upon the limited air support
he could muster. In the air the Italians were numerically superior,
particularly in the role of reconnaissance and high-level bombing, but
they were short of *naval* 'air' and lacked an understanding of *naval*
requirements, and had nothing comparable with the torpedo bomber
squadrons which the *Illustrious* had brought out.

The Italian battle fleet, now comprising 5 battleships, 10 cruisers,
and 6 destroyers, had made a brief sortie when ordered to sea on
31 August to oppose Cunningham's fleet, and had been reported at
dusk by one of *Eagle*'s Swordfish to be 90 miles northward of Cunningham. It was already too dark for an effective torpedo strike so Cunningham stationed the fleet to cover the west-bound convoy during the night,
expecting battle the next day. A dawn search failed to reveal the Italians
who had altered course for home, 'because the British had shown no
intention of seeking an encounter'[8] and despite the fact that the 'Italian
naval forces at that moment were in magnificent condition as to effectiveness, readiness for action, and fighting spirit'. They had lost a great
opportunity to strike before Cunningham's considerable accession of
strength.

The captain of the *Calcutta*[9] gives a first-hand account of part of the
operation:

'Two AA cruisers, *Calcutta* and *Coventry*, took part in operation HATS but neither had the fuel endurance to do the whole trip from Gibraltar to Alexandria without refuelling. So when well west of Malta we were detached and ordered to proceed at maximum speed to Malta, refuel and rejoin the party at about dawn the next day, when Admiral Cunningham with the Eastern Fleet would be waiting to take the force on to Alexandria.

'As usual, as we were joining up, there was a fair-sized air attack. We, after non-stop practice in home waters, had become pretty proficient and shot down several of the enemy planes which evidently impressed ABC.

'Soon after arrival at Alexandria I went to report to the C-in-C and was greeted with his usual charm cum bark. Without my getting a chance to say a word he rattled off "You shot pretty well coming out of Malta. I suppose you have got this bloody RDF stuff [radar]. Let me tell you straight away that I know it will always be breaking down but you are not going to have any days in harbour because of this".

'At last, when I was able to get a word in, I said, "But I haven't got RDF".

'"What the bloody hell do you mean by coming out here without it?" was the instant retort!!'

The Italians launched their eastward land offensive in the Western Desert on 13 September 1940: a half-hearted, long-expected affair forced on Marshal Graziani by Mussolini. There was disagreement as to how this should be met. Wavell favoured a withdrawal eastward to Mersa Matruh (see map 5) so as to extend enemy lines of communication prior to a decisive battle, whereas Cunningham and Longmore deplored the idea of surrendering territory and thus losing still more local control in the air so near Alexandria. In the event the Italians ran out of supplies at Sidi Barrani and halted there. The advance exposed their left flank to Cunningham's shallow draught ships, from whom they suffered bombardment almost nightly. Many of these were the 625-ton gunboats of the insect class that had served in China up the Yangste and West rivers, between the wars. They were later joined by other small craft and the 15-inch monitor *Terror*, and were to give great service on this coast in support of the British army.

Cunningham had repeatedly complained to the First Sea Lord that in the absence of long-range air reconnaissance his strategic moves were frustrated and severely handicapped; without exact and reliable information of enemy fleet movements, operations could easily fail or prove fruitless or unnecessarily hazardous. Furthermore he complained of the insufficiency of his destroyers of which about a third were continually defective and awaiting refit in the limited facilities available at Alexandria, thus often holding up operations of his capital ships for want of an anti-submarine screen. Responsibility for the safety of the fleet, and with it the support of British forces in the Western Desert, was his and his alone, and it must have caused considerable and continuing anxiety. Cunningham was excessively irritated therefore to receive a 'prodding' signal from the Minister of Defence 9 September implying that he had been insufficiently offensive against the Italian fleet and hoping that more would be done with the arrival of the *Illustrious* and *Valiant*. For a man always offensive in outlook, and himself unhesitatingly critical when need arose, such interference seemed unwarranted, especially in view of the handicaps he suffered. Churchill for his part regarded a little prompting or prodding as necessary for everybody, in conformity with his 'action this day' policy. He was the inspiration for a Britain that had lagged sadly in the 1930s and which needed prodding. For all his tantrums he was the country's saviour in her hour of need, and without him Britain was lost. Fortunately, the First Sea Lord Sir Dudley Pound was one who had quickly appreciated Churchill's great qualities and his indispensability, first upon Churchill's return to take over the Admiralty in 1939, and still more so in 1940 when he had become Prime Minister and Minister of Defence.

'I have the greatest admiration for WC,' he had written in January 1940 to Admiral Sir Charles Forbes, Commander-in-Chief Home Fleet, who like Cunningham resented interference, 'and his good qualities are such and his desire to hit the enemy so overwhelming, that I feel one must hesitate in turning down any of his proposals.'[10] Again in a letter to ABC 30 March 1940, Pound says 'I find Winston admirable to work with'.[11] This was not the result of blind veneration but was in keeping with his admiration and respect, qualities which were reciprocated by Churchill. Pound achieved far more by working *with* WC than by using the flat contradiction or total disagreement adopted by some. ABC was in a more remote position which probably accentuated his self-confessed 'tenacity of purpose' and his determination to carry out his task in command as he thought fit. In later days he said that he found Winston much tamer when one was at close quarters with him, a statement that reveals ABC's appreciation of the Nelsonic principle 'engage the enemy more closely'. It is evident that Churchill particularly missed his sympathetic relationship with Pound after the latter's death, and was less in sympathy with Cunningham's ideas.[12]

Cunningham's reply to the prodding signal was lengthy and detailed, indicating some of the many commitments for destroyers such as escorting slow convoys to Haifa, Port Said, and Cyprus. Using a destroyer in such a role was wasteful, as Cunningham had foreseen when as DCNS he had advocated the building of inexpensive small escort vessels. He also reiterated the need to continue to supply Malta with frequent convoys from Alexandria, each of which involved a complete fleet operation and a readiness for action in case they should have the good fortune to find the Italian battle fleet at sea.

During the carriage westward of troop reinforcements to Malta at the end of September 1940 in the cruisers *Liverpool* and *Gloucester*, escorted by the *Warspite*, *Valiant*, and *Illustrious*, the Italian battle fleet was sighted by one of the carrier's reconnaissance aircraft 120 miles to the northward. This consisted of four battleships and included the recently completed *Littorio* and *Vittorio Veneto* who not only had a speed of 31 knots, i.e. 7 or 8 knots in excess of ABC's battleships, but mounted 15-inch guns whose range of 47,000 yards ($23\frac{1}{2}$ miles) could outrange his best by more than seven miles. In conformity with well-established tactical principles, Cunningham 'after some thought decided to press on with the main object of landing troops in Malta, and no more was seen or heard of the Italians'.

Another convoy was run to Malta early in October 1940, and in view of the report of four Italian battleships on the previous occasion, Cunningham took his whole fleet to sea to cover the operation. Nothing was seen of the Italian fleet, but the destroyer *Imperial* was damaged by a mine off Malta. During the return, one of the cruisers, the *Ajax*, Captain E. D. B. McCarthy, spread on a line of bearing to the north-ward on a moonlight night, had a spirited action, 'handled with resolution and skill' according to ABC, against a destroyer flotilla of which she sank two and damaged a third. High-level bombing still took place during daylight, but early warning by radar, the presence of fighters flown off *Illustrious*, and the usual anti-aircraft barrage proved effective in taking a toll of the Italian bombers.

In view of Cunningham's uppermost aim to destroy the enemy fleet it is interesting to dwell on a feature of his character which was so much admired by the Italian navy. Because of the Italian Air Force bombing of the *Havock* who had lowered boats to pick up survivors from the *Bartolomeo Colleoni*, Cunningham was not in favour of British ships stopping to lower boats. On the morning following the *Ajax*'s action, the damaged Italian destroyer *Artigliere* was sighted by the British cruiser *York*, Captain R. H. Portal, who did not stop but dropped floats, allowed time for the Italians to abandon ship, and then sank her. Cunningham reported the position of the survivors to the Italian Admiralty in plain language. For this humane action he was chided by the 'authorities' but remained unrepentant, and did the same thing after

Matapan. 'I may have been wrong,'[13] he writes; 'but on this occasion the Italian destroyers *had* fought well. As for compromising the fleet's position, the *Ajax*'s action must already have caused the enemy to be aware of our presence.'

Cunningham had to make frequent trips to Cairo for discussions with Wavell and Longmore, both of whom requested him to shift his headquarters there. He firmly refused. Traditionally it would be wrong, he argued, and he wished to share the difficulties and dangers with his officers and men; while there was a possibility of meeting the enemy he could not consider leaving the fleet.

It was late in October 1940 that Franco told Hitler that he would not commit Spain until the Germans had shown a clear superiority in the Mediterranean by the capture of Suez. This put a stop to Grand Admiral Raeder's Mediterranean plan[14] that envisaged a lightning advance supported by sea and air, through Spain, Morocco, Tunisia, Libya, and Egypt to Turkey, and so to the Balkans, thus closing the Mediterranean to the British at both ends.

Mussolini was anxious to forestall any German move into the Balkans, and it was he who took the initiative by invading Greece (28 October 1940) without informing Hitler, and against the advice of his naval staff. The invasion drastically weakened Graziani's thrust towards Suez, and led at once to a British occupation of Crete, thus providing Cunningham with a valuable advanced fuelling and supply base at Suda Bay, and the opportunity to build a naval air base at Maleme, close to Italian convoy routes. On the adverse side however, Britain was now faced with the need to support Greece. Italy's failure to sustain the assault on Greece, ironically for Mussolini, accelerated the German advance through the Balkans, and quickened Hitler's fear that Britain would establish air bases in Greece within range of Rumanian oil.

Cunningham knew that with Greece now in the war as an ally, there would soon be a steady stream of convoys carrying British troops and war material across the eastern Mediterranean to the Aegean, within easy reach of Italian airfields in the Dodecanese. This would entail even greater commitments for his overworked destroyers and escort forces. He responded by taking the whole fleet to sea to a position west of Crete, to cover the passage of ships taking men and equipment to Suda Bay. Heavy Italian air raids took place on Suda Bay and Canea, but there was no report of the Italian fleet being at sea. The continued existence of the Italian battleships at Taranto, even if they never put to sea, nevertheless necessitated the retention of British capital ships in a state of readiness at both ends of the Mediterranean.

It was on the night of 11 November 1940 that Cunningham put his

long-planned assault on Taranto into operation. There was a suitable
moon, three-quarters full bearing south, wind and weather were appropriate, and RAF reconnaissance revealed that by the evening there were
six Italian battleships in the harbour, protected by nets and a balloon
barrage. The operation was timed to coincide with the passage of convoys
from Alexandria to Suda Bay and Malta, and the arrival through the
Sicilian narrows of further reinforcements for the Mediterranean Fleet,
comprising the battleship *Barham*, the cruisers *Glasgow* and *Berwick*,
and six destroyers, all to be escorted eastward from Gibraltar as far as
Sardinia by Force H under Somerville: this supplementary operation
was entitled COAT. In spite of bombing, the ships arriving in operation
COAT escaped damage but were late in joining the rendezvous with
Cunningham's fleet, only a day before the planned night attack. The
C-in-C signalled Somerville in Force H, 'I nearly caught a chill waiting
at rendezvous for a coat. I still have no trousers but propose to take off
Mussolini's shortly'.

ABC might have had personal memories of an occasion in the summer
of 1937 when the *Hood* paid a visit to Corsica. According to the assistant
secretary,[15] 'The Vice-Admiral was full of fun, taking an enormous
pleasure in life, work, and play. Once he came up the gangway of his
flagship *minus trousers*. He'd been trying for trout in the hillside torrents,
and been deprived whilst making an awkward crossing.'

Leaving Cunningham in a covering position to the southward, the
Illustrious, Captain D. W. Boyd, DSC, accompanied by four cruisers and
four destroyers, steamed to the flying off position, roughly 40 miles
west of Cephalonia, and 170 miles south-south-east of Taranto, and at
2040 flew off the first flight of 12 aircraft, and an hour later the second
flight of nine, carrying between them 11 torpedoes as well as flares and
bombs (see map 7). Simultaneously with this attack the cruisers *Orion*,
Sydney, and *Ajax* bombarded targets in the Straits of Otranto as a
diversionary attraction.

Nothing like this had ever been attempted before, although a year
later the Japanese were to perform a similar but more advanced assault
on the American Pacific Fleet at Pearl Harbor. Well might ABC 'spend
the night on tenterhooks', as he relates, having signalled *Illustrious*
'Good luck then to your lads in their enterprise. Their success may well
have a most important bearing on the course of the war in the Mediterranean.' Their success was great. The aircrews were jubilant on returning to the carrier after having been airborne for five hours: even
Lieutenant-Commander Williamson and Lieut. Scarlett, who had been
taken prisoner after being shot down in the leading aircraft, found
themselves treated by the Italian Navy as popular heroes. One other

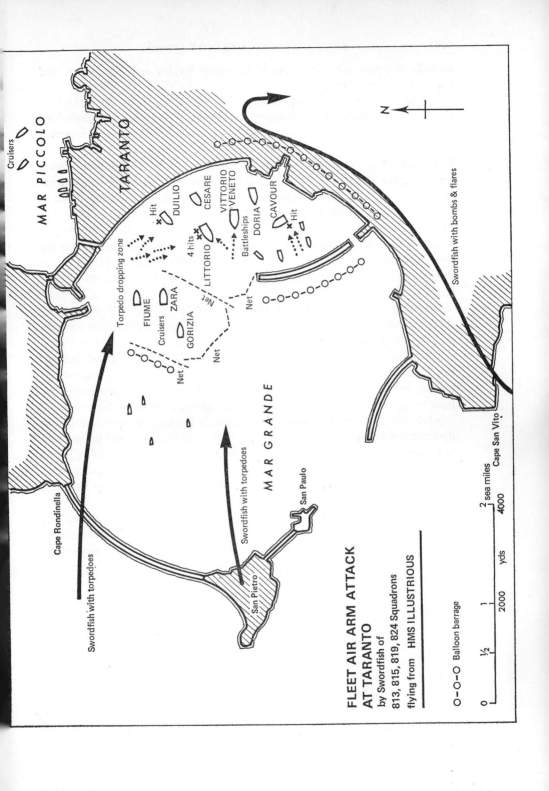

FLEET AIR ARM ATTACK AT TARANTO
by Swordfish of
813, 815, 819, 824 Squadrons
flying from HMS ILLUSTRIOUS

O—O—O Balloon barrage

MAR PICCOLO

Cruisers

TARANTO

Hit
DUILIO
CESARE
VITTORIO
VENETO
Battleships
DORIA
CAVOUR
Hit

4 hits
LITTORIO

Torpedo dropping zone

Net

Net

FIUME
Cruisers
ZARA
GORIZIA

Net

Net

Net

MAR GRANDE

San Paulo

Swordfish with torpedoes

San Pietro

Cape Rondinella

Swordfish with torpedoes

Swordfish with bombs & flares

Cape San Vito

N

0   ½   1   2 sea miles
0   2000   yds   4000

aircraft, together with its crew Lieutenants Bayley and Slaughter, did not survive the attack.

There was great keenness among the crews to repeat the operation the next night, but on the strength of a forecast of bad weather, Cunningham put a stop to the enterprise. As the *Illustrious* and cruisers rejoined the *Warspite* at daylight 12 November, Cunningham ordered a hoist of flags conveying a message, remarkable even for him for understatement, yet somehow fitting the occasion. It said briefly, '*Illustrious* manoeuvre well executed'. The whole operation had achieved considerable results, putting half the Italian battle fleet out of action, the new *Littorio*, the *Duilio*, and the *Cavour*, and profoundly affecting the naval strategical situation in the Mediterranean, for the Italians, in addition to losing three battleships, promptly moved the remaining three to Naples, and at once diminished the threat to British convoys proceeding to Greece and Crete.

Flag Officer Force H made to the Commander-in-Chief: 'Congratulations on successful debagging. If this goes on Uncle Benito will soon be singing alto in the choir.'

Cunningham was now also free to release his two older battleships, the *Malaya* and the *Ramillies*, which he regarded as more of an encumbrance and a liability than an asset owing to their low speed and the poor range of their unmodernised 15-inch guns. Congratulations poured in and Admiral Sir Andrew Cunningham's reputation spread rapidly, particularly at home where the people were hungry for good news. The same need had been expressed in the words of Admiral Sir John Jervis at daybreak on 14 February 1797 when bearing down on the enemy fleet at the battle of Cape St. Vincent: 'A victory is very essential to England at this moment.'

Cunningham's effective 'blow' at Taranto also left a far-reaching impression on both Turkey and Spain, and a realisation of the flexibility and extent of British sea power which confirmed them in their resolution to remain neutral and not succumb to Axis pressure to join them.

There was no resting on laurels following the crippling assault on the Italian battleships, and Cunningham's return to Alexandria for replenishment. Before dawn on 25 November 1940 he had sailed with the *Warspite*, *Valiant*, and *Illustrious* to proceed westward, first calling at Suda Bay to fuel destroyers and land troops, thence to steam to Malta to rendezvous with the rest of the fleet escorting a convoy to Malta, and there to meet an important fast eastbound convoy from the United Kingdom which was to be covered as far as the Sicilian narrows by Force H from Gibraltar. Opportunity was to be taken at the same time to pass the *Ramillies*, *Berwick*, and *Newcastle* westward out of the Mediterranean. Meanwhile, aircraft from the *Illustrious* and the *Eagle* were respectively to assault the Dodecanese and Tripoli.

The complexity of the operation, the hazards, and great distances involved can best be appreciated by a glance at the map on p. 110, which attempts to represent the complementary schemes being undertaken in this vast operation.

While waiting off Malta on 27 November for the eastbound COLLAR convoy which consisted of three fast merchant ships escorted by the 6-inch cruisers *Manchester* and *Southampton*, each carrying 700 RAF and military personnel, Cunningham intercepted signals indicating that Force H was in contact with the enemy south of Cape Spartivento, Sardinia. The *Ramillies* force had already been sent on, but could not join Force H for some hours. The Italian battle fleet of two battleships, seven cruisers, and 16 destroyers which had sailed from Naples 26 November was in the enviable position of being superior to either Force H or the *Ramillies* force, but failed to realise or make use of this fact in time. By the time that fire was opened between opposing cruisers the *Ramillies* force had joined Force H, and Campioni, realising that he had lost the opportunity to exploit his great superiority, decided to break off the action and withdraw. Somerville, having already sent off air strikes from the carrier *Ark Royal* which proved abortive, and now aware of his inferior speed, and conscious of his responsibility for the safe passage of the convoy COLLAR, decided to abandon the chase and rejoin the convoy.

Although the action off Cape Spartivento was indecisive, the objects of the whole operation were achieved, and convoys, troops, airmen, and minesweepers all arrived at their destinations. Nevertheless a Board of Enquiry was ordered by the authorities at home, to question the discontinuance of Somerville's chase. Cunningham considered this questioning iniquitous and told Pound that he was very sorry. He thought it 'intolerable that a Flag Officer, doing his utmost in difficult circumstances, should be continuously under the threat of finding a Board of Enquiry waiting for him on his return to harbour if his actions failed to commend themselves to those at home who knew little or nothing of the real facts of the case. . . . Not the best way to get loyal service.'[16]

The Board of Enquiry came to a decision entirely favourable to Somerville. But there was some talk of Somerville's relief.

It is interesting to read the correspondence between ABC and Pound at this time concerning a possible successor for Cunningham should he be 'knocked out'.[17] Pound suggested Admiral Sir Percy Noble, who was a good deal senior to ABC, and asked for the latter's views. Commander-in-Chief Mediterranean then gave his proposed selection and order as

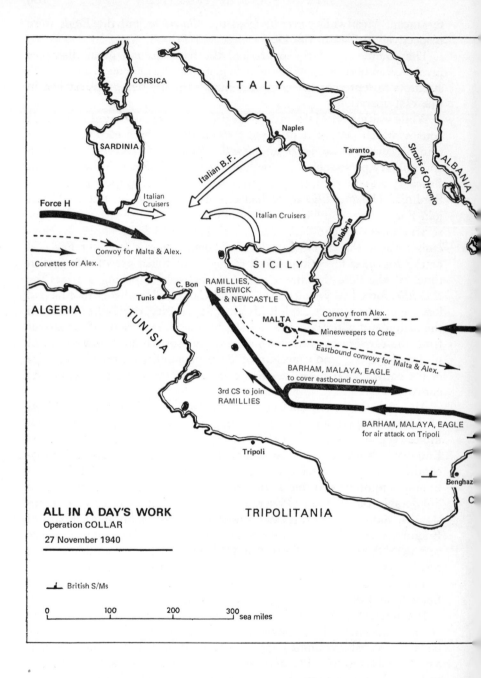

CORSICA

ITALY

SARDINIA

Naples

Taranto

Straits of Otranto

ALBANIA

Force H

Italian
Cruisers

Italian B.F.

Italian Cruisers

Calabria

Convoy for Malta & Alex.

Corvettes for Alex.

SICILY

C. Bon

RAMILLIES,
BERWICK
& NEWCASTLE

Tunis

MALTA

Convoy from Alex.

ALGERIA

TUNISIA

Minesweepers to Crete

Eastbound convoys for Malta & Alex.

BARHAM, MALAYA, EAGLE
to cover eastbound convoy

3rd CS to join
RAMILLIES

BARHAM, MALAYA, EAGLE
for air attack on Tripoli

Tripoli

Benghazi

C.

ALL IN A DAY'S WORK
Operation COLLAR

27 November 1940

TRIPOLITANIA

⊥ British S/Ms

0   100   200   300
                                    sea miles

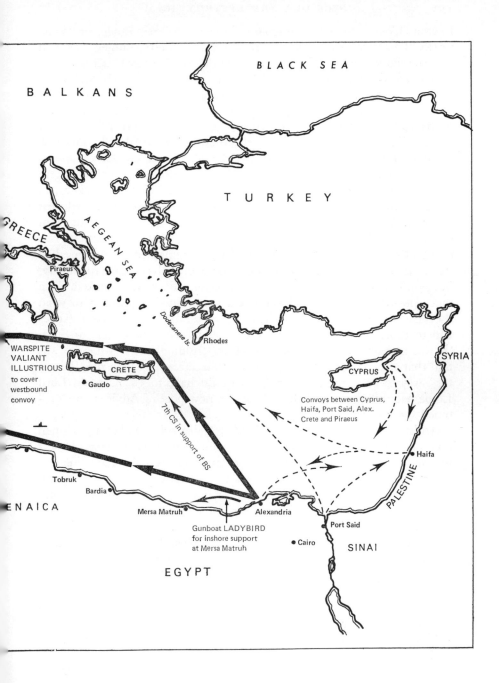

BLACK SEA

BALKANS

TURKEY

GREECE

AEGEAN SEA

Piraeus

Dodecanese Is.

Rhodes

SYRIA

WARSPITE
VALIANT
ILLUSTRIOUS
to cover
westbound
convoy

CRETE

CYPRUS

Gaudo

Convoys between Cyprus,
Haifa, Port Said, Alex.
Crete and Piraeus

7th CS in support of BS

Haifa

Tobruk

PALESTINE

Bardia

ENAICA

Mersa Matruh

Alexandria

Port Said

Gunboat LADYBIRD
for inshore support
at Mersa Matruh

Cairo

SINAI

EGYPT

Layton, Tovey, John Cunningham, Edward-Collins, Royle, or Whit-worth. The First Sea Lord himself was soon to be the subject of much criticism accusing him of permitting the Prime Minister to set aside the advice of his naval advisers. Cunningham regarded such 'malicious gossip' as cruel and unwarrantably unjust. This probably first arose over the appointment in August 1940 of Admiral of the Fleet Sir Roger Keyes as Director of Combined Operations. He was a great favourite of Churchill's, but was not so highly regarded by the naval staff. Towards the end of 1940 Keyes proposed that the island of Pantelleria, close to Sicily, should be captured, a project that was carefully considered and planned by the Chiefs of Staff, spurred on by the Prime Minister, in spite of opposition from Cunningham who considered it a 'wild-cat scheme'. He was already greatly concerned about the difficulties of getting essential supplies to Malta and Suda Bay. The project was eventually dropped, but the Prime Minister remained unconvinced of its futility at that time. Pound had got the plan shelved in his quiet way, but continued to receive odium from naval officers who looked for a more positive approach and wanted a determined opposition to what they considered to be 'half-baked' ventures. In October 1941 Keyes had to retire. He could never see eye to eye with the Chiefs of Staff. 'It was a shock to him,' wrote Pound to Cunningham,[18] 'when he was told that as he could not accept the new directive [in which the "Direc-tor" was to become "Adviser"], he would have to go.' Captain Lord Louis Mountbatten was selected for the new post of Adviser on Com-bined Operations.[19]

An important Conference was held at Cairo 4 December 1940 when final plans were discussed for Wavell's offensive in the Western Desert to start in five days' time. This campaign was aimed at forestalling any resumption that Graziani might make of his advance towards Egypt. Cunningham had formed an Inshore Squadron under the command first of Rear-Admiral H. B. Rawlings and later Captain H. Hickling, whose task was to provide support from the sea, not only in bombard-ment as required, but to provide water, food, and ammunition, and to take off the sick and wounded, and Italian prisoners. The planning and conduct of the campaign, known as operation COMPASS, were in the hands of Lieutenant-General R. N. O'Connor commanding the Western Desert Force. In a brilliant offensive in spite of severe problems concern-ing supplies of water, food, petrol, and ammunition, O'Connor with his bold and vigorous action achieved results beyond expectation. By 15 December 1940, all Egypt was free of Italian troops. On 21 January 1941 Tobruk was captured, and being swiftly cleared by the Royal Navy, was unloading ships within a week. The campaign came to an end with the surrender of 130,000 Italian prisoners and 400 tanks on 7 February 1941, cut off by O'Connor's lightning thrust to Beda Fomm some 50 miles south of Benghazi, after an advance of 500 miles.

With becoming modesty General Sir Richard O'Connor[20] pays tribute to the assistance from the Navy under Cunningham's direction, as follows:

'During the 1st Desert Campaign we were supported by the guns of the Royal Navy on a number of occasions – notably at Bardia and Tobruk. In addition, we received a large proportion of our supplies which were carried at great risk by the Yangtse gunboats *Aphis*, *Gnat*, and *Ladybird*; and the monitor *Terror* seemed often to be up our part of the world. [She was sunk by air attack off North Africa coast on 22 February 1941.] We owe much of our success to the gallant leadership of these small ships. Admiral Cunningham must have hated leaving them in these dangerous waters, supported against air attack by only shore-based aircraft which were short in numbers and had many other tasks to perform. We fully appreciated their sacrifice and realised that we could not have advanced without them.

'In my report on our operations, I stressed how much we owed to the Navy in both capacities, and I wrote personally to Admiral Cunningham on the subject.

'During this period I was in close touch with the Admiral, through his naval liaison officers who served us well, and I received a kind message to visit him on board his flagship in Alexandria if and when I had a day or two's leave and he was not at sea. So on one occasion I took advantage of this invitation by lunching with him in the *Warspite* and, on another, I dined with him and stayed the night in Admiralty House. He was kind enough to tell me a little of what was going on and what a burden the Navy had to carry. I was tremendously impressed by the Admiral himself and could well understand the admiration and affection in which he was held. I particularly admired the way he stood up to the heavy losses of ships and friends which occurred at this time. The high morale of the Navy, in spite of these losses, was mainly due to his example. He was greatly helped by Lady Cunningham.

'He was very kind to me and helped me in every possible way and I looked forward to my meetings with him.

'In Egypt the military command was a joint one, that is to say that, in addition to commanding their own Services, the Commanders-in-Chief held responsibility for general planning. The Admiral really disregarded this factor as, when I asked him one day what he thought of the Greek venture, he said, "I considered it was my job to transport the army wherever they wanted to go, if it was possible to do so from the

Naval point of view. They would get my full support." But I persisted – "But did you think it was a good plan strategically?" He answered, "If Wavell thought that it was a sound plan, that was good enough for me."

'I had six weeks commanding in Egypt at the end of the 1st Desert Campaign, but was ordered up again to the Desert after the German advance had got well under way, but I was too late to do any good and, with three other officers, I got captured by the Germans driving at night miles behind our lines. [7 April 1941 at Derna.] This, alas, ended my active co-operation with the Admiral.'

Cunningham considered O'Connor's capture 'a real tragedy', and comments on the supremely important result of the desert campaign in bringing the Naval, Military, and Air Commanders-in-Chief together in close co-ordination and co-operation. He had a great admiration for both Wavell and Longmore.

The clearance of the Italians from Cyrenaica gave renewed hope for Britain, and advantage was taken of this respite to revictual Malta and fly in more Hurricanes. The removal of hostile air bases hitherto flanking Cunningham's route to the westward was also beneficial. The main fleet continued such operations as covering convoys and bombarding and bombing enemy targets. Rhodes was assaulted by the *Illustrious* on 16 December 1940, and Valona in Albania was shelled by the *Warspite* and *Valiant* on 18 December 1940.

Cunningham paid a visit to Malta 20 December 1940 and remarks on the fact that they remained there for 40 hours completely undisturbed by any air attack. His reputation was high and he had difficulty when mobbed by enthusiastic Maltese singing 'God save the King' and 'Rule Britannia'. Opportunity had been taken of the presence of the fleet to pass a convoy through the narrows to the westward and to part with the *Malaya* at the same time. The destroyer *Hyperion* was lost due to a mine.

Generally the year 1940 ended in high hope for Cunningham, for British convoys were passing both ways through the Mediterranean and his fleet was taking an increasing toll of the enemy's convoys to Tripoli. The presence of the *Illustrious* had given local control of the air whenever the fleet had proceeded to sea. Moreover it now appeared from experience that the dangers to be sustained from Italian high-level bombing had previously been overrated.

Cunningham received confirmation in the rank of Admiral on 3 January 1941: a fitting day as it coincided with the bombardment of Bardia by the battleships *Warspite*, *Barham*, and *Valiant* in support of the ships of the Inshore Squadron; *Illustrious* also was in company, so that her Fulmars could give fighter protection, and her Swordfish could act as spotters for the accurate fall of shot on the target. 'Our task,' Cunningham writes,[21] 'was to prevent the large accumulation of enemy troops and tanks in the northern third of the area from taking the Australians in the flank while the latter went in to the attack. Indeed, we had to concentrate our fire on an area surrounded on three sides by our own troops.' Royer Dick remarks that 'the *Terror*'s guns were worn so smooth that her shells could be seen turning over and over as they bowled along towards the enemy armour'.

But already a shadow lay over the scene. Mussolini's fiasco in Greece had provoked German intervention in the Mediterranean. The Luftwaffe arrived in Sicily in January 1941; and Germany's campaigns in Greece and Libya were already under preparation.

The Luftwaffe Intervenes
(January 1941–March 1941)

Apart from losses in submarines, presumed to have run into minefields, the Mediterranean Fleet had so far suffered comparatively little, taking into consideration the damage and losses inflicted on the enemy. Elsewhere the losses of British warships had been severe, amounting at the end of 1940 to one battleship, two aircraft carriers, two cruisers, and a large number of destroyers and submarines, mainly due to German air and submarine attack. With the arrival in Sicily of Fliegerkorps X about mid-January 1941 the situation in the central Mediterranean dramatically changed. Hitler's directive was that it should 'attack the British Navy ... in Alexandria ... the Suez Canal ... and in the straits between Sicily and the north coast of Africa'. This force had obtained useful experience in Norway particularly in attacking ships at sea. With its initial number of 150 dive-bombers and 25 fighters, opposed locally by only 33 Hurricanes in Malta, it was steadily increasing, and supplementing those of the Italian Air Force already in Sicily, Sardinia, and the Dodecanese. Thus it posed a severe threat to Cunningham's command of the eastern Mediterranean. A new phase in the battle of Malta was about to open, with an intensity and persistence of bombing not previously seen.

Early in January Cunningham was again at sea with his whole fleet, except the *Barham* refitting at Alexandria, this time in execution of a complex and ambitious operation EXCESS, the main object of which was to pass through the Mediterranean from the west four fast merchant ships, three taking stores to the Piraeus for the Greek army, and one taking ammunition to Malta. Distributed among the merchant ships were 806 soldiers and airmen for Malta. The cruisers *Gloucester* and *Southampton* with two destroyers were carrying 500 soldiers and airmen from Alexandria for Malta, and were to go ahead of Cunningham, westward through the Sicilian narrows, to meet the convoy and take over from Force H, after which they would escort the four merchant ships eastward to rendezvous with the C-in-C's main force, the battleships *Warspite*, *Valiant*, and the carrier *Illustrious* 100 miles to the west of Malta. As in similar previous operations Force H would return to Gibraltar on completion of the task of escorting the eastbound convoy as far as the approaches to the Sicilian narrows.

Daylight on 10 January 1941 found the fast convoy proceeding eastward with its escort, having been met by Cunningham, but nevertheless in a position still west of Malta. An attack by Italian torpedo-bombers was foiled by the Fulmars from *Illustrious*, but an attack by 35 JU 87s and JU 88s achieved six hits on the *Illustrious*, the main target, wrecking her flight deck and half her guns, and setting her on fire fore and aft. Her captain (D. W. Boyd) was ordered to make for Malta, for although her Fulmars had destroyed six German planes she was now unable to operate her own aircraft. In spite of three further attacks in which she incurred further damage, she reached Malta late that evening having suffered in casualties 126 killed and 91 wounded. All her aircraft landed safely in Malta. The *Warspite* was also attacked, and according to Royer Dick, 'had a wonderful escape when a large bomb just missed the mast, and then hit the starboard bower anchor, but failed to detonate. Had it hit the mast, the bridge personnel and thus the Fleet command must have been obliterated.' The remainder of the covering force and escorts, together with convoys, suffered no damage, but the *Valiant*, in which Midshipman Prince Philip was serving, lost one man killed and two wounded from flying splinters. On the following day (11 January) the *Southampton* and *Gloucester* were both dive-bombed at noon, the former suffering such damage from an uncontrollable fire and loss of water that she had to be abandoned and sunk. The casualties in the *Southampton* were 80 killed and 87 wounded: those in the *Gloucester*, which was severely damaged, nine killed and 14 wounded.

In spite of the spirited defence put up by the naval Fulmars and RAF fighters, the *Illustrious* was again hit when Malta was heavily raided several times by Fliegerkorps X in the ensuing fortnight. Nevertheless temporary repairs were achieved, and as darkness settled over the island 23 January she crept out of the Grand Harbour and was soon steaming towards Alexandria at 24 knots. But for the determination of her captain (later Admiral Sir Denis Boyd, KCB, DSC) and the protection of an armoured flight deck, she would almost certainly have been lost 10 January. Though too disabled to be of any further use to Cunningham, she would make a welcome addition to any fleet after the extensive repairs to be undertaken in Norfolk, Virginia, under the lend-lease arrangements which had recently been sponsored by President Roosevelt at the instigation of Churchill. Her Fulmars and a squadron of Sword-fish were left behind at Malta to support both offence and defence. Her remaining Swordfish would go to the Western Desert to work with the RAF and to the new FAA station at Maleme in Crete.

Cunningham wrote of the *Illustrious* returning to Alexandria:[1] 'Her unexpected turn of speed resulted in her missing the cruiser squadron sent west to escort her, which was perhaps as well, as they were heavily bombed. However, she made contact with the covering battle squadron, and at noon 25 January, battle-scarred and triumphant, arrived at Alexandria and came into harbour cheered to the echo by the *Warspite* and other ships as she steamed slowly past.'

It was to be a matter of six weeks before another new armoured deck carrier, the *Formidable* (in which the author was serving), could arrive at Alexandria, having come round from the Atlantic via the Cape of Good Hope, only to be delayed when the Luftwaffe dropped mines in the Suez Canal, and finally being literally squeezed through the canal past a wreck. Her arrival also was cheered by other ships, but in the minds of the cheerers was 'How long will she last?' The heavy Luftwaffe attacks on Malta indicated that fleet operations could be undertaken only at considerable risk, and convoys through the central Mediterranean could no longer be run except at terrible loss. Sir Arthur Longmore, the Air Officer Commanding-in-Chief, whom Cunningham always found 'very understanding and sympathetic', assured him of all the fighter co-operation he could provide, but he was already receiving demands from the Greeks for aircraft assistance. In view of a continuing shortage of air support, the naval C-in-C was glad to have the three small anti-aircraft cruisers *Coventry*, *Calcutta*, and *Carlisle*, together with the new cruiser *Bonaventure* which was fitted with radar, an inestimable benefit for any group of ships at sea needing a warning of impending air attack. The use of the *Bonaventure* however was restricted, as she had already consumed three-quarters of her low-angle ammunition in an action against Italian destroyers in the narrows, and there was no reserve on the station.

In spite of Cunningham's great admiration for the feats of the Fleet Air Arm, especially after Taranto, there is evidence of his continuing traditional reliance on ships' gun power, particularly if such fire power could be massive and concentrated. This may well have been sustained by a despair of ever having even a modicum of air cover. In a letter to the First Sea Lord (10 February 1941) complaining of the blockage of the Suez Canal, which was delaying the arrival of the *Formidable* and preventing the departure of the disabled *Illustrious* and the vulnerable *Eagle* from Alexandria, he referred to Fliegerkorps X whose dive-bombing attacks his ships had had to suffer for nearly a month. 'We are trying some new methods against them,' he said. 'One which looks very promising is to make the destroyer screen put up an umbrella barrage over a particular ship, probably the carrier.' Provided ships were concentrated, these barrages proved fairly effective in deterring or upsetting dive-bombing attacks. It was not however possible to concentrate all the time; for example the carrier had to alter course frequently into wind, to fly on or to fly off, and any ship's speed or course might become erratic owing to a hit or a near miss. Cunningham continues his letter: 'I am also going to have 12 fighters in the air over the fleet when we encounter those gentlemen again. I haven't much doubt of the result.' In the event he was to find with the steadily increasing tempo that fighters were vulnerable and in constant need of maintenance and repair, and hence those available for service would rapidly decrease, as was happening at that very moment in Malta. There was also the problem concerning the right time to commit the fighters, and how many, for although the carrier's radar could give warning of approaching aircraft, it could not discern whether these were carefully timed decoys to get the Fulmars fruitlessly airborne or a planned attack. All this we were to learn very soon.

After the First World War there had been no lack of desire to press ahead with the development of the carrier, but generally speaking it was regarded as only a supplement to the battleship, which continued to be considered the backbone of the fleet.[2] The true story was only now beginning to emerge. The effectiveness of the torpedo-bomber had been demonstrated at Taranto: that of the dive-bomber in the attack by Fliegerkorps X upon the *Illustrious* and the *Southampton* during operation EXCESS. The Germans had carefully studied the British dive-bombing attacks by the Fleet Air Arm on German warships during the Norwegian campaign, and had made an intensive development of the technique, using the single-engined monoplane, JU 87, commonly known as the Stuka, capable of a speed of 220 knots and a bomb load of 1,100 lb. with radius of action of roughly 150 miles. To supplement this there was the bigger JU 88, a twin-engine monoplane with a speed of 260 knots and a radius of action roughly 600 miles, carrying a bomb-load twice that of the Stuka.

On conclusion of General O'Connor's lightning dash to Benghazi with the capture of the 10th Italian army of 130,000 Italians, Wavell wrote his dispatch and sent a copy to Cunningham, part of which gave due credit to the role played by ships and aircraft of the Royal Navy.[3]

'The Army owes much to the Royal Navy under Admiral Sir Andrew Cunningham for its support and prearranged bombardment previous to attacks on Sidi Barrani, Bardia, and Tobruk. Maintenance problems over a distance of 500 miles would have been insurmountable without the Navy's assistance in keeping open the sea supply lines, and in opening up the harbours at Sollum, Bardia, and Tobruk, thereby shortening the lines of communication and releasing motor transport.'

Cunningham was very proud of and well aware of the gallant work done by the little ships of the Inshore Squadron in spite of repeated bombing by the enemy from which they had practically no air defence. Even their quota of guns was meagre, and their casualties were great, with losses almost daily. Never should their dedicated contribution be forgotten. Cunningham refers to the fact that 'they were splendidly commanded by officers who soon showed their worth'. The captain of of one of them, H.M.S. *Chakla*, an old BI passenger ship converted in Alexandria to an 'auxiliary anti-aircraft cruiser', writes[4] of ABC '. . . that fine characteristic of his – to inspire the morale of ships under his command by showing his interest in them and by showing them they were not forgotten. I think we were one of his pet odd ships.' ABC himself writes of the *Chakla*[5] after she had been sunk in Tobruk harbour (29 April 1941): 'The *Chakla*'s latest feat had been the towing of the *Desmoulea*, a large disabled tanker, from Suda Bay to Port Said, escorted only by a trawler. Attacked six times on the way by bombers and torpedo aircraft she never broke wireless silence.'

When created GCB early in March 1941, Cunningham told his staff that he would rather have been given three squadrons of Hurricanes. It was a little later that same year that his old *Britannia* mate, Sir James Somerville, was appointed KBE, having already been a KCB since 1939. This was the occasion when ABC signalled him, 'Congratulations. Fancy twice a knight at your age.' Incidentally they were both then 58.

After long hesitation concerning the extent to which she might receive British assistance without incurring retaliation by Germany, Greece decided early in February 1941 to ask Britain for direct help from British troops. Wavell was then told by the British War Cabinet that there was to be no offensive beyond the western frontier of Cyrenaica, as it must now be held with minimum forces, while the largest possible land forces were to be sent to Greece. Operation LUSTRE, the transport of British troops to Greece, began on 5 March 1941. It continued for three weeks during which 25 merchant ships were bombed and sunk, mainly after arrival in Greek harbours.

Cunningham, whose ships were pressed to the limit, speaks of serious misgivings among the three Commanders-in-Chief concerning the wisdom of aid to Greece. There was no question that Britain was bound by treaty to help Greece, but little effective help could be given militarily, because of shortage of guns, equipment, and aircraft, and pressing needs that already existed. Rather would Cunningham have seen a continuation of the British army advance towards Tripolitania, with air support from the North Africa coast extending its influence to reach the supply routes to Malta. The plight of Malta was continually in his thoughts, just as it was with Nelson when the latter wrote in 1799 to the Russian Minister in Palermo:[6] 'Malta, my dear Sir, is in my thoughts sleeping and waking.' Already when the decision to send troops to Greece was taken, Cunningham was considering the even more difficult problem which would almost certainly arise with compelling urgency: how to get the British army *out* of Greece.

While Britain was considering the transport of troops to Greece from North Africa, Germany was sending troops and tanks to Tripoli, and on 30 March 1941 General Rommel's Afrika Korps, strengthened by the addition of a Panzer Division, struck eastward in a lightning offensive. In two weeks Wavell's depleted 'Army of the Nile' was driven back to the Egyptian frontier, losing Benghazi, Derna, and Bardia and, except for Tobruk, the whole of Cyrenaica. The Axis convoy route (see map 16) from Naples through the Sicilian narrows and along the Tunisian coast to Tripoli, though 600 miles in distance, was virtually under Axis air cover all the way, except for limited attacks that could be provided by the few aircraft in Malta; but by February 1941 it had become possible to base small British U-class submarines in Malta, and although it took a week or two for them to establish co-ordination with air reconnaissance, they were soon inflicting severe losses on the German troop and supply convoys. In addition, the *Upright* (Lieutenant E. D. Norman) sank an Italian cruiser, the *Armando Diaz*, in a night attack on 25 February.

The German high command, intent on encouragement, informed the Italian Navy that it was particularly gratifying that so many German troops had been transported to Tripoli with so few losses. It was not long however before they were complaining of lack of Italian fleet interference in Cunningham's transport of troops and supplies to Greece. Germany invaded Greece and Yugoslavia on 6 April 1941.

Meanwhile with the arrival of the *Formidable* (Captain A. W. La T. Bisset) at Alexandria 10 March, Cunningham once again received an accession of air strength which had the great merit of being under his command, and whose mobility and flexibility he intended to use to the full. The *Illustrious* had served him well for four months, before being knocked out. We in the *Formidable* had few illusions as we heard the greeting cheers from Cunningham's ships: the battleships *Warspite*, *Valiant*, *Barham*; the submarine parent ship *Medway*; the damaged

Illustrious, and the old carrier *Eagle* long overdue for a thorough refit. We should be the centre attraction in every dive-bombing sortie, but at the moment we were new, and had in addition to young and enthusiastic air crews, two complete squadrons (826 and 829) of Albacore (TSR) torpedo reconnaissance bombers, and 803 squadron, shortly to be supplemented by 806 squadron, of Fulmar fighters. Here were indispensable assets for a fleet, providing not only the benefits of a long-range armament and skilled naval reconnaissance, but also vital defence from enemy shadowers and bombers. Like the *Illustrious*, the *Formidable* was fast (31 knots) and had an armoured deck. But the question in everyone's mind in the fleet was 'how long?'

Acting Rear-Admiral Denis Boyd, who with ABC's enthusiastic concurrence was really the architect of the Taranto assault, and had distinguished himself in getting the *Illustrious* into the Grand Harbour and later to Alexandria, hoisted his flag in the *Formidable* as Rear-Admiral (Air). Very soon the *Formidable* was sailing with the battle fleet to cover a fast convoy of four ships with stores for Malta, which had been held up pending *Formidable*'s passage through the canal. Cunningham was anxious about committing his new carrier and convoy on such a hazardous mission, and made a signal (16 March) to Admiralty pointing out that the risk would be much accentuated if Malta's fighters were not reinforced by Hurricanes in time. The reason for his terse signal was that Mr. Anthony Eden had told him that the further delivery of Hurricanes by flying off west of Malta from a carrier which had brought them from England had been abandoned, owing to the great risk to the carrier. Mr. Eden (Secretary of State for War) and General Dill (Chief of the Imperial General Staff) had been visiting Cairo and Greece to discuss with the Commanders-in-Chief the extent to which help should be provided for the Greeks. Cunningham had felt unable to join them all in their visit to Greece, as he wished to be immediately available to sail in the *Warspite* with his fleet as soon as there was any chance of Italian warships being reported at sea. Captain Royer Dick therefore represented him in the visit to Greece.

In a letter to the First Sea Lord, 11 March 1941, Cunningham had twice stated bluntly that the Chiefs of Staff were badly misinformed about the 'state of our air force out here' and the 'real state of affairs' concerning Malta, where the enemy air force could mine the Grand Harbour and the many creeks whenever they chose to come. 'We must have large numbers of fighters rushed out to us if we are to make any headway, and, indeed, they are needed to save what may be a serious set-back.'

These were prophetic words, for in a few weeks the disastrous battle for Crete was to take place. Nevertheless Sir Dudley Pound made a personal signal to Cunningham in what the latter regarded as a 'tart reply'. It was decidedly pedagogic in tone, and glossed over complaints of the absence of adequate fighter strength throughout the command, in particular Malta, Crete, Tobruk, and the Cyrenaican coast generally. The intervention of the Luftwaffe was especially felt in these places, and since the disablement of the *Illustrious* in January 1941 Cunningham had had no illusions whatsoever about the impracticability of his ships operating close to enemy airfields.

Pound's 'tart reply' stated:

'1. The earliest date of getting Hurricanes to Malta by carrier is 28 March; delivery by this method has at no time been abandoned.

'2. Had *Ark Royal* been in *Illustrious*'s place, I am sure you are in no doubt what her fate would have been, but the risk to the carrier is but one of many factors taken into account. [The *Ark Royal*'s flight deck was not armoured.]

'3. I am not sure you fully appreciate events outside the Mediterranean. The Battle of the Atlantic is of supreme importance over all other commitments. The U-boat, mine and aircraft menace is not only on our own coasts but U-boats are already operating in the Freetown area and may be operating off Newfoundland. In addition there is the surface menace from a pocket battleship at large, one 'Hipper' class 8-inch cruiser at Brest and two enemy battle cruisers in the North Atlantic, against which all the capital ships of the Home Fleet and Force H are, with the exception of the *Nelson*, employed on convoy escort duty. While the situation lasts, Force H primary duty will be to the westward rather than the eastward.

'4. I trust you will disabuse Longmore that the reinforcement of Malta with Hurricanes will become a routine affair, which I suspect he hopes for. Although glad to use carriers as air transports in grave emergency, I feel this is wrong when it can be avoided by looking ahead sufficiently.'

The meaning of 'looking ahead' in the final sentence is not altogether clear and could hardly imply that either Cunningham or Longmore had failed to look ahead concerning the shortage of fighter cover. It probably refers to the fact that transport of aircraft, especially fighters, to the Middle East was taking place largely by merchant ships carrying crates to Takoradi on the Gold Coast, whence after disembarkation, uncrating, and reassembly, the aircraft could fly via Khartoum to Egypt. Such a process was affected by lack of equipment and skilled personnel, and was obviously very much slower than the process of flying off direct from a carrier either for Takoradi or for Malta, but the latter method put at risk and locked up at least two of the older unarmoured carriers for weeks at a time. Cunningham replied that drastic and early measures were needed to restore the situation at Malta, and emphasised again the 'present rather grim situation'. As he was always careful about the exact meaning of words, those who knew him would appreciate that 'rather grim' meant exactly what it said. He had an instinctive loathing of the word 'desperate', for in his mind seldom was a situation quite beyond hope. In his reply he once again told the First Sea Lord: 'You are not fully informed of the Middle East fighter situation.'

As a result of the intervention of the Luftwaffe in the Mediterranean, Cunningham had in February 1941 reopened the question of RAF co-operation with the Navy. Neither he nor Wavell had ever ceased to emphasise the importance of the air aspect in their operations, and they were critical of the limitations in the support given by the Middle East Air Command. Cunningham wanted a specially trained RAF Co-operation Group placed under his control, whose duties would be the defence of British ships. This was resolutely opposed by Air Marshal A. W. Tedder, who had been appointed Deputy to Longmore (29 November 1940) and who now engaged in what he refers[7] to as 'the long battle which Admiral Cunningham and I waged on the subject of a Coastal Command'. Despite the fleet's critical need, Tedder argued, not altogether convincingly, for concentration of aircraft under one authority, on the grounds of the devastating effect of division of fighter effort. He was not unaware of the terrible handicap under which the British fleet was now operating in the eastern Mediterranean, but nevertheless stated that in his opinion 'sea, land and air operations in the Middle East Theatre are so closely inter-related that effective co-ordination will only be possible if the campaign is considered and controlled as a combined operation in the full sense of that term'. There could be little sympathy for such a narrow policy at a time when Cunningham and those in the fleet were waiting for the unpredictable moment that the Italian fleet might put to sea.

Having worked up in the few days after arrival at Alexandria, *Formidable* embarked her squadrons from Dekheila and sailed with the battleships and a screen of destroyers on 20 March 1941, to cover a convoy of four ships which had left Alexandria the day before with stores for Malta. This was very much in the nature of a trial run, not only because of determined air attacks to be expected on the carrier, but also because of the continuing possibility of a sortie by Italian warships looking perhaps for the Malta convoy or ships proceeding to Greece. It was impossible to prevent news of ships leaving Alexandria from being transmitted to the enemy, but the weather proved an ally; a northerly gale and overcast sky frustrated significant reconnaissance. Nevertheless there were repeated attempts by JU 88s to get through, foiled every time on this occasion by the *Formidable*'s fighters and the umbrella barrage put up over the carrier. The expenditure of ammunition during these attacks was considerable; the rough sea all around was chopped by the fall of shot, and the grey sky darkened by innumerable brown puffs of smoke. The excitement was intensified by the blast of gunfire and the sight of a blazing JU 88 in its death dive to a final gigantic splash. The convoy reached Malta safely 23 March, though later bombed in harbour, and the fleet returned to Alexandria 24 March after its relatively uneventful sweep to the north-west. There had been no sign or reports of Italian warships being at sea but, as will be seen in the next chapter, Cunningham would not have to wait much longer.

Equally important with the accounts of those battles and major actions which were to consolidate imperishably his already great reputation, are the individual portraits of Cunningham given by those who saw him at this time. Perhaps the most amazing feature is that he revealed no sign of personal fatigue or excessive anxiety. Confidence in his leadership remained. But sickness had already deprived the Mediterranean Fleet of a number of its admirals, and now claimed Cunningham's Chief of Staff Rear-Admiral Algernon Willis who, according to the C-in-C, had literally exhausted himself. He had been indefatigable through three years of active and wearing employment. Cunningham writes of him in glowing terms, referring to his wise counsel, unfailing help, and far-seeing mind. A rising star in Captain Lord Louis Mountbatten was suggested by the First Sea Lord as a possible successor, with an alternative in Captain John Edelsten who also had a growing reputation. Cunningham[8] replied that he liked and admired Mountbatten, but that he was 'very junior still'. This might be considered a somewhat specious remark, since Edelsten was not much more than three years senior to Mountbatten; but they were vital years. Cunningham had seen Edelsten at work as Deputy Director of Plans at the Admiralty when he himself had served as DCNS, and considered him very sound. Edelsten joined in time to be present at the battle of Matapan, and it was he who over-heard a conversation about ABC between two sailors working on the upper deck of the *Warspite* as the ship secured for sea. 'Is the Old Man coming with us this time?' asked one; to which the other replied effusively, 'I should bloody well hope so. We're all right with him on board.'

According to his secretary[9] Edelsten used to speak feelingly of the air raids on Alexandria harbour when bombs and spent ammunition were falling thick and fast, whilst with the Commander-in-Chief he paced the deserted quarter-deck, observing the thunderous and lively scene. It shook him but appeared to leave Cunningham unmoved.

Smith also comments on ABC's reluctant but inevitable transfer of HQ ashore before the battle for Crete. 'When the intensity of combined operations called for constant touch with GHQ and AHQ in Cairo, Naval Command HQ were reluctantly moved from *Warspite* to the old Egyptian Customs building ashore at Gabbari (Alexandria), where the flagship was secured stern to the jetty. ABC's violent distaste for moving anything ashore was plain to see (and hear) in his scathing remarks about "soft arsed accommodation ashore". His influence,' Smith continues, 'was effective by the practical evidence of his outlook and conduct in a closely knit fleet far from home in a foreign base. By his unconscious example officers and men were fortified and carried by the character and performance of the C-in-C. It was perhaps a harsh tonic, certainly a bracing one; no other attitude could have sustained the long and costly task such as the Tobruk run.'

General Sir Richard O'Connor, then in command of British Troops, Egypt, until his capture on 3 April 1941, visited ABC in Alexandria frequently. Incidentally, Wavell's measure of the loss of O'Connor is succinctly revealed in his offer to exchange any six Italian Generals for O'Connor: an offer which was not accepted. O'Connor,[10] writing of ABC, says: 'Naturally we discussed personalities. As to Churchill, ABC had an admiration for his courage but could hardly forgive him for some of the insulting telegrams he received from him from time to time. Of his own service (no doubt amongst many others) he thought very highly of Admiral Tovey and Admiral Rawlings and Admiral Vian. He also thought that Admiral Sir Dudley Pound had done magnificently in spite of the P.M.! Of the Army, he was very fond of Wavell and thought him excellent. He found Auchinleck more difficult to get on with.' General Sir Claude Auchinleck relieved Wavell a few weeks after the battle for Crete, and ABC thought him a fine man, but self-opinionated in spite of his knowing 'damn-all' about the Navy.

O'Connor remarks on ABC's liking for Air Chief Marshal Sir Arthur Longmore, and ABC himself writes of Longmore as a true comrade and friend whose early upbringing in the Navy gave him a real understanding of naval problems.[11] ABC deeply regretted Longmore's departure in May 1941 when relieved in his appointment as Air Officer Commanding-in-Chief by his deputy, Air Marshal A. W. Tedder. There is a story here. As far back as November 1940 Longmore had asked for Tedder to be sent out from UK to become his Deputy. The Prime Minister was against this, so VCAS then appointed Air Marshal Owen Boyd whose pilot had the misfortune to land him in Sicily instead of

Malta on the way to Cairo. There is no account as to how these two fared as prisoners of war together, but the fact is that Tedder was then appointed in place of Boyd to the Middle East and thereafter went from strength to strength.

O'Connor concludes that Cunningham 'was at his best commanding the Fleet in the Mediterranean', and describes him as 'the greatest sailor since Nelson'. Cunningham's reputation for all time was shortly to be established by his victory off Cape Matapan 28 March 1941.

With the departure of Longmore, Cunningham was not happy with what he called 'the present lot in Cairo'. This is more readily understood when it is realised what a time of great adversity the latter half of 1941 was to be for Cunningham in particular. Tedder writes of Cunningham as a 'very refreshing old bird' when they first met in January 1941, and thought that there was a 'tremendous lot of kick in the old boy yet'.[12] ABC was then a young 58, keeping himself fit by tennis and golf whenever possible ashore in Alexandria. A year later Tedder was referring to 'the old man of the sea' as being 'rather a trial'[13] presumably because of Cunningham's continued insistence that 201 Co-operation Group RAF should come under the immediate control of the naval Commander-in-Chief Mediterranean. In spite of the 'long battle' to which Tedder refers, Cunningham describes him as being 'a nice enough fellow'.

One or two members of Cunningham's staff complain that ABC did not appreciate administrative or logistic problems, examples of which are given later. One, who prefers to be unnamed, writes: 'Broadly I would say that he was quite superb at sea, and unequalled during the Second World War. This not only applies to his tactics but also his friendliness especially when matters seemed to be going very badly indeed.

'In harbour was a different matter altogether, and here I believe he did us a great deal of harm. He refused to spend money on harbour defences, or allow enough men to serve ashore. Philip Vian was quoted to me as saying after a Flag Officers meeting in harbour, "The C-in-C ought to be put in a refrigerator as soon as we get back to harbour and not allowed out until we go to sea again".

'I feel that he was a classic example of a senior officer who has not had enough time on shore before taking over an important command.'

This officer also refers to Cunningham's well-known dislike of khaki for the Navy, even in war. He never really approved of tropical rig (white shorts and shirt), and in hot weather always himself wore 'number tens': white tunic with button-up collar and long trousers.

The following letter from a distinguished submarine officer[14] is useful in dispelling any suggestion that Cunningham lacked interest in the efforts of British submarines. Any such rumour may have stemmed from his dislike of the 'private navy' concept whereby some submariners, as also airmen, in early days, considered themselves as being apart from the routine navy, and tended to adopt irregular dress and an independent approach, perhaps in an attempt to distinguish the fact that they were different. In some respects this attitude was praiseworthy and understandable and could be seen also in the destroyer 'trade', though it would never have got very far with such a taut hand as Andrew Cunningham in command.

'My memories of ABC date from early 1941, when I arrived in Alexandria in command of H.M. Submarine *Triumph*, having been operating from Gibraltar and Malta during the preceding four months. Though I had not met him, I was well aware of his reputation, and it was with some trepidation that I presented myself on board the *Warspite* to pay my respects and report on a patrol which I did not think had gone particularly well, although I had managed to sink two ships.

'I found him reading my patrol report, and waited with increasing nervousness until he had finished. As he looked up his piercing blue, red-rimmed eyes, which I was later to discover could look so terrifying, were full of good humour. He was pleased about the two ships, but especially tickled by the fact that I had reported hearing a "hostile" dog bark while closing the shore one still and hazy night. He never forgot this, and whenever I met him in later years he invariably asked with a grin if I had "heard any hostile dogs lately".

'I left him, considerably cheered and enormously impressed by his buoyant and confident manner, and beginning to understand why morale in the Fleet was so high. Some time later, on return from a more successful patrol, I was lying in a bath on board the *Medway* when I was told that the C-in-C was walking up and down *Triumph*'s fore casing and wanted to see me at once. Again he was all smiles, congratulated me on a successful patrol, spoke to some of my sailors, but refused to go below, saying he didn't want to interrupt work. Very shortly afterwards we went past the flagship on our way to Gabbari Dock, and I received a severe bottle by signal because my ship's company looked like "a lot of bloody pirates". They were in khaki shorts and shirts, which was an authorised working rig for submarines, but anathema to ABC, who seldom wore anything but No. 10s.

'This was during the evacuation of Crete, but there was not the smallest sign of the appalling strain to which the C-in-C was being subjected, in common with the rest of the Fleet. We submarines, despite our heavy casualties, led a very different, almost sheltered life, compared with the surface ships. We took no direct part in Fleet operations, and we were almost the only ships allowed a period of extended notice in harbour. We naturally saw little of the C-in-C except for unexpected visits such as the one I have described, and, for the COs, occasional summonses to dinner in the flagship. Only later, after I joined the C-in-C's staff, did I realise just how sheltered our lives were. I have heard it said that ABC did not fully appreciate the efforts of our submarines in the Mediterranean. I never felt this at the time – quite the contrary in fact. The C-in-C was acutely aware of the value of the submarine offensive against the enemy's supply lines; of the multitude of "odd jobs" which they undertook, and of the high degree of risk involved in almost all of them'.

Further on the subject of Cunningham's attitude towards smartness, the captain of the *Phoebe* writes:[15]

'Andrew was a great stickler for correct uniform and always wore a white suit rather than shorts and a shirt. In our squadron [15th cruiser squadron] the OOW had to wear a white suit with a sword belt, in harbour, and peacetime smartness and cleanliness were the order of the day. This kept pride of ship and morale high. One day in Alexandria Andrew sent for Philip Vian [Rear-Admiral in command 15th cruiser squadron] who came on deck looking immaculate except that he was wearing a pair of white buckskin sandals over white socks. I said "You cannot go and see the C-in-C with those things on your feet", to which he replied "Why the hell not?" He got away with it!'

'After *Phoebe* was damaged and went to America to be repaired, Andrew sent me to the Western Desert as naval liaison officer to his brother Alan Cunningham, the first commander VIII Army when it was formed in the autumn of 1941. I was there for four months. Each time I reported to Andrew I changed from khaki into white uniform. But once I was met at the airport by one of the staff and told the C-in-C wanted to see me *immediately*. When I appeared in battle-dress, he blew his top and said, "What the hell do you mean by appearing before me like that?"'

Royer Dick has a comment on this attitude towards dress which leads one to believe that ABC may have become a little more lenient with the passage of years. He writes '. . . When I signed the Italian armistice in the middle of an olive grove in Sicily, ABC saw a photograph of it, sent for me, and asked what the hell I meant by being in a white shirt and shorts. I replied that firstly I had to conform surely to the soldiers and airmen present, and secondly that it was, I assured him, the first armistice I had ever signed, and I did not know the protocol. He looked suspiciously to see if I was pulling his leg, which I was, and then laughed.'

The vast change in the eastern and central Mediterranean scene brought about by the new German interest was rapidly taking place. By the end of March 1941 both Bulgaria and Yugoslavia had joined the Axis. Considerable British help was being given to Greece, not only in the matter of troops who could ill be spared from the Western Desert, but in tanks, guns, and aircraft. Though suffering regular air attacks Malta still held out, and Crete was becoming increasingly valuable as a supporting base for British shipping bound for the Piraeus and other Greek ports. However unlikely to succeed the Greek venture might appear strategically, with its diversion of effort and material from the Western Desert which Cunningham regarded as a vital region to hold, the political attitude was that it must be done, and must be seen to be done, in order to impress potential allies such as Turkey and the USA. In Cunningham's view, the loss of Malta would lead inevitably to a strengthening of the enemy advance eastward into Egypt, with the possible loss of Alexandria, and the compulsory evacuation of the eastern Mediterranean by his fleet.

But in spite of the deteriorating outlook for the British and the vulnerability of the regular convoys of British ships escorted only by light warships, there had been no appearance of the Italian fleet. Cunningham's great success at Taranto seemed to have acted as a warning that their valuable and splendid fleet could be better preserved if kept out of sight. The idea of a fleet in being that failed to pick off a few ripe plums such as the British transports, did not however appeal to the Germans. They thought, as we shall see in the next chapter, that the Italians needed only a little persuasion, and Cunningham's out-of-date ships could then be safely got out of the way: permanently.

Matapan (March 1941)

The following telegram describing the naval strategic situation in the Mediterranean was sent on 19 March 1941 to the Italian Naval Staff by the German Naval Liaison Officer in Rome.

'The German Naval Staff considers that at the moment there is only one British battleship, *Valiant*, in the Eastern Mediterranean fully ready for action. It is not anticipated that heavy British units will be withdrawn from the Atlantic in the near future. Force H is also considered unlikely to appear in the Mediterranean.

'Thus the situation in the Mediterranean is at the moment more favourable for the Italian Fleet than ever before. Intensive traffic from Alexandria to the Greek ports, whereby the Greek forces are receiving constant reinforcements in men and equipment, presents a particularly worthwhile target for the Italian Naval forces.

'The German Naval Staff considers that the appearance of Italian units in the area south of Crete will seriously interfere with British shipping, and may even lead to the complete interruption of the transport of troops, especially as these transports are at the moment inadequately protected.'

Here was a tasty piece of bait which the Italians naturally found irresistible. Inexorably they were being drawn into the very situation which they had always avoided: the risk of using their ships far from home and the possibility of losing 'a fleet in being'.

Shortly after noon on Thursday 27 March there came again the sudden bustle of preparation for leaving harbour. This was unexpected as *Formidable* had returned to Alexandria only three days earlier. Aircraft stores and ground crews were arriving, heavy arrester wires were being rigged across the flight deck, and the crash-barriers were undergoing test.

Formidable sailed at 1530, and about an hour later turned into wind to fly on the squadrons from Dekheila airfield. It was a lovely spring afternoon, the sky was almost a clear blue, and the wind was light.

Conjecture increased when the battle fleet also left Alexandria after dark. Soon we were steaming together at 20 knots to the north-westward: the three 15-inch battleships, *Warspite, Barham,* and *Valiant,* the armoured aircraft carrier *Formidable,* and an anti-submarine screen of nine destroyers, *Jervis, Janus, Nubian, Mohawk, Stuart, Greyhound, Griffin, Hotspur,* and *Havock.* All ships were darkened. The Commander-in-Chief was in the *Warspite.* Excitement grew when it was learnt that the Italian fleet had been reported at sea, presumably looking for a rich plum in the shape of a British troop convoy. There had been no major fleet action since the Battle of Jutland in 1916, and it was generally felt that one might be brewing now. All three of our battleships had fought at Jutland, 25 years earlier, and were very old in comparison with the new Italian battleships such as *Vittorio Veneto* and *Littorio.*

To cover the movements to Greece of troops and stores, Vice-Admiral Light Forces (VALF), Vice-Admiral H. D. Pridham-Wippell was operating in the Aegean Sea, with four cruisers *Orion, Ajax, Perth,* and *Gloucester,* and four destroyers *Ilex, Hasty, Hereward,* and *Vendetta.*

On receipt of a report from a British flying-boat early on 27 March, that a force of three Italian cruisers and a destroyer had been sighted 80 miles east of the south-eastern tip of Sicily, proceeding to the south-eastward, roughly in the direction of Crete, Cunningham had assumed the possibility of Italian battleships being at sea in support. If this were true he was anxious not to appear to be aware of their movements. It was fortunate that there was only one British convoy at sea, AG9 at that moment, and it was to the southward of Crete, bound for the Piraeus with troops. Cunningham directed that it should continue until dark, and then reverse course. The sailing of a south-bound convoy from the Piraeus was cancelled. He had also decided to keep the British battleships in harbour until nightfall. An Italian reconnaissance aircraft from Rhodes flew over Alexandria at 1400 that afternoon and reported seeing three battleships, two aircraft carriers, and an uncertain number of cruisers in harbour. Evidently the British were suspecting nothing.

There had been a noticeable increase in Italian efforts to watch the movements of the British Mediterranean Fleet, and this had led Cunningham to believe that an Italian fleet operation was imminent. He ordered Pridham-Wippell with his four cruisers and four destroyers to be in a position 30 miles south of Gaudo Island – a rocky islet 20 miles south of Crete – at 0630 the next morning, 28 March. The Royal Air Force had been asked to stand by with Blenheim bombers now in Greece, and were requested to provide air reconnaissance over the sea to the south of Crete.

Cunningham had his own private cover plan, going ashore during the afternoon with an obvious suitcase, to make it appear that he would be spending the night ashore. He returned to the *Warspite* immediately after dark; the fleet sailed at 1900. Brownrigg,[1] master of the fleet, wrote:

'We intentionally sent principal staff officers away by air during the day so as to allay all the Italian agents' apprehension; we also kept our awnings spread, and the Admiral invited people to dinner. As soon as it was dark we furled our awnings, the officers returned, and the dinner was cancelled.'

Excitement was high as the fleet sped north-westward on this lovely night, and, although we knew little as yet of either the composition of the Italian forces or their exact intentions, there was a feeling that we were on the eve of a major action.

There was just enough light to see across the flight deck at 0555 the next morning, as *Formidable* turned into wind, and flew off aircraft for search, anti-submarine patrol, and fighter patrol.

At 0720 our aircraft reported four cruisers and four destroyers in '34° 22 North, 24° 47' East steering 230°. Another reported that at 0739 she had sighted four cruisers and six destroyers steering 220° in 34' 05° North, 24' 26' East. When it became known that Pridham-Wippell had been ordered to rendezvous at 0630 south of Gaudo Island, conviction spread that his own force must have been the subject of the two separate reports from aircraft.

The situation took a dramatic turn at 0824 when an emergency signal from *Orion* was intercepted. This reported three unknown vessels at 0745 bearing north from her at a distance of 18 miles, steering eastward. These were the Italian 10,000-ton cruisers *Trieste*, *Trento*, and *Bolzano*, and three destroyers (see map 9), under the command of Vice-Admiral Sansonetti. Pridham-Wippell, correctly, believed the enemy cruisers to be armed with 8-inch guns which could outrange all four of his own 6-inch cruisers. He was also aware that they were faster by $2\frac{1}{2}$ knots. He therefore determined to head straight for Cunningham, now 100 miles to the south-eastward, with the idea of leading this superior cruiser force towards the British battle fleet. Course was altered to 140°, and speed was increased to 28 knots.

Unknown to Pridham-Wippell, there was an even stronger force (see map 9) which placed him in an exceedingly vulnerable position, for it consisted of three 10,000-ton 8-inch cruisers *Zara* (Vice-Admiral Cattaneo), *Fiume*, and *Pola*, two 8,000-ton 6-inch cruisers *Garibaldi* and *Abruzzi*, and six destroyers.

At 0812 the Trieste class cruisers opened fire with their 8-inch guns. The opening salvoes fell short of Pridham-Wippell's cruisers, but the range was slowly closing owing to the superior speed of the Italian cruisers, who now concentrated their fire on the *Gloucester*. The latter, though still out-ranged, was able to avoid being hit by 'snaking the line'.

The range had fallen to 23,500 yards by 0829. *Gloucester* now opened fire with her 6-inch guns, firing three salvoes, all of which fell short, but which caused the Italian cruisers to alter course away for a few minutes. When they regained a parallel course at 0837 they were still out of range of the British cruisers. The Italian salvoes were also falling short.

At 0855 the Italian cruisers suddenly ceased fire, and, turning a circle to port, withdrew to the north-westward. They had scored no hits and had been drawn some 50 miles closer to Cunningham who was steaming 310° (north-westerly) at 22 knots, distant only 72 miles. Pridham-Wippell decided to follow and shadow the Trieste group. At 0936 he reported the three enemy cruisers and three destroyers still in sight steaming 320° at 28 knots, distant 16 miles from him.

The first round had been fought without either side scoring a hit. The exact size and dispositions of forces generally remained obscure, and neither side was yet aware of the presence of enemy battleships. Pridham-Wippell was now steaming to the north-westward, about to fall into the same sort of trap that he had hoped to set for the Italians, for (as we see in map 9) the new 15-inch battleship *Vittorio Veneto* wearing the flag of Admiral Iachino, Commander-in-Chief of the Italian fleet, had been only a few miles distant on the port quarter of Pridham-Wippell in *Orion* as he raced to the south-east with the intent of drawing the Italian cruisers within range of the British battle fleet. The sudden breaking off by Sansonetti's cruisers at 0855 and their withdrawal to the north-west had been ordered by Iachino himself; he was unwilling to have his forces drawn any farther into the unknown, and was suspicious of Pridham-Wippell's retreat which did not to his mind accord with British tradition.

Cunningham ordered *Formidable* to range a torpedo striking force but decided to hold it until he could be certain about the presence of the Italian battle fleet. He did not want to reveal his strength until he could be sure of catching them.

Iachino now initiated a scheme for the annihilation of Pridham-Wippell's force. Though he had not himself sighted the British cruisers he knew that the Trieste group was being shadowed by Pridham-Wippell. He estimated that the British cruisers were some distance to the south-eastward of *Vittorio Veneto*. At 1030 he ordered his battleship to alter course to the eastward with the intention of working round to the northward of the British cruisers to take up station just out of sight on their starboard quarter.

As soon as he was in an advantageous position he intended ordering

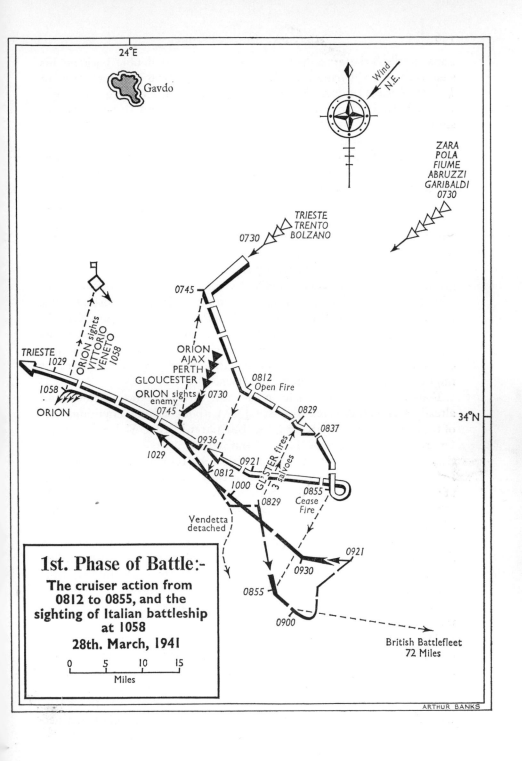

24°E

Gavdo

Wind
N.E.

ZARA
POLA
FIUME
ABRUZZI
GARIBALDI
0730

TRIESTE
TRENTO
BOLZANO

0730

0745

ORION sights
VITTORIO
VENETO 1058

ORION sights
VITTORIO
VENETO 1058

TRIESTE
1029

ORION
AJAX
PERTH
GLOUCESTER
ORION sights
enemy
0745

0730

0812
Open Fire

1058

ORION

34°N

0829

0837

0936

1029

0921

0812

GLOSTER fires
3 salvoes

0855
Cease
Fire

1000

0829

Vendetta
detached

0921

0930

0855

0900

British Battlefleet
72 Miles

1st. Phase of Battle:-

The cruiser action from 0812 to 0855, and the sighting of Italian battleship at 1058
28th. March, 1941

0   5   10   15
Miles

ARTHUR BANKS

Sansonetti's Trieste group to reverse course and double back on his
shadowers, thus driving them into the full fury of the 15-inch guns of
Vittorio Veneto. Pridham-Wippell's four 6-inch cruisers were to be sand-
wiched between Sansonetti's three 8-inch cruisers and a 15-inch battleship. Annihilation would be swift.

To us in the British fleet the composition of the Italian fleet was still
obscure. Messages continued to come in, but no further report of battleships was received. There was little hope of a surface action unless
enemy ships could be slowed down.

It was at the moment that our cruisers were being engaged that
Formidable's striking force had been ordered to range aircraft at 0833,
and these aircraft were shortly afterwards being fuelled, armed with
torpedoes, and having engines run up on the after part of the flight deck.
The crews came up to the briefing room in the island, where they were
given the latest information, such as we had, on enemy dispositions, and
wind and weather. At 0922, however, after news had been received that
the enemy cruisers had broken off action with Pridham-Wippell,
Cunningham decided to hold back the strike for a while. Before revealing the presence of a British carrier, he wished to be sure of being near
enough himself to be able to overtake and engage any enemy ship that
might be slowed down by such an attack.

Four Swordfish from Maleme in Crete, armed with torpedoes, had
already searched the area west of Crete without sighting anything. One
of these had suffered engine trouble, but all returned to Maleme by 0845.
On receipt of a message from Cunningham at 1005, three of these
Swordfish again flew off at 1050, having been refuelled and armed with
Mark 12 torpedoes. Flying at 9,000 feet they sighted the Trieste group
at noon steering 300° at 30 knots. Five minutes later they made a torpedo
attack on the rear cruiser, the *Bolzano*, but the enemy took avoiding
action and each torpedo missed.

At 0939 Cunningham had ordered the *Formidable* to fly off the six
Albacores that had been ranged on the flight deck for the last hour. His
aim was to attack the Trieste cruisers now being shadowed by Pridham-
Wippell. It was a providential decision, for Pridham-Wippell was
unaware of the grim fate which Iachino had planned for him: in fact
unaware of Iachino's presence at all.

At 1058 a look-out in the *Orion* suddenly sighted an unknown vessel
to the northward bearing 002° at a distance of 16 miles (see maps pp. 135
and 139). A minute later the ship had been identified as a Vittorio Veneto
class battleship. At the same moment she opened fire on *Orion* with her
15-inch guns. Pridham-Wippell immediately altered course to the southward and increased to full speed. The staff in *Warspite* were electrified

at three intercepted emergency signals made by Pridham-Wippell to his cruisers:

'Make smoke by all available means.'

'Turn together to 180 degrees.'

'Proceed at your utmost speed.'

According to the fleet gunnery officer ABC took one look at the signals and said, 'He's sighted the enemy battle fleet, and if you'd ever done any reasonable time in destroyers, you'd know it without waiting for the amplifying report. Put the enemy battle fleet in at visibility distance to the northward of him.'

At 1100 Sansonetti altered course to port with his Trieste division, in accordance with Iachino's plan for him to engage Pridham-Wippell from the starboard quarter.

Pridham-Wippell was now in a perilous position, pursued by Sansonetti, who with his superior speed would shortly be within range of him, and being fired on by *Vittorio Veneto* who found no difficulty in keeping up with him. The range was about 12 miles, and the battleship's fire was accurate though with too large a spread. She concentrated on *Orion* and soon scored a near miss which caused *Orion* some minor damage. Pridham-Wippell had ordered his force to make smoke, and with the wind light from the north-east, this began to be effective as a screen. Only one ship, the *Gloucester* (to windward of the other three) remained visible to the enemy who quickly shifted fire to her and repeatedly straddled her with 15-inch shell. The destroyer *Hasty* raced to close the gap and made smoke which soon effectively hid the *Gloucester* from the *Vittorio Veneto*.

At this critical moment, 1127, *Formidable*'s striking force arrived. Two German JU 88 fighter bombers had dived out of the sun into the formation, but were at once spotted by our two Fulmars. One was shot down in flames, and the other fled.

Iachino says how cheered he was when, at 1100, a look-out from the mast-head reported sighting six aircraft which looked like Italian CR 43 escorts. Here were the planes from Rhodes for which he had waited so long. His joy was short-lived. The planes were British. The battleship and all the destroyers in company opened up with anti-aircraft guns and machine-guns. Iachino saw the aircraft drop six torpedoes. He considered the dropping zone in each case to be more than 2,000 metres from *Veneto*.

In spite of *Formidable*'s determined attack, all the torpedoes missed *Veneto*. The attack, however, saved the British cruisers. *Veneto*, having had a narrow escape, broke off action and proceeded on a course 300° towards home at 28 knots. Pridham-Wippell, racing southwards at full speed under a smoke screen, failed to see the air attack that had arrived at such an opportune moment. Nor did he see *Vittorio Veneto* turn away to the north-westward, or Sansonetti doing likewise at high speed (see map 10). Pridham-Wippell now altered course to gain touch with Cunningham. At 1224 *Gloucester* sighted the screen of the British battle fleet bearing 046° (north-easterly). Cunningham, now only 45 miles to the east-south-east of Iachino, was chasing hopefully at top speed: a top speed, however, that would be quite insufficient unless the Italian ships could be slowed down by further aircraft attacks.

Formidable's log[2] for this day shows that flying operations were conducted on 21 separate occasions. Each operation might occupy only a few minutes but required an alteration of course into the wind which was upsetting when the whole fleet had to conform to these movements to ensure that the destroyer screen would remain effective. Essential routine operations severely limited the number of aircraft that could be made ready for the big strikes. She had a total of only 27 aircraft on board: 13 Fulmars, 10 Albacores (of which only five were fitted with long-range tanks), and four Swordfish. These had to cover all routine requirements, such as fighter protection and anti-submarine patrol in addition to the shadowing, mass reconnaissance, and offensive strikes needed in battle: a pitiably small force when compared with the large forces available in carriers in the Pacific Campaign of 1945.

The *Formidable* had been detached from the battleships soon after noon, to conduct her flying operations independently of the fleet and so allow the battleships to continue the chase at the maximum speed of the fleet, limited by the *Barham* to about 22 knots. As she turned into wind she quickly dropped astern of the battle fleet, feeling somewhat defenceless in the absence of their heavy guns, but reassured at the thought of the Italian fleet legging it for home 50 or 60 miles to the north-west.

The second strike of three Albacores and two Swordfish now took off to allow aircraft of the forenoon strike to fly on. The strike was to be accompanied by two Fulmar fighters. As soon as flying on had been completed, *Formidable* at 1244 shaped course at full speed to rejoin the battle fleet now out of sight beyond the horizon. It was then that she was attacked by two Italian S 79s coming in low and dropping torpedoes. The *Formidable* made two violent alterations of course sufficiently to miss both torpedoes, and course was once again resumed to close the battle fleet.

Formidable rejoined Cunningham at 1400. The fleet now presented a powerful spectacle with four 6-inch cruisers 16 miles ahead, and three 15-inch battleships and an armoured fleet carrier with 13 destroyers in

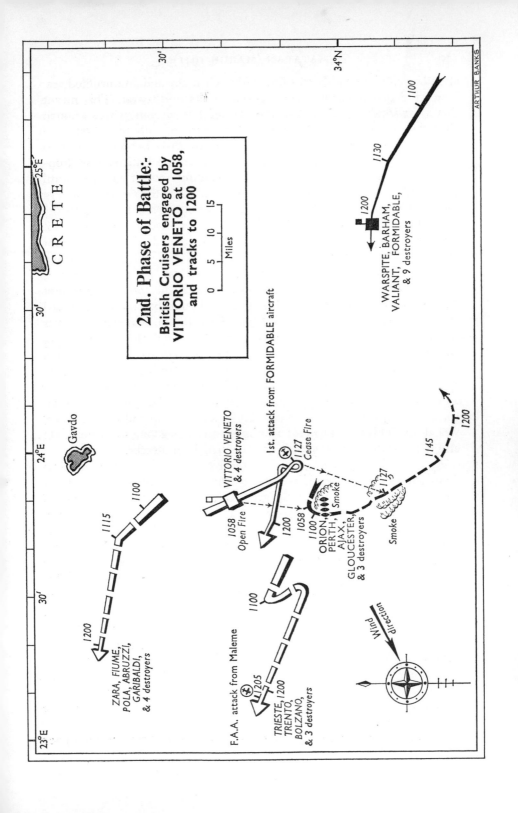

CRETE

25°E

30'

Gavdo

2nd. Phase of Battle:-
British Cruisers engaged by
VITTORIO VENETO at 1058,
and tracks to 1200

0   5   10   15
Miles

ZARA, FIUME,
POLA, ABRUZZI,
GARIBALDI,
& 4 destroyers

1200

1115

1100

1st. attack from FORMIDABLE aircraft

VITTORIO VENETO
& 4 destroyers

1127
Cease Fire

1058
Open Fire

1200

1058

1100

Smoke

ORION,
PERTH,
AJAX,
GLOUCESTER,
& 3 destroyers

1127

Smoke

1145

1200

F.A.A. attack from Maleme

1100

1205

TRIESTE, 1200
TRENTO,
BOLZANO,
& 3 destroyers

Wind
direction

WARSPITE, BARHAM,
VALIANT, FORMIDABLE,
& 9 destroyers

1200

1130

1100

34°N

30'

23°E

30'

24°E

30'

ARTHUR BANKS

attendance. The weather was fine with a clear sky and an unruffled sea. The wind had moderated and backed to the north-west. This meant that *Formidable* could fly on and fly off her aircraft without much alteration of course, and the chase could continue without interruption at a steady speed of over 22 knots. Little by little it became clear to Cunningham that his fleet, far from gaining on the Italians, was dropping farther astern. Iachino had been steaming 300° at 28 knots until 1400, and then dropped to 25 knots only because of the need to conserve fuel in his destroyers. This however was not apparent owing to the conflicting nature of individual aircraft's reports. Errors were not revealed owing to the vast distances which separated the three different Italian groups. Owing to *Formidable*'s shortage of aircraft, shadowing touch with the enemy had temporarily been lost. By 1400, however, three of the Albacores that had flown on with the return of the first striking force had been refuelled and ranged, and took off to locate and shadow the enemy again. By 1500 Mike Haworth, the lieutenant observer in aircraft 4F, had sighted *Vittorio Veneto* and reported her position, course, and speed. He arrived in good time to observe 829 Squadron's attack on the *Veneto* and remained until dusk sending regular reports.

Iachino's appreciation of the situation at 1500, based on the small amount of information received, was that, apart from the four Orion cruisers, only a single carrier escorted by a battleship and minor vessels was at sea. This group had inferior speed and was a long way astern. He still felt that the real danger lay only in British air attacks.

At 1420 *Vittorio Veneto* was attacked by Royal Air Force Blenheims from Menedi in Greece. Bombs were dropped at high level and fell close alongside. They threw up great columns of water but caused no damage. Half an hour later six more Blenheims attacked from a high altitude. Evasive action was taken and anti-aircraft fire opened. All the bombs fell into the sea. There were further attacks by Royal Air Force bombers at 1520 and 1700 on the Trieste group, and, although near misses were claimed, no hits were scored. Iachino complains that there was not a single Italian or German aircraft in the sky to defend them. 'I felt pretty well deceived,' says Iachino, 'by the lack of co-operation. We continued to remain for the rest of the day without any fighter cover.'

But Iachino was now to receive what he calls the most important attack on *Vittorio Veneto*, 'conducted this time with particular ability and bravery in aircraft which had evidently come from an aircraft carrier'. This was the arrival of *Formidable*'s second torpedo strike provided by aircraft of 829 Squadron led by Lieutenant-Commander Dalyell-Stead.

Iachino describes the machine-gunning of the bridges and upper works by the fighter escort, which momentarily surprised and paralysed his look-outs and gunners, and enabled three Albacores to continue their head-on attack and get close in. An immediate alteration of course was necessary, but before the ship began effectively to turn to starboard an interminable interval of time seemed to pass during which 'we all had our hearts in our mouths and our eyes fixed on the aircraft'. Iachino particularly mentions the aircraft which was leading and which showed very great skill and courage in approaching so close before dropping. He saw the torpedo fall in the water little more than 1,000 yards ahead of the ship just as the ship began to turn slowly to starboard. He also clearly saw the track of the approaching torpedo. The next few seconds seemed like hours. Machine-gun fire now opened, and the pilot who had come in so close was obviously in difficulty. Every gun concentrated on him. He turned sharply to his left, as if to cross *Veneto*'s course and escape to her starboard hand where the fire was less intense. Now he presented a full target to the forward machine-guns and received many hits. Suddenly his aircraft staggered, dipped violently across the track a dozen yards ahead of *Veneto*'s bows, and finally dropped into the sea about 1,000 yards on the starboard hand. 'And so died a brave pilot without the satisfaction of knowing that his attack had been successful', wrote Iachino. So died also Cooke, the observer, and Blenkhorn, the PO air gunner: a gallant end for three of our shipmates.

With *Veneto* swinging rapidly to starboard, a hit aft seemed inevitable. Seconds after the aircraft had crashed, the torpedo struck; just above the outer port screw 15 feet below the water line. The impact was tremendous. Thousands of tons of water were shipped. At 1530 the engines stopped. Slowly *Vittorio Veneto* began to list to port. Inch by inch she settled by the stern. Perhaps her fate was now sealed. She was stopped. Only 65 miles astern, still unknown to Iachino, was the British battle fleet closing at 22 knots. Three possible hits were claimed and reported by Rear-Admiral (Air), to which Cunningham replied, 'Well done. Give him another nudge at dusk.'

As the *Vittorio Veneto* listed to port and went down by the stern the engines stopped completely. Damage control parties rushed immediately into action, and the two starboard engines were started. Soon afterwards *Vittorio Veneto* was working up to 16 knots. Iachino states that by 1700 they were doing 19 knots and were able to keep this up. When hit at 1530 they were still 420 miles from Taranto, and Iachino complains bitterly at the lack of aircraft, 'not a single Italian or German', to defend them.

Cunningham had had no visual contact of the enemy by surface vessel since *Vittorio Veneto* had broken off action in the late forenoon. Aircraft reports continued to reach him throughout the afternoon, but there were differences concerning composition and disposition of Italian forces, and much uncertainty about their speeds. The general position still remained confused, so at 1644 Pridham-Wippell was ordered to press on at full speed, and the destroyers *Nubian* and *Mohawk* were sent on ahead of the battle fleet to act as a visual link between Pridham-Wippell and Cunningham. Two hours of daylight still remained, and if it were true that *Vittorio Veneto* had been really stopped or considerably slowed down, the chances of a decisive engagement before nightfall were quite high. But first to find the quarry.

In the *Formidable* six Albacores of 826 Squadron and two Swordfish of 829 Squadron were ranged and armed with torpedoes for the dusk strike, and, having been briefed, flew off at 1735 under the command of Lieutenant-Commander Gerald Saunt with instructions to land ashore at Maleme after the attack. Night landing was not at this time feasible in carriers owing to the dangers of revealing position to the enemy.

At 1810 Cunningham made a signal declaring his intentions for the night. The cruisers had been steaming at full speed for an hour and a half and there was good reason to believe that they would make contact before nightfall, though much depended on the extent to which the Italian fleet had been slowed down by *Formidable*'s afternoon torpedo strike.

'If cruisers gain touch with damaged battleship,' declared the Commander-in-Chief, '2nd and 14th destroyer flotillas will be sent to attack. If she is not then destroyed, battle fleet will follow in. If not located by cruisers I intend to work round to the north and then west and regain touch in the morning.'

It was not until 1820 that *Vittorio Veneto* was again sighted, this time by Lieutenant-Commander A. S. Bolt in the *Warspite*'s own Swordfish. Eleven minutes later Bolt made the first of his valuable reports. Others followed. It became clear that the enemy were still some 50 miles ahead of the British battle fleet, maintaining a speed variously estimated between 12 and 15 knots on a course of 300°. This indicated that the British battle fleet had an advantage of little more than 7 knots, or, at the most optimistic, 10 knots.

To reduce the 50 miles gap to 12 miles, so as to bring the Italians within gun range, would take four hours or more. Everything seemed to rest now on the torpedo attack by the destroyers immediately Pridham-Wippell's cruisers regained visual contact, but *Formidable* had high hopes of success from the dusk air attack with torpedoes.

At 1855 Bolt reported the enemy concentrating, composed of one battleship, six cruisers, and eleven destroyers. He followed this at 1914 by a message reporting the disposition of the enemy fleet in five columns; a formidable obstacle to any form of attack. But the situation seemed clear at last. The enemy forces were proceeding for home on a west-north-westerly course at 15 knots, only 45 miles from Cunningham.

At 1915 Pridham-Wippell was in radar and visual contact with some of the enemy. It was now dusk.

A difficult decision faced Cunningham. The *Warspite* had intercepted a signal at 1918, made by *Orion* three minutes earlier, reporting two un-known vessels ahead at a distance of 10 miles. As the sun had set, the possibility of a fleet action seemed remote. He now had a concise report of the Italian fleet, based on Bolt's messages, and was aware of probable hits in the dusk torpedo attack by *Formidable*'s aircraft. But there was considerable risk that he might be leading his own fleet into a dangerous position. The situation is best described in Cunningham's own words:[3]

'Now came the difficult moment of deciding what to do. I was fairly well convinced that having got so far it would be foolish not to make every effort to complete the *Vittorio Veneto*'s destruction. At the same time it appeared to us that the Italian Admiral must have been fully aware of our position. He had numerous cruisers and destroyers in company, and any British Admiral in his position would not have hesi-tated to use every destroyer he had, backed up by all his cruisers fitted with torpedo tubes, for attacks upon the pursuing fleet. Some of my staff argued that it would be unwise to charge blindly after the retreating enemy with our three heavy ships, and the *Formidable* also on our hands, to run the risk of ships being crippled, and to find ourselves within easy range of the enemy dive-bombers at daylight. I paid respectful attention to this opinion, and as the discussion happened to coincide with my time for dinner I told them I would have my evening meal and would see how I felt afterwards.'

There is a measure of Drake in this 'time to have dinner and beat the Italians yet' attitude. For a first-hand account of the Commander-in-Chief himself at this critical time we must read the comments of Barnard, the fleet gunnery officer.[4]

'The well-known steely blue look was in ABC's eye, and the staff had no doubt that there was going to be a party. Nevertheless, on paper the compact mass of the enemy fleet looked to the staff a pretty formidable proposition for any form of night attack. I think that ABC had probably made up his mind by about 2000 to send the light forces into attack and to follow up in person with the battle fleet, but he nevertheless, on this occasion, went through the formality of asking the opinion of certain staff officers. Neither the staff officer operations nor the master of the

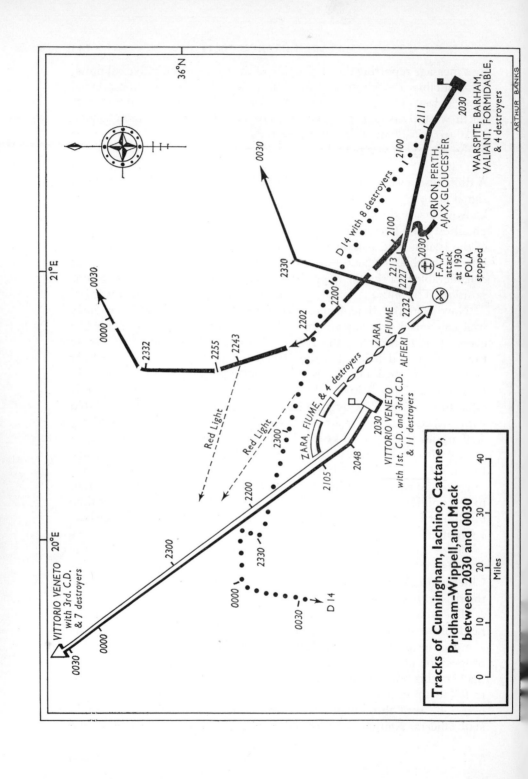

Tracks of Cunningham, Iachino, Cattaneo, Pridham-Wippell, and Mack between 2030 and 0030

36°N

21°E

20°E

ARTHUR BANKS

VITTORIO VENETO with 3rd. C.D. & 7 destroyers

0030

0000

2200

2330

2300

0000

D 14

0030

2332

2255

2243

2202

2200

Red Light

Red Light

0030

0000

0030

2330

D 14 with 8 destroyers

2100

2100

2111

2030

2213

2227

2232

2030

F.A.A. attack at 1930

POLA stopped

ORION, PERTH, AJAX, GLOUCESTER

WARSPITE, BARHAM, VALIANT, FORMIDABLE, & 4 destroyers

ZARA FIUME ALFIERI

ZARA, FIUME, & 4 destroyers

2030

VITTORIO VENETO with 1st. C.D. and 3rd. C.D. & 11 destroyers

2048

2105

2200

2330

0000

0030

D 14

Miles

0   10   20   30   40

fleet liked the idea much, and said so in their very different ways. The fleet gunnery officer said he was keen to let the guns off, but the battle-ships hadn't had a night practice for months and there might well be a pot mess with star-shells and searchlights if we got confused night action. ABC took one look at his supposed helpers and said: "You're a pack of yellow-livered skunks. I'll go and have my supper now and see after supper if my morale isn't higher than yours".'

It is amusing to compare the last comment with ABC's own reference to 'respectful attention' to staff opinion. It seems clear that Cunningham was determined not to let the onset of night rob his fleet of a victory which he now felt was near. At 2037 the 2nd and 14th Destroyer Flotillas were sent off under Captain Mack (D14) to attack, leaving but four destroyers with the battle fleet and *Formidable*, to deal with any attack that the Italians might decide to make (see map p. 144). The estimated bearing and distance of the enemy fleet from the Commander-in-Chief was deduced from Bolt's observations and given to Mack as 286°, 33 miles, at 2030; enemy course and speed were estimated as 295°, 13 knots. On receipt of Cunningham's signal Mack's eight destroyers drew away, increasing to 28 knots and steering 300°.

As we steamed to the north-west in line ahead with the fleet at the maximum speed of the battleships, all was relatively quiet in the *Formid-able*. This was a comfortable speed for us. We were now well to the west of Crete. The nearest point of land was Cape Matapan, 80 miles to the north-east of us. There was no moon, and a haze obliterated the stars. After the racket of the day, the vibration of high speed, the blasts of the assisted take-offs, the roar of aircraft engines, the whirr of the arrester wires, and the general excitement of the various phases of the battle, it seemed strangely quiet on board.

Formidable's aircraft had attacked with great gallantry at dusk, sup-ported by two Swordfish from the Royal Naval Air Station at Maleme in Crete. In spite of a withering fire from the concentrated Italian fleet, a hit had been scored on the 8-inch cruiser *Pola*: see map p. 144. She stopped immediately and drifted out of line. Iachino pressed on home-ward, unaware of *Pola*'s damage, and surprisingly having managed to increase speed to 16 knots. At 2048 he altered course to 323°. These two factors were to have grave consequences on D14's plan, his intention being to work round ahead of the enemy and then to attack: see map p. 144. In the event D14 crossed Iachino's track 30 miles astern of him at about 2320, still unaware of Iachino's changes of course and speed.

It was fully an hour before Iachino was informed of the *Pola*'s plight. It was then quite dark, and in conformity with Italian policy that they need expect no night fighting, he ordered the 8-inch cruisers *Zara* and

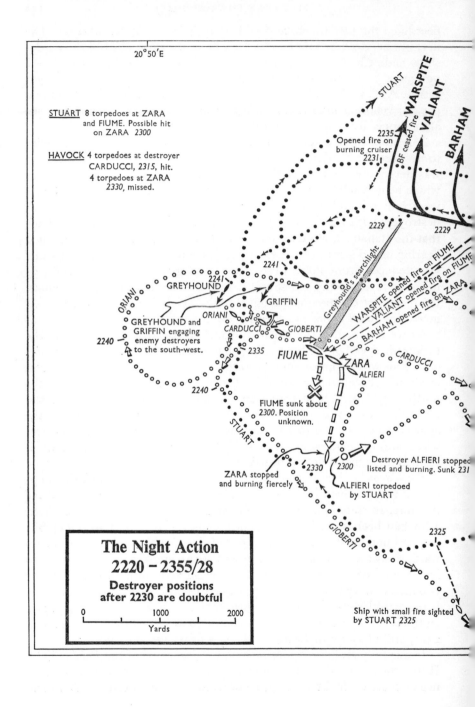

20°50'E

STUART 8 torpedoes at ZARA
and FIUME. Possible hit
on ZARA 2300

HAVOCK 4 torpedoes at destroyer
CARDUCCI, 2315, hit.
4 torpedoes at ZARA
2330, missed.

STUART

WARSPITE
VALIANT
BARHAM

2235
Opened fire on
burning cruiser
2231

BF ceased fire

2229

2229

WARSPITE opened fire on FIUME
VALIANT opened fire on FIUME
BARHAM opened fire on ZARA

Greyhound's searchlight

2241

GREYHOUND

2241

ORIANI

GRIFFIN

GREYHOUND and
GRIFFIN engaging
enemy destroyers
to the south-west.

ORIANI

CARDUCCI

GIOBERTI

FIUME

CARDUCCI

2240

ZARA

ALFIERI

2240

2335

STUART

FIUME sunk about
2300. Position
unknown.

2330

2300

Destroyer ALFIERI stopped
listed and burning. Sunk 231

ZARA stopped
and burning fiercely

ALFIERI torpedoed
by STUART

GIOBERTI

2325

The Night Action
2220 – 2355/28

Destroyer positions
after 2230 are doubtful

0   1000   2000

Yards

Ship with small fire sighted
by STUART 2325

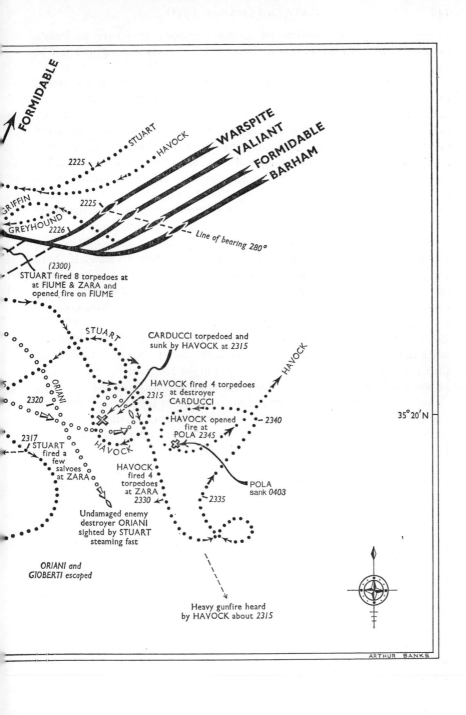

FORMIDABLE

STUART

HAVOCK

WARSPITE
VALIANT
FORMIDABLE
BARHAM

2225

2225

GRIFFIN

GREYHOUND

2226

Line of bearing 280°

(2300)
STUART fired 8 torpedoes at
at FIUME & ZARA and
opened fire on FIUME

STUART

CARDUCCI torpedoed and
sunk by HAVOCK at 2315

HAVOCK

HAVOCK fired 4 torpedoes
at destroyer
CARDUCCI

2315

ORIANI

2320

HAVOCK opened
fire at
POLA 2345

2340

35° 20' N

2317
STUART
fired a
few
salvoes
at ZARA

HAVOCK

HAVOCK
fired 4
torpedoes
at ZARA
2330

POLA
sank 0403

2335

Undamaged enemy
destroyer ORIANI
sighted by STUART
steaming fast

ORIANI and
GIOBERTI escaped

Heavy gunfire heard
by HAVOCK about 2315

ARTHUR BANKS

Fiume, with four destroyers, all under Cattaneo, to return to *Pola*'s assistance, while he with the remainder of his fleet continued on a course 323° home.

It was at 2111 that radar revealed the stopped *Pola* some miles ahead, in Cunningham's path. He believed this to be the *Vittorio Veneto*. With his three old battleships in company with the *Formidable*, screened by only four destroyers, *Greyhound*, *Griffin*, *Stuart*, and *Havock*, he steamed on at speed through the night, altering course slightly to port, steering 280° to close the stopped ship. At 2210 *Valiant*'s radar indicated that the stopped ship was only six miles on the port bow. Cunningham immediately ordered a turn of 40° to port together, handling his four great ships as he would have handled a division of destroyers. Main armaments were ready and all guns trained on the correct bearing to port.

Such a turn *towards* the enemy was unprecedented in a night action, for the drill had always been for the battle fleet to turn *away* if there were a possibility of being subjected to a destroyer attack. The master of the fleet writes: 'It was widely assumed on the bridge that enemy destroyers would be in company with the large enemy ship, and the Commander-in-Chief was recommended to turn *away*: BLUE FOUR. But he said, "If that's the enemy we will turn *towards* and find out what sort they are and how soon we sink them: FOUR BLUE".' It thus occurred that for the first time in a night action either in peace or in war a battle fleet turned towards an unknown force of enemy ships.

At 2220 Cunningham was only four miles from the stopped *Pola*, his ships about to open fire, when the massive shapes of darkened ships could be seen crossing the path of the battle fleet, from right to left in line ahead, at a distance of two miles bearing 250°. This was Cattaneo's *Zara* group arriving to stand by the damaged *Pola*. Here were seven ships; all unsuspecting and unready. Using a short-range radio signal, Cunningham turned his four capital ships back into line ahead, once again on a course of 280°: see map pp. 146, 147.

At 2227 the destroyer *Greyhound* opened her searchlight. Almost simultaneously *Warspite*, *Valiant*, and *Barham* opened fire with 15-inch broadsides; the range was now less than 4,000 yards. Broadsides were accompanied by 6-inch salvoes, and in a matter of seconds the night was lit by great orange fires in an unforgettable scene of devastation.

The captain of the *Griffin*[5] found himself in the unenviable position of 'being smack in the line of fire when the "battle-boats" opened up, and received a very curt "Get out of the way, you b.f." from ABC'.

At 2231 Cunningham made an emergency turn 90° to starboard to

10 *C-in-C Mediterranean, Admiral Sir Andrew Cunningham at Alexandria, August 1940*

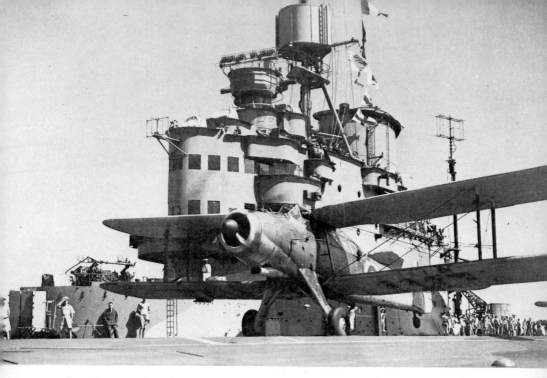

11 *An Albacore takes off from* HMS Formidable

12 *At Cairo, March 1940. Left to right: Eden, Dill, Cunningham, Longmore, Wavell*

avoid possible torpedoes fired by the enemy destroyers, and ordered his own screen of four destroyers to finish off the enemy. The *Formidable* had already turned out of line at 2227. The four destroyers were later joined by the 14th and 2nd Destroyer Flotillas who, lacking radar, had failed to locate the escaping *Vittorio Veneto*. Pridham-Wippell had also missed her, and was now ordered to disengage to the north-eastward to leave the field clear for destroyers and avoid all danger of our forces engaging each other in the dark. A rendezvous was ordered for 0800 the following morning 29 March: see map pp. 150, 151.

Now came the mopping up by Cunningham's destroyers. Of Cattaneo's *Zara* group only two destroyers escaped. The burning cruiser *Fiume* sank at 2315. The destroyer *Alfieri* was torpedoed by the *Stuart*, and sank at 2315. The destroyer *Carducci* was sunk by the *Havock* at 2330. The abandoned and burning cruiser *Zara* was found and sunk by the *Jervis* at 0240. The disabled cruiser *Pola*, long since abandoned, was sunk at 0403 by the *Jervis* and *Nubian*.

Following a dawn search which revealed little of importance, ships arrived at the rendezvous at 0800, and the Commander-in-Chief then set course for the scene of the night action. Over 900 survivors were picked up by his ships before German aircraft appeared compelling him to get under way and shape course for Alexandria. With great humanity Cunningham made a signal by radio direct to Rome, giving his position and asking that a hospital ship should be sent to pick up the considerable number of Italian sailors still in the sea, an act which Admiral Iachino[6] says 'demonstrated his noble and generous character'. To criticism that this might risk his whole fleet, ABC would have replied that his position was known in any case.

There had been a brisk flow of signals during the mopping-up period. One of these referred to the Italian prisoners.

'Prisoners when asked why they had failed to fire at us replied that they thought if they did we would fire back.'

Another was made in reply to C-in-C's query about the number of wounded prisoners on board:

'State of prisoners: six cot cases: fifty slightly injured: one senior officer has piles.'

To which Cunningham quickly replied:

'I am NOT surprised'.

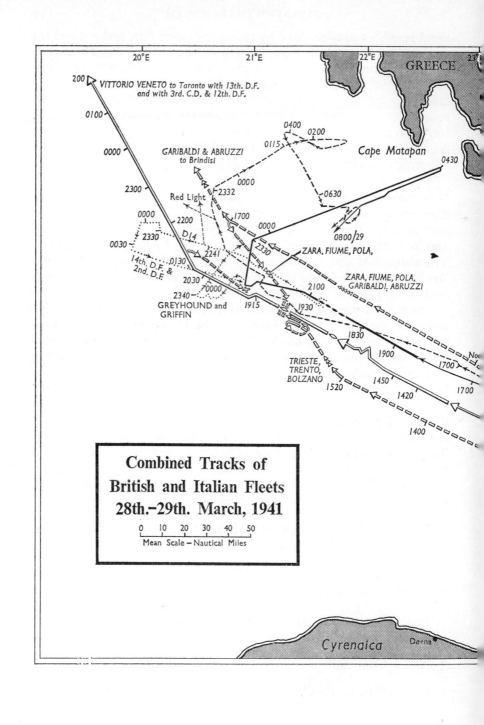

Combined Tracks of British and Italian Fleets 28th.–29th. March, 1941

0   10   20   30   40   50

Mean Scale – Nautical Miles

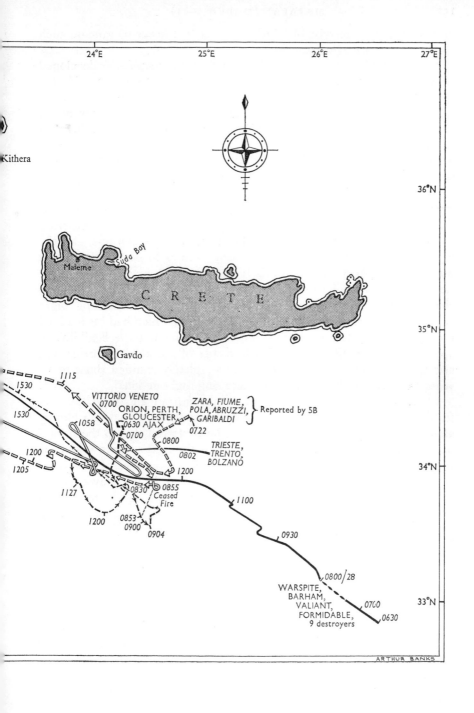

Kithera

36°N

Suda Bay

Maleme

C R E T E

35°N

Gavdo

1115

1530

VITTORIO VENETO
0700

ZARA, FIUME,
POLA, ABRUZZI,
GARIBALDI   } Reported by 5B

1530

ORION, PERTH,
GLOUCESTER,
0630 AJAX
0700

1058

0722

0800

TRIESTE,
TRENTO,
BOLZANO

0802

1200

1205

1200

34°N

1127

0830

1200

0855
Ceased
Fire

1100

0853
0900
0904

0930

0800/28

WARSPITE,
BARHAM,
VALIANT,
FORMIDABLE,
9 destroyers

0700

0630

33°N

ARTHUR BANKS

Perhaps it is this exercise of a little humour that keeps us sane on such momentous but tragic occasions.

The inevitable heavy dive-bomber attack on the *Formidable* developed a few hours later, but was repelled by the fleet barrage and *Formidable*'s fighters. On Passion Sunday (30 March) the victorious fleet passed safely through the Great Pass and entered the harbour at Alexandria, and on the following day a special thanksgiving service was held on board all ships.

Fuller details of the action together with statistics and technical particulars are given elsewhere.[7,8] It is necessary to mention here however the striking effect which Cunningham's victory had on his reputation. Taranto had established it for ever and had at the same time produced the satisfactory reduction of half the Italian battle fleet. In the case of Matapan the material reduction was much less, and the big prize, the *Vittorio Veneto*, had been allowed to escape. But there was a ring of naval history in this battle with its sequence of sighting, search, two phases of action in the forenoon, a timely reprieve, the long chase, the element of surprise on both sides, the devastating night action, and the mopping-up in the dark, to all of which had been added the realisation of two important new features, namely the flexibility of approach and drastic effect on battle tactics of the aircraft carrier, and also the far-seeing eye of radar which completely justified those many years spent by the Royal Navy in exercising night action.

Cunningham had not been slow to take full advantage of the new features, and in spite of the warning by his staff about charging blindly after the retreating enemy in the dark, he preferred this to the hazard of approaching enemy air bases at daylight the next morning, and the possibility of being drawn towards enemy submarines. Perhaps he remembered the risks taken by Admiral Sir Edward Hawke when chasing the French into shoal water at Quiberon Bay in a rising gale in 1759; or he may have had in mind those numerous occasions when British ships had been cheated of their potential victims when suddenly becalmed. He had accepted the risk and scored a notable victory which had provided a most welcome tonic for Britain.

Iachino had been sadly let down. When summoned to Rome to see Mussolini, the latter said:[9] 'Throughout the operation you had neither a single Italian nor a single German plane overhead. . . . I have ordered my Chief of the General Staff to have construction of an aircraft carrier begun at once.' Iachino says that the thought occurred to him that the fault was very largely Mussolini's, for it was his edict, before the war, that there should be no carriers, because shore-based fighters would be able to take care of the fleet. In fact Axis aviation had been more active during the battle than was realised, but had been ineffectual through poor communication, bad co-ordination, and misinterpretation of enemy reports; well-known problems which the Fleet Air Arm of the Royal Navy had spent great efforts trying to overcome, in spite of those barren years of two decades during which their administration had been withdrawn from the Admiralty. Under Cunningham the Fleet Air Arm had again added fame to that gained at Taranto, showing beyond doubt the benefits of surprise and flexibility of manoeuvre provided by an aircraft carrier, in addition to the enormous value of long-range search, attack, and local defence from both aircraft and submarine.

Taranto and Matapan provided lessons which were not lost on either the USA or Japan, nor on Mussolini for whom it was now too late. History shows so often that the lessons of war are forgotten or discarded in peace. Perhaps the long struggle between those who favoured the battleship and the big guns, and those who put their faith in the future of the aircraft carrier, will be perpetuated in a similar struggle characterised by the political moves of the sixties and seventies. Certain it is that complete reliance on the dominance and self-sufficiency of the missile at the expense of the superb mobility provided by naval aviation can lead only to the same sort of repentance experienced by Mussolini.

Cunningham had not only been visionary and confident about his Fleet Air Arm, but had an uncanny sense of good timing in their use. *Formidable*'s forenoon strike on the *Vittorio Veneto* at 1127 undoubtedly saved Pridham-Wippell's four cruisers from the annihilation planned by Iachino; and without her successful strike at dusk Cunningham would never have caught up or been confronted with Cattaneo's division that night. With his bold courage and admirable optimism Cunningham had also had great luck. He had been denied the big prize, largely because of Pridham-Wippell's misfortune in losing contact after dusk, when obliged to concentrate his force in the presence of unidentified ships reported by radar, and somewhat cramped by D14's force.

In his dispatch the Commander-in-Chief summed up Matapan as follows:

'The results of the action cannot be viewed with entire satisfaction since the damaged *Vittorio Veneto* was allowed to escape. The failure of the cruisers and destroyers to make contact with her during the night was unlucky and is much to be regretted. Nevertheless, substantial results were achieved in the destruction of the three Zara class cruisers. These fast, well-armed and armoured ships had always been a source of anxiety as a threat to our own less well-armed cruisers and I was well content to see them disposed of in this summary fashion. There is little doubt that the rough handling given to the enemy on this occasion served us in good stead during the subsequent evacuation of Greece and Crete. Much of these later operations may be said to have been conducted under the cover of the Battle of Matapan.'

Admiral Sir Charles Little sent a message to the Commander-in-Chief at Alexandria, 3 April 1941, on behalf of the term of cadets who had passed out of *Britannia* in June 1898:

'Your term-mates rejoice in your memorable achievements at the Battle of Matapan.'

In sending a copy of this message to term-mates, 'Tiny' Little, also known in *Britannia* as 'Lampy' or 'Six Foot of Gaspipe', wrote:[10]

'I am sure he will appreciate hearing from us all. I can so well remember his frequent Sunday afternoon fights in the "Brit" and bloody face, "meat phaz".

'It does not surprise us that his determination, natural gifts, and love of battle have ranked him with our greatest naval leaders.'

'Ranked with our GREATEST NAVAL LEADERS': could there be much greater praise? The spirit in the fleet was tremendous now. It was as well; for the British fleet was approaching a time of great adversity in the Mediterranean, and even the presence of a Cunningham could not compensate for the growing threat from the air.

Cunningham received in 1968 the great distinction of having one of the Divisions at the Britannia Royal Naval College, Dartmouth, named after him, thus being awarded a recognised position among the most distinguished Admirals of the Royal Navy during five centuries.

Withdrawal from Greece and Crete (April 1941–May 1941)

In retrospect the victory at Matapan appears as an encouraging interlude immediately followed by a series of adverse events. Axis troops invading British-held territory in Libya began by taking Mersa Brega on 1 April 1941. By 3 April they were in Benghazi, and the British army was in full retreat in Cyrenaica. Within a week the Axis had reached Egypt at Bardia and Sollum, by-passing Tobruk which Cunningham declared could be supplied from the sea if it was decided to hold it. Throughout a siege which was to last 242 days until the end of 1941, Tobruk was to remain in British hands, thanks to a courageous defence by Imperial troops and the unending efforts of the gallant little Inshore Squadron.

To add further gloom to the British cause the Germans launched their big offensive on Greece and Yugoslavia 6 April 1941. Within a few days a planned withdrawal of British troops to certain defence lines was being implemented, and by 21 April, after the collapse of Greek defence, the decision had been made to evacuate all troops from Greece. By this time practically all the Hurricanes that had been sent to Greece had been lost.[1] This adverse state of affairs for fighter defence was accentuated by the loss also of most of the Hurricanes that had been retained at Tobruk.

The position was not much brighter at Malta, but losses were alleviated by the arrival of 12 Hurricanes flown from the *Ark Royal* on 3 April, 23 more on 27 April, and 47 more on 21 May. Malta also received reinforcements in the shape of more warships when the light cruiser *Dido*, the fast new minelayer *Abdiel*, and six destroyers arrived in late April.

In an attempt to reduce the number of Axis convoys reaching Tripoli, Cunningham sent to Malta on 11 April 1941 a division of the 14th Destroyer Flotilla: the *Jervis* (Captain Mack, D14), *Janus*, *Mohawk*, and *Nubian*. Because of Luftwaffe activity during daylight hours, this force was able to operate only at night, guided by local reconnaissance reports.

High speed was required in order that the destroyers could complete a mission in darkness, and this meant a greatly increased consumption of fuel, a commodity becoming daily more scarce. Success however followed shortly, for in the early morning of 16 April, some 30 miles to seaward of Sfax, Mack destroyed two Italian destroyers together with an important convoy of five transports which they were escorting. The Italians put up a spirited defence, especially the escort commander Cristoforo who, though mortally wounded, fired three torpedoes in the last moments before his ship the *Tarigo* sank. The *Mohawk* was sunk, together with two officers and 39 ratings, but the loss of supplies suffered by Rommel's Afrika Korps was considerable and serious.

There had been an exchange of signals between Cunningham and the Admiralty following a suggestion by the latter that battleships should bombard Tripoli in an endeavour to wreck the port. Since this was 800 miles from Alexandria and almost as many from any British-held air-base that could be regarded as effectual, the project seemed impracticable to Cunningham, and hardly worth the enormous risk to the fleet, especially because of the presence of an active Italian airfield at Castel Benito near Tripoli. Early on 15 April, however, the Commander-in-Chief received a signal which stated that the Admiralty had decided that *Barham* and a 'C' class cruiser should be regarded as expendable, and used to block the port; they were to bombard at point-blank range as they approached the harbour, steaming to their final settling place.

The signal appears to have resulted from a directive by the Prime Minister that the prime duty of the Mediterranean Fleet was to stop all seaborne traffic between Italy and North Africa: 'Every convoy which gets through must be considered a serious naval failure.'

At a time when he was already faced with the likelihood of having to get the Army away from Greece, Cunningham was deeply concerned, especially as he felt that the Admiralty decision had been taken without sufficient knowledge of either Tripoli or local circumstances. He doubted the practicability of the operation, and felt that the inevitable heavy casualties which would result might undermine the whole confidence of the fleet in the Higher Command; at home as well as in the Mediterranean. Accepting the lesser of the two evils, Cunningham said he would prefer to bombard with all his battleships and accept the risks. It would appear that the reception of the news of Mack's great success about this time inclined the Admiralty to accept Cunningham's recommendation, and elicited a congratulatory message from the Prime Minister. Perhaps the Mediterranean Fleet were not doing so badly after all.

No time was to be wasted. Cunningham planned to combine the

return passage from Tripoli with the escorting of three empty merchant ships from Malta: an essential preliminary before running in another convoy to Malta. 'We really did not expect to get away with it,' Cunningham[2] writes, 'without having a ship disabled, either by air attacks or in one or other of the minefields.'

At 0630 Friday 18 April, unexpectedly for most of the ship's company the *Formidable* slipped and proceeded in company with the *Warspite*, *Valiant*, *Barham*, and destroyers, for Suda Bay, after flying on her fighter and bomber squadrons. Also in company was the fuel carrier *Breconshire* with aviation spirit and oil for Malta. Saturday was spent in fuelling at sea, until 1500, when in clear weather the fleet proceeded as if for Malta, and continued thus all of Sunday 20 April until dark, when course was altered for Tripoli and speed increased so as to be in position for the bombardment before dawn. Fighter protection from *Formidable*'s Fulmars had been excellent, various enemy aircraft being shot down before being able to reveal Cunningham's presence.

The battle fleet parted company with *Formidable* at 2100 in a position 60 miles from the coast, and continued inshore to look for the submarine *Truant*'s beacon light which was to shine to seaward in an accurately determined position four miles off the Tripoli harbour entrance, thus providing a fix in the dark before the bombardment.

Formidable's aircraft flew off at 0340 Monday 21 April. Cunningham's plan was that they should attack harbour works with high explosive and incendiary bombs and provide flares to illuminate the target area during the 40-minute bombardment by 15-inch and 6-inch guns, which was to begin at 0500. Swordfish of 830 Squadron and RAF Wellingtons, all from Malta, were to assist in the fire-spreading before the bombardment. Each ship of the bombarding squadron, which was composed of the three battleships and the cruiser *Gloucester* escorted by nine destroyers, was allotted a specific target, with two runs at a range of about seven miles.

Complete surprise was achieved, and all went according to plan except that immense clouds of dust and smoke obscured and confused observation of fall of shot. Otherwise it was a clear night. From the *Formidable* could be seen the great orange flashes and the red flares hanging in the sky slowly dropping over the horizon. Although 530 tons were dropped on Tripoli, the results of the bombardment were, as expected by Cunningham, disappointing. Ironically, more damage was done a few days later by an explosion in a single Italian ship.

The fleet now beat a hasty retreat for Alexandria, prepared especially on this first day of the return passage for unceasing and heavy air attacks. Surprisingly, however, though the weather was clear and *Formidable*'s fighters were ready, no attack developed. There were red warnings on the following day, with groups seen approaching on the radar screen; but again the fighters had the upper hand. The fact is that it was on these days that an almost unopposed Luftwaffe was giving overwhelming support to the German drive to cut off withdrawing Greek and British troops in Greece. On the way back to Alexandria, Pridham-Wippell's cruisers closed the coast of Cyrenaica to bombard.

'We had been incredibly fortunate,'[3] says Cunningham, 'or perhaps the objects of Divine favour. I had been totally opposed to the bombard- ment of Tripoli by the fleet from the outset, and was equally against a repetition of the naval bombardment which seemed to be in the minds of the authorities at home.' Cunningham was concerned about other commitments which he considered more pressing. He was also 'seriously annoyed' at the constant advice, not to say interference concerning the command of his fleet, from those who seemed to be unaware of the real facts of the situation. The feeling in the Mediterranean at this time was that decreasing local air strength was due to the greater consideration given at home to the bombing of Germany. 'The Tripoli operation,' reported Cunningham, 'had taken the whole Mediterranean Fleet five days to accomplish what a heavy bomber squadron working from Egypt could probably carry out in a few hours.' He was very soon taken to task in a long message from the Prime Minister, part of which stated that one Wellington squadron operating from Malta would have taken $10\frac{1}{2}$ weeks to drop the same weight of bombs as Cunningham had fired in shells in 42 minutes. And to his plea that the crux of effective naval attacks on the enemy convoys to Tripoli lay in a proper air support from Malta, he was told that he did not appreciate that the primary aim of the Air Force in Malta was to defend the naval base against air attack.

It is relevant to refer to a first-hand description of the Prime Minister at this time,[4] written by Captain Charles Lambe on 19 April 1941 after his first glimpse of Churchill, and which gives some idea of the great strain from which he was suffering.

'We were summoned to meet the PM after dinner in the underground Cabinet War Room. It was like a nightmare without emotion. The news from Greece and Yugoslavia and Libya was bad and the PM came in ten minutes late, very depressed . . . and desperately tired in a sort of coma almost. His speech was rather slobbery and very slow. . . . The general atmosphere of sycophancy and the old man's lack of grasp and understanding apparently, made me leave to walk home convinced for the first time that we could not win the war.'

Cunningham was now too busy with preparations for the evacuation of the Army from Greece to reply to the Prime Minister. As he saw it, the battle of the Libyan convoys could be won by the Navy only if supported by an adequate air force: one which could provide long-range fighters to give air cover to convoys in every area, short-range fighters for the naval bases, and long-range reconnaissance aircraft to give him as much information of the enemy's movements at sea as the enemy had of British naval movements. These were the requirements for which he had long been appealing, but were beyond the resources of the Air Command. Within a month the bitter lesson was to be learnt.

By 21 April, the day on which Cunningham was bombarding Tripoli, it became evident in Greece that German troops would very soon over-run the whole of the country, supported in the air by Fliegerkorps VIII and part of Fliegerkorps X. There was now great danger of British and Imperial forces being cut off in their retreat, and although the King of Greece and his government had consented that their evacuation should begin on 28 April, the date was now advanced to 24 April. The King spoke with deep regret at the collapse of his own forces on the British left flank, and of having been the means of placing British forces in such a perilous position.[5]

On his return to Alexandria, Cunningham had to work fast in order to implement Operation DEMON, as it was called. During daylight, 21 and 22 April, 23 Greek ships were sunk in coastal waters. The port of Piraeus had been wrecked on 7 April by the explosion of an ammunition ship. The plan was therefore to use all available destroyers, sloops, cruisers, and the two new infantry assault ships (LSIs), which were provided with landing craft instead of boats. There were also 19 troop-ships and a variety of small craft. Embarkation was to take place at six beaches (see map p. 165) within reach of the probable roads for troop withdrawal.

Pridham-Wippell's staff officer (operations)[6] writes about a dramatic moment during what he calls his only personal encounter with ABC:

'I was on board *Orion* when a signal came that the C-in-C wanted to see Pridham-Wippell or, failing him, his SO (O). I went over to *Warspite* and was shown into the cuddy. ABC said gruffly:

'"Where's your admiral?"

'"Ashore playing golf, sir."

'"Get him back at once and you're to sail to-night with all the cruisers and all the destroyers and take the Army out of Greece. Four assault ships and eight troop transports now in the Canal will join you and come under your orders. Captain Crooks will join your staff to help deal with the merchant ships."

'We, the staff in *Orion*, had privately thought and talked about the possibility – nay, probability – of an evacuation but the subject had never been mentioned by our admiral and was considered taboo.

'I gulped and began to ask questions:

'"How many soldiers, sir? What about air cover? . . . and fuel? . . . and anti-aircraft ammunition? . . . and boats? . . ." (I'd been at Dunkirk.)

'Drooping one eyelid (a well-known danger signal I'd heard about) he said, "Don't tell me you can't do it, boy! Get out of here! Raise steam and sail as soon as your admiral's on board!"

'We did; and brought away 50,000.'

SO (O) makes it all sound so easy. Though the numbers to be embarked were only a fifth of those to be brought off at Dunkirk, there were many great difficulties involved in the long sea passages and absence of maintenance support from a home base. Of even greater consequence was the enemy-held air superiority around all the beaches and sea approaches. For this reason embarkation had to be restricted to the hours of darkness up to 0300. The Dutch ship *Slamat* paid the penalty for remaining until 0415 when embarking troops at Nauplia, being found and bombed soon after daylight. The destroyers *Diamond* and *Wryneck* were sent to their aid, rescued 700 men, and were themselves then dive-bombed and sunk with all hands except for 50 survivors. Nevertheless apart from this and the loss of three troop-ships from whom some survivors were rescued by the destroyers *Hero*, *Hereward*, and *Defender*, the six-night operation was far more successful than could have been expected. Cunningham's signal at the beginning of DEMON had said that 'the object is to embark men, if possible with arms; but no material must be allowed to take precedence to men'.

At Kalamata on the evening of 28 April, following a successful embarkation of 8,650 men two evenings previously, it appeared from the sea that heavy fighting was taking place. A column of Germans had been able to crash into the town and take over the quays, capturing among others the naval embarkation officer and his signalman, and although this operation was suppressed in gallant counter-attacks by those troops who were waiting hopefully for Cunningham's ships to return, the impression wrongly interpreted by the *Perth*, lying ten miles off, was that the risk to the ships was too great for the small number that might be able to embark. This unfortunately led to the surrender of these troops at 0530 the next day. Nevertheless it did not prevent the Navy from having another go on the two successive nights when all looked hopeless. Cunningham sent the *Isis*, *Hero*, and *Kimberley* to Kalamata on 29 and 30 April, under the command of Commander Casper Swinley who had already on 26 April helped to embark 4,527 at Nauplia, and was later awarded the DSO for his persistence in the face of great difficulty.

Many men had to be left ashore on the last night of evacuation, having been overtaken by events, but of the total landed in Greece during the preceding weeks, about 80 per cent, a little over 50,000, were taken off. Of these, about one-third were taken to Crete to swell the garrison, and the remainder to Egypt. Many had returned with weapons, but it had not been practicable to bring away guns or heavy equipment and supplies.

It was again on the very day that Cunningham was bombarding Tripoli, 21 April 1941, that consideration was being given by the Defence Committee in London to a disturbing report from Wavell that a German panzer division had been identified in the Western Desert, and the disparity in strength in favour of Rommel was growing. Nevertheless Rommel's supply line from Tripoli was now over 1,000 miles long, and two of his attempts to capture Tobruk had been defeated. Wavell already had in mind an operation BATTLEAXE to be undertaken as soon as he could mount an armoured assault. The Prime Minister proposed once again the short cut through the Mediterranean. A convoy of fast ships (operation TIGER) containing large armoured reinforcements was about to leave the United Kingdom for Egypt. Instead of going round the Cape of Good Hope it was to turn eastward at Gibraltar, thus saving nearly 40 days. As the need was great, Cunningham agreed, although no such attempt had been made since the Luftwaffe had dramatically appeared early in January 1941, sinking the *Southampton* and disabling the *Illustrious*.

In addition to the fast convoy of 15-knot merchant ships loaded with tanks and Hurricanes from the United Kingdom, to be taken to Alexandria, operation TIGER was to offer an opportunity of passing two vital convoys, a fast and a slow, from Alexandria to Malta, each with close escort covered by Cunningham's carrier and battleships. With the destroyers playing a major part in the evacuation from Greece from 24 April to 1 May, it had not been possible to provide a screen for the battleships, which had therefore been compelled to remain in harbour at Alexandria. The destroyers had been fully employed, except for those requiring boiler cleaning and essential repair, without a break since early March. The *Formidable* had also proceeded to sea on 29 April in the direction of Crete, with 16 Fulmars on board, to escort cruisers engaged in evacuation of troops to Egypt. Compared with conditions to be experienced less than a month later, air activity at sea was on a reduced scale, presumably because of the Luftwaffe's widespread activities over the shores of Greece.

Reinforcements for Cunningham in the shape of the newly modernised 15-inch battleship *Queen Elizabeth*, the cruiser *Fiji*, and the light cruiser *Naiad*, were to accompany the main TIGER convoy from the United Kingdom throughout its journey to Alexandria. Opportunity was to be taken by Cunningham's light forces to bombard Benghazi both on the westward passage to Malta and on the return journey to Alexandria. The principal convoy was to be escorted from Gibraltar by Force H for the first half of the eastward passage through the Mediterranean. Long-range fighter protection for the passage of the TIGER convoy eastward of Malta was to be provided by 15 twin-engined monoplane Beaufighters flown to Malta via Gibraltar.

Cunningham was to go to sea yet again in the *Warspite*, his flagship, though it was becoming increasingly clear that communication was limited when he was at sea, so often at a time when the passing of orders and the receipt of intelligence were not only vital but very considerable. Once more it was deeply felt as a good omen to have 'the old man' with us, particularly as the whole notion of attempting such an operation during the long clear summer days of May appeared hazardous in the extreme. Cunningham was not only concerned about the fact that his cruisers and destroyers had had no respite during the withdrawal from Greece, and that there was hardly one of them that was not urgently in need of repair, but he was also worried about the state of the ships' companies. On 3 May 1941 he wrote to Sir Dudley Pound[7] saying that he had noticed 'signs of strain among the officers and ratings'. Surprisingly, he himself revealed no falling-off in his optimism and resolute leadership, and again the fleet was perhaps to be 'the object of Divine favour'.

The Mediterranean Fleet and Force H were both timed to sail from their respective ends on 6 May. Cunningham's battleships and the carrier were delayed by the fact that the harbour entrance had been mined the day before. The heavy ships had to be taken out individually by a force of sweepers. Scarcely had the operation begun when Vice-Admiral Malta signalled Cunningham that his harbours were mined, and he had no sweepers that could sweep magnetic mines. The Commander-in-Chief sent for his 'silent, imperturbable' fleet torpedo officer who in about an hour produced a signal directing VA (M) to blast a channel into Malta with depth charges. The scheme was a triumphant success. Captain Carne may have had this episode in mind when he wrote:[8]

'Many people found ABC a difficult chap to get on with but when I got to know him and he had realised that my brain only worked at a third the speed of his, we got on pretty well. I don't know how many times he didn't say to me when some technical difficulty was being encountered with minesweeping, paravanes, magnetic mines, degaussing, or what have you, "I have had to deal with many technical gadgets in my time and when one has gone wrong I have found that there are two things I could do, either get a new technical gadget or a new technical officer, and I have invariably found that the more satisfactory alternative was to get a new technical officer".' On completion of TIGER, Carne was promoted and given command of the anti-aircraft light cruiser *Coventry* in the Mediterranean Fleet.

To resume: the *Formidable* had hardly cleared Alexandria harbour with the battleships, and flown on her air squadrons, when a thick and persistent sand-storm reduced visibility to a thousand yards. And all of the following two days wonderful cover was provided by extensive low cloud, so unusual for May in the Mediterranean, and the visibility remained poor. On the fourth day, 9 May, in addition to low cloud there was occasionally thick fog. On this day we were near Malta, met the eastbound convoy and reinforcements, and then resumed course to the eastward. Luftwaffe air raids were foiled by the Beaufighters and *Formidable*'s Fulmars, and no heavy attack developed. But we were unfortunate in losing two Fulmars on 9 May, one crashing on the flight deck, the other force-landing in the sea, and another on the following day, 10 May, when taking off from the catapult. The weather cleared, and a heavy attack on the fleet developed after nightfall 10 May, with sufficient light provided by a brilliant full moon. A tremendous umbrella barrage of fire was put up by the fleet which continued for about two hours before the last attackers were driven off, having missed the convoy altogether. This kind of barrage against an unseen enemy proved very costly in ammunition. There were no further attacks, and by 1030 on 12 May the precious cargo of 238 tanks and 43 crated Hurricanes were safely at Alexandria. Only one of the convoy had been lost, and that by a mine in the Skerki Channel. The fleet had suffered no ship loss, and Benghazi harbour had been successfully bombarded on the night of 7 May by the *Ajax* and three destroyers under Captain McCarthy. This force had also met and destroyed an enemy convoy of two ships carrying transport and ammunition. 'I afterwards heard of lurid tales of motor lorries hurtling through the air, right over the destroyers,' wrote Cunningham. Five destroyers under Captain Mountbatten also carried out a bombardment of Benghazi on the night of 10 May, and were later subjected to persistent dive-bombing in the moonlight, but without hurt.

Except for the unfortunate loss of our Fulmars and with them those gallant young airmen, TIGER had worked out very successfully, thanks to the miracle of persistent bad weather varying from sand-storm, mist, fog, and low cloud almost down to the mast-head. Providence had again worked in Cunningham's favour. 'It was bound to be all right with the old man there,' was the feeling in the fleet. The Admiralty regarded the operation as a 'memorable achievement'; a masterly understatement which Cunningham thought might indicate conclusions that he had exaggerated the dangers. 'Before long the dismal truth was painfully to be brought home to them,'[9] he wrote.

He reported on 13 May 1941 that during the period covered by the bombardment of Tripoli and the TIGER convoy the fleet had expended 40 per cent of the stock of anti-aircraft ammunition. He was also worried about the shortage of fleet fighters. The *Formidable* had brought with her 806 Squadron of Fulmars when she arrived 10 March, but during two very active months which included two hard fought convoy operations, the bombardment of Tripoli, the battle of Matapan, and the evacuation from Greece, she had suffered severe loss and wear and tear from the need to have almost constant fighter patrol over the fleet. In carrier operations aircraft were liable to suffer extra stress from accelerated take-off, flight deck arrester wires, and the crash barrier, and this increased the demand for maintenance and spares.

A constant worry was Malta, subjected to almost continuous air attack, to an extent which required the temporary abandonment of stationing light forces there, except for submarines which continued to play great havoc with the enemy transports. On 15 May VA (M) reported that seven Hurricanes had been lost in three days, and many aircraft were daily being damaged on the ground.

It was also known that a German assault on Crete was imminent. The peril in which it stood was all too clear, for the Germans were by now in full control of Rumania, Bulgaria, Greece, and many of the Aegean islands. Daily from 14 May 1941 there were 'softening up' bombing attacks upon Crete, increasing in intensity, and aimed at destroying gun emplacements and defence posts at Maleme, and also at the smaller airfields at Retimo and Heraklion farther east.

Official opinion was that Crete could be held, provided that the assault was airborne only. This was based on the principle that the Germans would be unable to land heavy guns, tanks, vehicles, and reinforcements, except by sea. It was therefore expected that they might attempt a seaborne landing in support of an airborne assault, the prevention of which would become the Royal Navy's role. In view of the possibility of continuous German and Italian air attacks around Crete, and the absence of any substantial Royal Air Force strength closer than 500 miles, together with the added chance of a sortie from the Italian fleet, it was evident that Cunningham's task would be stretched to the limits.

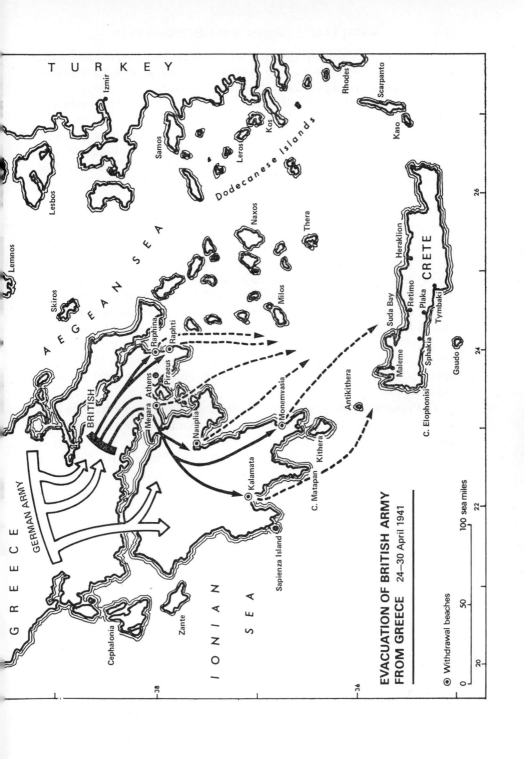

EVACUATION OF BRITISH ARMY FROM GREECE 24–30 April 1941

◎ Withdrawal beaches

0   20   50   100 sea miles

In addition to British shore-based air cover around Crete being non-existent, the *Formidable* was now lying at Alexandria, with her complement of 16 Fulmar fighter aircraft reduced to four.

It was not until 30 April, after six different commanders in the previous six months, that Major-General B. C. Freyberg, VC, CB, CMG, DSO, had assumed command of the British and Imperial forces in Crete. Less than three weeks later the airborne assault began. Although British intelligence had knowledge of German intentions, it was still uncertain whether the assault would be airborne, seaborne, or both. This fact severely limited Freyberg's plans for defence, for in the event he had to allow flexibility so as to be prepared for all three.

The German plans were for air landings of 13,000 troops to take place at Maleme on the forenoon of the first day, and at Retimo and Heraklion that afternoon: see map p. 165. These were to be followed by mainly seaborne landings of 9,000 mountain troops with guns, tanks, and heavy stores, transport being provided by steamships and caiques. There was the prospect that these might be escorted by units of the Italian fleet. Facilities for unloading British supply ships which arrived at Suda Bay were limited, and were subjected to ever-increasing bombing attacks during daylight hours. Between 30 April and 20 May, 15 supply ships arrived, of which eight were sunk or damaged while in harbour.

The operation for the airborne assault on Crete was originated by General Student, and was to involve 700 bombers and fighters, 530 transport aircraft, and 72 gliders. Hitler had agreed to the operation only after assurance from Goering that it could be conducted entirely by air and completed in a few days. Hitler was already preparing for his drive into Russia and was concerned at the threat to the Ploesti oil-fields posed by the British retention of Crete, but was reassured by Goering that the planned role for the Luftwaffe in the Russian campaign would not be delayed. The assault was scheduled for 17 May but delayed until 20 May because 2,500,000 gallons of aircraft fuel had to be brought by sea down the Adriatic coast from Trieste.

Cunningham had given much consideration to naval requirements to prevent enemy seaborne landings regardless of enemy air superiority, and at the same time to be ready to meet any sortie by the Italian fleet.[10] He decided to station four different forces in order to carry out nightly sweeps in the enemy approaches to Crete, withdrawing from dangerous areas at night. These would cover: a position well to the westward of Crete (against the possible appearance of heavy units of the Italian fleet); an area between Cape Matapan and Sapienza Island; the area Antikithera to Piraeus (against landings west of Retimo); and the area Kaso to Leros (against landings at Heraklion and Suda).

With four dispersed forces at sea, Cunningham considered it imperative to direct the naval side of operations from his HQ at Alexandria, where positions of all ships could be plotted hour by hour on a large-scale chart in the war room close to his office, and from which communications would be unhampered. Air reconnaissance was arranged but this was thin.

In addition to preventing German seaborne landings, the Navy had to provide for reinforcements and supplies to the British and Imperial troops ashore in Crete. A battalion of the Leinster Regiment with full equipment was landed at night on 15 May at Heraklion by the cruisers *Gloucester* and *Fiji*. Two nights later, the special service ship *Glengyle* landed 700 men of the Argyll and Sutherland Highlanders at Tymbaki, an anchorage on the south coast of Crete, 25 miles over the mountains from Heraklion.

The allocation of areas sounds fairly straightforward, but the reader need not stretch the imagination far to realise the immense amount of signalling required to pass instructions and counter-instructions concerning night intentions during the constant expectation of the enemy assault and the continued preparedness to squash any seaborne expedition. During this phase *Greyhound* (Commander W. R. Marshall-A'Deane, DSO, DSC) passed to Rear-Admiral E. L. S. King, before regrouping, 'The road to Crete is paved with Night Intentions'.

The composition of groups at daylight 20 May (the morning of the German airborne assault on Crete) was:

Force A : Queen Elizabeth and *Barham* under Vice-Admiral Sir Henry Pridham-Wippell, having been relieved by Force A 1;

Force A 1 : Warspite, Valiant, and five destroyers *Napier, Hereward, Decoy, Hero, Hotspur* under Rear-Admiral H. B. Rawlings, 100 miles west of Crete;

Force B : Gloucester, Fiji, and two destroyers *Greyhound* and *Griffin* under Captain H. A. Rowley, on passage to rendezvous with Rawlings;

Force C : Naiad, Perth, and four destroyers *Kandahar, Kingston, Nubian*, and *Juno* under Rear-Admiral E. L. S. King, southward of the Kaso Strait;

Force D : Dido, Orion, Ajax, and four destroyers *Isis, Kimberley, Imperial*, and *Janus* under Rear-Admiral I. Glennie, west of the Antikithera Channel.

It was during the preliminary phase on 18 May that the first Victoria Cross to be awarded to the Mediterranean Fleet during the war was won by Petty Officer A. E. Sephton, the director gunlayer of the anti-aircraft cruiser *Coventry*. South of Crete the *Coventry* had gone to the assistance of the hospital ship *Aba* which was being attacked by seven Ju 87s. The latter then transferred their attack to the *Coventry*, raking her with machine-gun fire, and a bullet passed through Sephton's back. Though in great pain Sephton refused help and continued to direct the fire until the attackers were driven off. He died the next day. His action may well have saved both the *Coventry* and the *Aba*.

As soon as he heard that the air assault on Crete had begun, on Tuesday 20 May, Cunningham ordered those forces that were at sea to close Crete, but to keep out of sight of land during daylight. The constitution of forces would vary because of the constant need for refuelling. Over and above the requirements for both strategic and tactical moves, therefore, there had to be unremitting consideration for expenditure of ammunition and fuel, factors which were to prove crucial in the battle of ships against aircraft.

Following its night sweep into the Aegean which had produced nothing more than an encounter with motor-boats, King's Force C withdrew through the Kaso Strait just before sunrise on Wednesday 21 May, being joined then by the *Calcutta* and that afternoon by the *Carlisle*. Both of these anti-aircraft cruisers were fresh from Alexandria. King's Force C suffered several aircraft attacks from daylight onwards as he proceeded southwards from the Kaso Strait, being bombed almost continuously for the four hours between 0950 and 1350 either by Italian high-level bombers or by German dive-bombers, all of whom revelled in the absence of fighter opposition. Great havoc was performed however by the guns of the cruisers *Naiad, Perth, Calcutta, Carlisle*, and the destroyers *Kandahar, Kingston, Nubian*, and *Juno*. At 1249 the *Juno* was hit by a bomb during an Italian high-level attack, which penetrated her magazine and exploded. She sank in two minutes. Six officers and 91 ratings were picked up by the destroyers. But there was great loss of life, including the First Lieutenant Walter Starkie, an officer highly regarded in the service, who had relinquished his job as Flag Lieutenant to the Commander-in-Chief for a more active life in destroyers. His widow was Cunningham's niece. A petty officer, Edwin Lumley, blown over the side and badly burned, swam 40 yards in a thick layer of floating oil to rescue a shipmate in difficulties.

The formidable size of the naval forces remaining to the south-west of Kithera, refuelling and awaiting reports of enemy convoys that might be at sea, can be gathered from the following list:

Force A 1: The battleships *Warspite* and *Valiant*, and the destroyers *Napier, Decoy, Hero,* and *Hotspur* under Rawlings;

Force B: The heavy cruisers *Gloucester* and *Fiji,* and the destroyers *Griffin* and *Greyhound* under Rowley;

Force D: The light cruisers *Dido, Orion, Ajax,* and the destroyers *Janus, Kimberley, Hasty,* and *Hereward* under Glennie.

During the afternoon of Wednesday 21 May a Maryland of the RAF No. 39 Squadron reported groups of small craft escorted by warships proceeding southward from the island of Milos towards Crete, in a position about 80 miles north of Retimo. Glennie's Force D was to go in at dusk, while Rowley's Force B stood guard in the Antikithera Strait to prevent any Italian naval forces breaking in from the west. Rawlings's Force A 1 was to be in a strategic position to the south-west ready to give support as required. Meanwhile King's Force C was to re-enter through the Kaso Strait and resume patrol of the eastern section during the night in search of enemy seaborne forces.

Aided by radar, Glennie's Force D encountered the reported enemy troop convoy at 2330 Wednesday 21 May when 18 miles north of Canea, steaming for Suda Bay, headed by the Italian destroyer *Lupo.* This desperate measure with scant naval support followed the serious setback received by the German air assault on the first day. More than half were sunk, and a thousand troops were killed or thrown into the sea. Glennie called off his scattered force at 0330 Thursday 22 May. His flagship the *Dido* had only 30 per cent ammunition remaining, and he felt little justified in carrying out the previously planned sweep to the northward at daylight with the prospect of a heavy day of air attacks ahead. Cunningham ordered Glennie's force to return to Alexandria with all dispatch. While endorsing Glennie's opinion that the *Dido* was in no condition to comply with orders to sweep northward, Cunningham considered that the *Ajax* and the *Orion* should have remained to assist other forces, for they were still comparatively well off for ammunition.

During the night of Wednesday 21 May Freyberg's counter-attack to regain Maleme airfield was mounted. Almost all the ground lost had been recaptured by dawn, but the airfield itself remained in German hands, and from dawn onwards big JU 52s arrived at the rate of almost one a minute, each transport plane depositing 40 fully equipped men.

Meanwhile Cunningham had ordered Force B, *Gloucester, Fiji, Griffin,* and *Greyhound,* to break off their patrol off Cape Matapan and to proceed with dispatch into the Aegean to Heraklion where the harbour was reported to be in enemy hands. No enemy was sighted but Rowley's force was continuously dive-bombed from sunrise onwards, until at

0830 on this Thursday forenoon he had rejoined Rawlings's Force A 1 well west of Kithera. The wear and tear and fatigue had been enormous, and the expenditure of ammunition was on a scale that could not be long maintained.

Thursday 22 May was to be a particularly sad day for Cunningham's fleet. Positions at daylight were as follows: Rawlings with his Force A 1 was about 45 miles south-west of Kithera, proceeding to the north-westward, shortly to be joined during the forenoon by Rowley's Force B after his sweep into the Aegean, and Mountbatten who had sailed from Malta with his five destroyers of the 5th Destroyer Flotilla the previous evening. King's Force C was in the Aegean off Heraklion beginning a sweep to the north-westward. Glennie's Force D would shortly be on its way to Alexandria for replenishment.

Air attacks on King's ships began at 0700 and continued incessantly on this Thursday forenoon. After an hour and a half of continuous attacks from the air, Force C sighted a single caique carrying German troops. King's position was then only 60 miles south of the island of Milos, one of the German advanced bombing bases. The caique was sunk by the *Perth*. At 1010 an Italian destroyer (the *Sagittario*) was reported together with five small sailing vessels. By this time Force C was only 25 miles south of Milos. The *Perth* had rejoined the rest of the force, but the *Naiad* was labouring some distance astern, under very heavy air attack. The whole force engaged the *Sagittario* which retired behind smoke after firing torpedoes. The convoy consisted of 38 caiques carrying 4,000 troops to be landed at Heraklion, together with small steamships loaded with guns and tanks, and had already been recalled as a result of Glennie's action in the early hours of Thursday 22 May, though King was not to know about that. He now had to make a crucial decision. His ships were running short of ammunition and had to be kept together for mutual support. He made his decision, recalled the destroyers from the chase and proceeded westward. Cunningham considered King's decision a faulty one, and believed that the destruction of this large convoy would have justified severe losses. With characteristic comment he stated that the safest place for King's force was among the ships of the enemy convoy. This may appear to be sound, but it assumes a degree of recognition and discrimination among the enemy bombers not borne out in operations.

During his withdrawal to the westward King was bombed continuously for three and a half hours. The light cruiser *Naiad* had two turrets put out of action, the *Carlisle* was hit, and the *Perth* had her armament control damaged.

Meanwhile Rawlings with Force A 1 and Force B had been patrolling

20 to 30 miles westward of the Kithera Channel, 'serving a useful purpose' as he put it, 'by attracting enemy aircraft'. Ships always found it
consoling when under heavy air attack to see that there were other ships
to share the load. As soon as he heard that King would be withdrawing
from the Aegean, Rawlings decided to meet him in the neighbourhood
of the Kithera Channel. At 1225 upon hearing further of the *Naiad*'s
reduced speed and Force C's need for support, Rawlings steered for the
Channel at his maximum speed of 23 knots, with the intention of entering the Aegean.

As King's sorely pressed Force C approached the Channel, a Messerschmitt dived at the *Carlisle* spraying the bridge with machine-gun fire,
and killing her commanding officer Captain T. C. Hampton. At 1312
King's anti-aircraft shell bursts were sighted by Rawlings, and 20
minutes later the Forces C, A 1, and B joined, and withdrew together
to the south-westward. At this very moment, 1332, the *Warspite* was
dive-bombed by three Messerschmitts, and her speed reduced to 18
knots. Shortly before this a large caique had been sighted, and the
destroyer *Greyhound* ordered to sink her. Rear-Admiral King being
senior to Rear-Admiral Rawlings now assumed command of the combined forces.

In spite of the concentrated and incessant bombing attacks around
Crete, skilful manoeuvre together with lively anti-aircraft fire from the
ships of the fleet had so far resulted in little loss and relatively small
damage. The situation was now to take a drastic turn on this calamitous
day, Thursday 22 May. The first casualty was the destroyer *Greyhound*,
too vulnerable away from the main body. She sank in 15 minutes, her
guns firing to the last. King at once detached the destroyers *Kandahar*
and *Kingston* to pick up survivors, and later ordered the heavy cruisers
Gloucester and *Fiji* to stand by the rescuing destroyers, while the remainder of the fleet retired south-westward. He was unaware of sadly depleted
stocks of ammunition in Force B.

The rescuing ships were taking such a pasting that at 1456 King,
now aware of limited ammunition, ordered the ships to withdraw after
dropping boats and rafts, and then to join him. By 1530 the *Gloucester*
and *Fiji* were seen to be coming up at high speed astern of the main
force. Twenty minutes later, the gallant *Gloucester* which had survived
so many bomb attacks in the past was seen to receive several hits. She
was brought to a standstill enveloped in raging fires, her upper deck a
shambles. The *Fiji* closed to drop floats and boats, but in view of the
intensity of air attacks and a shortage of ammunition and oil fuel her
captain reluctantly decided that the *Fiji*, together with the destroyers
Kandahar and *Kingston*, must withdraw to the southward. They were

hotly pursued by aircraft. At 1710 *Fiji* reported her position as 24 miles 305° from the south-west corner of Crete. Her luck forsook her when she fell a victim to a single Messerschmitt coming out of the clouds in a shallow dive. Her end was near, for at 1915 another single aircraft hit her above 'A' boiler room with three bombs. She had by then expended all her 4-inch ammunition. The *Kandahar* (Commander W. G. A. Robson) and *Kingston* (Lieutenant-Commander P. Somerville) returned to the scene after dark, and succeeded in picking up 523 out of a total of 780. Commander W. R. Marshall-A'Deane, who had been picked up by the *Kandahar* after the loss of the *Greyhound*, assisted in the rescue work. Seeing a man in difficulties in the water, he dived in and swam to his assistance, but was not seen again. For his gallantry he was posthumously awarded the Albert Medal.

On this sad day 22 May for the Navy, the position ashore in Crete was not a very happy one for the Army. Following the unsuccessful dawn counter-attack to regain control of the Maleme airfield from the Germans, the withdrawal of British troops to a new defensive line farther east was begun. Enemy troop carriers continued to arrive all day at Maleme, though at great cost. There was no slackening of determination among the gallant defenders, but already towards the end of this third day it was obvious that the Germans had made up considerably for their slow progress on the first two days.

Disembarkation of reinforcements and supplies for the defenders could take place only at night, and approach to and withdrawal from the island had already become extremely hazardous. Nevertheless on this afternoon of Thursday 22 May, at Alexandria, the special service ship *Glenroy* (Captain Sir James Paget, Bart.) embarked 900 men of the Queen's Royal Regiment, the HQ Staff of 16th Infantry Brigade, and 18 vehicles, and sailed for Tymbaki on the south coast of Crete.

The intention was that Crete must be held. Though the position strategically had changed vitally with the loss of the airfield at Maleme, nowhere was the coast in enemy hands, and all enemy convoys had turned back. Nightly patrols continued off the north coast, the main brunt being borne by destroyers. Two of Mountbatten's 5th Destroyer Flotilla were set upon early on 23 May while withdrawing westward after a successful sweep in the Aegean. The *Kelly* and the *Kashmir* were both sunk, but the *Kipling* (Commander Aubrey St. Clair Ford) managed to pick up 281 survivors including both captains, Captain Mountbatten and Commander H. A. King, and in spite of severe bombing got to within 80 miles of Alexandria before running out of fuel. She was assisted into harbour by the *Protector* which had been sent out to meet her. Here was a case of an isolated ship 'getting away with it', but her good fortune was particularly appropriate in view of the resolution and courage shown by her gallant captain and crew.

The special service ship *Glenroy* had sailed for Tymbaki on Thursday afternoon 22 May, escorted by the anti-aircraft cruiser *Coventry* and the sloops *Auckland* and *Flamingo*. In view of the great naval losses suffered that day, Cunningham at 1117/23 signalled her recall. This was done after consultation with General Wavell, under the impression that: 'It appeared to be sheer murder to send her on.' To Cunningham's amazement, the Admiralty sent a direct message to the *Glenroy* ordering her to turn north again. It was much too late, so Cunningham ordered the *Glenroy* back to Alexandria and informed the Admiralty that if she had proceeded north she would have arrived at daylight, the worst possible time for air attacks. 'The less said about this unjustifiable interference by those ignorant of the situation the better,' wrote Cunningham.[11]

A signal from the Admiralty informed him (and who should know better?) that the outcome of the battle for Crete would have serious repercussions, and that it was vital to prevent seaborne landings in the next day or two, even if further losses resulted. Cunningham replied at some length, stressing the fuel and ammunition situation which existed in practically all ships. The Chiefs of Staff in London had also asked for an appreciation, to which Cunningham replied that the scale of air attack now made it no longer possible for the Navy to operate in the Aegean, or vicinity of Crete, by day. He could not guarantee to prevent seaborne landings without suffering losses which, added to those already sustained, would seriously prejudice the command of the eastern Mediterranean.

The Chiefs of Staff replied that the fleet and the Royal Air Force must accept whatever risk was entailed in preventing considerable enemy reinforcements. 'Singularly unhelpful', writes Cunningham, who delayed replying until 26 May.

Early on Friday 23 May at about 0200, the destroyers *Decoy* and *Hero* had embarked from a village on the south coast no less a person than King George II of Greece, together with members of the Royal Household, in accordance with a plan arranged with *Noic* Suda Bay. The King had narrowly escaped from his house at Perivolia shortly before it had been surrounded by Germans. Reinforcements were still being landed in Crete by fast ships such as the *Glenroy* and the *Abdiel*, but at great loss.

Cunningham was well aware of the prolonged strain under which his ships were working, and the mounting depression induced by growing losses. The humid weather and low cloud added gloom to the situation. He broadcast the following signal to the fleet, which raised hopes and stirred desire for immediate action.

'The Army is just holding its own against constant reinforcement of airborne troops. We must *not* let them down. At whatever cost to ourselves, we must land reinforcements and keep the enemy from using the sea. There are indications that enemy resources are stretched to the limit. We can and must outlast them. *Stick it out.*' Under these circumstances we were glad to learn that the *Formidable* would be proceeding to sea, having collected and repaired a few broken-down Fulmars.

On Sunday 25 May *Formidable* sailed, and after flying on fighter and bomber squadrons joined Force A under Pridham-Wippell, consisting of the two battleships *Queen Elizabeth* and *Barham*, and the destroyers *Jervis, Janus, Kandahar, Nubian, Hasty, Hereward, Voyager*, and *Vendetta*.

Pridham-Wippell's Force A steamed to the north-west at 21 knots. At 0330 a striking force of four Albacores took off as *Formidable* turned into the wind in a position 100 miles south-south-west of Scarpanto, to bomb airfields in Scarpanto, followed later by four Fulmar fighters. Complete surprise was achieved and all aircraft had returned safely by 0700. On being joined by *Ajax* and *Dido* who had been on night patrol, Pridham-Wippell proceeded southward, and *Formidable*'s Fulmars were able to frustrate the enemy's attempts to get through. At 1320, however, when well and truly in 'Bomb Alley', Pridham-Wippell's squadron was attacked by 20 dive-bombers from North Africa.

The following eye-witness account by the author, who was in the *Formidable*,[12] may add a little realism to a narrative which must necessarily be brief:

'At 1320, by which time we were 150 miles from the Kaso Strait, a force of about 20 bombers were seen on the radar screen, approaching from North Africa. They were greeted by a barrage of fire from the whole squadron in sufficiently open formation to permit ships to take rapid avoiding action. The sky was full of white puffs and brown blobs of smoke. Jagged bits of steel rained into the sea like gigantic hailstones. We were hurtling along at maximum speed, but the noise of the ship's vibration was out-rivalled by the roar of gunfire and the blast and crackle of the pom-poms. Soon we could see the swarm of Stukas silhouetted against bright sunlight. They were already peeling off undaunted by the gunfire. Their target was obviously the carrier.

'Violent avoiding action was immediately taken in answer to the captain's order for "Hard a-port" followed next by "Hard a-starboard". The *Formidable* responded instantly, heeling sharply to starboard as her head turned to port: then, seconds later, to port as her head came back again. But all of us on the bridge could see the relentless approach of the Stukas. And now we could hear the whistle of bombs. A mountain of filthy black water shot up close on our starboard bow and rose to 80 feet. Five seconds later there was another mountain, even closer and higher. Millions of crystals of water glittered in the sunlight as they fell. Then there were two in quick succession. We continued to weave. The next one hit. We were immediately on fire on the starboard side forward. A bomb had penetrated one of the 4·5-inch gun turrets. The explosion had blown out the ship's starboard side below the fo'c'sle. The fire appeared to be spreading, but the sea was calm, and the hull was still sound below the water-line.

'The firing from the fleet continued; and still the bombers peeled off to dive. There were further near misses, and then a gigantic jolt in the *Formidable* when the whole ship seemed to lift from aft. A 1,000-lb. bomb had gone right through the after starboard 4·5-inch gun sponson and exploded under the starboard quarter. It was an uncanny sensation as the stern violently lifted, and then fell: shuddering like a tuning-fork vibrating about its fixed end. It was all terrifying yet in some odd way exhilarating. It was also satisfying to be able to share some of the experiences suffered by our ships during the last six days.

'In a while the attack fizzled out. The bombers had withdrawn, doubtless with claims of a carrier and destroyer sunk; for the *Nubian* also had received a bomb hit which had blown her stern off and wiped out her after guns.

'*Formidable*'s fire was got under control, and watertight bulkheads were sealed off from the seven compartments which were open to the sea. Our catapult for accelerated take-off was out of action, but we were able to land on two Fulmars, and continued to operate fighters until dark, after which we parted company with Force A and proceeded to Alexandria attended by an anti-submarine screen of four destroyers. The *Nubian* was detached. Escorted by the *Jackal* she was able to return to Alexandria under her own steam, steering on her two screws in the absence of a rudder.'

Stick it out? What were our feelings now? For the destruction of a few enemy aircraft and minor damage to Scarpanto airfield, the *Formidable* had been so severely damaged that she would be out of use for several months. We had suffered ten casualties and were once again reduced to half a dozen serviceable aircraft. The only carrier in the eastern Mediterranean was now useless and it would be a very long time before another was available.

News of the damage to the *Formidable* and *Nubian* reached Cunningham while he was writing a reply on Monday 26 May to the Chiefs of Staff. 'It is not the fear of sustaining losses,' he said, 'but the need to avoid losses which will cripple the fleet without any commensurate advantage which is the determining factor in operating in the Aegean. As far as I know the enemy has so far had little success in reinforcing Crete by sea.

'The experience of three days in which two cruisers and four destroyers have been sunk, and one battleship, two cruisers, and four destroyers severely damaged shows what losses are likely to be. Sea control in the eastern Mediterranean could not be retained after another such experience.'

Cunningham went on to say that the enemy's supply by sea had not yet come into the picture. Enemy reinforcements and stores were able to come in at will by air, quite unchecked by any British air action. The sight of a constant and unhindered procession of JU 52s flying into Crete was likely to affect the morale of British troops.

He also stressed the fact that his men and ships were nearing exhaustion, having been kept running almost to the limit of their endurance since the end of February when the decision had been taken to send the British Army to Greece.

He complained that he had not received the reconnaissance aircraft he had so earnestly requested. Only adequate air reconnaissance would permit him to keep his ships far enough away by day, to avoid serious loss, pending the moment when the enemy committed his convoys to sea.

On the following day, 27 May, the battleship *Barham* was damaged. But there was just one piece of heartening news that reached us at Alexandria. It was of the sinking of the German battleship *Bismarck* which had sunk H.M.S. *Hood* in the Denmark Straits three days earlier. She had been successfully hunted in prolonged operations involving many British ships in the North Atlantic. History is full of incidents where the hunted ship slips through the net of overwhelming strength, but in this case the *Bismarck* had been fairly caught and forced to pay the inevitable penalty. This was particularly encouraging after all our recent heavy losses in the Mediterranean, and helped us to face the grim reality that Crete was now as good as lost.

The Germans had at times been near collapse in their attack on Crete, but their overwhelming air superiority had decided the issue, not only by direct assault against a spirited and gallant defence, but in the provision of information about tactical positions and movements. By 27 May it had been decided that British and Imperial troops should withdraw before a strong rearguard, and be evacuated by the Navy, mainly from the little port of Heraklion, and the fishing village Sphakia on the south coast which could be reached only by a tortuous road and path across the central mountains, ending in a steep descent to open beaches. This would involve much boat work.

Cunningham made it quite clear that 'Whatever the risks, whatever our losses, the remaining ships of the fleet would make an all-out effort to bring away the Army'. His attitude concerning the task of rescuing the Army is revealed in his oft-quoted remark that 'It takes three years to build a ship: but 300 to build a tradition'. But he warned Wavell that the moment might come when terrible losses could be inflicted from the air; to save numerous lives, surrender might then be more humane. Tedder promised all available help that could be raised from the RAF in the Middle East.

'And so we wearily turned to planning another evacuation,' wrote Cunningham, 'with fewer ships, far less resources . . . and our seamen and ships worn to the point of exhaustion.'

'But it has to be remembered,' said Cunningham in his dispatch, 'that the Navy's duty was achieved and no enemy ship, whether warship or transport, succeeded in reaching Crete.' And, thanks to Cunningham's victory at Matapan, neither were the Navy's operational intentions foiled at any stage by the Italian fleet.

The fact that the retreat to Sphakia had already begun, lessened in no degree the need for fighting, but it was expected that the Luftwaffe would make an all-out assault on ships at sea. Except for the brief period of *Formidable*'s operation against Scarpanto airfield, the fleet had been without fighter defence. The RAF had however now promised some fighter cover, though this could be only spasmodic owing to the great distances involved. Group Captain C. B. R. Pelly (later Air Chief Marshal Sir Claude) was attached temporarily to Cunningham's staff at Alexandria to co-ordinate the operation of RAF fighters with the movements of ships. A military liaison officer, Major-General J. F. Evetts (later General) was also attached. Cunningham paid warm tribute to the close co-ordination achieved by these two officers.

The plan was that embarkation of troops should be confined to the three hours immediately following midnight, in order to allow ships four hours of darkness on each side of this period for steaming, and to be as far as possible from enemy air bases during the hours of daylight. Troops from the Suda area would come off at Sphakia, and those from Heraklion were to embark at Heraklion harbour. Those from Retimo could most easily retreat to Plaka, and be taken off by H.M. ships calling in there: see map 14. An RAF aircraft dropped a message phrased in slang so as to be unintelligible if picked up by the Germans, ordering withdrawal to Plaka. It was never received, for the commanding officer Lieutenant-Colonel I. R. Campbell continued the defence until Friday 30 May when, with ammunition and rations spent, he was forced to surrender, not realising that rescue would be available just ten miles away on the south coast.

At 0600 on Wednesday 28 May, less than 24 hours after the decision to evacuate, Force B, under Rawlings, flying his flag in the *Orion* accompanied by the cruisers *Ajax* and *Dido*, and the destroyers *Decoy*, *Jackal*, *Imperial*, *Hotspur*, *Kimberley*, and *Hereward*, sailed from Alexandria for Heraklion harbour. Their object was to embark the whole of the Heraklion garrison of 4,000 that night.

Two hours later Force C, under Captain S. H. T. Arliss in the destroyer *Napier* accompanied by the *Nizam*, *Kelvin*, and *Kandahar*, sailed from Alexandria carrying additional boats for beach work off Sphakia, and small arms and provisions for those troops who could not be embarked that night.

The two forces on their missions of mercy were to have vastly different experiences, perhaps because of the German preoccupation over the stubbornness of the Heraklion defenders. Arliss arrived off Sphakia without incident, and by 0300 on Thursday 29 May had taken off nearly 700 men, and landed urgently needed rations for the 15,000 yet to come. Among the *Napier*'s passengers were three women, one Chinaman, two children, and a dog. The force was attacked by JU 88s, but arrived safely at Alexandria 1700 on Thursday 29 May. This augured well, but there was as yet no news of the arrival of Force B from Heraklion.

It had been the intention that the whole force of 4,000 should be brought off from Heraklion in one lift; hence the size of Rawlings's Force B. Steering at speed for the Kaso Straits, Rawlings encountered nothing until 1700/28 when, 90 miles from Scarpanto, his force was subjected to a series of air attacks, and at 1920/28 the *Imperial* (Lieutenant-Commander C. A. De W. Kitcat) received a near miss and damage to her steering which was to have grave consequences later in the operation. At 2010/28 the *Ajax* sustained damage and casualties and was at once ordered back to Alexandria.

Rawlings arrived off Heraklion at 2330/28, and by 0320 on Thursday 29 May the whole of the Heraklion garrison, amounting to some 4,000 troops, had been smoothly embarked, an operation performed in complete darkness, and without alarming the enemy. The rearguard had had to hold a covering position to the end, and break off in small numbers. But this Thursday 29 May 1941 was indeed to be a sad day for soldier and sailor alike.

At 0320/29 the squadron proceeded to sea working quickly up to 29 knots. Most of the troops were soon asleep in spite of their cramped quarters on the mess decks below. The congestion can be imagined when it is realised, for example, that the *Orion* was now carrying 1,000 troops in addition to her complement of 550 officers and men, and the destroyers 300 in addition to their ship's complement of 150 officers and men.

The squadron had just reached maximum speed, steaming in formation for the Straits at 0345, when *Imperial*'s steering gear failed, and her rudder jammed. Rawlings had to make a quick decision. He could wait while *Imperial* diagnosed the trouble and if possible put it right, meanwhile imperilling the whole squadron and the 4,000 troops; or he could abandon her after removing the troops. He decided on the latter and flashed a signal to the *Hotspur* (Lieutenant-Commander C. P. F. Brown) 'Take off crew and sink *Imperial*', adding, as the squadron resumed passage, 'Make for Alexandria'. Cunningham later remarked that this decision could not be cavilled at, but he thought it might have been wiser to remove the troops only, and let ship and crew take their chance on a struggle home.

It was the belief in the *Hotspur* that this was now to be their own fate. Transfer of troops would take up another precious hour. With the coming dawn they were likely to be alone in the Kaso Straits, no more than 30 miles from the enemy airfield in Scarpanto. At 0445, only a few minutes before the beginning of twilight, with a total of 900 men on board *Hotspur* worked up to full speed and steamed eastward for the north-east corner of Crete. A whole hour had passed, and by now Rawlings must be 30 miles farther on.

In the process of hugging the coast and passing inside a small island near the north-east point of Crete, so as to cut the corners, indistinct grey shapes were suddenly seen from the *Hotspur* in the twilight. It could be an Italian squadron. As the light grew behind the dark masses, the silhouettes of British ships were recognised. Rawlings had proceeded at a reduced speed of only 15 knots.

'It's the *Orion*,' went up the cry. The utter relief is described by the *Hotspur*'s first lieutenant:[13]

'Never have I been so "pro" anybody as I was pro-Rawlings at that moment. We did not know him well, but on hearing about him later one realised that Rawlings could never leave an undamaged ship in the lurch if he could get there to add his support.'

It was Rawlings who had taken the battleships into the Kithera Channel to save the cruisers on 22 May. Now he had reduced speed to wait for the *Hotspur*.

At 0600 the dive-bombing began. Sometimes the attacks were concentrated on the two cruisers *Orion* and *Dido*, sometimes on individual ships of the destroyer screen. A hail of gunfire met every attack. The first lieutenant of the *Hotspur* describes the scene:[14]

'Down they came screaming out of the half-light one after the other. The Captain stood on the bridge. He had already been there 24 hours. As the leader turned vertically down on us from starboard, he swung the destroyer hard over to starboard, and for the next seven hours he drove us with amazing precision, watching each bomber as a cat would watch a bird, and then, as they dived on us, he would throw the *Hotspur* hard over towards them, so as to force them to be diving steeper and steeper on the way down, which tended to make them pull out early to avoid getting past the vertical. . . .'

No sooner had the dive-bombers completed their attack than they would return to Scarpanto for reloading, unworried by fuelling problems for the few miles involved.

At 0625 the *Hereward* (Lieutenant-Commander W. J. Munn) was hit amidships, and fell away astern of the squadron. Rawlings was forced once again to make a quick decision. Should he stand by the *Hereward*, thus gravely imperilling the rest of his squadron and the troops on board, or must he abandon her to her fate? He chose the latter, a decision later endorsed by Cunningham as undoubtedly correct. When last seen the *Hereward* was making slowly for the coast of Crete, her guns firing. A large number of survivors were picked up by Italian motor-boats and were made prisoner.

Rawlings continued southward at 30 knots still hopeful of fighter protection. At 0645 however the *Decoy* received a near miss which affected her speed, and Rawlings was now compelled to reduce to 25 knots. At 0730 a bomb fell very close to the *Orion*, causing a further reduction of the speed of the squadron to 21 knots. Soon after 0730 a Stuka raked the *Orion*'s bridge, mortally wounding Rawlings's flag captain, G. R. B. Back, and also slightly wounding Rawlings. In the *Dido* (Captain H. W. V. McCall) B turret had been completely destroyed by a bomb. At 1045 a wave of 11 JU 87s dived in succession on the *Orion*, determined to sink her. Almost hidden by smoke and towering splashes, she emerged still able to steam, but evidently badly hit and temporarily out of control. The results were appalling, for a bomb passed through the bridge to explode below on the stokers' mess deck where the space was crowded with soldiers, of whom there were in all 1,100 on board. Casualties amounted to 260 killed, 280 wounded.

There were no further dive-bombing attacks, and at 2000 Force B arrived at Alexandria. *Orion* then had only two rounds of 6-inch H.E. ammunition left, and but 10 tons of fuel. Cunningham described the scene:[15]

---

13 *Italian Commander-in-Chief, Admiral Angelo Iachino, at Matapan*

14 *Italian cruisers* Zara, Pola, Fiume *and* Garibaldi *seen from the* Abruzzi *early on the morning of Matapan. A sad fate awaited three of them*

15 *Cruisers* HMAS Perth, HMS Ajax, *and* HMS Orion *at Matapan, as seen from* HMS Gloucester

'Rawlings brought his shattered squadron into Alexandria. . . . I shall never forget the sight of those ships coming up harbour, the guns of their fore-turrets awry, one or two broken off and pointing forlornly skyward, their upper decks crowded with troops, and the marks of their ordeal only too plainly visible. I went on board at once and found Rawlings cheerful but exhausted. The ship (*Orion*) was a terrible sight and the mess deck a ghastly shambles'.

Of the 4,000 soldiers taken off at Heraklion at the beginning of this long day, 29 May, 800 had been killed, wounded, or (in the case of those in the *Hereward*) captured. Not many more than 3,000 soldiers had been rescued, with the substantial loss of many seamen and stokers and two destroyers, and the sustaining of damage to the *Orion* and *Dido* which would keep them out of service for months. Some of the destroyers had escaped damage, and there was still a cruiser or two to assist in the further evacuations, all from Sphakia, which were to take place during the following three days. Exhausted ships' companies carried out the work of fuelling, ammunitioning, and preparing for action and embarkation, driven by pity and sympathy for those soldiers still left in Crete, until a final halt had to be called. RAF fighters now provided fighter defence for the return passage, nevertheless the cruiser *Calcutta* was lost, and the *Perth, Napier*, and *Kelvin* were damaged.

At the cost of three cruisers and six destroyers sunk, two battleships and a carrier out of action, with damage also to five cruisers and eight destroyers, some 17,000 men had been evacuated. It was still possible to boast of an unbroken tradition. The Navy had kept its pledge 'not to let the Army down'. About 12,000 men were taken prisoner in Crete, but many escaped surrender to the Germans and roamed the island, while others adapted abandoned motor landing craft or boats, and steered under improvised sails for the North Africa coast, with implacable gallantry, taking a week or more under conditions of extreme hardship and deprivation. The Royal Navy lost 1,828 officers and men killed.

Cunningham's dispatch after the battle brings out well the tragedy of the losses suffered by the Navy in supporting and rescuing the Army, and pays due tribute to the officers and men who were involved. He writes:

'It is not easy to convey how heavy was the strain that men and ships sustained. Apart from the cumulative effect of prolonged sea-going over extended periods it has to be remembered that in this last instance ships' companies had none of the inspiration of battle with the enemy to bear them up. Instead they had the unceasing anxiety of the task of trying to bring away in safety thousands of their own countrymen, many of whom were in an exhausted and dispirited condition, in ships necessarily so

APPROXIMATE NUMBERS DISEMBARKED AT ALEXANDRIA

Date	Force	H.M. Ships	From	Number
Prior to 27 May	—	—	—	112
27 May	—	Abdiel, Hero, Nizam	Suda	930
29 May	Force B (Rawlings)	Orion, Dido, Kimberley, Decoy, Jackal, Hotspur	Heraklion	3,486
	Force C (Arliss)	Napier, Nizam, Kelvin, Kandahar	Sphakia	680
30 May	Force D (King)	Phoebe, Glengyle, Perth, Jervis, Janus, Hasty	Sphakia	6,029
31 May	Force C (Arliss)	Napier, Nizam	Sphakia	1,510
1 June	Force D (King)	Phoebe, Abdiel, Jackal, Hotspur, Kimberley	Sphakia	3,710
		By Sunderland aircraft	Sphakia	54
				16,511

overcrowded that even when there was opportunity to relax, conditions made this impossible. They had started the evacuation already over-tired, and they had to carry it through under conditions of savage air attacks such as had only recently caused grievous losses in the fleet.

'There is rightly little credit or glory to be expected in these operations of retreat, but I feel that the spirit of tenacity shown by those who took part should not go unrecorded.

'More than once I felt that the stage had been reached when no more could be asked of officers and men, physically and mentally exhausted by their efforts and by the events of these fateful days. It is perhaps even now not realised how nearly the breaking point was reached, but that these men struggled through is the measure of their achievement, and I trust that it will not lightly be forgotten.'

On conclusion of the final evacuation Cunningham received a personal message from General Sir Archibald Wavell which was promulgated to the fleet:

'I send to you and all under your command the deepest admiration and gratitude of the Army in the Middle East for the magnificent work of the Royal Navy in bringing the troops back from Crete. The skill and self-sacrifice with which the difficult and dangerous operation was carried out will never be forgotten, and will form another strong link between our two services. Our thanks to all and sympathy for your losses.'

On the same day Tedder sent the following message:

'May I express on behalf of myself and the Royal Air Force, Middle East, our admiration of the way in which the Royal Navy has once again succeeded in doing what seemed almost impossible.'

Major Ian Manson, one of those thousands who were evacuated,[16] writes:

'The odds were against us from the start, one can't fight aeroplanes with bayonets. The German dive-bombing and machine-gunning from the air was terrific. The evacuation involved a journey over steep mountainous country of about 50 miles on foot, marching by night and fighting rearguard actions by day. . . . New Zealand will never be able to thank the Royal Navy enough for its work at great cost of men and ships, in evacuating us from Greece and Crete.'

Here are words of which Cunningham's Fleet might well be proud. It would take years to recover from those terrible losses of men and ships, but a tradition of centuries had been maintained.

The Mediterranean Fleet in Adversity (June 1941–December 1941)

Before leaving the story of Crete it is necessary to examine the question as to whether Cunningham should have attempted a further evacuation after the morning of 1 June. It has been said that he should have risked one more on 2 June. It has also been said that his decision not to do so was induced by the haunting memory of Rawlings's return on 29 May with his battered Force B, having lost the *Imperial* and the *Hereward*, and suffered crippling damage to the *Orion* and the *Dido*, in addition to losing 800 troops killed, wounded, or captured, from the 4,000 embarked that morning at Heraklion. Cunningham certainly never forgot that day, but he was not the man to allow emotion to sway his better judgment; and he was resolved that his ships should embark troops as long as it was practicable to do so. According to Royer Dick, it was at a moment of deep perplexity, when presented by his staff with a grim picture of the likely disastrous consequences, that ABC had replied that it took the Navy three years to build a ship but 300 years to build a tradition; 'and to all present it shone out like a beam'. He was however greatly concerned about the limitations imposed on a ship's fighting capacity when crammed with troops.

The difficulty in the exchange of information was not the least of the problems attending evacuation, for the Crete headquarters were in a cave at Sphakia from the forenoon of Wednesday 28 May until finally overrun, and radio communication on a resurrected set became only sporadic.[1] As a result it was not possible to keep Cairo and Alexandria informed of the changing state of availability of troops to be evacuated, nor was it possible to predict exactly how long it would be before embarkation would become impracticable altogether. The original estimate at Sphakia was that Friday 30 May must be the last morning of evacuation, but after consultation with Wavell that day, Cunningham agreed that there should be a further attempt in the early hours of Saturday 31 May, and a final effort on the morning of Sunday 1 June. It seemed then, owing to limited information of the most recent situation, that this might achieve complete withdrawal. These deliberations were confirmed on Saturday 31 May when Cunningham received a visit from Wavell, Freyberg (who had been flown from Crete by flying-boat), and Mr. Fraser (Prime Minister of New Zealand). Again, in spite of conflicting reports as to the number still to be taken off, and they were unfortunately very far from the truth, there was general agreement that the final evacuation by Force D under Admiral King flying his flag in the *Phoebe* (Captain G. Grantham) would suffice if all five ships of the force were filled to capacity.

Perhaps it is not generally realised by the critic that the round journey for each ship involved a gruelling passage of some 800 miles, with frequent and extended periods of action and manoeuvring at full speed, and in the case of destroyers, the need for refuelling and ammunitioning before being available for a second run. Each operation occupied the best part of two days. If therefore, as in the case of the *Phoebe, Nizam*, and *Napier*, a ship had to operate an embarkation on alternate days, there was practically no time for recovery between any two operations.

Guy Grantham[2] the captain of the *Phoebe* writes:

'The last but one trip we did to Sphakia we brought a full load (6,000) to Alexandria and berthed at Mahmoudieh Wharf about 2300 Friday 30 May. The C-in-C and Kelsey (*Naiad*) were waiting on the jetty and, when we had secured and had the brows in, came on board and Andrew said, "That was to have been the last trip, but you have got to do one more run, sailing at 0545 to-morrow morning." I told him we were very short of fuel and had practically no ammunition left and everyone was pretty well whacked. He then said that *Naiad*'s crew would take over all watchkeeping, fuel and ammunition ship, while I and my ship's company turned in and got some sleep. And so it was. We sailed on time [at 0545 Saturday 31 May with *Abdiel, Kimberley, Hotspur*, and *Jackal*] and did the last run, and took off 3,710 from Sphakia on the morning of Sunday 1 June. Whether another run could have been successfully carried out I do not know. Army communications were poor or almost non-existent, and I do not think anyone in Egypt had any clear picture of the situation in Crete at the time we left. Certainly our passengers were unable to give any clear or coherent report.'

The final evacuation for Sunday 1 June having been decided and agreed at two meetings, Cunningham saw no reason to change, even when Major-General Weston of the Royal Marines arrived at Alexandria

Ship losses in Greece and Crete operations, April/May 1941.

Legend:
- ✗ Warships sunk, destroyed or severely damaged.
- ⊙ Transports sunk, destroyed or severely damaged.

GREECE

Nauplia

Ulster Prince
Glenearn
Kalamata
Slamat
Diamond & Wryneck
Pennland

Athens

C. Matapan

KITHERA ✗ Naiad
✗ Warspite
Greyhound ✗
Gloucester ✗
ANTIKITHERA

⊙ Costa Rica
Widnes & York
Canea
Maleme
Sphakia
Tymbaki
Heraklion ✗
CRETE

Imperial ✗ KASO IS.
✗ Hereward
Plaka
Orion & Dido ✗

SCARPANTO
RHODES

TURKEY

✗ Fiji
✗ Kelly & Kashmir
✗ Juno

Perth ✗
Nizam ✗
Napier ✗
Formidable & Nubian ✗
✗ Barham
✗ Kelvin
✗ Calcutta

Derna
Tobruk
LIBYA
Bardia
Mersa Matruh
EGYPT
Alexandria

0   50   100
Miles

~ARTHUR BANKS~

early on Sunday by flying-boat, and reported that there were still 5,000 troops in Crete. In truth there were double that number, but they were short of food and incapable of further resistance. They had already been instructed by Weston to capitulate, before he had left Crete in accordance with orders from Wavell. On this Sunday morning Cunningham received a signal from the First Sea Lord saying that if there was any reasonable chance of embarking any substantial formed body on the morning of 2 June the attempt should be made. Cunningham in his reply reported the situation as described by Weston, and said that in the circumstances no further ships would be sent. It was on this day that the anti-aircraft cruiser *Calcutta* was sunk, when only 85 miles from Alexandria, bringing Cunningham's Crete losses to 9 ships sunk, and 17 damaged, in addition to the loss of 16 light craft: see map 15. To cover the supply of Tobruk and Malta and to harass the enemy's supply lines to Libya, he now had but 14 serviceable ships left, including the battleships *Queen Elizabeth* and *Valiant*, and no carrier.

The captain[3] of the *Calcutta* writes:

'My ship had got back to harbour during the middle watch of the last but one day of the Crete evacuation and, immediately after breakfast, I went to the Commander-in-Chief's office. Knowing that the final evacuation was to be made that night I was confident of at least two days and nights in harbour during which I and my ship's company would be able to get some much needed rest and sleep.

'Imagine my feelings therefore when, in the Operations Room, I was told I was to sail again at 2300 that night, meet the party returning from Crete and escort back to Alexandria any ships whose speed might have been reduced, thereby enabling the main body to carry on at high speed. I must have been fairly near the end of my tether because, I am afraid, I let loose a torrent of vituperation and abuse at the staff.

'ABC, whose office adjoined the Operations Room, must have heard me as the door opened and, without saying a word, he beckoned me to come into his room. Having sat me down he said, "Now, what's the matter?" I replied, "I know to-night is the final evacuation. My ship's company is tired out. I am tired out. And now I hear we have got to go to sea again at 2300 to-night."

'Most Commanders-in-Chief would have given a very severe ticking off to a junior Post Captain for such an outburst; not so ABC. He understood the strain we had been under for long weeks. He talked to me very quietly, like a father, explaining everything including his own misery at being shore-bound whilst the ships of his fleet were being decimated. After about a quarter of an hour he asked, "Now are you happy to go out to-night?"

'Of course I was.

'His method of dealing with me increased my loyalty and affection so that I returned to my ship thinking, "What a very great man".

'My ship was sunk at about 0900 next morning by a low flying aircraft coming in out of the sun (we had not got radar). *Coventry*, who was with me, picked up our survivors, and ABC himself was waiting on the jetty when *Coventry* returned to harbour. He came on board and as he and I walked up and down the quarterdeck, he was in tears.'

Many speak of the humanitarian side of this great sailor, and it is fitting to reproduce below a copy of a card which was displayed in each room of the Commander-in-Chief's house. Most of the rooms were kept for officers whose ships had been sunk in action or seriously damaged, and who came for a short interval of rest. Admiral and Lady Cunningham had had their own personal tragedy when Walter Starkie was lost in the *Juno*, and felt that the words on the card would provide solace for those becoming overborne by the strain of war in the Mediterranean.

INTERVAL

Be still, and give its ease to your tired mind;
Let the rare silence like a river flow.
If there were war it was long, long ago,
If there were noise, it went out with the wind;
Time battles on, maybe; aye, life itself is so,
A little while the torch burns faint and low
And deeds are but dim shadows on a blind;

This is that hour, unmindful of alarms:
Think on a sunny meadow and green leas,
Grey cropping sheep and little curled-up farms
And let the vision bear you where it please.
It is because of moments such as these
That brave men can take up their arms.

Another view of Cunningham at this time comes from the captain of the *Dido*[4] who also says that it is quite 'UN-TRUE that ABC never quite recovered from the sight of *Orion* and *Dido* returning to harbour after evacuating from Heraklion'.

'We arrived,' he continues, 'at Alexandria near the end of April 1941 to get a most friendly welcome from the C-in-C. He told me that we could have exactly 48 hours in harbour before being required to patrol around Crete. That was the last rest we were to have for a month. Our role before the final evacuation was to prevent German forces landing on the island. This entailed constant patrolling subject to everlasting air attacks. Our returns to Alexandria were more often dictated by the necessity to top up with ammunition rather than shortage of fuel. At the end of one particularly anxious expedition to bring out all the gold in Crete and escort out several troop-ships the C-in-C came on board to find out how things had gone. The first question he asked me was, "How are the sailors?" I replied they were all pretty tired. "Tired?" he questioned. "Why are they tired, they had a night in harbour last Thursday." Feeling pretty weary myself I replied, "Well, sir, if you consider that it's a night in harbour when you arrive at sunset, ammunition ship till 10.00 p.m., turn out in the middle watch to repel an air raid and sail at dawn, I don't." "Well," he said, "maybe you've got something on your side."

'Our final episode of that period before we were damaged beyond local repair was the evacuation of troops from Heraklion [on that sad Thursday 29 May 1941]. ABC came on board that night whilst we were disembarking troops in Alexandria. Looking pretty done up himself, after hearing my account of our wonderfully lucky escape from being blown up and sunk he turned to me and said, "Well, you can't make an omelette without breaking eggs – and you haven't made a bad omelette".' The omelette in this case was the evacuation by *Dido* of 1,100 troops.

Mountbatten, who had lost two destroyers of his flotilla, reported[5] that the 'whole Fleet would do anything for ABC. They have the utmost confidence in him'. Nevertheless ABC had told Mountbatten that he felt like going out in a destroyer into the thickest of the bombing and getting killed or else like resigning.

Cunningham felt particularly sad about the loss of 1,828 officers and men, and the sinking of three cruisers and six destroyers, some of which he considered would still be afloat had he himself been at sea to control movements. In a letter[6] to the First Sea Lord (30 May 1941) he wrote: 'The sending back of *Gloucester* and *Fiji* to stand by the *Greyhound* was another grave error, and cost us two further ships.' Both had been short of AA ammunition, and in a position less than 30 miles from an enemy airfield. Cunningham refers to his anxiety for the state of mind of the sailors, and questions whether he himself should remain in command. 'I hear,' he continued, 'that the PM has removed Longmore (replacing a 1st class man with a 2nd class in my opinion).' Longmore had been superseded as AO Commanding-in-Chief, ME, 1 June 1941; in Cunningham's eyes he could do no wrong. Wavell also was shortly to be superseded, being relieved by General Sir Claude Auchinleck on 5 July 1941. Cunningham felt that he himself should go if there was any lack of confidence in him.

'It may be,' Cunningham continued in his letter to the First Sea Lord, 'that the PM or the Admiralty would like a change in command of the fleet out here. If this is so I shall not feel in any way annoyed, more especially as the happenings of the last few days may have shaken the faith of the personnel of the fleet in my handling of affairs.' It was clear to those serving in the fleet that the reverse was the case. Never had Cunningham's stature been higher. Out of defeat he had snatched the miracle of yet another evacuation. Despite his own inner sorrow, he continued an exterior of good cheer and optimism. 'Just a little stroke of luck,' he remarked in a letter to a friend 12 June 1941, 'and the tide will turn and we shall be off again.'

'We always felt,' comments Royer Dick, 'that Crete was lost only by a hair, and had fighters been available we should have won the day. But the fighters instead of coming back to Crete were expended trying to protect the troops in Greece; an understandable but mistaken decision.'

Cunningham's lack of appreciation of Tedder arose because of frustration of his long-stated request for an RAF Co-operation Group. 'I soon gathered,' writes Tedder,[7] 'that Cunningham was pitching his demands high. . . . I could give no support to such ideas.' Referring to the army survivors from Crete, Tedder continues: 'I was soon conscious of a first-class hate working up against the RAF for having "let them down in Greece and Crete".' It is a relief to read however that 'personal relations were very friendly', and Cunningham writes of Tedder that he 'is a nice enough fellow'. Tedder emphasised that shortages were not confined to the air side, but extended to 'anti-aircraft guns, tanks, motor transport, submarines and light naval craft'.

During the last few days of the evacuation, RAF long-distance fighters and bombers provided gallant assistance whenever possible, but were limited by the great distances involved, and the loss of so much maintenance equipment during the recent withdrawal from Greece.

It is interesting to examine Cunningham's argument[8] that the struggle to hold Crete was worth while.

'Looking back,' he writes, 'I sometimes wonder whether the loss of the island was really such a serious matter as it seemed at the time. Had we defeated the German attack and held the island the problem of its maintenance and supply would have been extraordinarily difficult. We should undoubtedly have required a large garrison, and though it is true that the defence could primarily have been entrusted to the Greeks, the drain on our slender resources of arms, ammunition, and equipment available in the Mediterranean would have been heavy. Moreover, all the ports available for landing supplies were on the north coast within easy reach of enemy airfields.

'The Royal Air Force would also have had to be maintained in considerable strength in Crete. This would have involved the construction of new airfields. When one considers all the extra equipment and supplies necessary for the RAF, to say nothing of maintaining the troops, it is difficult to see how the necessary masses of stores could have been landed on the limited beaches on the south coast of Crete, and have been transported over the mountains.

'On the other hand, it is not to be denied that the retention of Crete would probably have done away with much of the difficulty of supplying Malta during the critical phases that were soon to come upon us. It was the German air force in Crete and in Cyrenaica on the flanks of our convoy route to Malta that made the maintenance of that island from the east so costly and hazardous.'

Cunningham refers to the serious effect on Germany's Balkan campaign which was caused by Britain's struggle in Greece and then in Crete. Germany had begun her march through Yugoslavia and Greece on 6 April 1941, and this campaign involved 27 divisions and a third of the total Panzer strength of the German army. Her detention and tremendous losses in Crete not only frustrated Hitler's designs on Syria and Iraq but seriously delayed his attack upon Russia.

Cunningham continues:

'The German army reached the outskirts of Moscow in October 1941, by which time the early frost had begun to interfere with its movements. Its arrival in front of Moscow five weeks earlier would probably have led to the capture of that city, the importance of which it is difficult to exaggerate.

'Our defence of Crete, therefore, may have served its purpose in the overall pattern of the war.'

Perhaps even more serious for the Germans was the virtual destruction of Fliegerkorps XI in the struggle for Crete, and the enormous losses in men and equipment which precluded any possibility of a similar assault on Malta or Cyprus. With the withdrawal of Fliegerkorps VIII for the Russian campaign, Fliegerkorps X now had to cope with the whole of the eastern Mediterranean from Malta to Suez, and was concentrated mainly in Crete and Cyrenaica. Cunningham however never ceased to press for more air strength, and although there was little hope of regaining the northern flank, his faith rested in the recapture of the southern flank. With British airfields in Libya again, the Luftwaffe activities could be pushed westward, thus relieving the pressure on Egypt and the supply lines to the Western Desert. The fleet might then operate in the central Mediterranean with reasonable protection from fighters, and torpedo-bombers could be brought to bear against any

Italian fleet offensive aimed at Egypt. The Italian Navy had made no appearance in strength during the struggle for Crete, and had suffered no loss. Their four battleships and 11 cruisers therefore now well outnumbered Cunningham's two battleships and three cruisers. From June onwards American shipping was bringing vital supplies through the Red Sea to Suez, since the Red Sea was no longer regarded as a 'combat zone', and was safely in British hands: there was however real danger from enemy bombs and mines to all shipping.

Alexandria now began to receive night air raids, during which mines and bombs were dropped over a period of two hours from 30 or 40 German aircraft, the most favoured nights being those when the moon was bright. During these attacks, carried out in the face of a fleet barrage and smoke screens, mines falling into the harbour were observed and reported, and then dealt with during daylight hours. Little damage was done to the fleet, but there were many casualties ashore which had such a demoralising effect that Cunningham feared the possibility of dockyard work coming to a standstill and Alexandria ceasing as a discharge port. The raids continued sporadically, gradually decreasing in frequency and weight after the German invasion of Russia.

Hitler's lightning campaign to eliminate Russia began on 22 June 1941, and was at first everywhere successful. By December his troops were on the outskirts of Leningrad and Moscow; they then froze to a halt.

The transference of German attention to Russia resulted in a breathing space for British forces in Egypt. British troops were sent into Syria and Iraq in June, and on into Asia Minor and Iran, to frustrate German designs and to safeguard British oil supplies. Offshore support was provided by a squadron under Admiral King using Haifa as headquarters. This consisted of the *Phoebe, Ajax*, and *Coventry*, together with six destroyers and the special service ship *Glengyle*. Such a move stimulated the Turkish will to resist Axis intimidation, and also supported Russia.

Fulmar fighters of the FAA were sent to Palestine to provide air cover for King's squadron and supply ships. It was regrettable to find hostility from the French forces in Syria, whose single-seat fighters were far superior to the Fulmars. Swordfish based on Cyprus effected reprisals however, by torpedoing several French ships. An armistice on 10 July brought an end to these local interruptions by the French, and British troops were soon in control over the whole of Syria.

Meanwhile Cunningham's crippled ships were being patched sufficiently to enable them to undertake the long voyages to shipyards where they would be rendered serviceable. When the *Warspite* left on 24 June the Commander-in-Chief shifted his office ashore to the Gabbari Docks in Alexandria. There was great pressure 'in high places' for him to transfer to Cairo, a move to which he was utterly opposed, particularly as he flew with Dick to Cairo at least weekly to attend C-in-C meetings. He considered it bad enough to be ashore in Alexandria while conducting directly the operations of the Mediterranean Station, and had every intention of shifting his flag when practicable to the *Queen Elizabeth*, which he did in September 1941 when the *Barham* returned to the fleet. He already had his own excellent naval liaison officer in Captain H. G. Norman serving in Cairo. To maintain a liaison with Cunningham's staff, Wavell had appointed Lieutenant-Colonel R. B. Moseley,[9] an officer of the Yorkshire Dragoons, as a personal 'go-between'. It is of interest to read the views of this soldier, especially as he had started service life at Osborne in 1913, as a naval cadet, and had seen much service at sea in the First World War. It should be realised that (certainly during the war) the Commander-in-Chief of a substantial fleet would hold a staff conference every day, and that this could easily become swollen, though in the case of Cunningham the 'waffle' and the numbers attending were kept as low as practicable.

'I reported to Alexandria,' writes Moseley. 'GHQ Cairo gave me virtually a blank cheque to keep close touch with the Navy, attend all Commander-in-Chief conferences, explain the implications of what had been discussed at them, and generally keep GHQ informed of naval movements and thought. They (the Navy) had been prone to disappear to sea keeping wireless silence when important decisions were wanted by Wavell. I was given the rank of Lieutenant-Colonel.

'I was shown to a desk in an office used by the more junior officers of Commander-in-Chief Mediterranean's staff, and allowed to see an assortment of signals. I found it difficult to find out what was going on and was not informed about C-in-C conferences, etc. After a few days I went to ABC and said, "I realise, sir, what you are thinking of me. Either I was a failure in the Senior Service and axed or I wilfully deserted and converted myself into a 'Pongo' in which case I must be mad. In neither case would I be of any use to you. I would like you to know I deliberately made myself a horsed soldier and have no regrets!" He roared with laughter, and seemed to understand immediately. Very soon I was seeing the most top secret papers and signals and attending intelligence meetings, etc.

'I was an immense admirer of ABC. He was a very salt sailor but a great man of few words but staunchly loyal to his service and country. I enjoyed the twinkle in his watery eye and his great sense of humour.'

Wavell left Cairo 7 July in an exchange of appointments with the Commander-in-Chief India, General Sir Claude Auchinleck. Cunningham was a shrewd judge of men, and it is therefore of interest to read his comment which says:[10] 'I had the greatest admiration for Wavell. He was cool and imperturbable . . . and steadfastly refused to be riled by the prodding messages to which he, like myself, was at times subjected. . . . Never once did he have the good fortune to fight with all the resources he really needed. Assuredly he will be recognised by posterity as one of the great Generals to be thrown up by the war, if not the greatest.'

Cunningham was in a position to realise the considerable amount of political and administrative work involved in Wavell's vast command additional to purely military requirements. Such duties were taken over by Mr. Oliver Lyttelton, when appointed (28 June) to represent the British War Cabinet. As chairman of the Commanders-in-Chief Committee, Middle East, he was unbiased and successful, though at first suspiciously regarded and referred to as the 'commissar'. There appears to have been general apprehension[11] by the Commanders-in-Chief that higher authority at home might soon appoint a supreme commander, on the grounds of incompatibility between the three service chiefs concerning allocation of air strength. The word 'supremo' had unhappy connotations. Cunningham's view was that a 'supremo' was unnecessary except perhaps among allies, and even then it would be necessary to clarify all relationships exactly. In stating that much better results were to be obtained by a selection of men who were determined to support each other loyally for a common end, he presumably had very much in mind his own happy association with Wavell and Longmore. The question was to rise very much to the fore within the year, and was to be beset at first with difficulties in those cases where relationships were not happy ones. The matter as it affected Cunningham will be dealt with later.

With the German Luftwaffe in Crete to the north of 'Bomb Alley', and Cyrenaica to the south, it was no longer practicable to send convoys from Alexandria to Malta. The isolated fortress of Tobruk continued to be what Cunningham called 'a running sore to the enemy', but at a cost of many small ships and courageous crews. Supply to Malta by convoy from the west with Force H continued, and the situation eased temporarily with the transfer of Luftwaffe squadrons from Sicily to the Russian front. Submarines operating from Alexandria and from Malta were effecting great destruction in enemy supplies to Libya. Nevertheless there were to be losses among this gallant group, including the *Upholder* whose captain Lieutenant-Commander M. D. Wanklyn had in May 1941 been awarded the Victoria Cross. Light surface forces could once again be based at Malta, and a small squadron Force K was sent out from the

United Kingdom under Commodore W. G. Agnew, composed of the light cruisers *Aurora* and *Penelope,* and the two destroyers *Lance* and *Lively.* In a skilful early morning action on 9 November 1941 they attacked and sank all seven ships of a heavily protected Italian convoy. Later in the same month they sank two large supply ships, and on 1 December a tanker, an ammunition ship, and the destroyer *Damotto,* 60 miles north-west of Tripoli.

On 13 December 1941 a flotilla of destroyers, the *Sikh, Legion, Maori,* and *Isaac Sweers* (a Dutch ship), under Commander G. H. Stokes and on the way to Alexandria to reinforce Cunningham's flotillas, sank two Italian cruisers, the *Barbiano* and *Giussano,* in a brilliant night action off Cap Bon in eastern Tunisia. The Italians had no proper facilities for a night action, and as stated earlier were discouraged, as a policy, from accepting such.

Malta continued to be the key in the increasing struggle over lines of communication in the central Mediterranean. For reconnaissance, defence, and attack it had to have more aircraft, and these continued to arrive by sea from a carrier. Fleet Air Arm Swordfish and Albacores continued to operate, not only as torpedo-carriers, but also as flare-droppers when co-operating with Wellington bombers. By December 1941 Cunningham achieved at last, with Air Ministry agreement, his demand for an RAF Co-operation Group: the Naval Co-operation Group No. 201 at Alexandria. Cunningham found that this provided also an effective channel of communication with the AO C-in-C in Cairo, and matters could now be instantly referred. Only by air power supported by sea power could Malta survive. Only with Malta's survival could Cunningham continue to attack Italian supply routes to Rommel's campaign in North Africa, and weaken it (especially in stocks of petrol) and ultimately stop it: see map 16. In November 1941 63 per cent of the cargoes sent to Libya were cut off, and the rate was increasing. If Rommel could be thrown out of Cyrenaica the fleet could operate with fewer hazards from the air, and the destruction of convoys would become cumulative. Thus can it be seen how closely were events intertwined, and the opportunity for a build-up offered by any temporary respite. Two factors had materially helped Cunningham: one was radar, which gave early and accurate warning, day or night, of the enemy disposition of attacking aircraft or ships; the second was the ability of his ships to fight at night. Mussolini wanted and hoped for Tunisia, so as to shorten the journeys of his supply ships and reduce the hazards, but France refused to co-operate.

Hitler did not entirely neglect the Mediterranean during his advance into Russia. Against Raeder's advice not to weaken the Atlantic

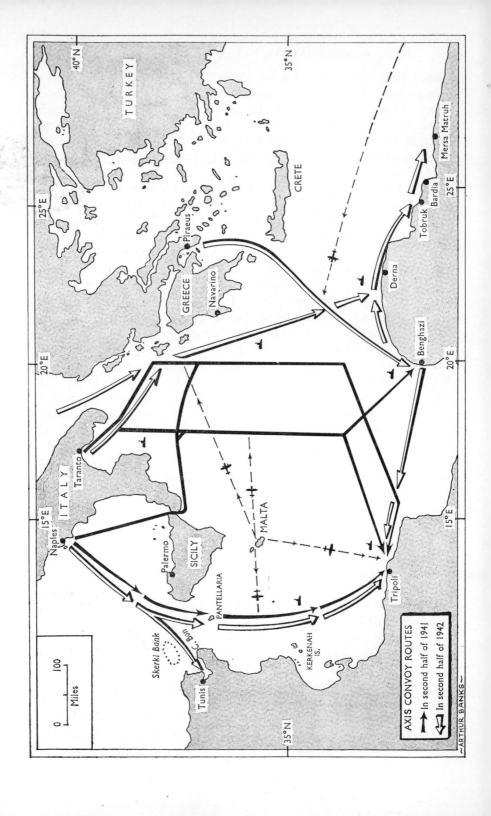

16 *C-in-C's operational staff in* HMS Queen Elizabeth, *late 1941. Left to right: Culme-Seymour, Dick, Edelsten, ABC, Bousfield, Wood, Brownrigg, Hubback, Norman*

17 *The First Sea Lord, Admiral of the Fleet Sir Dudley Pound, on board* HMS Prince of Wales *with* US *Chiefs of Staff in Argentia Bay, Newfoundland, August 1941, for agreement on the Atlantic Charter*

18 *The destroyer* Kipling *emerging from a smoke screen threatens the Italian battleship* Littorio *at the second battle of Sirte, March 1942*

19 *August 1942: the American tanker* Ohio *is helped into Grand Harbour, at a critical stage in Malta's history*

20 *Part of the massive assault convoy for the North Africa landings, November*
1942

21 *View of part of the covering force for the North Africa landings, November 1942 as seen from* HMS Formidable. *Left to right:* Renown, Rodney, Duke of York, Victorious

submarine offensive, six U-boats were sent into the Mediterranean in September 1941, and this number was in due course increased to 25. Before the end of the year five U-boats had been detected and sunk in the Straits. Improved German mines were also laid.

On 1 November Cunningham was delighted to welcome Rear-Admiral Philip Vian who assumed command of the 15th Cruiser Squadron in succession to Vice-Admiral King. Vian already had a distinguished record of service as a fighting sailor, and Cunningham regarded him as a considerable addition of strength to his fleet. British ships in the Mediterranean were now however to experience a time of great adversity.

Among British losses in the next few weeks were the carrier *Ark Royal* of Force H on 14 November, 25 miles from Gibraltar after being torpedoed; the battleship *Barham*, sunk on 25 November off the Libyan coast by U331 (von Tiesenhausen) after skilful penetration of a strong destroyer screen; the light cruiser *Galatea*, sunk off Alexandria by U557 on 14 December; the cruiser *Neptune* and destroyer *Kandahar*, mined 20 miles north-west of Tripoli 19 December.

Cunningham had taken the *Queen Elizabeth*, *Barham*, and *Valiant*, and eight destroyers, to sea 24 November 1941 to cover a force consisting of the cruisers *Ajax*, *Neptune*, *Naiad*, *Euryalus*, and *Galatea*, under Admiral Rawlings, in a search for two Italian convoys bound for Benghazi. Cunningham[12] describes the loss of the *Barham*, an event almost as shocking as the loss of the 'mighty' *Hood*. 'Patrolling between Crete and Cyrenaica, I was sitting in my bridge cabin in the *Queen Elizabeth* having tea. I suddenly heard and half felt the door give three distinct rattles, and thought we had opened fire . . . then I saw the *Barham*, immediately astern of us, stopped and listing heavily . . . a minute or two later there came the dull rumble of a terrific explosion as one of her main magazines blew up. It was ghastly to look at, a horrible and awe-inspiring spectacle.'

The fleet gunnery officer[13] describes Cunningham's reactions:

'I was duty staff officer on the bridge when *Barham* was hit. ABC was having tea in his sea cabin, and the juddering of the door had ABC up before I could call him. It was then that he showed such a speed of decision and action as I have never seen before or since.

'He increased the speed of the fleet and altered the zigzag. He detailed destroyers to hunt and those to pick up survivors, and gave attention to many other items. He asked no advice and required no reminders from the whole staff who were up by this time, and there was nothing he forgot.'

There were but 450 survivors, including Vice-Admiral Sir Henry Pridham-Wippell, flying his flag in the *Barham*, out of a complement of 1,311.

The Chaplain[14] of the *Queen Elizabeth* writes:

'I was having tea in our gunroom when we heard an almighty explosion and went out to see what was happening. I went up to the signal-deck, and from there saw the *Barham* with smoke pouring out going in a circle and gradually heeling over. Large numbers of the ship's company could be seen on the hull, like a swarm of bees, and then about four and a half minutes from the original impact *Barham* blew up – turrets, guns, and other bits of ironmongery were hurled into the air. It seemed like the *Hood* and most of us expected only a handful of survivors. I looked up to the flag deck and there was ABC – showing no signs of emotion – giving orders for the disposition of the fleet – the destroyers allocated to save life and to hunt the submarine, as if it was a copybook exercise in naval warfare.

'What was going on in the minds of our own ship's company I don't know. If it had not been for a zig or zag shortly before the enemy submarine fired her torpedoes we would have been the recipients not the *Barham* (at least that is what most of us thought), and furthermore we had been in company with the *Barham* some time and all had friends amongst her ship's company. I asked the captain if I could say some prayers from the broadcaster in the lobby. He referred the request to ABC who gave his permission on the understanding, which I explained before asking the ship's company to join in thought with the prayers, that if an order was given this clearly must interrupt the prayers, and particularly asking those on look-out not to allow their concentration to be interrupted. The sense of the whole ship's company being united during that time of prayer was quite apparent. I was glad ABC did not refer to these prayers later when I had come to know him much more intimately, but I did speak of this after his death, to his wife, who said that this had clearly made a deep impression on him.'

Worse was to follow. Courageous Italian swimmers had long been developing attacks in which they piloted sea chariots. There had been many failures. On the night of 19 December 1941, however, three of them, piloted by de la Penne, Marceglia, and Martellota, managed to enter Alexandria harbour unobserved while British destroyers were passing through the open gate. They mined the battleships *Queen Elizabeth* and *Valiant*, and a tanker, and thus at one fell swoop brought about a dramatic change in the balance of naval power. The fact that Japan had entered the war less than a fortnight earlier, without a declaration of war, and had sunk the American battle fleet at Pearl Harbor, and three days later had sunk H.M. ships *Prince of Wales* and *Repulse*, added heavily to what had become a very grave situation.

Cunningham now had only the light cruisers *Naiad*, *Dido*, and *Euryalus*, and the anti-aircraft cruiser *Carlisle*, in the eastern Mediterranean, and the *Penelope* and *Ajax* at Malta, with no possibility of receiving battleships because of the new situation in the Far East. Nor was there any immediate prospect of receiving a carrier. The *Illustrious* and *Formidable* were still completing repairs in America, and the new carrier *Indomitable*, earmarked for the Far East, had run aground.

Fortunately the two Alexandria battleships settled vertically and in shallow water, so that it was a month or two before the enemy realised their own advantageous situation, and Cunningham took every precaution to maintain the deception. Bishop Fleming recalls to mind a copy of the *Illustrated London News* a short time later, which had 'a splendid picture of Divisions on board the flagship of the Mediterranean Fleet – actually stuck to the bottom'.

Yendell writes: 'On this morning as I was arriving at the office I thought the *Queen Elizabeth* looked a little "funny", then saw a submarine alongside and that *Queen Elizabeth* was lower in the water with a slight list. But for colours that day ABC had the Press down; and photographs of colours and ABC were in the papers the next day (with no sign of list or submarine) and I believe it was months before the Italians knew the result of the attack.'

Admiral Glennie says: 'My most vivid memory of him was on the quarter-deck of the *Queen Elizabeth* after she and *Valiant* had been savaged by Italian midget submarines. I went down to see him and was met with: "If you've come with your damned sympathy I don't want it." Brave words in view of the severity of the blow.'

Rear-Admiral Creswell[15] had charge of the security of the port, as Port Admiral. 'It may be of interest,' he wrote, 'to tell you what happened after that dreadful morning when the two battleships were disabled. I went over and offered Cunningham my head to put in the hole, and he said, "It's not your fault at all." There was later a Court of Inquiry in which I was, I suppose, the prisoner. The inquiry was utterly frank and all the truth came out except one item. Some time before, I had asked Cunningham for an Extended Defence Officer for the boom, and got a reply that my demands for officers were insatiable.

'A few days later one of Cunningham's staff came over and said, "We were expecting a come-back from you." I replied, "No. If Cunningham says that, then that is that." I think the Court must have known of this and fished a bit as to whether I had ever had more officers refused me, but I evaded the matter.

'Incidentally we defeated future attacks by the simple expedient of burning our searchlights continuously spread out to the widest possible beam, and submersibles always thought they had been spotted and made off.'

The Admiralty once again was forced to consider the advisability of withdrawing from the eastern basin of the Mediterranean, but decided against. The future looked darker than ever. Rommel stood at the gates of Egypt, though still denied possession of Tobruk, whose maintenance by the British inshore squadron had cost Cunningham 25 warships, five merchant ships, two hospital ships, and many of their brave ship's companies. The Luftwaffe returned in strength to Sicily in December 1941, and Hitler sent Marshal Kesselring to Rome to organise the neutralisation of Malta.

Although the outlook was bleak, Britain, led by an unflinching Churchill, could be cheered by the thought that her resistance every-where was stubborn. The knowledge that America was now her ally, though still reeling under the sudden assault at Pearl Harbor, was encouraging. In early December 1941 the Russians had stopped Hitler's armies before Moscow, and for them a terrible winter lay ahead. The Axis held control of the air in the central Mediterranean, and thus prevented Cunningham from exercising his moral ascendancy, but Gibraltar, Malta, and Suez still lay in British hands.

Many of Cunningham's subordinate admirals had had to be relieved because of sickness or fatigue, while he, despite his continued great load of responsibility for two and a half years, appeared to be as fit as ever, and still retained his optimism and humour which were so neces-sary in maintaining the morale of the fleet. Every day, when practicable, he indulged in recreation ashore, either golf or tennis. His Fleet for some 18 months had dominated the Mediterranean at Taranto, Mata-pan, and in many another action, but thereafter the need to lift out the Army from the military disasters of Greece and Crete in operations of which the Navy would always be proud, had deeply eroded the balance of control at sea. There was no let-up in the active operations by Cunningham's forces, and the enemy appeared to be unaware of the opportunities that existed. Never was good leadership more necessary than at this time of adversity. The following account written by his staff officer (operations)[16] gives a first-hand glimpse of the period:

'One of the oddest jobs was when submarines were required to provide power to keep *Queen Elizabeth* [then fleet flagship] afloat after the Italian human torpedo attack on 19 December 1941. I had by this time been relieved in command of *Triumph*, and, as Commander (Submarines) in *Medway*, it fell to my lot to be called from my bunk to organise the operation.

'It was shortly after this that I was abruptly removed from the "sheltered" submarine world to relieve Commander M. L. Power as SO (O) on the C-in-C's staff. Of course we all realised the gravity of the situation, but nobody could have guessed it from the C-in-C's demeanour. I was virtually a stranger to the C-in-C and knew almost nothing of the problems which confronted me. The C-in-C's offices had by this time been established ashore at Gabbari; though the C-in-C still used the flagship. I found myself sleeping in a cubicle which was part of the Main Signal Office, woken by messengers with almost every signal which arrived during the night, and deafened by the constant clatter of typewriters and teleprinters. Many of the signals required me to telephone the C-in-C and propose action, in the sure knowledge that there would be some facet of the situation which I had not appreciated, and which he would be on to in a flash.

'It was some time before I felt any sort of confidence in dealing with these nocturnal crises, or with the ordeal of the morning staff meeting, held in the C-in-C's office. These were, for me, the most unnerving parts of my initiation. Apart from reporting on whatever operations which might be in progress, I was subjected to a regular grilling over the "Daily State". This document showed the whereabouts, condition, and employment of every ship in the fleet, down to the smallest local defence patrol boat or harbour minesweeper. It was my business to know it exactly, and to be prepared to answer any question about any ship.

'I found myself frequently acting as the champion of various destroyers and other small ships whose turn for boiler-cleaning had come round, and were so shown on the Daily State. The C-in-C never accepted this without question – indeed, without a positive inquisition. He demanded chapter and verse in every case – how long since the last boiler-clean, what other defects she had, how long since her last operation, what was planned for her next, and so on. In fact he usually knew all the answers even better than I did, but his unswerving aim was that the fleet should always be ready for sea, and he expected it to "live on its fat" as far as maintenance was concerned. Only with the greatest reluctance would he ever allow a boiler-clean to proceed. I recall a long tussle on behalf of a trawler at Aden which, according to the Flag Officer Red Sea's anguished signals, could hardly get the water in her boiler to simmer, only being allowed the bare minimum time to boiler-clean after her third or fourth request. Even so, she didn't escape his usual stricture, that she was becoming "velvet-arsed"!

'It was during these dreaded boiler-cleaning contests that his eyes assumed their most baleful expression, and he made the curious gestures with his hands down the front of his monkey jacket which resulted in a high degree of polish, usually seen on the seats of desk-bound trousers. There is no doubt that he drove the fleet to the limit, and, in so doing, drove himself harder than any of us realised at the time. Yet he never questioned the submarines' rest periods, and gave his Captains (S) at Malta and Alexandria a completely free hand in operating their flotillas. I know that this trust was very highly appreciated by both of them.

'One of my very early tasks at a staff meeting was to report that my late ship, the submarine *Triumph*, was overdue and must be considered sunk. He looked at me for a long time, his eyes sad, and then said very quietly, "Poor *Triumph*". He never referred to her again.

'I gradually learned to take the staff meetings in my stride, and it would be quite wrong to give the impression that they were always an ordeal. Often they were a riot of laughter, and enlivened by two little games of which he was extremely fond. He loathed the Signalese expression "Come up", and any staff officer unguarded enough to report that so-and-so had "come up" with a signal would be greeted with roars of delight and ordered to put a piastre in the "come-uppance box" which he kept on his desk. Similar fines were imposed on anyone referring to No. 201 Naval Co-operation Group RAF (HQ at Ras-el-Tin at that time) as "201 Group". The words "Naval Co-operation" were obligatory, and were, indeed, a reflection of the battle he had fought with his fellow Cs-in-C in Cairo to get an RAF Group specifically detailed and equipped for Naval Co-operation.

'I don't know what he did with the fines, but I suspect he used them to buy the boiled sweets which he always kept in a tin on his desk, and which he sometimes used as a peace offering after a stormy scene. I shared an office with Tom Brownrigg (Master of the Fleet), Michael Culme-Seymour (SOO 2) and Douglas Alston (misleadingly entitled Staff Officer Intelligence Afloat). This adjoined the C-in-C's office, with a connecting door and another door on to a balcony which ABC used as a "stern walk", and which gave him a good view of the harbour. We never knew when he wasn't going to erupt into our office. Often enough it was to take one of us to task about something, eyes gleaming, hands massaging his monkey jacket, language pungent. Equally abruptly he would be gone, nearly always to return a few minutes later with his box of boiled sweets, his blood pressure perceptibly lower, to offer one to his late victim.

'I never knew ABC to use Christian names or nicknames. He referred to people, and addressed them either by their job title (e.g. COS, FEO, RA(D), etc.), or by their surnames. From the time I joined his staff he always addressed me as "Woods", but previously I had always been "*Triumph*", which, I confess, gave me a considerable feeling of pride.

The only exception to this rule was Captain Boustead (Chief of Intelligence Staff). ABC professed to treat all intelligence as somewhat lunatic guesswork. "No deductions," he would say. "Give me the facts. *I* will make the deductions." He had such a gift for getting the essentials out of signals and documents that he really knew it all. He could never resist pulling COIS's leg, and every morning he would ask him, "Well, Bouser, any dirty stories this morning?" COIS was usually able to oblige, but if he failed, out came the "come-uppance" box.'

Boiled sweets and fines may sound trivial alongside the more significant items in the command and administration of a fleet, but it is often the trivialities and a sense of humour that enable the sailor to endure the rigours and monotony of ship life in wartime. In one destroyer leaving Alexandria for Crete to attempt yet another rescue operation, a sailor was heard to remark as he inflated his Mae West: 'This is all the ruddy air support I'll get this trip.'

James Munn, captain of the *Hereward*, lost off Crete 29 May, was taken prisoner that day. Shortly beforehand he had stayed with the Cunninghams during a period of boiler-cleaning. He had been Flag-Lieutenant to ABC in the *Hood* in 1937, and had also served in the *Coventry* when ABC was RA(D) Mediterranean. He remarks that ABC mellowed a lot after his destroyer days. He also comments on the kindness and hospitality of the C-in-C and Lady Cunningham. 'At Alexandria,' he writes, 'their house was often full of people who were tired, or who had lost their ships, or were in need of a rest. I remember Denis Boyd being there on one occasion and he could not stop talking about and blaming himself for the damage to the *Illustrious*. ABC was always in good form and after dinner made us all lie down on the floor and throw ping-pong balls into the electric light bowl hanging from the ceiling. I wrote home to my family saying I felt certain we would win the war.'

Despite his own personal tragedy, great losses, and heavy responsibilities at this time of adversity, Cunningham remained the great inspiration for the officers and men of the Mediterranean Fleet.

In Adversity: Defiance
(January 1942–March 1942)

The year 1941 had ended with the relief of Tobruk, and with British troops driving Rommel's Afrika Korps out of Cyrenaica. General Auchinleck, having succeeded Wavell, had taken over an accumulation of armour and equipment which had arrived via the Cape and Suez. His determined drive was brought to an end on 6 January 1942, however, at Agadebia near the border of Tripolitania, largely due to outrunning supplies and the sudden deterioration of the British position in the Far East. The situation was worsened in December 1941 by the transfer of Fliegerkorps II from the Russian front to Sicily and North Africa.

Within a few days Rommel began a counter-attack. He recaptured most of Cyrenaica in a fortnight and drove Auchinleck back to Tobruk. By 7 February he occupied Gazala. 'Bomb Alley' was once more very much under the control of the Luftwaffe. Two convoys of tanks and fuel were safely escorted to Africa by the Italian fleet in January 1942, unmolested by Cunningham's ships. Meanwhile air attacks on Malta increased, and her situation was becoming critical and her striking power negligible.

Despite the arrival of Fliegerkorps II, which had struck particularly hard at Malta while Italian convoys were on passage, the Naval Co-operation Group No. 201 of the RAF, which Cunningham had demanded for so long, provided reconnaissance and fighter protection, and made it possible to transfer fuel in the *Glengyle* and the *Breconshire* from Alexandria to Malta, and, when opportunity offered, for those tankers which were empty to return to Alexandria. For a few weeks, with great urgency, each side concentrated on getting its own convoys through, generally at the expense of offensive action, though each would inevitably have to endure air attacks. The British plan was for Vian's 15th Cruiser Squadron to escort ships westward from Alexandria until they were met by

Force K and then taken on to Malta. Even before the mining of the *Queen Elizabeth* and *Valiant* in harbour on 19 December 1941, Cunningham had found it impracticable to take the battleships to sea, because of the disproportionate number of destroyers that would be required to act as an anti-submarine screen. There had been a screen of eight destroyers when the *Barham* was torpedoed 25 November 1941, and even this had proved inadequate. When consulted by Cunningham, Vian expressed a preference for available destroyers to be at hand with his own cruiser squadron, rather than allocated as a screen for the battle squadron; thus he would forego battleship support. On 17 December 1941, towards evening, while escorting the *Breconshire* to Malta, Vian had encountered Admiral Iachino, in the *Littorio*, who with a strong force which included four battleships and heavy cruisers was escorting an Italian convoy to Tripoli. However it was believed by Iachino that Cunningham must also be at sea with his battleships, so when Vian made a bold attack with his cruisers and destroyers at sunset, Iachino withdrew to the northward under the impression that Vian, in showing such boldness, must have battleship support in the rear. This brief encounter, subsequently termed the First Battle of Sirte, enabled the *Breconshire* to get safely to Malta.

On 11 March 1942 Vian's flagship the cruiser *Naiad* was sunk by a U-boat, during an operation in which his forces failed to find an Italian convoy which had been reported on passage for Africa. Vian and his flag captain Guy Grantham (whom ABC described as 'that most brilliant and very capable officer') were picked up by destroyers, and returned to Alexandria. Vian (*Action This Day*, p. 84) refers to the fact that Grantham was picked up, completely exhausted, after ferrying non-swimmers to a raft. Three days later Vian hoisted his flag in the newly arrived cruiser *Cleopatra*, and took Grantham as his flag captain.

The Second Battle of Sirte which took place 22 March 1942 was not quite so straightforward as the First Battle of Sirte. There was now no battleship in the eastern Mediterranean, even had Vian wanted one. Few fast supply ships were available, maintenance problems were increasing, and in fact the general situation had never looked so gloomy. Control of the central Mediterranean, especially in the air, had shifted so much into Axis hands that in late February 1942 the Italians had been able to run a large convoy with battleship and cruiser cover without loss, in spite of RAF and FAA sorties. Tobruk, which had been supplied by the small ships at such great cost and sacrifice, was still in British hands, but after the recent reverses in Libya its tenure was extremely insecure, and the same could now be said of Malta whose supplies of aviation spirit and oil fuel were getting very low. Cunningham was

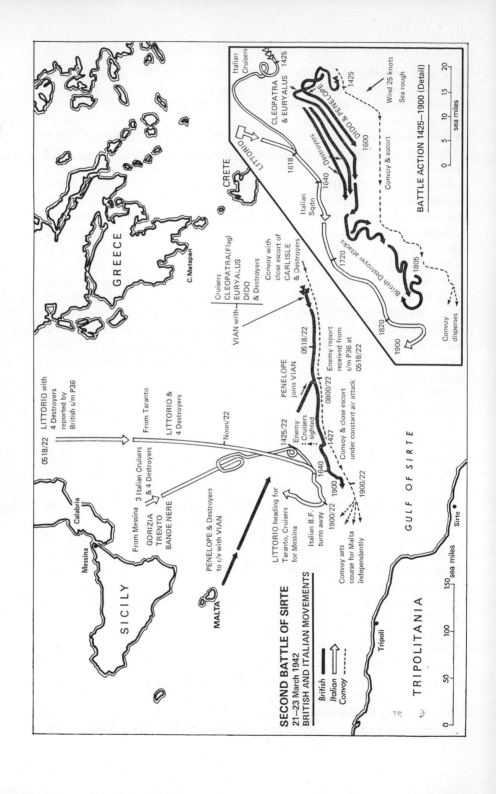

SECOND BATTLE OF SIRTE
21–23 March 1942
BRITISH AND ITALIAN MOVEMENTS

British ▬▬▬
Italian ⇨
Convoy ╍╍╍

SICILY

Messina

Calabria

GREECE

C. Matapan

CRETE

0518/22 ——▶

LITTORIO with
4 Destroyers
reported by
British s/m P36

From Taranto
LITTORIO &
4 Destroyers.

From Messina 3 Italian Cruisers
& 4 Destroyers

GORIZIA
TRENTO
BANDE NERE

Noon/22

1425/22

Enemy
Cruisers
sighted

1427

1640

1900

MALTA

PENELOPE & Destroyers
to r/v with VIAN

LITTORIO heading for
Taranto, Cruisers
for Messina

Italian B.F.
turns away

Convoy sets
course for Malta
independently

1900/22

1900/22

1900/22

GULF OF SIRTE

Sirte

Cruisers
CLEOPATRA(Flag)
EURYALUS
DIDO
& Destroyers

VIAN with

Convoy with
close escort of
CARLISLE
& Destroyers

PENELOPE
joins VIAN

0518/22

0800/22

Enemy report
received from
s/m P36 at
0518/22

Convoy & close escort
under constant air attack

TRIPOLITANIA

Tripoli

Sirte

0   50   100   150
sea miles

BATTLE ACTION 1425–1900 (Detail)

Italian
Cruisers

1425

CLEOPATRA
& EURYALUS

DIDO & PENELOPE

LITTORIO

1618

Italian
Sqdn

1640

Destroyers

1600

1720

1805

1820

1900

1425

Wind 25 knots
Sea rough

Convoy & escort

British Destroyer attacks

Convoy
disperses

0   5   10   15   20
sea miles

however resolved that everything possible should be done to save Malta.

An attempt was to be made to get four supply ships into Malta from Alexandria as a matter of primary importance, with a co-ordinated effort on the part of all three Services. The Army long-range desert group was to create a diversion by raiding airfields behind the enemy lines. The RAF Naval Co-operation Group No. 201 was to provide air reconnaissance, and with the FAA 826 Squadron (ex-*Formidable*) was to bomb western airfields. The RAF was also to attack airfields in Crete and Cyrenaica to keep enemy aircraft grounded. Lunar considerations governed the timing of the operation. The convoy, consisting of the *Breconshire, Clan Campbell, Pampas*, and *Talabot*, sailed from Alexandria at 0700 20 March, escorted by the *Carlisle* (Captain D. M. L. Neame) and six destroyers, the *Sikh* (Captain St. J. Micklethwait), *Zulu* (Commander H. R. Graham), *Lively* (Lieutenant-Commander W. F. E. Hussey), *Hero* (Commander R. L. Fisher), *Havock* (Lieutenant-Commander G. A. G. Watkins), and *Hasty* (Lieutenant-Commander N. H. G. Austen).

At 1800 the same day, Rear-Admiral Vian in the *Cleopatra* (Captain G. Grantham) left harbour with the *Dido* (Captain H. W. McCall) and *Euryalus* (Captain E. W. Bush), and four destroyers, *Jervis* (Captain A. L. Poland), *Kipling* (Commander A. St. Clair Ford), *Kelvin* (Commander J. H. Allison), and *Kingston* (Commander P. Somerville).

Vian's force and the convoy passed safely through Bomb Alley, thanks to diversionary attacks on enemy airfields and cover from fighter defence as previously arranged, and was met early on 22 March by Force K from Malta, now reduced to the cruiser *Penelope* (Captain A. D. Nicholl) and the destroyer *Legion* (Commander R. F. Jessel): see map 17. On the previous day he had also been joined by six 'Hunt' class destroyers that had carried out an anti-submarine sweep in advance between Alexandria and Tobruk. Cunningham himself, it will be remembered, had been responsible for the inception of these light relatively slow destroyers whose great assets were endurance and 4-inch anti-aircraft guns. Of the original seven that had begun the sweep, one, ironically, had been torpedoed by a U-boat. Early 22 March Vian received a report from submarine P36 that an Italian squadron had put to sea from Taranto. He was now some 120 miles north of Benghazi, beyond fighter protection from Egypt, and still 250 miles eastward of Malta. This meant that the convoy would have at least another 24 hours at sea plodding westward. He estimated that the Italians would attempt to intercept that afternoon, and he aimed at holding them off from the convoy until dark, hiding the supply ships to the south by the use of heavy smoke screens through which his force, now divided into six divisions, could penetrate and withdraw at will.

From 0930 onwards, air attacks were made on Vian's force, and on the convoy round which the close escort of 'Hunt' class destroyers had formed. During the forenoon, attacks were principally from Italian torpedo and high-level bombers, and in the face of heavy gunfire were not particularly dangerous. Later in the day came heavier and more dangerous attacks by JU 88s, and the sky over the convoy was full of dark grey shell bursts. The expenditure of ammunition was tremendous. A fresh south-easterly wind was increasing and an ugly sea was rising, but Vian knew exactly what he would do, and each of his divisions understood his intentions from previously practised manoeuvres.

At 1427 the *Euryalus* reported enemy ships to the northward distant 12 miles, two hours earlier than expected. The sea was now rough with a moderate swell. Vian at once led out to the northward with his five striking divisions making smoke, and turned the convoy and its close escort to the south-westward. The ships sighted were in fact the 8-inch cruisers *Gorizia* and *Trento*, and the 6-inch cruiser *Bande Nere* in company with four destroyers. There were a few brief exchanges of ineffectual gunfire at long range. Then the Italian cruisers were seen to alter course to the north-west. Vian signalled Cunningham at Alexandria 'Enemy driven off', and proceeded southward with his divisions to join the convoy which was now under heavy air attack, with *Carlisle* and the Hunts putting up a spirited anti-aircraft fire. But the Italian force had only fallen back to join Admiral Iachino in the battleship *Littorio*, in company with three Italian destroyers. With Iachino they were now steaming south-westward at high speed to intercept the convoy, and were sighted at 1640. Vian at once turned the convoy to the south, and with his divisions all making smoke, again led off northward to intercept the powerful attacking squadron: a modern battleship, three cruisers, and seven destroyers, now to be confronted by four British light cruisers and 11 destroyers.

The direction of the wind, still increasing from the south-east, was most favourable for Vian. His heavy blanket of thick smoke drifting towards the Italians presented a blinding screen, obscuring any sight of either the British convoy withdrawing or of Vian's five divisions advancing upon the Italians. Iachino was as unwilling to approach the screen as he was to engage in a night attack, whereas Vian, under cover of smoke, wished to close to a range suitable for his smaller guns and from which torpedo attacks could be made. At 1644 *Cleopatra* had been hit by a salvo from the *Bande Nere* which caused casualties. Vian was concerned that the Italians would try to work round behind his smoke, either westward or eastward, in order to sight their major objective, the convoy. Firing was sporadic and only feasible when the flashes of guns could be sighted, or a ship dimly seen through the smoke screen. For two hours over this rough sea the battle of wits continued, the Italians scoring many hits, but continually being headed off, more especially by the threat of torpedoes.

The following is a first-hand account by Admiral Sir Guy Grantham,[1] captain of the *Cleopatra* at the battle.

'Philip Vian had all the COs of HM ships and the merchant ships to a conference on board before we sailed. He explained to them what he thought would happen and what he intended all ships should do. In the event his forecast was correct and the only signals he had to make to start the action were "Enemy in sight" and "Engage the enemy bearing . . ."'

'As you know an almost continuous smoke screen was used to shield the convoy and its Hunt class escort, and for much of the time *Cleopatra*, from before the foremost funnel, was showing ahead of the black cloud, except when doubling back and before popping out again to see what the Italian ships were doing. We got a lot of the gunfire and being close straddled by 15-inch shells was quite a noisy experience; they made a tremendous bang when they hit the water. At the same time we were being bombed and we could see the convoy being attacked by many waves of bombers. We used our three forward turrets for firing at the enemy ships, and the two after turrets against aircraft.

'We, in *Cleopatra*, were hit only once, by a 6-inch shell which I saw coming apparently straight at me, though it sheered off at the last moment and hit the starboard fore corner of the bridge, where Philip normally stood or sat on his stool chair. I was in my usual position, port fore corner; he was luckily having a quick look at our position in the chart house. That shell killed 14 and brought down all our W/T aerials. But it did not harm the main armament director and we were able to continue firing normally.

'The action started at 1427 when the enemy light forces drew back on the enemy battleship and heavy cruisers, and it then began again at 1640. I had forgotten to wind my watch the night before and the day seemed endless. When we were getting low in ammunition I looked at my watch (1730) and said to the Admiral, "I don't think we shall have enough rounds to last until dark." It was heavily overcast at the time and he said it would be dark in under half an hour, as of course it was. The enemy withdrew at high speed at dusk.'

In Alexandria Cunningham was watching every reported event on a large chart in his war room, experiencing 'the mortifying bitterness of sitting behind the scenes with a heavy load of responsibility while others were in action with a vastly superior force'.[2]

Colonel Moseley[3] describes the scene:

'One of the most thrilling and memorable events in my life was attending the ops room during the whole of Admiral Sir Philip Vian's escort of a vital convoy to Malta with his light cruisers, when the Italian battleship *Littorio*, heavy cruisers, and escorts, came out to intercept. The excellence of naval communications meant that ABC had his operations table plotted with the movements of both forces, and he received all signals and sightings as they were made. Never once did he interfere though continually making such comments as "Good boy!", "That is correct", then "Now is the time for a daylight destroyer attack", "One hit on a *Littorio* and they will all group round in protection". A few minutes later came the signal from Vian for his destroyers to attack. "There you are, he is right again." No other comment while he paced up and down. Then the dramatic claim of a hit and ABC's great joy. The Italians did as he said. Finally Vian's "night dispositions" and intention to withdraw. Here ABC intervened for the first time. "The convoy will need the *Carlisle*'s anti-aircraft protection entering Malta, we must instruct Vian to detach her." It was a great experience to be at his side during so thrilling and important an occasion. His confidence and infectious enthusiasm kept his entire staff at their best.'

By 1855, after receiving torpedo attacks at a range of 6,000 yards and with approaching darkness, Iachino deemed it essential to break off action and return to base. The sea was so rough on the return passage that his ships suffered serious damage, and the destroyers *Scirocco* and *Lanciere* which had survived the action foundered in the gale. The cruiser *Bande Nere* was so badly damaged that she had to be sent to Spezia for repairs, and was sunk by the submarine *Urge* while on passage. The *Urge* had already had the distinction of torpedoing the battleship *Vittorio Veneto* on 14 December 1941, putting her out of action for several months.

Although the convoy had been saved and sent on to Malta in the hope that they would cover most of the distance before daylight, while Vian, now particularly anxious about his fuel and ammunition shortage, immediately turned eastward into the gale, the morning of 23 March saw a renewal of the Axis air attacks on the convoy. The *Penelope* and the *Legion* had detached from Vian to return to Malta with the convoy and the Hunt class destroyers, together with the *Carlisle* and the damaged destroyers *Havock* and *Kingston*. Anti-aircraft fire had to be drastically curtailed owing to shortage of ammunition, and the four supply ships had to run the gauntlet of attacks all the way to the Grand

Harbour. Some protection was afforded by Spitfires and Hurricanes from Malta, but these were in disarray following four days of concentrated Axis air attacks. Soon after 0900 the *Talabot* and *Pampas* entered Malta's Grand Harbour, to the great relief and joy of spectators who watched from the battlements regardless of falling bombs. About this time the *Breconshire* was hit and disabled while still eight miles from the breakwater. Her deep draught and the rough sea frustrated immediate attempts to tow her in, until the following night when she was taken into Marsa Xlokk. Two days later she was hit by a bomb and set on fire. Cunningham speaks highly of her Captain C. A. G. Hutchison, DSO*, OBE, who had brought her safely through so many perilous occasions, and calls him a fine seaman and stern disciplinarian. Hutchison modestly attributes much to his *Britannia* training.[4] The *Pampas* and *Talabot* were also hit while in harbour, presenting easy targets for the Stukas from Sicily that now so greatly outnumbered Malta's fighters. The *Clan Campbell* had been sunk by a bomb 20 miles from harbour. Of the 26,000 tons of cargo and oil fuel, brought from Alexandria at such great cost, only about a fifth was safely unloaded. Nevertheless every bit and every drop was needed, for Malta was close to collapse under the new onslaught which had begun in March 1941. In the face of tremendous hazards the operation had been a bold and brilliant achievement.

'You will remember,' continued Grantham, 'that the *Breconshire* reached Marsa Xlokk and was later sunk in shallow water. They got most of the stuff out of her. If the *Talabot* and *Pampas* had been deliberately beached at the top of Grand Harbour, they would have managed to unload practically everything they were carrying and would have saved a big salvage operation after the war.'

Vian arrived at Alexandria about midday 24 March, his ships having suffered damage from heavy seas despite reduced speed. Woods[5] refers to 'a tremendous reception by the ships in harbour. I was on the stern-walk with the C-in-C and COS, and a moving moment it was. ABC was unnaturally silent at first, but then all his delight burst out, and he cheered with the rest of us.' His silence may have been due to information which he had received earlier that he was due for a new appointment.

Endured hardship and constant tough action might be expected to make men reproachful; yet such experiences seem in practice to bring out the best in men, and it is certain that ABC was aware of this. The captain of the *Dido*,[6] next senior to Vian in Force B, had brought the *Dido* back to the Mediterranean in December 1941 after four months of repair in America following disablement during the battle for Crete. His ship had been pretty constantly at sea, ever since, running supplies to Malta, with extra jobs thrown in by the Commander-in-Chief. It was less than ten days before sailing for what was to become the Second Battle of Sirte that Vian's flagship the *Naiad* had been sunk. McCall writes:

'On returning from one of these trips on 11 March 1942 *Naiad*, his flagship, was torpedoed and sunk in the middle of the night; this left me, as senior captain, in command of the force. Luckily he together with practically the whole ship's company were picked up by destroyers. But I was distinctly worried about him, as walking ashore with him just before that operation, he was exceedingly stiff as a result of unaccustomed riding on a horse, and I imagined that swimming about in a cold sea wouldn't have done him any good at all. I knew that in a few days' time we were due to try and force through the biggest convoy yet to Malta. After getting into harbour I therefore went ashore to find him in bed in the C-in-C's house. Anxiously asking ABC if he thought Philip would be fit enough to get to sea in command, he replied, "Yes you needn't worry. We are feeding him up on all the stout he can take, and he will be all right. But it's not very nice for you to see your flagship sunk like that. And the answer is a bit of offensive action. So in two days' time you will take the squadron with you and bombard Rhodes".'

This offensive action was carried out in the early hours of 15 March by *Dido*, *Euryalus*, and six destroyers, with McCall in command; and within a day or two the ships were due to sail westward on a most hazardous operation.

'One of his staff told me,' continues McCall, 'that when we were about to get back into Alexandria after Sirte he broke up a staff conference, saying, "Come on, come on, we must get out of here and give a proper welcome to my magnificent Fleet."

'Service under "our greatest sailor since Nelson" and to have commanded one of his ships in war was a wonderfully fortunate experience to have had. Provided one stood up to him it was also entirely satisfying knowing you could count on friendship and backing.'

Cunningham considered the action in the Gulf of Sirte to be one of the most brilliant naval actions of the war, if not the most brilliant, and commented on the heavy and accurate Italian gunfire. He regarded it as an act of Providence that there was not more considerable damage among Vian's ships during the battle, and still more so that not one was sunk. Vian was created KBE for his fine performance, and various decorations were bestowed on those who had taken part in the battle.

Attacks by the Luftwaffe were still increasing and had reached such a pitch that all ships had to leave Malta as soon as they could steam. The *Carlisle* and Hunt class destroyers sailed for Alexandria 25 March, and the *Havock* and *Penelope* as soon as they were patched up. The *Kingston*

22 *At the opening ceremony of the Allied* HQ *in Algiers, 17 November 1942.*
Left to right: *front row, Michelier, Clark, Cunningham, Anderson, Darlan*

23 *At Cunningham's villa, Algiers, February 1943*

24 *Combined Chiefs of Staff conference at Casablanca, January 1943. On the left, King, Marshall; on the right, Dill, Portal, Brooke, Dudley Pound, Mountbatten, Ismay*

and with her, her gallant captain, was destroyed in dock. Nevertheless it was still the intention to hang on to Malta at all cost, and in April 1942, the month of Malta's supreme trial, vital supplies were run in by sub-marines, and ammunition in the fast minelayer *Welshman*. Also more fighters were flown in.

But Sirte was to be the last operation under Cunningham's direction for a few months, for his new appointment was to relieve his old *Britannia* class-mate Admiral Sir Charles Little as head of the British Admiralty Delegation in Washington, and he himself was to be relieved by the victor of the River Plate Battle, Admiral Sir Henry Harwood. Cunning-ham was to haul down his flag (1 April 1942) in the Command which he had held since 1 June 1939 and in which he had made an imperishable reputation, holding tremendous responsibility for nearly three years during which his fleet, though often outclassed materially, had main-tained a moral ascendancy over the Italian Navy.

Cunningham disliked leaving the Mediterranean Fleet, particularly at a time when their fortune was at its lowest ebb, but he had always made it a rule not to question any appointment. In a letter to the First Sea Lord he mentioned that one of the most difficult jobs now was keeping up the morale of the sailors. It was not easy to sit in an armchair and send ships to sea, fully realising the hazards and hardships involved.

'If one went oneself it would make all the difference,' he concluded. This had always been the case, though not quite in the intended sense. It was still a fact that the men of the fleet had the greatest respect for the Commander-in-Chief's defiant attitude, and his fortitude and resolution. His presence had been a continual inspiration.

The Combined Chiefs of Staff, Washington (June 1942–October 1942)

For the reader to appreciate Cunningham's close and successful association with the Americans, it is important to understand the developing and changing scene of Anglo-American relationships. The author was privileged to see much of this at close quarters, when sent to Washington in September 1941 as a liaison officer, having arrived at Norfolk, Virginia, a few days earlier in the disabled *Formidable*. This was before Pearl Harbor, and although American policy was for help, where possible, short of war, there was a decidedly neutral attitude in general. To many Americans the prospect of their going to war seemed remote. The successful Japanese assault on Pearl Harbor (7 December 1941) therefore came as a shattering shock. It was interesting to witness not only the surprise but the sudden change in attitude. Until this moment we British officers had, of necessity in a neutral country, worn plain clothes. Now we sallied forth in uniform, as did the American forces, and there was a common bond, and an end of references to the 'phoney war'.

From the beginning however there had been a keenness among the American armed forces to hear first-hand of our own experiences and to develop Anglo-American understanding for the common good. There had been the offering of 50 old American destroyers in September 1940; the passing of lend-lease arrangements in March 1941 (time of Matapan); and, after a month or two of preliminary staff talks, the institution of a British Admiralty Delegation in Washington in May 1941 (at the time of the battle for Crete). The initial talks were on a high level, conducted in great secrecy, and produced Anglo-American agreement that if Japan should enter the war, thus bringing America in on the side of the Allies, the aim should be to knock out Germany first, while containing the Japanese.

The BAD provided common services for what was to become the British Joint Staff Mission, Washington. It was also intended in the beginning to form the administrative nucleus of a trans-Atlantic Admiralty should the Germans launch a successful invasion upon Britain: this alarming prospect became more remote as soon as the Germans invaded Russia in June 1941.

The Head of the Mission was Admiral Sir Charles Little, and the Army and RAF representatives were initially Lieutenant-General Sir Colville Wemyss and Air Marshal A. T. Harris (later Sir Arthur). The civilian head was Eric Seal (later Sir Eric). The US Chief of Naval Operations at this time was Admiral Stark with whom Little formed an excellent and understanding friendship. In addition to having a Joint Planning Staff and Joint Intelligence Committee, the British Mission was supported by other Committees as the need arose. The term 'Joint' signified the military services of one nation. The term 'Combined' was also soon to be introduced, signifying the combination of British and American military services: an allied committee as distinct from the national.

The term Chief of Staff is so overworked as to be confusing at times to the non-service reader. As is well known, the Royal Navy, the Army, and the Royal Air Force each has its professional head for whom the generic term is Chief of Staff; the specific terms being respectively Chief of the Naval Staff, Chief of the Imperial General Staff, and Chief of the Air Staff. This is straightforward, but it is necessary to remember that the term Chief of Staff also has its use, for example, as a title for the senior officer on a Commander-in-Chief's staff, and for instance the right-hand man of the President of the USA, Admiral Leahy. For a small command such as that of a junior admiral, the more rational term Chief Staff Officer is preferred to that of Chief of Staff.

As soon as America came into the war, Churchill went to Washington, taking with him Beaverbrook (then Minister of Supply), and the three British Chiefs of Staff, Pound, Dill, and Portal. This crucial Washington Conference, ARCADIA, opened on 22 December 1941 and continued until 17 January 1942. There had already been an Anglo-American conference at Argentia Bay, Newfoundland in August 1941, some four months before the Japanese assault on Pearl Harbor. Churchill had taken passage there in H.M.S. *Prince of Wales*, and jointly with Roosevelt agreed on the terms of the Atlantic Charter which, among other matters, resolved that the aggressor nations should be subdued. It was at the Washington Conference in December 1941 that the Combined Chiefs of Staff became established, whose constitution was defined as the 'British Chiefs of Staff (or accredited representatives) and their US opposite numbers'. Hitherto the US had had no formal arrangement for regular consultation between their Army and Navy, and they now set up a USCOS committee on lines similar to the British COS committee. An important item arising in the combined discussion for an agreed American and British policy, a Churchillian touch, was entitled 'The closing and tightening of the ring round Germany'.

The Combined Secretariat was defined as the body of officers duly appointed by the CCS to maintain records. It would be hard to appreciate the formidable difficulties which may attend the recording of agreements and disagreements in words acceptable to all parties concerned. This particularly applies in Anglo-American discussions where certain words and phrases have a different significance, despite the mistaken belief that the British and Americans speak the same language. The formation of the CCS committee and its declaration of grand strategy were events of the highest consequence: General Sir Alan Brooke called it 'the most efficient organisation that had ever been evolved for coordinating and correlating the war strategy and effort of the Allies'.[1]

Upon the return of the Prime Minister with Pound and Portal to London in mid-January 1942, Field-Marshal Sir John Dill, who had already been relieved at home as CIGS by Brooke, remained in Washington to head the BJSM and to serve as Chairman of the Washington Committee representing the London British Service Chiefs. The BJSM were thenceforth to meet the USCOS every Friday, assisted by the Combined Planning and Intelligence Staffs, to agree on the strategic direction of Allied forces and the allocation of man-power, munitions, and shipping. Their function was not only advisory in making agreed recommendations to Roosevelt and Churchill, but executive as soon as final agreement was reached. A weekly meeting of the BJSM was also held at the British Embassy to co-ordinate and progress the work of the various missions.

With the addition of the gigantic resources of America now brought to bear, this should have been a time for optimism, but it was instead one of growing concern, for the enemy was almost everywhere successful; in Russia, the Pacific, and the Atlantic, as well as in the Mediterranean. America had not been ready for war, and upon entry naturally wished to appropriate for herself much of the war material previously allocated to Britain. Both countries had vastly more transport need than could be satisfied by available shipping, and what shipping was in use was being quickly reduced at an alarming rate by increasing U-boat warfare, especially in the first half of the year 1942, when shipping losses amounted to 4,000,000 tons. General Marshall was gravely concerned because a large proportion of the shipping allocated for the transfer of the growing US Army across the Atlantic was being sunk by the enemy. 'The losses by submarine off our Atlantic seaboard and in the Caribbean,' he wrote, 'now threaten our entire war effort.' This shortage of shipping made the task of meeting Russia's continuous demand for an immediate Allied second front quite impracticable.

Almost half of 1942 had elapsed before Cunningham joined the CCS Washington on 25 June, to relieve Admiral Sir Charles Little. A few days earlier Tobruk had fallen to Rommel who, by the end of June, in a lightning thrust eastward reached El Alamein, only 60 miles from Alexandria. The situation in Malta looked grimmer than ever, for in spite of 183 Spitfires flown in by the *Eagle* and the American carrier *Wasp* during April, May, and June, and a double convoy operation (HARPOON from the west, and VIGOROUS from Alexandria) in June, it was possible only to get in two supply ships, for the loss of the cruiser *Hermione* and two destroyers.

The happy, progressive relationship which existed initially in the CCS, Washington, toughened considerably during 1942, a development largely due to what appeared to be a mutual jealousy between the US Army and the US Navy, exacerbated by a conflict of personalities. In spite of seemingly hostile attitudes which appeared from time to time, differences of opinion *were* reconciled, and vital decisions taken. It is valuable to record extracts of reports by observers who were there at the time and who attended the meetings or who worked in Combined committees in the solution of knotty problems, and some of these are given below.

With Dill as Chairman of the BJSM, there were Admiral Cunningham (recently raised to the dignity of a Baronet of the United Kingdom in the King's birthday honours) representing the First Sea Lord, Lieutenant-General G. N. Macready (representing the CIGS), and Air-Marshal D. C. S. Evill (representing the CAS). Cunningham, as Head of the BAD, had Rear-Admiral Wilfred Paterson as his Chief of Staff, but Captain Royer Dick, previously on his Mediterranean Staff, now joined him in Washington as his Deputy Chief of Staff for CCS work. On the American side, with Admiral Leahy (as Chairman of the USJCS, and representing the President), were the opposite numbers of the British COS in London; they were General George Marshall (CSO to the US Army), Admiral Ernest King (CNO and C-in-C of US Fleet), and General Henry Arnold (Commanding General the USAF).

Soon after the institution of the CCS at the time of Pearl Harbor, the BJSM moved headquarters from the limited offices at the British Embassy to the palatial Public Health building in Constitution Avenue, which faced on to the US Army Department and the US Navy Department. This was before the building of the Pentagon. British liaison officers were based mainly in the Public Health building, but had frequent and regular access to their opposite numbers across the road.

Cunningham's arrival coincided with the advent of the hot, damp season in Washington, and whereas American forces then assumed their khaki uniform jackets or shirts, officers of the Royal Navy were expected to wear No. 10 dress: white tunics and white drill trousers. This requirement was relaxed at a later date, after Cunningham's departure from Washington. Fortunately, most buildings in that beautiful modern non-industrial city were air-conditioned, winter and summer.

It had been generally agreed that if it did not prove possible to launch an emergency attack in North-West Europe in 1942 (operation SLEDGE-HAMMER), then the major invasion (operation ROUNDUP) which was to be the death blow to Germany, must be delivered before September 1943. ROUNDUP would be delivered across the English Channel by combined Anglo-American forces; a build-up of American-forces in Britain (operation BOLERO) should therefore take place in the meantime. There was however considerable disagreement as to the timing and practicability of such operations. The Americans, with as yet little experience of transport problems and the unavoidable delays in the building of shipping, landing-craft, airfields, military equipment, and all associated tasks, were aiming at an early date, with the realisation that the Japanese must be held at bay until the Germans were defeated. The British, with experience of Dunkirk, and the difficult provision of forces for the Middle East, were against any premature assault that could lead to failure and perhaps permanent disaster. The Russians however were demanding immediate action by the West, to relieve their perilous situation on the Eastern Front. This seemed to indicate the need for an alternative and immediate operation to forestall the possible collapse of Russia. SLEDGEHAMMER must be dropped because it was not feasible. ROUNDUP might have to be postponed because of delays in BOLERO and shipbuilding. A new operation was now to be considered, called GYMNAST, to be launched in October 1942, and was to comprise an Anglo-American landing in North-West Africa. GYMNAST, later re-named TORCH, met opposition, particularly from Admiral King who was apprehensive about the effect of such an operation on American holding operations in the Pacific. He declared that it would be impossible to provide the shipping and escorts. General Marshall condemned GYMNAST as expensive and ineffectual.

Cunningham found King a difficult character, able and dedicated, but not always co-operative, and often rude and overbearing. Perhaps it was jealousy or envy, a sense of grievance or due to an awareness of Britain's lonely role up to the time of Pearl Harbor. Cunningham also noted the inter-service jealousy which existed between the American Army and Navy, sometimes carried to extraordinary lengths. He admired Marshall for his sincerity and honesty of purpose, and found Leahy charming and courteous, always ready to smooth the difficulties.

Leahy[2] wrote of him: 'Cunningham was my favourite because, in the first place, he was a splendid sailor. He was a daring, experienced, and successful British sea commander, worthy of the tradition of Britain's Nelson. Cunningham was also the best expert in the Allied navies on strategy and tactics in the Mediterranean theatre, which was a focal point of attention of both the Combined and Joint Chiefs when I assumed duty. I presided over the meetings of the Combined Chiefs in the regular Friday sessions.'

It is interesting to read the following impression[3] by one who saw a great deal of the CCS members at this time in their highly responsible task of producing an acceptable and workable strategy. The sketch is also of interest in revealing ABC's tenacity in his relationship with Churchill.

'The British element was pretty influential primarily due to Dill who had the complete confidence of Marshall and indeed his deep friendship. This had its effect throughout American circles, and very soon after he had got settled in, Admiral Cunningham had achieved a high esteem as well. One has to remember that at this time Cunningham was *the* successful British Commander of the war. When he was appointed to Washington, he found on arrival in London prior to taking up the post, that he was to be treated as being on the same level as his juniors who had no high command experience. He quite rightly refused to accept the appointment unless this matter was rectified, but there was stubborn opposition and it was discovered that this came from the Prime Minister himself. Cunningham remained firm, and eventually the Prime Minister asked him to dinner with the idea of softening him up. He did not know his man. Despite an harmonious and hospitable evening, when the time came to leave, Winston said, "Well, good-bye, Admiral, and I look forward to hearing great things of you in Washington." He received the astringent reply: "I do not know if I shall be going until the problems raised have been cleared up." I well remember the Admiral telling me of this next morning with quiet glee. Winston was a man who knew determination when he saw it and gave way. This was not of course personal pique on the Admiral's part but because he well knew that he would have the toughest time dealing with the American Navy, and

King in particular, and it was vital that it should be realised he carried the guns for the task and the full confidence of London.

'The British Washington representation consisted of Dill as undoubted Chairman and leader, with Cunningham as deputy, although this was never an official appointment. But the Airman and General were never in the same standing and this is no reflection on them. Leahy was a man of much determination and shrewdness and, even as important, he wielded great influence with the President, and the Americans well knew that his support was vital if they were to get anything past Roosevelt. He had considerable political ability and, what was more, a highly judicial mind which made him ideal as the Chairman of the CCS. This was a great boon from the British viewpoint, for there were many and sometimes acrimonious discussions in the CCS not so much between the nations as between the Services, and it was a frequent occurrence that the intervention of the British often solved the situation. For instance the best medium as between the US Army and Navy was often the Royal Navy, as the latter seemed to be able to talk to the Army in a way not possible for the US Navy, and it was in this field that ABC often excelled with his aura of a successful Commander at sea. There was however great and enduring difficulty with "Ernie" King. He felt that the place for the US effort was in the Pacific, and thus grudged not only sending ships to Europe but had the constant fear that they would be swallowed up in the British Fleet. "I am not going to have US ships hoisting the White Ensign", was a remark I heard him make to ABC on one occasion when we were pressing for US carriers to help with the submarine war. But in the end a real respect and even liking developed between these two very strong characters. These men were running a great war and had great responsibilities to their country and to those they were leading and directing into battle. They were prepared to fight very hard and rightly so to ensure that their forces were properly equipped, in sufficient force and properly supported. If therefore an individual considered that this was not so in a particular instance it was natural for him to pursue his point of view to the last ditch.

'An instance of the skill with which Leahy conducted matters was on an occasion when Ernie King was in the blackest of moods at a CCS meeting, and after a longish discussion in which he was disagreeing with his colleagues and with Leahy, he got to his feet saying that he had other things to do than sit here arguing, and proceeded to walk to the door. This was, of course, gross discourtesy to the Chairman. Leahy did not turn a hair but as King was walking towards the door, he switched the subject completely and said to ABC in mild tones, "With regard to the provision of aircraft carriers in the Atlantic I have been talking to the

President . . .' King froze in his tracks as this was a matter on which he had the strongest views, and there he was stuck half-way to the door having brusquely said that he was off, but not daring to risk leaving. Leahy appeared to notice nothing and went gently on, talking about his discussion with the President, while King stood first on one leg and then on the other. And then after having thus made his rebuke amply clear he left matters with some innocuous remark which showed that King could in fact quite safely have left. The whole thing was a lesson in gentle control and I do not think that King was likely to forget it even though no actual word of rebuke had been uttered.

'The personalities were widely different, which made it all the more interesting. First there was Admiral Leahy, rather schoolmasterish and sedate. Then King, an evident leader whom one could but respect if not like. Marshall quiet, reserved, and not with much sense of humour, but of complete honesty and firmness of purpose: somewhat difficult of approach, but a man of the calmest judgment and finest character, deeply respected. "Happy" Arnold, the airman, a shrewd swashbuckling type of much force of character and determination to get his own way, but I would not have put him in the same category as those already mentioned. Dill was the epitome of the English gentleman as the Americans always imagine them to be, and this is high praise. As a consequence Dill was able to do so much more than one would have expected of this manifestly able but quiet-spoken and apparently unassertive man. ABC had the undoubted respect and appreciation of all concerned after the initial "running in" period when he was being summed up. The measure of his success was that it was the Americans who insisted that he and only he could lead the Navies for the North African invasion. Our own people were not so percipient.

'One incident I recall which should be recorded. It was ABC who talked of it to me. He said that the CCS meeting in London came to a grinding halt, as is well known, having failed to agree over the next move since the British were unalterably opposed to any invasion of France in 1942, the Americans being strongly in favour. In the end a decision was finally reached out of session by personal discussion between those concerned. So much so that the eventual draft was produced sitting on General Marshall's bed in the small hours. The interesting thing is that these eight or so men, all of undoubted good faith, signed a paper which at the next stage was totally differently interpreted by the two sides.'

This obviously refers to the visit to London (see Ismay, p. 249) of General Marshall and Mr. Hopkins (the President's personal representative) in April 1942, to get agreement on SLEDGEHAMMER and

ROUNDUP, and indicates how essential it is that the records of discussions should be explicit, especially when connotation of expression
may differ on each side. There is no record of Cunningham attending
these talks, but it is likely that he was an observer during the ten days
of consultation in April, in London, prior to going to Washington; he
marked well the points of ambiguity and individual interpretation. At
this time the Americans thought that the British were opposed to an
invasion of North-West Europe because of memories of those years of
attrition and trench warfare in the First World War. They believed that
the British were more concerned with meeting the needs of their struggle
in the Middle East and the Indian Ocean, a task which the Americans
regarded as unessential and a dispersion of effort. The June 1942 collapse
of British forces in the Western Desert as a result of Rommel's lightning
advance eastward brought about a considerable change of American
outlook.

It was one thing for a man of the stature of Cunningham to have to
put up with 'Ernie's' tantrums, but quite another for the 'lower orders'
of the BJSM working in the Operations Division with their opposite
numbers in the Navy Department. It is worth recording the picture as
seen by one of those commanders.[4]

Referring to ABC and King:

'Both were tough, both had been successful in different ways, both
were dedicated but to different causes. I believe they admired each
other for their toughness but differed in almost everything else.

'ABC was broad, stocky, and wore immaculate full whites, and had
been a "salt horse". King was tall and wore US Navy Air uniform, and
was very wedded to Naval Air. ABC had a great sense of humour. King
appeared to have little of that commodity.

'ABC had led a Fleet to victories in the Mediterranean, and was the
admiration of his own country. King had put the US Navy on its feet
again after Pearl Harbor, building up morale and ships by his own
leadership and untiring energy, for which his country was justly proud
and grateful.

'King was naturally bent on revenge for Pearl Harbor, and throughout his period of office he never really appeared to accept the agreed
priorities, always trying to direct the available effort to the Pacific.

'ABC inherited from his predecessors a well chewed bone of conten-
tion, splinters of which penetrated to the lower levels. He probably did
more than most in getting things straight, and in correct priority. The
bone was never really buried for long, it kept on being dug up at conferences at the highest level, but ABC knew what was right and stuck
to it.

'ABC was always very approachable and liked to hear what went on "over the road" (i.e. he was in the Public Health building, and I had an operational liaison office in the Navy Department).

'Another problem was the US Navy's antipathy to their own Army, obviously shared by King. There was an occasion when the US Army came to our Army to see if they could persuade our Navy to persuade their Navy to provide escorts for some convoy! However let it never be forgotten that nothing could have been better than relations I had with all my opposite numbers.

'One of our greatest problems was liaison over the Battle of the Atlantic. It must be remembered that the US had traded 50 reserve "4-stackers" to us for bases; these ships would have been of great use to them on their East Coast.

'Very soon after America was forced into the war by Japan, the U-boats found the East coast of America the most happy of all hunting grounds. Ships carrying cargoes, vital to the Allied war effort, of oil and bauxite from the Caribbean, were sailing independently unescorted to US and Canadian ports. Moreover they were silhouetted against the undimmed lights of the great American seaports. They were picked off one by one as long as the torpedoes lasted, and U-boat replenishment in Mid-Atlantic kept them on station for a considerable time.

'A British trained escort group and numbers of other British anti-submarine craft together with a coastal command unit based on Quonsett helped to patrol the coast; but it was some time before Admiral King would agree to ships being put into convoy, in spite of great pressure from us. Convoy eventually stopped the rot.

'Great strides were made however in jointly defeating the U-boats. The use of VLR (very long-range aircraft), small carriers, support groups and above all the rapid building of escorts in America, Canada, and UK were all co-ordinated and eventually effective.

'The Admiralty submaring tracking room, and methods of keeping it up to date, was reproduced daily in the Navy Department and this helped us in joint escorting of Allied ships and convoys, including both the "Queens".

'When the PM visited the President at the White House the PM's war room was moved to the dining-room of the White House, and a message came through as a "must" that the President was to have a similar picture of all the war theatres. I was given a special pass to the White House, and for the first time had a special view of the PM's war room, with full explanation. As I came out of the door I almost walked into the President's wheeled chair being propelled by the PM, cigar in mouth, both roaring with laughter over some joke, at a time when the war could not have been worse! It gave me a great feeling of certain success.

'Another President's "must" might be of interest. He promised the PM to send a large number of Sherman tanks, as they came off the line, round the Cape to Egypt for the 8th Army. They were available in remarkably quick time, embarked in I think four merchant ships, and route and escorts worked out. One ship was torpedoed soon after they sailed, and another "must" was sent to the Navy Department to replace it at once and sail as soon as further tanks were available, which duly took place.

'One saw many examples of the greatness of the American nation, and some of their weaknesses; but all my experiences then, and since in NATO and at sea off Korea, add up to one conclusion. I would prefer to make friends of and work with Americans rather than any other nation outside the Commonwealth, and for the good of mankind it is essential that we should stick together, recognising and putting up with each other's weaknesses and idiosyncrasies.'

The offer of the 300 tanks and 100 guns was made personally by Roosevelt to Churchill when the almost shattering news of the surrender of Tobruk was handed to Churchill during his visit to the White House in June 1942, and was preceded by the President's question 'What can we do to help?'[5] In six of America's fastest ships, the material arrived in time to play a big part in the victory of Alamein: such was one example of the immeasurable asset of the trust and friendship between those two staunch allies, Churchill and Roosevelt.

Despite doubts on the score of dispersion of effort, and in conformity with the policy of tightening the ring round Germany, and because an attack must be launched somewhere in the West in 1942 to relieve pressure on the Russians, it was decided that SLEDGEHAMMER would be abandoned, and instead operation TORCH should be launched before the end of October 1942. This decision was taken by Roosevelt in late July, counselling his representatives Marshall, Hopkins, and King, who had flown to London on 18 July, to agree with Churchill and the British COS who were resolute for a landing in North-West Africa. From the American point of view a landing in North-West Africa was less distasteful than sending American troops to serve under a British Commander-in-Chief in Egypt. It was agreed that TORCH should be under the supreme command of an American, a soothing of sore feelings that Churchill was quite ready to offer.

In Washington Cunningham had been outspokenly in favour of TORCH, and in a signal to the First Sea Lord on 21 July had said: 'It would go a long way towards relieving the shipping problem once the short route through the Mediterranean was gained. It would jeopardise the whole of Rommel's forces and relieve anxiety about Malta. It would shake Italy to the core and rouse the occupied countries.' Cunningham was also very much aware that Allied airfields along the North Africa seaboard would permit once more the passage of convoys through the Mediterranean: success would bring incalculable gains.

It was on 26 July 1942 that Eisenhower, whose rise to fame had been dramatic, was informed by Marshall that he was to be Supremo, or more exactly Commander-in-Chief Allied Expeditionary Force. A year earlier Eisenhower had reached the temporary rank of Colonel, but since June 1942 had been in England, commanding the build-up of United States Forces (BOLERO), in the rank of lieutenant-general. Major-General Mark Clark was to be the American Task Force Commander, and the British Task Force Commander was to be Major-General K. A. N. Anderson, General Sir Harold Alexander having already been appointed to relieve Auchinleck as Commander-in-Chief Middle East, and Lieutenant-General Sir Bernard Montgomery having assumed command of the Eighth Army in the Western Desert, both in mid-August 1942.

Eisenhower was determined to achieve what he called overall unity, and insisted that each Command must be an integral part of an Allied Force responsible to him as overall commander. His proposal that there should be a single Allied Naval Commander, directly responsible to him, was questioned both in London and in Washington, but he won his point thanks to the convincing influence of Cunningham speaking to the CCS Washington with the authority and experience of a former Commander-in-Chief Mediterranean. In London, Admiral Sir Bertram Ramsay was provisionally nominated for this role, but it was soon realised that there was no officer more fitted to take up this command than Cunningham himself. The fact that he had no fondness for his relatively non-executive post in Washington seemed to indicate that he should be released for this important and exacting command, with Ramsay acting as his deputy.

'Cunningham's selection as Naval Commander Allied Expeditionary Force,' writes Dick,[6] who was to become his Chief of Staff, 'was as the result of American not British insistence, and was largely due to Leahy and Marshall, and was in fact backed up by Bedell Smith who was in the CCS Washington office until he went to join Eisenhower in London as his Chief of Staff.'

In August Cunningham was told definitely that he was to be the Allied Naval Commander of the Expeditionary Force (ANCXF) but the appointment was to be kept secret, and although he would visit

TORCH planning headquarters in London, Lady Cunningham was to remain in Washington as part of the cover to give the impression that he would be returning in due course.

After meeting Cunningham for the first time, Eisenhower wrote:[7] 'He was the Nelsonian type of admiral. He believed that ships went to sea in order to find and destroy the enemy. He thought always in terms of attack, never of defence. In spite of his toughness, the degree of affection in which he was held was nothing short of remarkable.' Eisenhower's affection and confidence grew rapidly, for by late September he was telling Marshall how favourably he had been impressed by Admiral Cunningham. 'I strongly suspect that you may have lent a helping hand toward getting him into this job.' And three days later Ike was pressing Marshall to accept the policy that Cunningham should be his senior naval commander rather than merely a staff officer.

It would be wrong to permit the impression to grow that combined planning was one long bicker. On the whole it went very smoothly, and the fact that so much successful agreement was achieved is due to the patience and intelligence of all those concerned. Many firm and lasting Anglo-American friendships were formed, but also a few strained relationships developed, usually as a result of undue sensitivity over some phrase which might seem to criticise the British; or, in reverse, the Americans. One of the CCS planning staff[8] writes:

'We were discussing the allocation of a batch of the much needed LSTs then coming out of the yards. They had been ordered for us in the first place but now there had to be a share-out and my brief was, I suppose, to get at least a fair share. A recently arrived junior admiral was being extremely unpleasant and wanted to keep the whole batch; in the end he said to me in front of a big Staff meeting, "I wouldn't mind letting some go if I thought for a moment that you damned Britishers would use them offensively!" This was too much for me and I got up and walked out, saying that I was not prepared to discuss the matter any further with him. I was followed by several US officers apologising and asking me to come back.

'I went straight across the road to where ABC had his office and told him the story. Without a word he picked up his cap, told the Secretary to let Admiral King know that he was on his way over and walked off. Within a few minutes he was back and sent for me. "Don't worry," he said. "I don't think that sort of thing will be said to you again".'

To offset this, the following from the same planner reveals a nice touch of typical American charm:

'I was "in attendance" at a meeting of the Combined Chiefs of Staff when the command arrangements for TORCH were being discussed and Admiral Ernie King was being extremely difficult about the Naval proposals, objecting to any US Naval units being placed under British command.

'The Casablanca force for TORCH was to be entirely a US affair and King did not want it to become part of the whole force, commanded, until the landings took place, by Cunningham as Allied Naval Commander under Eisenhower. The meeting became pretty acrimonious, and eventually General Marshall, who was in the chair, said he wondered what the US Admiral concerned thought about it. This was Admiral Hall, a most delightful person whom I got to know quite well later, and he, sitting back from the "High Table" with the planners, said in a quiet voice, "It would be a privilege to serve under Admiral Cunningham".'

The attitude of a group of touring American senators towards the role of British commanders is summed up in the question they put to Secretary Stimson at a later date: 'If Cunningham commands the naval forces, Tedder the air forces, and Alexander the ground forces, what in hell does Eisenhower command?' The obvious answer was that, 'He commands Cunningham, Tedder, and Alexander', and this seemed to satisfy their concern.

Marshall at first showed little enthusiasm for TORCH. There was even less from King, who disliked the idea of permitting US naval forces to be placed under British command. He accepted however a compromise whereby an American naval force would be under the American Commander-in-Chief Atlantic until it passed east of a certain longitude, when it would become subject to the orders of Eisenhower and hence directly under Cunningham, the Allied Naval Commander.

So much has been said about King's attitude concerning his ships serving under British command, that it is of special interest to refer to a letter[9] from the First Sea Lord to Cunningham (24 August 1942) which indicates a more rational approach in the early days of help from USA when Britain stood alone. 'I do not quite understand your remark,' writes Pound, 'about King having a fixed determination not to place any US ships under British command; because we have had their ships working under C-in-C Home Fleet for a very long time.'

In general the Americans were anxious to confine the landings to the Casablanca area on the Atlantic coast of Morocco, whereas the British, anxious to make the best use of a maritime superiority, were urging that landings should be at least as far east as Algiers so that a quick advance to Tunisia would be possible. Cunningham was greatly in favour of making a landing as far east as Bizerta.

In mitigation of King's attitude, it must be remembered that the US

Navy after the crucial battle of Midway was shortly to face the trial of Guadalcanal. But British maritime strength was also continuing to meet sudden reductions, the most recent being the sinking of the old carrier *Eagle* and two cruisers in the Mediterranean in August 1942, during operation PEDESTAL. Out of 14 merchant ships in this heavily escorted convoy, only five reached Malta (including the American-built tanker *Ohio*). Nevertheless this, together with more Spitfires flown in to Malta, was sufficient to save the island for another spell. With the prospect of TORCH, Malta's future began to look more assured.

It was at this time, prior to the detailed planning for TORCH which was to take place in London, that Cunningham did so much to clear the air about the prospects of TORCH, and to dismiss the fears which the US Chiefs of Staff might have in such matters as the security of Gibraltar, the risks from minefields and submarines, the vulnerability of the northern flank should Spain become involved, and the problems of maintaining a large force in the Mediterranean. In his case familiarity with similar problems in the eastern Mediterranean in times of rarer opportunity had bred supreme confidence, but what was most stimulating now was the task that confronted him of organising the biggest Allied landing ever attempted and 'the use of maritime power suddenly to descend on widely separated parts of the enemy held coastline'.[10]

25 HMS Nelson *at Algiers, March 1943.* Left to right: *Eisenhower, Cunningham, Willis*

28 *Sicily landings 10 July 1943: unloading on the beaches soon after dawn*

Allied Naval Commander North Africa Landings (November 1942– February 1943)

Cunningham's appointment to Washington had more than fulfilled the hopes of those responsible. With his tremendous energy and high prestige he had contributed much to the mutual respect between the Allies, and specifically towards the agreement for the launching of TORCH which he regarded as an essential step. Moreover his new appointment as the obvious choice, uniquely qualified for the role of ANCXF, together with the mutual regard and confidence which formulated at once between him and Eisenhower, gave promise of great success. Allied fortunes had been at their lowest ebb in midsummer 1942, yet with the approach of autumn the tide was seen to be steadily turning. The Japanese had been defeated at Midway and were being held in the Pacific. The Russians were holding the Germans at Stalingrad. The submarine menace was being arrested in the Atlantic, and in the Middle East equipment and armour as well as men and aircraft were at last pouring in. Auchinleck had stopped Rommel at El Alamein in mid-July, and his successor Alexander was building up for a big offensive in October.

Divergence of opinion and opposition concerning operation TORCH now faded, and enthusiasm grew. SLEDGEHAMMER had been dropped, and the question as to which year must be selected for operation ROUNDUP was tacitly dropped. What might have been the fate of SLEDGEHAMMER was illustrated by the tragic raid on Dieppe (19 August 1942) by Canadian troops and British commandos. Though well planned by Combined Operations Headquarters, this gallant effort, appeared to be doomed to failure through bad weather, compromise, and ill luck. However there were many lessons which helped considerably in later operational planning.

Briefly, the object of TORCH can be defined[1] as being:

'To capture North Africa from Casablanca to Tunisia, in order to cut Axis sea and air communications in the Mediterranean, and to secure our own; and, in co-operation with Allied forces in the Middle East, to capture the whole southern shore of the Mediterranean.'

TORCH D-day had originally been selected for 30 October 1942. Any earlier was too soon for the completion of plans and the issue of orders, and would allow insufficient time for the marshalling of troops, transport, and landing-craft. There was little possibility in any case for the training which was so necessary for landing-craft crews in embarkation and disembarkation and, even more important, the accurate manoeuvring to ensure arrival at a predetermined point on the beaches at the right time. Cunningham was much concerned about this matter of training. To defer D-day however would increase the risk of weather deterioration, and provide the Germans with more time to strengthen resistance in Tunisia. By the end of September a compromise had been reached and it was agreed that the date for the assault should be 8 November 1942.

There were to be three main landings with 70,000 assault troops in all as follows (see map p. 231):

At Casablanca, in French Morocco on the Atlantic seaboard, the landings were to be carried out by American soldiers escorted and covered by a Western Task Force composed of American ships, the assault to be planned and operated from the US, the ships coming under Rear-Admiral H. K. Hewitt, USN, and the troops under General G. S. Patton. Reinforcement convoys were to follow at regular intervals from the US.

At Oran, some 500 miles farther eastward, and within the Mediterranean, there was to be a Central Task Force, all British ships under Rear-Admiral H. M. Burrough, to escort and cover the landing of those American troops who would come from Britain.

At Algiers, yet another 250 miles farther eastward, there was to be an Eastern Task Force, all British ships under Commodore T. H. Troubridge, to escort and cover the landing of British and American troops from Britain. The British First Army under Lieutenant-General Anderson was to land after the port of Algiers had been secured.

The degree of planning involved can be imagined, the greatest difficulty being the provision of adequate troop-ships, transport, landing-craft, escort vessels, and warships, and this would require the temporary cessation or reduction of existing convoys elsewhere. Cunningham

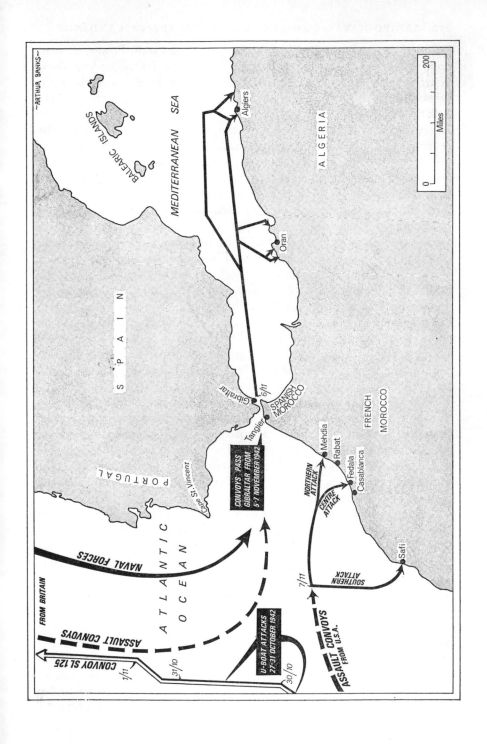

~ARTHUR BANKS~

BALEARIC ISLANDS

MEDITERRANEAN SEA

ALGERIA

Algiers

Oran

S P A I N

P O R T U G A L

Cape St. Vincent

Gibraltar

Tangier

SPANISH MOROCCO

FRENCH MOROCCO

Mehdia
Rabat
Fedala
Casablanca

Safi

NORTHERN ATTACK

CENTRE ATTACK

SOUTHERN ATTACK

7/11

ATLANTIC OCEAN

NAVAL FORCES

FROM BRITAIN

ASSAULT CONVOYS

CONVOY SL 125

7/11

31/10

30/10

ASSAULT CONVOYS FROM U.S.A.

CONVOYS PASS GIBRALTAR FROM 5-7 NOVEMBER 1942

U-BOAT ATTACKS 27-31 OCTOBER 1942

6/11

0   200

Miles

gathered three members of his old Mediterranean staff, Power, Brown-rigg, and Barnard, to work with his Chief of Staff Commodore Dick, to write the plans and prepare the necessary written instructions for ships. All the preliminary work for the landings, except that by the Americans at Casablanca, was done at Norfolk House in London. Close co-ordination was maintained with the Americans at every step. The orders laid down the duties and movements for close on 300 naval vessels, battleships, aircraft carriers, cruisers, minelayers, auxiliaries, destroyers, submarines, sloops, corvettes, and light craft, and dealt with the exact timing of 400 ships of different size and speed, passing through the eight-mile width of the Straits of Gibraltar.

Cunningham referred to Gibraltar as the hinge-pin of the whole operation. On 1 November 1942 he hoisted his flag there as Allied Naval Commander, taking command, under Eisenhower, of the maritime side of the whole operation, his command extending eastward from the Straits of Gibraltar to cover all that part of the Mediterranean to the west of the Narrows at Cape Bon. Both Eisenhower and Cunningham had offices in a tunnel burrowed in the Rock. Cunningham also had an office in the dockyard, and speaks of the thrill of being once again amongst the sea-going Navy. He and his personal staff lived at The Mount, the official residence of Flag Officer Gibraltar, Vice-Admiral Sir Frederick Edward-Collins.

Although the operation was not due to take place until 8 November there were, from early October, many advance convoys with special personnel for Gibraltar, and an unending train of colliers, tankers, annunition ships, tugs, destroyers, and auxiliaries, for all of which new re-fuelling arrangements had to be effected. Cunningham sent for Captain G. N. Oliver, who had been his gunnery officer in the *Rodney* in 1930, and had him appointed to Gibraltar.

'In the autumn 1942,' writes Oliver,[2] 'I was summoned by ABC to Norfolk House, whither he had been smuggled home from Washington to be Naval Commander of the TORCH landings in North Africa. He sent me to Gibraltar as Commodore (Flotillas), to attend to the numerous destroyers escorting the TORCH convoys as they approached the straits. They had to detach from their convoys in relays and pop into Gibraltar to refuel and pick up their operation orders, special charts, fresh provisions, etc., and be generally briefed before going on. All this was very necessary. So let it never be said, at least on this occasion, that ABC neglected administration.'

Cunningham says that Gibraltar stood up well to the superhuman exertions demanded. Force H, still based on Gibraltar, and now under Vice-Admiral Sir Neville Syfret, was specially reinforced as a safeguard against the possible appearance of the Italian fleet, and consisted of the battleships *Duke of York* (Flag) and *Rodney*; the battle cruiser *Renown*; the carriers *Formidable*, *Victorious*, and *Furious*; the cruisers *Bermuda*, *Argonaut*, and *Sirius*; and 17 destroyers. The Eastern and Central Task Forces, composed largely of cruisers and destroyers for close cover of the landings and bombardment of any opposition from shore artillery, had in addition carriers to give local fighter protection. These task forces were to be reinforced by Force H as requisite, provided there was no overall requirement to oppose strong enemy forces at sea.

Command in the air was divided into an Eastern Area which covered Gibraltar, the sea to the east of Gibraltar, and the coast of Africa east of longitude 1°E, under Air-Marshal Sir William Welsh of the RAF; and a Western Area which covered French Morocco as far east as longitude 1°E, under Major-General James Doolittle of the USAF. The RAF at Gibraltar shared an operations room with the Navy in the tunnel, wherein the progress of convoys in the Atlantic and the presence of reported German submarines could be seen on large charts on the walls. Although resources were still limited, the days of dire shortage were past, and Cunningham speaks of the 'outstandingly fine work' of the RAF operating from a congested airfield on the North Front of the great Rock.

German submarine activity began to increase in October 1942, following receipt by them of reports of many ships assembling in the ports of Great Britain and America. It was realised that a large Allied expeditionary force was to be shipped overseas, but German deduction was that it would take the form of an assault on Dakar; U-boats were accordingly massed around Madeira and the Azores. In consequence a large British convoy, SL 125, homeward bound from Sierra Leone, was intercepted in the vicinity of the Canary Isles and Madeira, and during four successive nights lost 13 ships. It may have been largely for this reason that all the TORCH convoys, including those from America, had the incredible luck to get through the Straits unscathed, and mostly unseen. The element of surprise was complete. Even after the appearance of an invasion fleet within the Mediterranean, German deduction was that it was a large convoy for Malta, or possibly reinforcement for the Western Desert. The Flag Officer at Freetown (Rear-Admiral F. A. Pegram)[3] wrote to Cunningham: 'I have nothing but admiration for the perfectly astounding feat you achieved in getting the XF to North Africa unscathed. Watching the progress of convoys from this end we were left with the impression that a miracle had occurred.'

There were of course other reasons for this great success, and Cunningham lists the precautions[4] that had been taken. 'Good routing, and good escort work and handling of convoys entered into it. Additional anti-submarine vessels patrolled the Bay of Biscay. Heavier surface forces patrolled between Iceland and Greenland, and between Iceland and the Faroes, in case German heavy ships tried to break into the Atlantic. The demands upon Coastal Command of the RAF were heavy. Bomber Command was called upon to provide escort to the convoys, and together with the Eighth USAF carried out precision bombing of the U-boat bases in the Bay of Biscay and Brest.'

The Allied Naval Commander had every reason for satisfaction. He it was who for two and a half years had endured shortage and limitation, especially in the air, and met it all with resolution through triumph and adversity, never faltering, but maintaining inspiring leadership and courage worthy of those great admirals and traditions of the past. And how much more satisfying must it have been in the realisation that this operation was a combined effort with two great nations giving their all in a determination to stamp out evil aggression.

The landings at Algiers and Oran, timed for 0100 8 November, were successful, detailed reconnaissance having been carried out by sub-marines working off-shore, and navigation of landing-craft being assisted by submarines acting as beacons. Nevertheless errors were made by some of the craft who were set westward along the coast by a current of four knots.

At Algiers initial resistance was slight, and by daylight the assault troops were ashore. Two local airfields were quickly captured, one of them, Blida, by FAA Martlets working from the *Victorious*, the other by RAF Hurricanes from Gibraltar in support of ground troops. There was however fire from the French Navy who manned guns in the harbour, and this was not finally silenced by the British bombarding ships until the evening of 9 November, when all French resistance ceased there. General Mark Clark as Eisenhower's Chief of Staff flew into Algiers that evening, and Cunningham sent his own Chief of Staff Commodore Dick, who with his many other accomplishments was also a fluent French speaker.

The assault on Oran, which was on a larger scale than that at Algiers, proved to be a much tougher problem. French destroyers there went out to attack the invasion shipping, and were met by warships of the covering force. The local airfield was operating American Spitfires by the evening of 8 November. Nevertheless the city did not capitulate until noon 10 November.

At Casablanca Admiral Hewitt met bad weather and heavy surf at 0000 7 November, but on the strength of a forecast of improving con-ditions decided to stick to the original plan, and was able to carry out the landings successfully from 0400 8 November, though with some losses. One of the principal objectives was the airfield at Port Lyautey. There was considerable resistance from the French Navy at Casablanca, but bombardments from the American ships covering the landings were able to neutralise the French fire. In landings at three separate places 31,000 troops and 250 tanks went ashore under Patton, and by 10 November, when Admiral Darlan broadcast to all French troops to cease resistance, the Americans had attained most of their objectives.

Cunningham's chief criticism of the operation was that there had been no time for proper training, and this had led to a delay in some of the schedules, misdirection, and some losses due to inexperienced handling of landing-craft. But in words which could have been uttered by General Wolfe two centuries earlier he said, 'We could not afford to wait, and the risk of embarking on these large-scale operations with inadequate training was deliberately accepted in order to strike when the time was ripe.'

'Cunningham was deeply disappointed,' writes Dick, 'at his failure to get the Americans to agree to landings much farther east despite utmost pressure. They were so apprehensive that Franco would allow Gibraltar to be attacked and the refusal was chiefly political. It was evident later how right ABC had been. The Allies paid a heavy price for the error.'

In his official dispatch on TORCH, Cunningham paid tribute to the sound planning by his deputy and rearlink, Admiral Sir Bertram Ramsay, and to the 'courage, determination, and adaptability of the Merchant Navy'. He concluded also with a most important point, eulogising the 'spirit of comradeship and understanding' and saying: 'The embodiment of that spirit was exemplified in our Commander-in-Chief General Dwight D. Eisenhower: we count it a privilege to follow in his train.'

On 14 November 1942 the Allied Naval Commander sent a message[5] to every merchant ship, British and American, as follows:

'In my message to you before this operation started I called on you for all your efforts in a hazardous operation of supreme importance to our countries.

'The response has been all and more than I hoped and I thank Captains, Officers and Men alike for the courage, efficiency and resolution with which they played their part.

'My pride in the work of the Merchant Navy and the confidence that I have learned to place in them after two years of hard warfare in the Mediterranean has been proved yet again. This was my first contact with United States ships and I emphasise that this message applies with equal force to them in this operation.

'I send Captains, Officers and Crews my thanks and wish them God-speed.'

(Signed) ANDREW CUNNINGHAM
Admiral

Meanwhile the Eighth Army, after taking up the offensive 23 October 1942 under Montgomery, had by 4 November broken out at El Alamein and were chasing westward with Rommel in full retreat. Admiral Harwood's inshore squadron was supporting the Eighth Army's rapid advance through Cyrenaica, and re-establishing the supply ports along that coast. Tobruk was regained on 13 November, and Benghazi was captured on 20 November, giving British forces once more an advanced airfield only 350 miles from Malta.

On 11 and 12 November the ports of Bougie, Djidjelli, and Bone were seized as an extension of the TORCH landings, principally for the purpose of reinforcing by sea the First Army in its drive eastward towards Bizerta and Tunis. Land communications were lamentably poor, and newly captured airfields were swamped with heavy rain so that shore-based fighters were late in getting established. The result was that these ports became easy targets for enemy bombers from Sardinia and Sicily. Many valuable ships were lost.

By the end of November the First Army was bogged down in appalling conditions, still some 40 miles west of Bizerta, suffering torrential rain, quagmires, and steadily deteriorating land communications. The Axis partners, having been completely surprised by TORCH, now began to rush troops by air into Tunisia, and tanks and guns by sea, maintaining their long-held supply route across the Narrows. In view of their local maritime inferiority, and an air superiority which could not hope to last much longer, this was an unwise step, although it might appear to put a stop temporarily to the effectiveness of the Anglo-American invasion. Liddell Hart[6] has commented on this point:

'A failure to gain immediate success has at times turned out very advantageously by helping towards fuller success and making final success more sure. . . . It was due to the Allies' original advance on Tunis from Algiers, in November 1942, that Hitler and Mussolini were encouraged to send a stream of reinforcements there, across the sea, where the Allies were eventually able to trap them six months later and put two Axis armies in the bag – thus removing the chief obstacle to their own cross-sea jump from Africa into Southern Europe.'

From the beginning of the TORCH landings there was much vacillation among the French leaders in Africa, and acute suspicion and mistrust concerning the attitude of the Vichy government. Long before the landings it had been assumed by the Americans on the basis of reports from their representative in North Africa, Mr. Robert D. Murphy, that there would be bitter resistance towards the British because of their treatment of French ships at Dakar and Oran after the fall of France in 1940, but they hoped themselves to be welcomed as saviours in a good cause. Despite secret talks in North Africa in October, which were attended by Major-General Mark Clark, the position remains obscure, the main reason being a fear among those French generals and French admirals who were anti-Vichy and anti-Pétain, of showing too much readiness to support the Allies. The matter was greatly complicated by other circumstances, a most important one being the knowledge that the Germans had plans in minute detail, operation ATTILA,[7] for the seizure of that part of France as yet unoccupied, together with the French fleet at Toulon. It was fairly certain that this would be put into execution if the Allies occupied North Africa. On 11 November, by local agreement, Admiral Darlan became the political head in French North Africa, and General Giraud (who had been smuggled out of France), the military commander of all French forces. On the basis that Hitler had broken the armistice with France by his move to occupy Southern France, Darlan made a signal to Admiral de la Borde, the Commander-in-Chief of the French fleet at Toulon, inviting him to sail the fleet direct to West Africa and to assume co-operation from Allied Naval Forces.

The reply from de la Borde was an uncompromising refusal, said to be expressed in one extremely unparliamentary French word.

Darlan also telephoned Admiral Esteva, Cunningham's old friend (see p. 71), and now Resident General in Tunis, telling him to denounce the Axis and declare for the Allies. Cunningham also sent a message to say that assistance would be rushed to him. But it was too late. The Germans were already flying into Tunis, and had taken Esteva hostage. 'I have a tutor at my elbow,' he replied.

Another complicating circumstance in the political tangle at Algiers was the fact that General de Gaulle had declared himself uncompromisingly for Britain in her support for the Free French. Any Allied agreement with Darlan in Algiers therefore raised acrimony in both the British and the American Press.

Cunningham flew with Eisenhower from Gibraltar to attend a meeting at Algiers on 13 November. There they both met Darlan for the first time. The Commander-in-Chief Expeditionary Force emphasised that the immediate object was to fight the Germans, and Darlan agreed. Cunningham then insisted that Darlan should again try to persuade de la Borde to take the French fleet away from Toulon. He deplored the delay in getting in touch with Esteva at Tunis caused by the initial parleying with Darlan. Both Cunningham and Dick considered Darlan without scruple in pursuing the interests of his country to which he was completely devoted, even if misguided. Once decided on a course however, in this case to work with the Allies, he carried out his engagements unswervingly. The British Press strongly disapproved of treating with Darlan.

'Once more,' writes Cunningham,[8] 'I bitterly regretted that bolder measures had not been taken in operation TORCH, and that we had not landed at Bizerta, as I had suggested. Esteva was a true patriot. He loathed the Germans, and I am quite sure he would have welcomed the Allies.' Esteva was eventually brought to trial before the High Court of Justice in France in March 1945, found guilty of treason, and sentenced to imprisonment for life. Darlan was assassinated by a young fanatic on Christmas Eve 1942, and was given a State funeral which was attended by Eisenhower and Cunningham. There was real fear that there might be attempts to assassinate one or both. There was never any doubt in Cunningham's mind, in the circumstances, that the agreement with Darlan was the right one. Though the bulk of the population was apathetic, the agreement enabled the Allies to get on with the task of fighting the Axis with the co-operation of the French Army in North Africa. As Cunningham had forecast, Franco kept Spain neutral throughout the TORCH landings, not through any love for the Allies, but because he felt that the Allies must be successful.

The Germans marched into southern France announcing that they would not occupy Toulon, as had Bonaparte in 1793. Nevertheless this they did suddenly in the early hours of 27 November, intending to seize the French fleet. Admiral de la Borde was ready, and immediately scuttled his ships. For this action he was tried and condemned to death by the Vichy government, a sentence later commuted to imprisonment for life. Five submarines succeeded in getting away, of which two reached Algiers and one Oran. One reached Barcelona and was promptly interned in accord with Franco's determination to remain neutral. Of the 61 ships scuttled, one was a battleship, two were battle cruisers, and seven cruisers.

On 24 November Eisenhower had moved his headquarters permanently to the Hotel St. Georges in Algiers, followed the next day by Cunningham who occupied a villa in the same garden. Although there were air raids daily, Cunningham was able to appreciate the comforts of a fine house and garden of palms and flowering shrubs, which had been suddenly abandoned by fleeing wealthy Axis collaborators. He settled in with his Chief of Staff, Secretary, and Flag Lieutenant, and himself mentions the triumphant success of Watts, his coxswain, who after an expedition of 20 miles into the country returned with six hens and a cockerel.

His chief aim was to establish Bone, 250 miles east of Algiers, as an effectual unloading port and a forward supply base for Anderson's First Army. Here he based a small squadron of cruisers and destroyers known as Force Q under Rear-Admiral Harcourt, for the task of night operations in the Narrows against Axis supply routes to Tunis: night operations would be preferable to daylight operations because of the enemy's present air superiority. To take charge of the much bombed port of Bone, Cunningham now brought Commodore Oliver forward from Gibraltar. It is interesting to read Oliver's account[9] and praise of Anglo-American relations during that difficult winter when approaching a stalemate.

'ABC's purpose was twofold, to build up First Army and to sink supplies going to the enemy. This went on incessantly, with varied success, until the enemy defeat.

'I cannot remember ever having any written orders or instructions from ABC. He had said what he wanted. Anything else could be dealt with by signal. He visited us at Bone and, very occasionally, I would be summoned and fly to Algiers, when something was brewing, for discussion and to enjoy the welcoming hospitality of ABC's villa.

'I'm sure that the success of those Anglo-American operations owed much to the good relations prevailing between the RN and USN and indeed between the RN and the US Air Force and US Army. (We were a complete mixture.) This was certainly inspired from the top, by ABC and by Ike, for whom ABC had a very staunch friendship and respect. Any sign of friction was quickly dealt with, the offender, whether British or US, finding himself drafted away out of the theatre of operations at once. The buzz soon got round.

'At Bone, the coastal forces operating against the enemy supply routes, all RN at first, soon became international with the arrival of the US PT boats operating together, sometimes under RN and sometimes under USN command.'

Malta was again relieved by the fast minelayers *Manxman* and *Welshman* from Alexandria, and a four-ship convoy protected for much of the way by fighters from advanced desert airfields that had been recaptured. The submarines, which had done such gallant service, were reinforced, and FAA torpedo-bombers moved into Malta's airfields. Force K, of 1941 fame, was also re-instituted, and this, in combination with Force Q from Bone, the submarines, and many skilfully laid minefields, brought about Axis losses of more than 40 ships a month in November and December 1942.

Though the cold, rain, and mud had bogged down Anderson's army temporarily, while the Axis were reinforcing Tunisia, supplies and troops continued to pour ashore in the wake of the TORCH landings, and naval forces pursued their task of escort and coverage, greatly helped in the west by aircraft of Coastal Command and the USAF working from Gibraltar and North Africa. There were nevertheless losses among the regular convoys due to mines, bombing, and U-boat attacks, the last named remaining the greatest menace. The Italian fleet still retained their powerful ships in harbour where they remained as a constant threat, though considered unlikely to emerge because of extreme need of oil fuel. Force H paid occasional visits from Gibraltar to Mers-el-Kebir and Algiers, 'mainly' as Cunningham said 'to show the French population that we had large ships operating on their doorstep'. Conditions at Bone however were still most hazardous for all ships, and after the newly arrived *Ajax* had received severe damage which necessitated her leaving the station, doubts were expressed about the wisdom of maintaining Force Q there. 'I had to harden my heart,' says Cunningham, who knew that improved defences were on the way, and signalled Harcourt that he must 'stick it out'. He went on to say that 'if our ships withdrew we were playing the enemy's game'.

The problem of running an enormous fleet at short notice from an unprepared base such as Algiers may not be fully appreciated. The following brief extracts from letters reveal some of the difficulties, as well as the optimism and initiative required.

From the Fleet Medical Officer:[10]

'There could have been no better choice for Naval Commander in TORCH than ABC straight from Washington, and he had the advantage that after TORCH the sea command was virtually a British fleet, gradually assimilating the American and French elements. Administratively it must have been an enormous headache; I would think that nobody appreciated in advance that it would overnight become a Command as big as the whole pre-war Navy. As a result an expeditionary force staff became a Fleet organisation without many of the requisites such as personnel, and somewhere for them to live and work; transport; communications.

'ABC had to inform the Admiralty that he was waiting longer for his mail than Nelson who had similarly complained in about 1800. There was no provision for equipping survivors except army battle dress, and Merchant seaman survivors seemed not to have been provided for in advance; as indeed also the released prisoners ex H.M.S. *Manchester*. Replacement medical stores did not exist, except a little at Gibraltar until it was possible to get a load out about May 1943 and find somewhere to set it up in Algiers. One RNVR four-striper looked very smart in the uniform of a Chief PO in US Navy (how he acquired that I do not recall).'

A leading Telegraphist[11] saw the picture from a different angle:

'Just after the North African landings, the naval barracks were bombed. As an emergency measure the survivors were kitted out with Army battledress, in the absence of naval uniform. When going on watch at the Hotel Saint Georges at 2000 one night, we stood aside at the entrance to allow ABC to pass. However he stood to one side with his Flag Lt. and waved us in. He pulled me out of the crowd and stood watching – battledress blouse, bellbottoms, khaki shirts, "pussers" flannels, army boots, etc. He turned to Flags and said, "Jacob himself couldn't match this lot" and then he asked me why. I explained and he grunted, "Carry on, my boy." We were fully kitted within a couple of days with kit flown from Alexandria. Whenever he appeared in the wireless office (situated in the old ballroom) we all of us felt that he took a personal interest in us all. He never seemed tired – even at 2 a.m. when we changed watches, and in the early days we were under considerable pressure with constant air raids, very poor accommodation and heavy work. I'm sure that we all subconsciously felt that if the old man could stick it, so could we. It is very difficult to define the feeling he inspired – I suppose this is the sign of the born leader.'

One of the biggest problems lay in the maintenance and repair of ships, and the following extract by the Fleet Naval Constructor[12] may reveal ABC in an unusual role though quite in character:

'Salvage preliminaries were under way on one of the Navy's precious escort sloops driven ashore at Algiers in a violent storm, when the C-in-C arrived on the harbour breakwater and got his first glimpse of this sorry and embarrassing situation. After passing a few preliminary "thoughts" by megaphone he departed.

'In less than half an hour he returned and with great gusto shouted "FNC I've got the biggest pump in North Africa for you", and pointed to the shore end of the breakwater, where lo and behold I could see the city of Algiers finest fire engine, resplendent in all its colourful and sparkling array, and "rearing to go".

'He ranks with the greatest "sea-dogs" of all time. We who served under him in the Mediterranean actions were indeed most privileged.'

One of the joys of working with Americans was the suddenness and sincerity with which they would sometimes make charming gestures. The following incidents are typical. On Christmas night 1942, just before Cunningham's guests were due to arrive at a small dinner party ABC was giving, Eisenhower, with his villa in the same grounds, asked if he could go and see him. He arrived with the guests, and by order of President Roosevelt presented ABC with the American Army Distinguished Service Medal. Cunningham says that it was quite unexpected, and he was greatly touched at the kind things said.

Admiral Oliver describes the occasion of ABC's departure from his Algiers headquarters some months later. 'For several days at set times there were unmistakable noises of military ceremonial from the lawn beneath his office windows. When one of the staff enquired what was afoot, his US opposite number proudly answered "We hev a liddle *sur*-prise for your Admiral Cunning-*HAM*". On the morning of his departure, he was seen off with a full US ceremonial Guard and Band.'

The arrival of January 1943 brought great optimism, and there were already hopes of knocking Italy out of the war, even though there was still much land fighting to be done to defeat the enemy in Tunisia. The Russians had begun their offensive at Stalingrad, and the Germans were in retreat. All the more surprising was it therefore that Axis troops were pouring into Tunis. Meanwhile the Eighth Army were steadily moving towards Tripoli, reducing the gap between them and the First Army, and raising hopes that the capture of Tripoli would shorten supply routes, but not fully aware that the Germans already had a plan for destroying the wharves and blocking the harbour.

In the middle of January Cunningham was summoned to Casablanca, where Roosevelt and Churchill and the Chiefs of Staff had arrived to confer on the next step in grand strategy, to take place as soon as the enemy had been driven from North Africa: an event which was optimistically regarded at that time as being only a matter of two or three months away. Though the American view still favoured the direct attack across the English Channel, they realised that it could not be done in 1942, and were prepared to accept the traditional British plan of attacking the 'soft underbelly' of Europe. There was some difference of opinion as to whether the operation should be a landing in Sardinia (BRIMSTONE) or the capture of Sicily (HUSKY), for there were telling arguments in favour of each.[13] Cunningham seems to have had a leaning towards Sardinia, on the grounds that it could have been captured more quickly and more cheaply, and provide just as readily air protection for shipping passing through the Narrows, but these arguments did not convince Portal or Pound or Brooke. A decision was made to adopt HUSKY, more particularly because the Russians might regard the capture of Sardinia as a relatively small contribution towards a second front, whereas a successful landing in Sicily seemed to have endless possibilities, the most attractive being the presence of Allied airfields at this strategic cross-roads in the Mediterranean. The main problem was 'when could it take place?' In this matter Churchill would brook no avoidable delay.

Eisenhower was to be Supreme Commander of HUSKY, with Alexander in command of all the land forces under Eisenhower, including the Eighth Army when it entered Tunisia. Cunningham was again to be the naval Commander-in-Chief, and Tedder was now selected to be the air Commander-in-Chief. Alexander was to be responsible for the detailed planning of the operation.

There had been much advocacy by Tedder towards the end of 1942, in consultation with Portal, the CAS, for a unified single command of the air forces comparable with Cunningham's unified single command of naval forces. Eisenhower was at first doubtful if this would work, but was later convinced and ready to have the benefit of Tedder's 18 months of practical experience of operations in the Middle East. By this time Tedder[14] had become less critical of Cunningham than had been the case when he had considered him 'rather a trial. I don't know how much longer we can carry on with him' (January 1942). Now he regarded Cunningham as 'the live wire' at Algiers. Moreover he was able to report to Portal with enthusiasm that he had 'told Cunningham our views about future Air Command in the Mediterranean, and he agreed with them'.

Tedder had become an expert in the Western Desert in combining air and surface operations, and in providing the army with close tactical air support. Both Tedder and Cunningham became great friends of Eisenhower who placed complete reliance in them, and it is apparent that they both had considerable influence over him, because of this confidence. Alexander also in due course impressed Eisenhower with what Churchill called his 'easy smiling grace' and 'contagious confidence'. After the Tunisian campaign Eisenhower wrote his own personal note about his leading commanders.[15] He ranked Cunningham first 'in absolute selflessness, energy, devotion to duty, knowledge of task, and in understanding of the requirements of Allied operations'. Tedder he ranked a close second but thought him 'not quite as broad-gauged as he might be', implying a tendency to see only from the air point of view. Though Ike regarded Alexander as sound, he remarked on 'a suspected unsureness in dealing with certain of his subordinates'. He amplified this by suggesting that the only thing 'the very able dynamic' Montgomery needed was a 'strong immediate commander'. Eisenhower's personal note also referred to Anderson being 'an earnest fighter completely devoted to duty'. Of Patton, the best fighting general America had, he considered there was too much flamboyancy, but he would

keep him whatever the cost. Mark Clark he regarded as 'the best organiser, planner, and trainer of troops'.

While at Casablanca, the First Sea Lord discussed with Cunningham
the desirability of extending his sphere of command to cover the whole
of the Mediterranean, a change which Cunningham felt was necessary,
since operations would be directed to the same purpose of frustrating
enemy communications everywhere in that sea, and of securing those of
the Allies. No decision was however reached at that time.

On returning to Algiers after the conference, and following a visit to
the port installations under Rear-Admiral John Hall, USN, Flag Officer
in Charge at Casablanca, Cunningham found that 12 officers and six
ratings of the Women's Royal Naval Service had arrived from Gibraltar
in two destroyers, thenceforward to be called the Wrens' Special. These
were forerunners of many more to come, and ABC speaks warmly of
their arrival. Always smart and well disciplined, though not subject to
the Naval Discipline Act, the Wrens who helped out in those somewhat
outlandish places during the war always remained a credit to their
Service and a testimony of the far-sightedness of their founder.

On 21 January 1943 Sir Andrew Cunningham, Bart., was promoted
Admiral of the Fleet, the highest rank in the Royal Navy, entitling him
to fly the Union Flag in place of the flag of St. George's Cross which he
had flown in various forms since 1932. At Colours on this day his Union
Flag was hoisted in H.M.S. *Maidstone*.

29 *Italian surrender seen from* HMS Warspite, *10 September 1943; squadron taking station astern of* HMS Valiant

30 *Bomb-damaged* Warspite *bombarding German guns ashore*

31 *Teheran Conference November 1943. Standing behind Stalin, Roosevelt and Churchill are, left to right, Dill, Marshall, Voroshilov, King, Arnold, Brooke, Portal, Cunningham, Leahy*

Prelude to Victory in the Mediterranean (March 1943–August 1943)

By February 1943 a decision had been taken concerning sea areas of responsibility, and on 23 February Admiral of the Fleet Sir Andrew Cunningham resumed the title Commander-in-Chief Mediterranean Station. His command now included those waters through which Allied forces would pass on their way to Sicily. This was all that sea to the west of a line joining the toe of Italy to the Tunisia–Tripolitania border, and embraced not only Sicily but also the island of Malta, and the whole of the Tunisia coast in which at that time Axis forces were so strongly entrenched, thereby dominating (at very great cost) the narrow seas which formed their principal supply route. East of this boundary was the Levant Command, responsibility for which was assumed by Admiral Sir John Cunningham (no relative of ABC) on 5 June 1943.

That gallant officer, Admiral Sir Henry Harwood, victor at the Battle of the River Plate, December 1939, who had relieved ABC midsummer 1942, had fallen on luckless times during his command in the Mediterranean, and more latterly had aroused Churchill's impatience because of intransigence on the part of Admiral Godfroy in committing the Alexandria French fleet to the support of the Allies after the landings in North Africa.[1] Although with Churchill Montgomery had paid tribute to the speed at which the port of Tripoli was re-established, he (Montgomery) also severely criticised the preparations which had been made by the Navy: this was on 26 January 1943, three days after the Eighth Army's occupation of Tripoli. Harwood's health was already failing, and he was relieved temporarily in March 1943, as Commander-in-Chief, Levant, pending Sir John Cunningham's arrival. ABC wrote that Harwood 'had always been most co-operative and helpful in every way'.

ABC writes of his considerable personal gratification at becoming Commander-in-Chief Mediterranean Station again, and at having once again in his command Malta, that island for whose success he had struggled so fiercely and so wisely since Italy had entered the war. It was apt that forces working from Bone and from Malta, whose objective was the disruption of the Axis supply line to Tunisia, should be under the same command. The long list[2] of British Commanders-in-Chief, Mediterranean Station, an historic title which began in 1711 and ended in 1967, and includes for 1802 the immortal name of Vice-Admiral Lord Nelson, shows in addition to Sir Andrew Cunningham only two other holders of the title who returned for a second period of command: they are Rear-Admiral Sir Richard Hussey Bickerton, Bart., first in 1802, and again, after Nelson's death, in 1805; and Vice-Admiral Sir Pulteney Malcolm, first in 1828 and again in 1833.

Cunningham (meaning Sir Andrew unless otherwise specified) flew to Malta at the end of February 1943 to see naval establishments and the dockyard facilities for ship repair and maintenance. He flew in an American Fortress arranged by Eisenhower's Chief of Staff, Bedell Smith, whose stock remark on such an occasion appeared to be 'Admiral, the whole of the American Air Force is at your disposal', and typifies the mutual friendship and esteem which had developed between ABC and the Americans. Harold Macmillan, Minister Resident at Allied HQ, later Prime Minister of the UK, was less fortunate, for on one occasion he suffered severe burns in a Hudson provided for him by the RAF. He describes 'the great sensation' when Sir Andrew Cunningham visited him in hospital in Algiers.[3]

'Everyone is tremendously excited. Nobody cares much about a poor old civilian Minister; but an Admiral of the Fleet, with gold from cuff to elbow, and "Flags" with gold all over him; well you can imagine how my stock has risen.

'Incidentally, the Admiral has brought me some very good news of the battle here, which has comforted me. He is a splendid man and absolutely first-class and a most amusing and agreeable companion. He is not surprised at the failure of the RAF to take anyone safely anywhere. "For myself," he says, "I generally travel American." This, of course, is just naughtiness and to tease the Air Chief Marshal and others.'

Having explained in his book that the accident was due to the pilot forgetting to remove the cover from some gadget, Macmillan follows with acclaim for Tedder, who also went to visit him in hospital.

'Tedder is really a most interesting man,' he writes. 'He has that rare quality of greatness (which you can't define but you sense). It consists partly of humour, immense common sense, and a power to concentrate on one or two simple points.'

At the end of March 1943 the Eighth Army broke through the Mareth Line and advanced rapidly to the north, thus permitting the use of the small port of Sfax, only 150 miles from Tunis, and by the end of April, the larger and less damaged port and harbour of Sousse which was only 75 miles from Tunis. Cunningham's cruisers and destroyers had been operating throughout the winter from Bone, and though according to Oliver, the Port Commodore, 'they suffered . . . fairly severely both at sea (torpedoes and mines) and in harbour (bombs), they were immediately replaced'. Operating from both Bone and Sousse, MTBs were a constant and nightly menace to Axis shipping, as were submarines of the 8th and 10th Flotillas, and also the FAA Swordfish and Albacores operating in co-ordinated attacks with the RAF from Malta. Almost half of the supplies of stores, ammunition, and petrol being carried to Tunis and Bizerta for the Axis armies were destroyed. German U-boats now found it impracticable to enter through the Straits of Gibraltar, and were suffering heavy losses in the Mediterranean. ABC refers particularly to the achievements of three little ships of the Royal Canadian Navy, the *Ville de Quebec*, the *Port Arthur*, and the *Regina*, which accounted for three U-boats in 26 days.

Cunningham describes the plight of the pilot of a naval aircraft which crashed into the sea east of Cape Serrat in Tunisia, who reached shore in a rubber dinghy only to sink into quicksand. Having been rescued by Arabs he was taken to a hut from which he saw German soldiers passing. That night he started off alone, walked through the German lines, and eventually reached the safety of British troops. Cunningham himself wished he could take a more active part in the fighting; he was very much aware of the heavy loss of life in his ships, from bombs, torpedoes, and mines, and also of those adventurous night operators in MTBs, and in British submarines performing such outstanding work in torpedoing Rommel's supplies.

With the benefit of lessons learned during TORCH, considerable training was taking place in the operation of landing-craft of all types now being assembled at Djidjelli and other ports in preparation for HUSKY, the landing in Sicily. It should be realised that the allocation of craft from which tanks or guns or infantry could be landed quickly and safely on a sandy beach was a relatively new idea, and presented many problems and much scope for improvement. Limitations in size and complexity were necessary in order that fast and considerable production could proceed, for without them a landing would be slow and impracticable.

The following story by Captain Grindle[4] is of direct interest, and is a reminder of the problem facing all commanders: that of avoiding the increasingly cumulative growth of staff officers and personnel; the administrative tail.

'In the early autumn of 1942, when ABC left Washington, ostensibly on a routine visit, it fell to me to see him off at Washington airport, I being on the Combined Chiefs of Staff set-up. As we said good-bye he said to me, "Don't stay too long here – a year is quite enough in this atmosphere." Within a few weeks I was relieved and when I reported to the Naval Secretary I was handed a copy of a signal from ABC in Algiers.

'The signal read roughly as follows: "Please send me a two-balled two-fisted so-and-so to become the senior British liaison officer with General Mark Clark and to represent me on all matters concerned with use of landing-craft!"

'When I took up my appointment as Director of Landing Craft (Mediterranean) I asked ABC what powers I had particularly in relation to signals to other authorities. He replied, "You'll soon find out and if you make the same mistake twice you'll be on your way home." This was the standard he set and it certainly worked because he saw virtually every signal made during the previous day, at about 0630, and brought those that he wished to query to the Staff meeting over which he presided daily at about 0815. One soon learnt whether one had exceeded one's powers: he did not spare his words on these occasions and COS, Royer Dick, was just as likely to get a rocket as any other of the eight or nine staff officers who were attending. On these occasions it was interesting to hear him refer more often than not to the Captain of the ship to whom a signal was addressed by name rather than to the ship itself – this applied even in the case of small escort destroyers and woe betide anyone who made a signal giving advice or instructions bordering on the obvious or which could be regarded as telling the man on the spot his job.

'Soon after I took over what was an entirely new job, it became necessary to ask for technical staff to man the various landing craft bases we were establishing along the North African coast in preparation for the assault on Sicily. The signal I had drafted went through the various staff channels leading up to the C-in-C himself, since it was obviously a policy matter. Neither the Captain of the Fleet, in whose province it lay, nor COS was able to persuade the C-in-C to approve it – he always challenged any attempt to build up a big administrative tail. The matter was critical so I was told by COS to take the signal in myself.

'Now the Admiral's normal timetable was to leave the Headquarters for lunch at about 1300 and return about 1630 having had tea; he would then stay until about 2000 when he returned to the villa for dinner: 1700 was regarded by everyone as the optimum time to tackle him on a difficult subject so on this occasion I was allocated the 1700 audience.

'I went in and asked if the signal could go – only to be met with what could almost amount to a torrent of sarcastic abuse and a charge of Empire-building. Nothing I could say appeared to have any effect so that in the end I was driven into saying: "Well, sir, if it doesn't go off I may as well go home and get another job." This aroused further abuse and I was sent ignominiously out of his presence.

'A few minutes later the COS came to my room and said, "What on earth have you been saying to the Admiral? He's fuming with rage and is almost having a heart attack – really you must not talk to him like that." I replied simply that, as we all knew, the signal had to go and that I had reckoned that I had to get it approved somehow, everyone else having failed.

'After a very short interval the Admiral's orderly came into my room – "The Admiral wishes to see you, sir." Now, I thought, comes the crunch, and I went in with very considerable trepidation. ABC stood up and in a few very strong words told me I had been extremely impertinent; that he was very angry indeed and that I must never speak to him, or anyone else, like that again. I muttered some sort of apology only to be cut short by, "Here's your damned signal – go and send it off." I withdrew and ten minutes later the orderly again came into my room, this time with a message – "The Admiral says that he will be leaving in his car a few minutes after eight o'clock. Will you please be at the door then and he will take you back to dinner at the Villa."

'The result was a very pleasant evening instead of yet another late night in the office; ABC was nothing if not hospitable and I was sent back to my own quarters – slightly the worse for drink – at midnight.'

There is a story that Churchill once complained to Sir Alan Brooke that the administrative tail was like a peacock's: far too large; and received the astute reply that the peacock would be absurdly unbalanced without it.

An appointment which ABC welcomed was that of Air Vice-Marshal Sir Hugh Lloyd to command the North-West Africa Coastal Air Force, whose task was the defence of shipping up to the Tunis-Tripoli frontier. Lloyd had done particularly well in Malta during the difficult years 1941 and 1942, and was thoroughly acquainted with naval requirements. He took pains to provide Cunningham with a Beaufighter and a young night-fighter pilot, which the C-in-C found of considerable use in his frequent visits to the outlying parts of his Command. By this time Cunningham had been allocated an official aircraft, a Dakota manned by a USAF crew, but though this was comfortable for long journeys he preferred the high speed of the Beaufighter for most journeys. A lucky escape is related by ABC's Chief of Staff, Commodore Royer Dick:[5]

'He was flying from Algiers to Bizerta in a Beaufighter which had been allotted to him and of which he was terribly proud. With him was his personal pilot, and myself. Just as we were about to take off Philip Vian put in an appearance, I forget why, and asked if he could have a lift. ABC agreed most reluctantly as I could see, and this rather surprised me as ABC was very fond of him as well as holding him in the highest esteem. So we took off and after about an hour Vian leant over and shouted "Is it all right that there is fuel and oil coming out over the port wing?" "Nonsense, perfectly all right," said ABC, furious that anyone should seem to criticise his pet toy. At that moment came the call from the cockpit "Stand by for forced landing" and down we came in the desert, the pilot having just managed to see an apology of a landing strip. Now you would have thought that having got away with what to put it mildly was a lucky escape that there would be mutual congratulations all round. Not at all. ABC turned round in a fury to Vian and said: "There you are you see, I told you something would go wrong. Two lucky men in one place cancel out and this is the result." And this was not said in jest. The taut atmosphere did not last long of course, but it was an interesting reaction.'

In this study of Cunningham we can be concerned only briefly with details of plans and appointments for HUSKY, but one appointment which is of particular interest because of ABC's long fight for a *naval* unit of the RAF, is that of Air Vice-Marshal T. H. Langford-Sainsbury to command No. 201 Naval Co-operation Group[6] consisting of three squadrons of fighters and (equally important in Cunningham's view) eight squadrons of reconnaissance aircraft. This group, together with the coastal units, and those for Gibraltar, Malta, and the Middle East, would complete the protection of all shipping in both the eastern and the western basins of the Mediterranean. All were under the overall command of Tedder. Ships with embarked forces destined to invade Sicily from the eastern basin of the Mediterranean were already building up by the long route round Cape Horn. Meanwhile the Axis continued their stubborn but now hopeless defence in Tunisia.

Changes in senior appointments were taking place. In March 1943 Vice-Admiral A. U. Willis, formerly COS to Cunningham in the *Warspite*, had been appointed to the command of Force H with his flag in the *Nelson*. In order to cover a force of five Italian battleships and two heavy cruisers whose interference, though unlikely because of an acute fuel shortage, always remained a possibility, Force H was supplemented by a reserve division of two battleships from the Home Fleet, and thus comprised six battleships *Nelson, Rodney, Howe, King George V, Warspite,* and *Valiant,* two armoured-deck aircraft carriers *Formidable* and *Indomitable,* and six light cruisers and 18 destroyers.

Also Vice-Admiral H. Kent Hewitt, USN, whose task it was to land US forces under General Patton in Sicily, was appointed, under Cunningham, to the command of all US naval forces in the Mediterranean, and set up his headquarters alongside those of Commander-in-Chief Mediterranean, in the Hotel St. Georges at Algiers; an arrangement which ABC regarded as most convenient, and ideal for whole-hearted co-operation. Admiral Sir Bertram Ramsay, who was to command the British assaulting squadron which was to take Montgomery's troops to Sicily, had his planning headquarters in Cairo, as did Montgomery. Patton's planners were near Oran. Such wide dispersion resulted in delay in concluding an agreed plan for HUSKY. Moreover Alexander, Montgomery, and Patton were still very actively engaged in rounding up Axis forces in Tunisia.

Early in May 1943 the First Army and the Eighth Army struck their final blow at the German–Italian bridge-head that had kept them at bay throughout the winter in Tunisia. On 7 May Allied forces entered both Tunis and Bizerta. Axis resistance collapsed, suddenly aware of the fact that there was no possibility of evacuation from Tunisia across what was now a hostile sea. No longer were the Sicilian narrows dominated by Axis forces. On 8 May Cunningham made his historic signal to all Allied naval forces:

'SINK, BURN, DESTROY. Let nothing pass.'

An attempt at mass withdrawal on the lines of the Dunkirk evacuation had been expected, and Cunningham had 'scraped up' more destroyers and light coastal craft from all over the Mediterranean and the Levant, for the purpose of frustrating any such attempts.

'I knew most of the destroyer captains,' wrote Cunningham.[7] 'Some of them, and many more of their ships' companies, had endured the agony that our men had had to face during the evacuation from Greece and Crete two years before. We called the operation RETRIBUTION, not in any spirit of revenge or because we intended to slaughter defence-less survivors in the water, as the Luftwaffe had done in 1941; but because we hoped, and most earnestly, that those of the enemy who essayed the perilous passage home by sea should be taught a lesson they would never forget.'

In addition to the hazards from minefields, destroyers suffered the danger of attack from those Allied aircraft untrained in ship recognition.

ABC writes of Lieutenant-Commander S. W. F. Bennetts, famed, as he says, for 'his extensive knowledge of the lesser-used terms of the English language', who when thus attacked let fly on the radio with words that surprised even the Americans. On the radio could be heard, spoken with apparent admiration, the remark, 'Say, I guess this guy's friendly.' Bennetts's probably unprintable response to this has not been recorded.

Liddell Hart[8] remarks on the irony of the fact that the failure of the Allies to make an early capture of Tunisia was in the long run immensely to their advantage. 'The complete capture of the eight divisions in Tunisia, including most of Rommel's veterans and the pick of the Italian Army, left Italy almost naked of defensive covering.' The total bag was believed to be something of the order of a quarter of a million troops, plus military equipment and stores. Cunningham signalled all ships on 13 May after the official surrender, and paid tribute especially to the recent work of the light forces by day and by night in harassing the enemy, thus discouraging any real attempt at evacuation by sea.

Command of the sea, assisted by a growing defence from the air, had enabled the Allies to support with complete success the land battles in North Africa. It now posed a threat of invasion of the Axis fortress anywhere between Spain and Greece. Hitler thought that the Allies were more likely to land in Sardinia and in Greece than in Sicily, and his opinion was strengthened upon receipt of what appeared to be high level secret correspondence obtained by the Germans from a body washed ashore on the Spanish coast: a successful British ruse referred to later as the 'Man who never was'.

By 15 May 1943 Cunningham was able to report to the Admiralty that the passage through the Mediterranean was clear. The first eastbound convoy to reach Malta unopposed since 1940 arrived 24 May, and thereafter regular convoys passed right through from Gibraltar to Alexandria. The mines and wrecks in the harbour of Bizerta were steadily cleared, with Commodore Oliver in charge of salvage, and all the mined approaches to Tunisian ports were swept. By the end of May channels had been cleared sufficiently to permit the entry of 10,000-ton 'Liberty' ships.

Bizerta, Tunis, Sousse, Sfax, and Tripoli were now to become assembly ports for the landing-craft required for HUSKY. Immense convoys, sometimes of over 100 merchantmen, with a score or so of escort vessels, made their way eastward, suffering sometimes, though not to a great extent, from the attentions of U-boats and also from German bombers based on Sardinia, Sicily, and Crete. One reason for losses being light was the excellent co-ordination that existed between naval forces, the RAF, the USAF, and strategically placed bases along the North Africa coast. (See map p. 256.)

Although the Mediterranean was now open, the three Italian islands of Pantelleria, Linosa, and Lampedusa, all manned with Italian garrisons, remained in a position of strategic advantage. Pantelleria however was the only one of importance, mainly because it had an airfield, admittedly small, but nevertheless in a commanding position in the Sicilian channel, from which fighters could operate over the landing beaches. Cunningham thought it should be captured, and Eisenhower decided in favour. Prepared for some opposition, Cunningham planned for a bombing and bombardment as a softening up prior to an assault with landing-craft. In the event the island fell easily into Allied hands on 11 June 1943.

It was on the following day that HM King George VI arrived at Algiers by air from London to visit the fighting men in North Africa. 'A most representative parade was assembled', writes Cunningham, which included 5,000 British sailors and Royal Marines, 600 sailors of the USN, and 1,200 officers and men of the Merchant Navy. On 19 June, His Majesty embarked with Cunningham in the light cruiser *Aurora* for passage to Malta where he received tremendous acclamation and demonstrations of spontaneous loyalty and affection. ABC refers to this as the most impressive of all the memorable spectacles he had ever witnessed. He must have had no little concern for security measures. Four destroyers were in company as anti-submarine precaution, a large fighter escort roared overhead, and mine-sweepers cleared the approaches to the Grand Harbour. The Royal visit raised morale everywhere in Allied-occupied territory, and was a complete success, setting the seal, as it were, on the resumption of the command of the sea.

The HUSKY naval plan under Cunningham's direction was a complex pattern of moves from various points leading to a night landing of some 160,000 Allied troops with 14,000 vehicles, 600 tanks, and 1,800 guns. The number of British and Imperial troops was almost twice that of American troops involved. As a diversion to attract the enemy's attention away from the actual beach landings, warships were to bombard various ports at dawn.

The military plans for HUSKY suffered a number of changes, original intentions being an American landing on the west coast of Sicily, with a view to the early capture of the port of Palermo, and a British landing on the south-east corner to aim at the capture of Syracuse, Augusta, and Catania. Montgomery, engrossed in his own battle, did not find time to study the plan in detail until late April, and then called for greater concentration of the assaulting forces, and an expectation of more severe opposition than that catered for. Such concentration had already been suggested earlier by Alexander, who was rash enough to state that command of the sea would be diminished by dispersion. Cunningham's view was that dispersion of assaults could in no way alter the command of the sea. He believed that amphibious operations should be employed on a wide front to reduce the vulnerability of a concentrated mass of shipping. More important in his view was the early capture of the local airfields, and in this he was supported by Tedder.

'Apart from my general conviction,' writes Cunningham,[9] 'that in amphibious operations the landings should be dispersed, I again insisted that it was essential to secure the use of the airfields at the earliest possible moment to safeguard the mass of shipping lying off the beaches. Tedder also entered strong objections. The Eighth Army plan would leave 13 airfields in enemy hands, far too many for effective neutralisation by air action.'

On 28 April 1943 Cunningham made the following signal to the First Sea Lord: 'I am afraid Montgomery is a bit of a nuisance; he seems to think that all he has to do is to say what is to be done and everyone will dance to the tune of his piping. Alexander appears quite unable to keep him in order. . . . Just over two months off "D"-day, and the commanders all at sixes and sevens, and even if we do get final agreement, someone will be operating a plan he doesn't fully agree with. Not the way to make the success of a difficult operation.'

A member of Cunningham's staff says that the first plan (Palermo and Catania) would have been just as well, and if accepted could have been implemented earlier with adequate preparations and less difficulty over the beach landings.

The plan was recast early in May, and final approval of it by the Combined Chiefs of Staff was received on 13 May, a week after the Axis collapse in Tunisia. The revision of the plan had caused regrettable delay in preparations and the invasion date had to be put back to 10 July. The British Eighth Army were to land in five sectors between Syracuse and Cape Passero the south-east corner of Sicily, and the American Seventh Army would land in three sectors on the south coast (see map p. 256), the initial objectives being Augusta and Syracuse and all the airfields in south-east Sicily. The new DUKW amphibious vehicles in conjunction with the LST tank-landing ships were to solve many of the problems of maintenance over the beaches. Another innovation which was an improvement on the TORCH landings was the use of 'shore to shore' assaults whereby troops would be already embarked in landing-craft at the start of the journey from Malta or North Africa, thus obviating the necessity for the lengthy and hazardous off-shore transfer from transport to landing-craft in the vicinity of the landing beaches.

In a message to all ships and naval units, Cunningham left no doubt in the minds of the recipients, concerning the crucial importance of this vast enterprise, and the risks that must be accepted. 'We are striking for the first time at the enemy in his own land. Our object is clear and our primary duty is to place this vast expedition ashore in the minimum time and subsequently to maintain our military and air forces as they drive relentlessly forward.

'Great risks must be accepted. I rest confident in the resolution, skill, and endurance of you all to whom this momentous enterprise is entrusted.'

As a measure of Cunningham's stature at this time one cannot do better than refer to a letter from Sir John Dill:

'BJSM Washington,
11 June 1943

'My dear Cunningham,

When lunching alone with Marshall today he dilated on how much your selfless support to Eisenhower had meant to him, and more important to the smooth running of affairs in North Africa. I do not tell you this for your personal gratification but that you may know how completely the Americans (including King) trust your judgment and will accept your considered opinion. You will still I feel have a vastly important part to play in keeping the balance in all that lies ahead.

Yours ever,
J. G. Dill.'

The landings in Sicily on 10 July 1943 achieved complete surprise, a surprise accentuated by the fact that a fresh north-westerly wind sprang up on the day before the operation, causing the enemy forces to assume that 'to-night at any rate they cannot come'. This wind caused much sickness and difficulty in the landing-craft, but mercifully began to ease after midnight.

The naval assault forces comprised 2,590 warships, landing-craft, and small ships. Airborne troops were sent in early to capture enemy airfields, and suffered considerably from the strong wind, some crashing into the sea and being rescued by small craft. Resistance was surprisingly light and immediate objectives were soon seized. Rocket-equipped landing-craft proved to be very effective.

Cunningham in overall naval command had his headquarters at Malta, the most suitable base from which to issue communications for

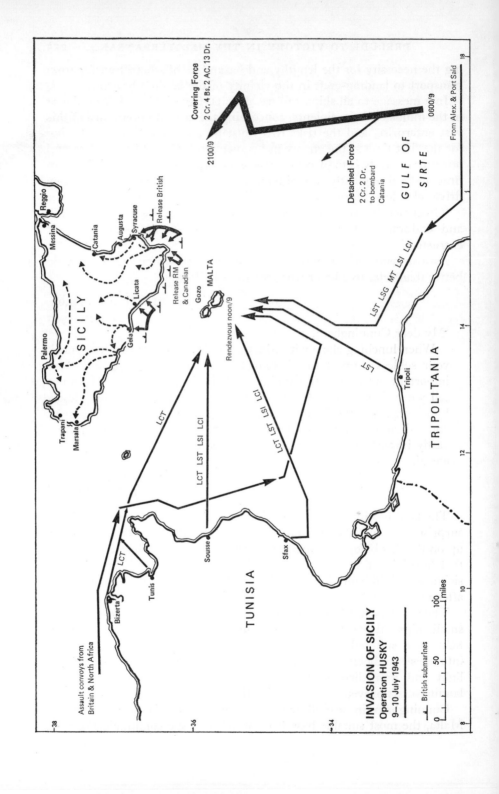

INVASION OF SICILY
Operation HUSKY
9–10 July 1943

operating the fleet. His was the great responsibility for landing 160,000 troops and all their equipment at the right time and at the right places. Ramsay was commanding the naval forces for the British eastern assault on Sicily, and Hewitt the naval forces for the American southern assault. Under Ramsay, in command of the British expedition from the Middle East, was Rear-Admiral Troubridge; that from North Africa and Malta was under Rear-Admiral McGrigor; and the convoy from Britain was under Rear-Admiral Sir Philip Vian. Under Hewitt were Rear-Admirals Kirk, Hall, and Conolly. ABC regarded this as 'a fine team of most able and experienced officers': see map p. 256.

A strong covering force of four battleships, two fleet carriers, four cruisers, and 17 destroyers to the east of Sicily was provided by Willis's Force H, while two of his battleships covered the western basin. Harcourt's cruiser and destroyer force provided inshore support for the army. British submarines acted as navigation beacons at seven beaches, and eight submarines lay in readiness in strategic points in case the Italian fleet left port. Eisenhower, as overall commander of the operation, was at Malta, with Alexander his deputy, and Montgomery. The RAF and USAF continued to keep their headquarters at Tunis, an arrangement which Cunningham blames for subsequent lack of complete co-ordination. Initial air cover was good, and shipping losses small. Remembering 1941 and 1942 Cunningham remarked that it was 'almost magical that great fleets of ships could remain anchored on the enemy's coast . . . with only such slight losses from air attack as were incurred'.

Although the initial landings were carried out quickly and successfully, the enemy thereafter fought hard, conducting a skilful retreat to Messina which lasted 38 days. After an initial check, Patton made a spectacular advance, occupied airfields in the north-west, and took Palermo on 22 July. He then pressed on eastward, accomplishing on the way, a series of three seaborne amphibious 'left hooks' aimed at landings behind the retreating enemy. Cunningham referred to them as 'a striking example of the proper use of sea power'. Regrettably, in spite of Patton's 'left hooks' the Germans were always able to keep ahead of him and avoid being trapped. Warships were kept busy answering calls for bombardment, repelling aircraft in concert with the air forces, opening up ports, and attacking enemy submarines of which 11 were sunk and one captured intact before the end of July. The most stubborn opposition put up by the enemy was in front of the British Eighth Army. Ships stood by off the east coast, ready to take off troops if necessary, so as to land them in the rear of the enemy if required. This service was not implemented, with the result that the defenders were driven back towards Messina where many of them, about 100,000, were able to escape to the mainland with great quantities of guns, vehicles, and equipment, greatly assisted in their withdrawal by the converging coast lines at this point. There was lack of co-ordination on the Allies' side in the latter half of the operation, probably due to the service commanders not being together in one headquarters.

Cunningham in his dispatch brought out the point that: 'No use was made by the Eighth Army of amphibious opportunities. The small LSTs were kept standing by for the purpose . . . and landing-craft were available on call. There were doubtless sound military reasons for making no use of this, what to me appeared, priceless asset of sea power and flexibility of manoeuvre: but it is worth consideration for future occasions whether much time and costly fighting could not be saved by even minor flank moves which must necessarily be unsettling to the enemy.' Such a policy was successfully adopted by the Americans during the Korea war of 1950–53.

Morison[10] has referred to HUSKY as a 'poor strategic plan, better calculated to push the Axis forces out of Sicily than to trap them in Sicily'. 'But,' Morison continues, 'its chief weakness lay in the refusal of the USAF to co-operate, largely because General "Tooey" Spaatz was wedded to the concept of "strategic" air operations – which meant the USAF fighting its own war. He planned to devote practically his entire strength to fighting the Luftwaffe and the Royal Italian Air Force. The amphibious expedition sailed and landed with no promise of tactical support from the air, and almost none did it obtain.'

German reinforcements brought into Sicily at the end of July were not for the purpose of maintaining a defence, so much as to conduct a delaying action to cover the evacuation of Axis forces from the north-eastern triangle of mountainous country. Liddell Hart[11] writes: 'The ably organised withdrawal across the Straits of Messina was carried out . . . without suffering any serious interception or loss from the Allied air or sea forces. Nearly 40,000 German troops and over 60,000 Italians were safely evacuated . . . the Germans brought away nearly 10,000 vehicles, 47 tanks, 94 guns, and 17,000 tons of equipment.'

When the Allied forces entered Messina on 17 August most of their quarry had escaped. The question as to why such a successful evacuation was permitted by the Allies with their preponderance of sea and air strength has been much discussed and is well covered by Roskill.[12] It must be realised that the straits, which were only $2\frac{1}{2}$ miles wide at the narrowest point, were strongly protected by batteries on both sides. In spite of these, light craft and sometimes heavier ships operated in these waters, the main thought then being to prevent the passage of reinforcements to Sicily. No attempt however was made to produce a co-ordinated plan to subdue the batteries until the first evacuations were well under way, and even then little effective action seemed to follow. It is certain that the matter was raised by Cunningham's staff, but Cunningham himself admits to paying insufficient attention to the matter. His staff were of the opinion that he paid attention all right, but could never forget the fate of some of the heavy ships sent in to bombard the gun batteries in the Dardanelles in 1915, and was therefore against the use of ships for this purpose.

Admiral Oliver[13] writes: 'With reference to the alleged failure to stop the escape of enemy forces from Sicily across the Messina Straits into Calabria. In a letter to me, dated 28 November 1953, ABC wrote:

". . . I am at the moment engaged in a long discussion by air mail with Morison the USA Naval Historian. He wants to know why the Navy and the Air didn't stop the four German divisions and some Italians getting back to Italy from Sicily. I don't think he realises the difficulty of stopping anyone trickling back over a journey of under 20 minutes. Still I have the sort of feeling that the Cs-in-C never discussed it!! I may be wrong though my memory is not what it was."

'I believe, myself, that an attempt to prevent this traffic by surface forces would have been hazardous and costly in the extreme by day and much less than effective by night. One has only to look at the chart to appreciate this, bearing in mind the numbers of enemy batteries mounted on both sides of the straits. Perhaps something might have been done less hazardously by round-the-clock air attacks, but I fancy that the Air Forces had many other calls to meet at that time; moreover, we had not yet at that time developed dive- and rocket-bombing to anything like the extent we did later on – following the example of our enemies.'

On the air side, plans seemed to be equally paralysed until it was too late, the Tactical Air Force being employed in local support of the Army, and the Strategic Air Force being already committed against targets in Italy. 'The correct policy,' says Roskill, 'was for the strategic bombers to attack terminal ports until they made embarkation imposs-ible, and for the tactical bombers to neutralise the coastal batteries sufficiently to enable our warships to seize control of the narrows; and had a joint plan been made to accomplish those objects, it is difficult not to believe that we could have stopped the evacuation.' Ironically the greater part of the Axis traffic crossed by day, and moreover Axis air activity was negligible.

ᴐ   unningham concludes that Eisenhower should have called a meeting of the three Commanders-in-Chief. It is evident that all the leaders were stretched to the limit at this time, concerned more about the next step than day-to-day problems. Increasing strength and success had perhaps caused the Allies to lean more on the strategical than the tactical aspect of warfare. Moreover it must be realised that there were many continuing and urgent political problems to be sorted out, in addition to the purely military difficulties that occurred daily. As an example, Ambrose[14] refers to the details of seven telegrams addressed to Eisenhower on one day, each conflicting with the others, and arriving from vastly different sources.

Cunningham praised the Allied Merchant Navies for their great part in what Churchill called 'an undertaking of the first magnitude'. During the actual operations, and the transport of men and material to Sicily from Great Britain and the United States, no more than 85,000 tons of shipping had been lost. British naval losses were two submarines, three torpedo-boats, and some landing-craft, but the aircraft carrier *Indomitable* had been hit by an aircraft torpedo, and the cruisers *Cleopatra* and *Newfoundland* were torpedoed by U-boats. These three ships were, however, able to reach Malta safely. On completion of the occupation of Sicily, Cunningham was presented with the Grand Cordon of the Legion of Honour by General Giraud at a colourful ceremony in Algiers.

Much gratification for Cunningham followed the receipt of the following dispatch from General Alexander:

'On the Navy fell the weight of what was in some ways the most arduous, detailed, and vital part of the operation: the task of conveying, assembling, and directing to obscure and unlit beaches in an enemy territory, an Armada of 2,000 ships and craft. I must mention only in passing the assistance of naval gunfire on the beaches, and the silent strength of the covering forces waiting, and hoping, for the appearance in defence of its native soil of that fleet which once claimed to dominate the Mediterranean. It is a theme of which the Royal Navy and the US Navy are justly proud.'

In Victory: Magnanimity (September 1943)

Italian morale was low. There was much talk of having been let down by the Germans, and thoughts of surrender were spreading. There was no enthusiasm for a long hard defence in Italy. On the authority of the King of Italy, Marshal Badoglio took over as head of the government from Mussolini on 25 July 1943, by which time plans were already being discussed for an Allied amphibious landing at Salerno (operation AVALANCHE), to the south of Naples, in September, and for which operational orders were complete by the end of August: see map 20. Peace feelers had secretly been put out by Badoglio, but it was known that the Germans were tightening their grip on Italy, and reinforcing lines of defence.

A provisional armistice between Italy and the Allies was signed (3 September 1943) by which the Italian armed forces were immediately to cease hostilities, and the Italian fleet and aircraft were to be transferred to the Allies. The text also included many other items of co-operation. Early hopes that this would mean the end of the war in the Mediterranean soon proved false, for the Germans fought with renewed vigour, and treated those Italians who supported the Badoglio government as traitors.

In operation BAYTOWN, carried out under the command of Rear-Admiral McGrigor, the British Eighth Army crossed from Sicily to the mainland of Italy (3 September 1943), landing in the vicinity of Reggio, and using the narrow stretch of water across which the Axis forces had withdrawn almost a month previously. Supported by a heavy bombardment from monitors and battleships, they met only weak opposition, for the Germans who had escaped from Sicily were already regrouping in a region round Naples. The Navy had promised the Army that they would ferry 5,000 vehicles in five days. ABC claims delightedly that by working all out, sometimes a dozen trips a day, 5,300 vehicles were taken across the Straits in *three* days. Such an achievement was reminiscent of the enthusiasm of those earlier days when *Scorpion* held the record for coaling ship, and the *Rodney* swept the board at the fleet regatta, mainly due to the will of the man in command who was not prepared to accept second place.

Cunningham, with his usual audacious outlook, had at first favoured a landing near Rome. This was dropped in favour of Salerno (with Naples as the objective), when it was realised that Rome would initially be beyond the range of any Allied shore-based fighters, and also that Germans were pouring into Italy from the north. Even Salerno was beyond the range of all but the modern Allied fighters, and it was therefore planned that there should be a Force V of five of the new British escort carriers, commonly known as Woolworth carriers having been built in America, under Rear-Admiral Sir Philip Vian with his flag in the cruiser *Euryalus* (Captain Eric Bush). These were to provide fighter cover for the beach landings. In addition Willis's Force H would prevent any enemy warship interference, and with two armoured carriers (our old friends the *Illustrious* and *Formidable*) would provide anti-submarine patrol as well as fighter cover over the battle fleet. As in operation HUSKY the three Commanders-in-Chief, under Eisenhower, were to be Cunningham, Alexander, and Tedder; but for this operation AVALANCHE all their operational headquarters were to be in the Tunis area. To ensure maximum communication facilities, Cunningham decided to operate from a ship moored alongside at Bizerta. This was the headquarters ship *Largs* with highly specialised communication installations. He points out[1] that 'in staff matters the Navy has a different system from the Army. It is not our custom for the Commander-in-Chief to delegate operational or other important decisions to anyone except perhaps his Chief of Staff. He deals with them himself, and signs all important orders with his own hand.'

Commanders for the landing at Salerno, which was fixed for 9 September 1943, were Vice-Admiral Hewitt for the Navy, and General Mark Clark for the Army. The Fifth Army under Clark consisted of the British X Corps and the American VI Corps, all of whom were to be landed on a 15-mile length of beach stretching south-east from Salerno which itself was some 30 miles south-eastward of Naples. Commodore G. N. Oliver was to be Northern Attack Force Commander, responsible for the British landing at the northern end of the beach; while Rear-Admiral John L. Hall, USN, was to be Southern Attack Force Commander, responsible for the American landing at the southern end; both were under Hewitt. Oliver[2] writes:

'After I had been hauled in, in the autumn of 1942, to work under

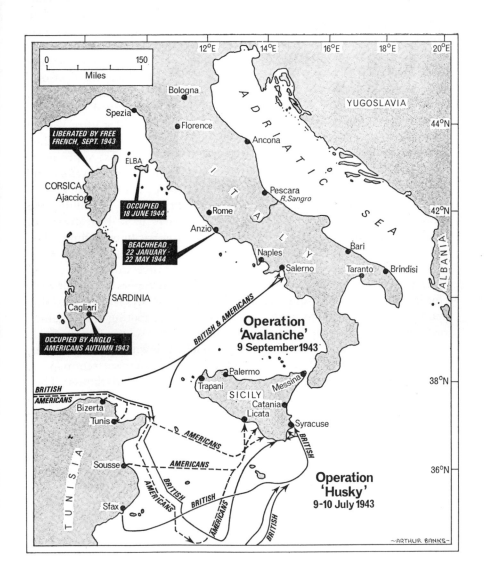

Miles
0 ————— 150

12°E 14°E 16°E 18°E 20°E

Bologna

Spezia

LIBERATED BY FREE FRENCH, SEPT. 1943

ELBA

CORSICA
Ajaccio

OCCUPIED 18 JUNE 1944

Rome

Anzio

BEACHHEAD 22 JANUARY - 22 MAY 1944

Naples
Salerno

SARDINIA

Cagliari

OCCUPIED BY ANGLO - AMERICANS AUTUMN 1943

Florence

Ancona

A D R I A T I C

YUGOSLAVIA

44°N

Pescara
R.Sangro

I T A L Y

42°N

Bari

Taranto   Brindisi

S E A

ALBANIA

BRITISH & AMERICANS

Operation
'Avalanche'
9 September 1943

Palermo

Trapani

SICILY

Messina

Catania

Licata

Syracuse

38°N

BRITISH
AMERICANS

Bizerta

Tunis

T U N I S I A

Sousse

Sfax

AMERICANS

AMERICANS

BRITISH

AMERICANS

BRITISH

BRITISH

BRITISH

36°N

Operation
'Husky'
9-10 July 1943

~ARTHUR BANKS~

ABC as Commodore (Flotillas) at Gibraltar, he sent me up to Bone as Senior Officer Inshore Squadron. At the end of June 1943, I was made Commodore of Force N and sent to Algiers with my little team to plan, with the British X Corps and the US Navy. At the Salerno landings, RN and USN ships and craft were entirely interchangeable. For the actual assault I had the US Rear-Admiral Conolly under me, because he didn't want to miss the assault and preferred to "take his coat off" just for the occasion rather than detail a more junior officer for the job.

'For about the first week at Salerno the soldiers depended very much on ships' gunfire; the bombarding squadrons and flotillas were kept at full strength in spite of losses from radio-controlled bombs, and, when things got rather sticky on shore, *Warspite* and *Valiant* were promptly sent in to reinforce the bombardment, with a promise of *Nelson* and *Rodney* as well. ABC never hesitated to take risks when necessary.'

The British convoys used Bizerta and Tripoli for assembly; the Americans used Algiers and Oran. All convoys passed westward of Sicily to give the impression of a move towards Sardinia, calling when necessary at ports on the north coast of Sicily to refuel. The force comprised some 700 vessels, and both Attack Force Commanders had heavy ships for bombardment, as well as minesweepers and light craft for inshore work. Shuttle service and follow-up convoys from the loading ports to Salerno were to begin as soon as a secure footing was obtained ashore.

The first waves of assaulting troops touched down on 9 September, as in the invasion of Sicily, about an hour before sunrise: see map 21. This was in accordance with the Army's wishes for darkness. They hoped thereby to achieve surprise. For the same reason, there was no preliminary air bombing or naval bombardment. The Navy's preference was for an assault after dawn, so that the allocated approach and landing positions could be attained accurately and in accordance with the time schedule. The Navy also felt that a preliminary softening up was well worth any loss of surprise that might result. Such a policy was to be adopted eventually, for the June 1944 landings in France, but regrettably not at Salerno where, despite the precautions aiming at surprise, the assault encountered strongly prepared positions, with the Germans firing heavy guns at the landing-craft, and their troops contesting possession of the beaches.

The news of the cessation of hostilities by Italian armed forces had been publicly announced by Eisenhower and Badoglio on the previous evening, 8 September, as the assault convoys were approaching Salerno. The announcement produced a more stringent attitude in the Germans, at the same time giving false hope to many of the Allied invaders that the Italians were no longer opposed to them, and might now intervene on their behalf. But the armistice[3] had not been achieved without equivocation and vacillation on the part of those Italians in close contact with the Germans, and the position in some matters was obscure. One thing was clear however: that was that the Italian fleet was to be immediately transferred to 'such points as may be designated by the Allied Commander-in-Chief'.

In the meantime, although initial German opposition to the landings at Salerno had been temporarily overcome, and the beaches were in Allied hands, penetration by the Allies had not been extensive, and there was a five-mile gap between the British and American assault forces. This gap the Germans endeavoured to exploit by a well-developed counter-attack. By 13 September the situation was becoming critical. The Germans were able to use mobile guns in the hills beyond the bridge-head. Moreover they now had at their disposal a potent new weapon in the shape of radio-controlled bombs launched and directed by aircraft, which proved to be an instant menace to the bombarding ships of the Allies. The American cruisers *Philadelphia* and *Savannah* both suffered severe damage, as did the British cruiser *Uganda*.

On 14 September the increasing weight of German attack forced the Americans to give more ground on their beaches, and Admiral Hewitt stopped unloading supplies, in case withdrawal became necessary. He signalled Cunningham for heavy bombardment which was soon provided by the arrival of *Warspite* and *Valiant* (as already described by Oliver) with a screen of six destroyers from Malta. Reinforcements were brought in by the British cruisers *Euryalus*, *Scylla*, and *Charybdis* from Tripoli. There was great surprise therefore when a request was received from General Clark that day, to prepare plans for the withdrawal of troops at one sector, with a view to transferring them to another.

Cunningham[4] writes:

'Oliver gave it as his firm opinion that considering enemy opposition and the nature of the beaches for re-embarkation, the operation of transferring troops from one attack area to the other was not to be contemplated. Now that the troops were ashore, the only thing was to stay and fight it out with all the support the Navy could give them in the way of gunfire. . . . The further progress of the troops depended on our ability to keep the beaches open, and to go on unloading men, guns, ammunition, and stores.

'I consider that General McCreery [Commander of X Corps] and Commodore Oliver displayed most commendable firmness and resolution in adopting the attitude they did. Any evacuation or partial evacuation from one or other of the narrow Allied beach-heads would have

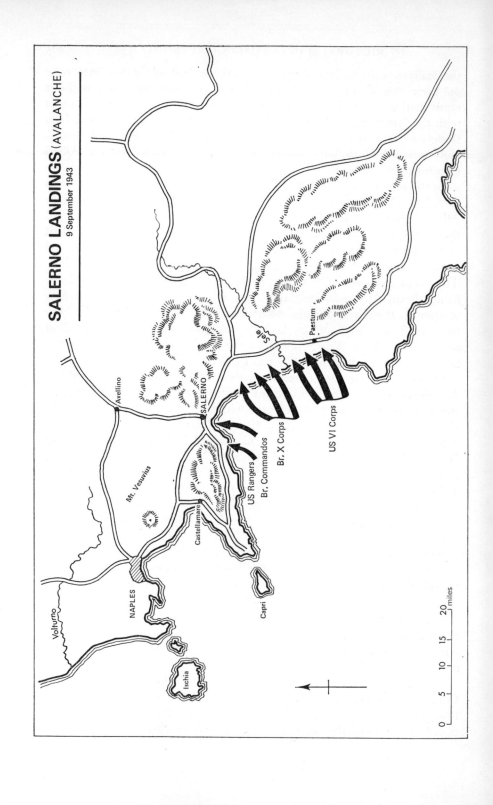

SALERNO LANDINGS (AVALANCHE)

9 September 1943

Volturno

NAPLES

Castellamare

Mt. Vesuvius

Avellino

SALERNO

Sele

Sele

Paestum

Ischia

Capri

US Rangers

Br. Commandos

Br. X Corps

US VI Corps

0   5   10   15   20 miles

resulted in a reverse of the first magnitude; an Allied defeat which would have completely offset the Italian surrender, and have been hailed by the Germans as a smashing victory.'

An account of the situation in detail is given by Roskill,[5] who concludes that on 14 September 'withdrawal in the face of heavy pressure could only result in utter disaster. By the evening, the situation, though still dangerous, had improved somewhat, and Admiral Hewitt ordered a partial resumption of the unloading.'

Cunningham embarked in the destroyer *Offa* on 17 September to visit the operational area. Having called on Hewitt he then went on with him to the British landings farther north, and had lunch in the *Hilary* with Oliver, the latter in the words of ABC 'as ever on the crest of a wave: calm, imperturbable, and completely optimistic'.

After frustration of the German counter-attack the Allied build-up grew rapidly. On 16 September the advance forces of Montgomery's Eighth Army gained touch with Clark's Fifth Army, and by 1 October Allied troops were in Naples, and naval clearance parties were beginning the task of restoring the port to normal use. The continued Allied advance through Italy, though subject to temporary setbacks and delays due to the early onset of winter, was now no longer in doubt. The Allies already had a firm foothold inside the Fortress of Europe.

On 16 September the *Warspite*, completing her third bombardment of the day, was hit and severely damaged by a radio-controlled bomb, which also inflicted many casualties. With all boilers out of action she was towed through the Straits of Messina to Malta; a most difficult operation, for at one stage she broke loose and drifted sideways through the Straits. This gallant old ship was very popular in the Royal Navy. Cunningham had flown his flag in the *Warspite* both in peace and in war, and, in 1940 and 1941 particularly, had seen much action in her in his unrelenting efforts to 'seek out and destroy' the Italian fleet. In due course she was to be repaired and would take part in the bombardment of enemy emplacements at the Normandy landings in June 1944. 'I know of no ship with a worthier fighting record,' Cunningham wrote.

Only a few days earlier, on 10 September, the *Warspite* in company with the *Valiant*, after being detached from Force H, had on Cunningham's instructions, met off the coast of Africa, north of Bone, the Italian squadron which had sailed from Spezia in the very early hours of 9 September. A special route west of Corsica had been prescribed for the Italian squadron, which comprised three battleships, six cruisers, and eight destroyers. The battleships were the new 15-inch, 46,000-ton, 30-knot *Roma*, and her two slightly older sister ships the 15-inch, 41,000-ton, 30-knot *Vittorio Veneto* and *Italia* (previously named

Littorio). Although the ships slipped from Spezia unobserved, they were attacked by German planes flown from the South of France, using the new radio-controlled bombs. The *Roma* was sunk with heavy loss of life. The *Italia* was slightly damaged, but with the *Vittorio Veneto* and the rest of the force, proceeded on her way, to be met by the *Warspite* and *Valiant* the next morning. From Taranto on 9 September a squadron comprising the two 12½-inch, 29,000-ton, 26-knot battleships *Doria* and *Duilio* and two cruisers sailed for Malta. Unmolested by the Germans they arrived safely the following day. A sixth battleship, the 12½-inch, 29,000-ton, 26-knot *Cesare* succeeded in escaping from Trieste. Her sister ship the *Cavour*, still rebuilding at Trieste after being sunk at Taranto 1940, was captured by the Germans. Other ships also arrived, singly or in small groups, but many were lost either in action or from scuttling. 'In all,' writes Rear-Admiral de Belot,[6] '5 battleships, 8 cruisers, 7 destroyers, 24 torpedo-boats, 40 submarines, 19 corvettes, 32 MTBs, an aircraft supply ship, 3 mine-sweepers, and various auxiliaries went over to the Allied side, along with about 100 merchant ships totalling 170,000 tons. Once again,' he continues, 'Admiral Cunningham showed himself to be a great commander: he avoided all vexatious requirements, required no purging of the staffs, and took only essential security measures.' This victorious operation was appropriately named GIBBON, to commemorate the decline and fall of Mussolini who in his untimely and unwise decision of June 1940 had cast in his lot with Hitler, hoping to be in time to collect the lucrative spoils of a speedy and prosperous war. But for the presence of Cunningham in the Mediterranean he might well have succeeded.

Bragadin[7] complains of the use of the term 'surrender' in relation to the delivery of the Italian fleet into Allied hands, and some authors have avoided this offensive word. But Cunningham, with his directness and his feeling for the exact sense of words, uses it without restraint. To surrender means to yield; and this is exactly what the Italian ships were now doing under the orders of the man who had been their most vigorous opponent, and whom they had defied for three momentous years in those confined waters of the so-called *mare nostrum*. This great sailor now behaved with magnanimity towards the ships and men whom he had previously sought to destroy. He had been a senior commander at the conclusion of the First World War in which one of the most dramatic occasions had been the German naval surrender. Both the *Warspite* and the *Valiant*, now acting in their same role, had been present at the spectacular surrender of the German fleet 21 November 1918; almost a quarter of a century earlier. 'As the naval representative at those fascinating negotiations in Sicily,' writes Dick, 'I was quite clear that this was in fact a surrender however much the Italians claimed, and they certainly did, that they were only there to come in on our side.'

Cunningham however was not to be deterred by any sentiment while there was action to be taken. As soon as he knew that the Italian fleet was committed to submission on 8 September, it occurred to him that there could be little opposition at Taranto to stop the Allies from occupying that port, provided that action was taken immediately. Eisenhower, agreed, and it was decided that the 1st Airborne Division, then at Bizerta, should be lifted that very evening by ships of the 12th Cruiser Squadron, *Aurora, Penelope, Sirius,* and *Dido,* in company with the cruiser mine-layer *Abdiel* and the US cruiser *Boise.* The operation was not without risk, for little was known about the minefields or the manning of forts and batteries. To make certain, Cunningham adopted the bold measure of ordering Vice-Admiral, Malta (A. J. Power), to hoist his flag in the battleship *Howe* and to take the battleship *King George V* and four destroyers under his command, for the purpose of meeting the ships that had embarked troops at Bizerta, and then to escort them to Taranto. Preceded by mine-sweepers, Power entered the harbour at Taranto late on the afternoon of 9 September, met no resistance, and disembarked troops and stores. Regrettably the *Abdiel,* that fine fast ship with a wonderful war record, struck a mine on the following day and sank with heavy loss of life. The port and harbour of Taranto were soon in full use, however. The troops occupied the town, and boldly marched north to join the Eighth Army with the promise of early reinforcements direct from Alexandria. In due course, thanks to full co-operation by the local Italian naval authorities, all the important naval bases in the south of Italy were available for use by the Allies.

'The Airborne division was chosen,' writes Dick, 'because no other troops were available. This was most fortunate because they had just that extra flexibility and enterprise. We always thought that a run of the mill division would have dug itself in. Instead the Airborne division rushed up to Foggia (using the ordinary train service), and that was the vital target, for thereafter the whole of that complex was available to the Allies. Had the Germans called their bluff there were ample troops to drive the Airborne division out.'

It was at 0600 on 10 September that the Italian ships were met by the *Warspite, Valiant,* and destroyers. The flagship was boarded by ABC's Staff Officer Plans, Captain Tom Brownrigg, previously Master of the Fleet; the Italian ships then formed in line astern of the two British battleships with destroyers on each flank. For Cunningham this was probably his finest hour. He writes with great feeling of embarking in the destroyer *Hambledon* (Lieutenant-Commander G. W. McKendrick) with Eisenhower and Royer Dick, to watch the assembly of ships ceremoniously passing Bizerta on their way to Malta.

'To me,' he says,[8] 'it was a most moving and thrilling sight. To see my wildest hopes of years back, brought to fruition, and my former flagship the *Warspite*, which had struck the first blow against the Italians three years before, leading her erstwhile opponents into captivity, filled me with the deepest emotion and lives with me still. I can never forget it. I made a signal congratulating the *Warspite* on her proud and rightful position at the head of the line.'

There were many present who will remember the approach of the Italian ships and the dramatic moment of sighting them at 15 miles, no longer as targets in a director sight, yet still providing the thrill of identification. For some with memories of Calabria, Matapan, and Sirte, the moment was full of wonder; for others there was pathos and recollection of shipmates lost; but for all was the great feeling of triumph at last. On the evening of 10 September the Commander-in-Chief ordered that 'the Italian fleet having scrupulously honoured the engagement entered into by their Government, officers and ships' companies are to be treated with courtesy and consideration on all occasions'. On the following day Cunningham made his stirring and unforgettable signal to the Admiralty:

'Be pleased to inform Their Lordships that the Italian battle fleet now lies at anchor beneath the guns of the fortress of Malta.'[9]

In view of Cunningham's chivalrous reference to the scrupulous behaviour of the Italians, it is interesting to read extracts from a report by an officer[10] who saw a different side, when given the responsibility for berthing the three Italian battleships *Duilio*, *Cesare*, and *Doria*, in Marsa Xlokk Harbour, Malta, 9 September 1943, an operation 'not without incident'. . . .

'11. At last we entered harbour and *Oriania* [tug] promptly parted her wire in trying to haul us [*Cesare*] towards our berth well to windward. When ordered to push, *Oriania* stove a hole in herself on a projection, so a large manilla (of great age) was run from *Cesare* but promptly parted. As we were drifting across the harbour an anchor was let go and providentially *Oriania* produced her last and biggest wire, and in due course we middled, about 1600.

'13. Except for the Doctor, who took an active interest, and the Captain when on periodic visits, I heard no Italian officer give an order on the forecastle.

'14. By 1915, after 5 hours' work on the forecastle, only interrupted when an issue of wine was made, or when the rating working the cable holder was refilling his pipe, the *Cesare* was moored.

'15. I then went on board the *Doria*. . . . Lt.-Cdr Cowburn had been unable to board her outside due to the swell. He told me that on his arrival they had no chart in sight and intended mooring by eye. He rigged the chart table and laid out his chart, but whilst getting a fix his chart was folded away and the chart table unrigged. After discussion, whilst the ship drifted to leeward, he was able to convince them of the necessity of mooring in the assigned position.

'19. The day's work was certainly an experience to all concerned. The moments of peril and periodic brisk feats of agility necessary to remain whole on the forecastle were more than compensated for by the knowledge gained of Italian seamanship and of the help they got in times of stress by dramatic appeals to their parents, grandparents, and numerous quite obscure saints.'

With the transfer of the Italian fleet to Allied control, the need for cover by the battleships of Force H in the Mediterranean ceased to exist, and covetous eyes began to be cast, typified by the following signal from Admiral Sir Bruce Fraser, Commander-in-Chief of the Home Fleet.

'From C-in-C HF to C-in-C Med.
'Your light so shines before men that they see your good works and magnify the number of ships we expect to be returned from the Med.
08 2122 Sept.'

To which ABC replied in non-committal language:

'We have been gathering Wops to-day, Wops to-day, Wops to-day.
Who will you send to fetch them away, fetch them away, fetch them away,
On a calm September morning.
10 1103 Sept.'

The retention of the heavy ships had been more than justified during the critical situation of 14 September and the following two days when the great naval guns were brought to bear and were almost continuously in action against the German concentration of troops and the gun batteries in the hills flanking and dominating the Salerno beach. They had been denied their appropriateness for softening up *before* AVA-LANCHE; without them on 14–16 September it is certain that the whole operation would have ended in disaster for the Allies. The Germans themselves attributed their own failure to the devastating effect of the naval guns. Nor should it be forgotten that it was the presence and mobility of the British aircraft carrier that provided a local air strength which was not in the first few days possible for shore-based aircraft.

Cunningham's report on AVALANCHE included the following:

'That it succeeded after many vicissitudes reflected great credit on Admiral Hewitt, USN, his subordinate commanders and all those who served under them. That there were extremely anxious moments cannot be denied. I am proud to say that throughout the operation the Navies never faltered and carried out their tasks in accordance with the highest traditions of their Services. Whilst full acknowledgement must be made of the devastating though necessarily intermittent bombing by the Allied Air Forces, it was the Naval gunfire, incessant in effect, that held the ring when there was danger of the enemy breaking through to the beaches and when the overall position looked so gloomy.'

Cunningham found the Italian force too large to be kept at Malta, and sent the *Vittorio Veneto* and the *Italia* to Alexandria, escorted by the *Howe*, *King George V*, and six destroyers.

A correspondent[11] provides an Italian admiral's view of Cunningham.

'I was stationed at Fayid in 1943, as CRE Canal Area. This included the Bitter Lake in which two Italian warships were interned – the *Vittorio Veneto* and *Italia*, two beautiful ships. The Area Commander asked me to deputise for him and see the Italian admiral regarding a request he had made to allow his sailors ashore for recreation. I was duly piped aboard and taken down to the Admiral's cabin. We discussed the business, then he asked if I would like to see the ship. He took me over and I was particularly interested in a catapult arrangement for launching the spotter plane, but I could not see how or where the plane returned to the ship and voicing this to the old admiral I said: "I suppose you have to heave to, for the plane to settle on the water, and then winch it aboard." "WHAT; STOP THIS SHIP WITH CUNNINGHAM IN THE MEDITERRANEAN? Not likely, the plane has to go ashore!!"'

The Italians were in a position somewhat similar to, though not altogether the same as, that faced by the French in June 1940, concerning which Cunningham had shown so much patience and understanding despite the forceful prodding from home. Rear-Admiral de Belot, of the French Navy, writes of him at this time as having 'directed British and Allied naval forces in masterly fashion. To Frenchmen,' he continues, 'he will remain one of those foreign commanders who best understood France's mournful situation.'

The fact that Italy had been knocked out of the war proved the correctness of Anglo-American strategy and the wisdom of the policy of attacking the 'soft underbelly' of Fortress Europe. Yet agreement on such policy had not been easily reached. At the TRIDENT conference held in Washington in May 1943, while the battle for Tunis was still raging, the American view was that TORCH and its sequels in the Mediterranean would swallow all such resources as were available, and perhaps lead to still further postponement of OVERLORD (ex-ROUNDUP), the cross-Channel operation which was to be launched from England, planned at that time for May 1944, for the final defeat of Germany. The attitude of the American COS was understandable, for although they had from the beginning agreed on priority for the defeat of Germany over that of Japan, they nevertheless had their problems of finding sufficient resources of trained manpower, shipping, landing-craft, and air strength to meet demands in the Pacific. Moreover the situation in the Indian Ocean, Burma, and the Dutch East Indies, and those places where Japan was retaining a firm hold, did nothing to produce optimism about the future.

At the QUADRANT conference in Quebec in August 1943 it was already known that the Germans had been thrown out of Sicily and that Eisenhower had recommended that the next move should be an assault on the Italian mainland, but, as expected, the most important item on the agenda was the consideration by the CCS of the plans that had been produced for OVERLORD, and there was careful analysis, at the instigation of Brooke, of the relationship which must exist between the cross-Channel and Italian operations. They could not be discussed in isolation.

The British COS succeeded[12] in getting the principle of flexibility and the interdependence of the two operations accepted and recorded, but only by abandoning what had been called the Stand-Still order which had required that Eisenhower should keep everyone and everything for his further Mediterranean assaults: seven battle-tested divisions together with shipping and landing-craft, the latter of fundamental importance to Cunningham.

It was at QUADRANT that a Supreme Allied Commander, South-East Asia, was nominated. It had been agreed at TRIDENT (Washington, May 1943) that he should be British. Cunningham was offered this appointment but was not enthusiastic: 'too old a dog to learn new tricks'. Churchill however nominated acting Vice-Admiral Lord Louis Mountbatten, then serving as Chief of Combined Operations, for the appointment.[13] This was highly acceptable to Roosevelt and to the JCS, and heralded a successful era for the Allied war in the Far East.

Although there was still a limitation of resources in all theatres, the crucial shortages of 1941 and 1942 were over, nor was there any doubt in Cunningham's mind that victory over the Germans must now follow, even though the long road to Berlin would prove hard and tragic. Overshadowing a general optimism was the news from home that the First Sea Lord, Sir Dudley Pound, was gravely ill. That he was failing had been obvious for some time, and he himself had more than once talked of resigning and of Cunningham relieving him in the appointment of First Sea Lord. For more than four years he had borne heavy responsibility and had never spared himself from the great load of administrative work and his counsel on the COS Committee.

The prospect of moving from the Mediterranean scene which had been his passionate interest for four years, to take over the considerable administrative problems of the First Sea Lord, even though it meant occupying the senior post in the Royal Navy, could not have been a congenial one for Cunningham, especially as the fruits of his long command were now being harvested. On 1 October 1943 Allied troops entered Naples. Meanwhile the Germans had speedily evacuated Sardinia and were now withdrawing from Corsica in operations in which Allied ships were supported by cruisers and destroyers of a Free French squadron. Allied acquisition of airfields in these two islands was to help considerably in the planning of the next amphibious operation, SHINGLE, which aimed at a landing at Anzio, close to Rome.

Sir Dudley Pound had attended QUADRANT with the Prime Minister and the British COS in August, and had suffered a stroke before returning home in the battle cruiser *Renown*. He partially recovered but suffered a second stroke after arrival in England, which left him paralysed and brought about his death on 21 October 1943: the anniversary of Trafalgar. Ismay[14] writes: 'He was a master of his profession, a sailor to the very depths of his being. . . . There had been a good deal of chaff about his habit of apparently sleeping through important meetings. But on the mention of the word "destroyer" or of any harbour, he was wide awake at once, and showed that he had been following the discussion more closely than many of those who had their eyes open. He was a brave, generous character, and a willing horse if ever there was one.'

'His greatest achievement,' says Roskill,[15] 'lay perhaps in the steadying influence he exerted in high places . . . he was in the Prime Minister's confidence from the beginning, and retained it to the last.'

As soon as it was known in the Navy that Pound was failing, the general opinion was that Cunningham would succeed to the senior post, because of his tremendous prestige. Churchill was reluctant to allow Cunningham to leave the scene of his great successes. His first choice was Admiral Sir Bruce Fraser, at that time Commander-in-Chief Home Fleet. An outstanding officer, Fraser had served in the early years of the war in the very demanding job of Third Sea Lord and Controller of the Navy, with great success and without showing signs of fatigue. He had soon won Churchill's confidence. Cunningham on the other hand had frequently replied to Churchill's prodding signals in terse unyielding phrases, and it is certain that the Prime Minister in consequence intended not to risk having another Jacky Fisher as First Sea Lord. Fraser however declined Churchill's offer, indicating that whereas he himself had the confidence of his own fleet, Cunningham had the confidence and support of the whole Navy. He asked Churchill to weigh the matter longer.

On 28 September Cunningham was ordered home for consultation, and before leaving informed Eisenhower of the situation. The latter, aware of his reluctance to relinquish his Allied command for an office desk, assured him that it would be his duty to accept the appointment of First Sea Lord if offered.

Cunningham[16] has written: 'I knew that the office desk was not my strong suit. My own feeling was that however grieved I might be at leaving the Mediterranean it was my duty to go to the Admiralty if it were felt throughout the Service that I should go.' It certainly was felt, for he received assurances from many senior officers, including members of the Board of Admiralty: in particular the Deputy First Sea Lord Admiral Sir Charles Kennedy-Purvis who had previously assisted him at the Admiralty in 1938; and the Second Sea Lord Admiral Sir William Jock Whitworth. When Mr. A. V. Alexander, the First Lord, finally convinced the Prime Minister that Cunningham was the appropriate choice, Churchill welcomed the new First Sea Lord with grace, and the appointment was made on 5 October. Admiral Sir John Cunningham was thereupon appointed to succeed Sir Andrew as Commander-in-Chief Mediterranean, and the latter met him at Algiers on 6 October for the turnover.

Uppermost in mind at this time was the subject of the Dodecanese islands Kos, Leros, and Samos, which had been occupied by British troops after the Italian surrender. Kos had been recaptured by the Germans on 3 October, and the prospect of holding on to Leros and Samos, or of ousting the Germans from Rhodes, was now very much in question by Eisenhower and all the Commanders-in-Chief Mediterranean and Middle East, especially because of a lack of landing-craft. This involved considerable flying for Cunningham, including a trip to Cairo where at the wish of the Prime Minister he had to confer with Mr. Anthony Eden and others. But by 14 October he was packed and ready to leave Algiers. There was a tremendous send off, with Eisenhower and Tedder in attendance; and British, American, and French admirals and generals, and senior officers and officials of every kind. A well rehearsed American ceremonial guard and band provided the generous 'liddle *sur*-prise' already referred to on page 242.

Cunningham felt deep emotion at his departure ceremony, and records: 'I found difficulty in expressing myself when saying farewell to all my faithful friends and comrades. We had passed through troublous times together; but had won through in spite of everything. I was leaving my beloved ships, and the gallant people who manned them. It was a great wrench.'

He concluded his farewell message:

'To you all who have fought and endured with such courage, tenacity, and determination, I send my heartfelt thanks and appreciation. We still have far to go, but I know well that the spirit of our countries will carry us through to the day when we can return to enjoy the blessings of the land with the fruits of our labour.'

Great Sailor

Unlike the War Office or Air Ministry, the Admiralty was an operational headquarters as well as an administrative department, and possessed a vast, stoutly protected War Room called the Citadel, where large charts displayed the actual or likely positions of all important warships and shipping. This was manned continuously and was greatly instrumental in providing vital information for the increasingly successful operations against U-boats. From the very beginning of the war the Admiralty had stressed the right to exercise control widely over naval operations, as made clear in a message[1] from the First Sea Lord to Commander-in-Chief Home Fleet, Admiral Sir Charles Forbes at that time, on 18 August 1939:

'There may be occasions when you are at sea keeping W/T silence when later information makes it necessary to alter your disposition. This can only be done by the Admiralty. I suggest it be recognised that it will be necessary for the Admiralty to order dispositions but Admiralty control will cease as soon as possible.'

Such a policy had proved highly successful, for example, in the finding and sinking of the *Bismarck* in May 1941; but there were also regrettable occasions, such as the Admiralty order to scatter received by arctic convoy PQ 17, July 1942, which was followed by exceptionally heavy losses of ships from the convoy.

Having lost the great Mediterranean command by his elevation to the top post in the Royal Navy, and with recollections of unwelcome 'prodding' and interference from home during his Mediterranean years, Cunningham was resolved to keep intervention in operational matters to a minimum. In any case he was now heavily burdened with Naval Staff problems, many of which had accumulated since Pound's departure. With what a former member of his staff[2] called 'his astonishing decentralisation and reliance on his staff', he was able to cope effectively with the load of administrative work and also to play an effectual part as the new Royal Navy representative on the British COS Committee. Such representation was not altogether to his liking, for he preferred making decisions to arguing at conferences.

'I had an almost complete lack of staff training,' Cunningham[3] writes, 'and have to confess to an inherent difficulty in expressing myself in verbal discussion, except when really roused. I had neither the ability nor knowledge of Brooke and Portal, nor their experience in dealing with members of the Government. Hence I looked forward with trepidation to the meeting of the COS Committee, with the Prime Minister often present.'

There were probably others who had doubts at first, but Brooke was enthusiastic and wrote:[4] 'Andrew Cunningham's arrival in the COS was indeed a happy event for me. I found in him first and foremost one of the most attractive of friends, a charming associate to work with and the staunchest of companions when it came to supporting a policy agreed. His personality, charming smile, and heartwarming laugh were enough to disperse at once those miasmas of gloom and despondency which occasionally swamped the COS.'

The First Sea Lord's daily routine usually began at 0900 with his being briefed on current operations and anti-submarine activities. This was followed by the daily COS meeting at 1030. The afternoon would be spent in dealing with a mass of papers or seeing people, and work would continue until after dinner, except on Mondays when the COS would attend a Cabinet meeting to review the progress of the war. Cunningham complains that it was physically impossible to give more than cursory consideration to the flood of signals and mass of papers which he had to see, and he had to rely on the staff to cope with a mass of detail. He comments on the fact that he was well served by helpful and efficient staff officers. He had no operational responsibility for NEPTUNE, the naval part of operation OVERLORD in June 1944, which was to be the greatest amphibious operation in history; but he relied on the appointments of commanders of proven merit, worthy to continue in the Cunningham tradition. The Allied Naval Commander was to be Admiral Sir Bertram Ramsay, with Rear-Admiral Sir Philip Vian commanding the British naval assault across the Channel, and ABC's old friend Rear-Admiral Alan Kirk, USN, commanding the Americans. The well-tried Commodore G. N. Oliver, of whom Cunningham had such a high opinion, was to have one of the sub-commands of the British naval assault.

The officer[5] who served as Naval Assistant (usually a captain) to Cunningham as First Sea Lord writes:

'I got the impression that ABC was not happy as CNS. He loathed polishing his backside on an office chair, and longed to be out in the field again. Nevertheless he was extremely conscientious, and did everything he could to help his Commanders-in-Chief and the fleet at sea. He was loath to interfere with the man in charge on the spot, unless he was convinced he had some information that his subordinate had not. This was possibly the result of back-seat driving from Whitehall when he was C-in-C Mediterranean.

'I used to try and write his speeches for him, not with great success. He always learnt his speeches off by heart, having only the opening words of each paragraph in front of him in case his memory failed, but it never did.

'I remember him telling me just before he retired, that he would probably have to make a good many more speeches up and down the country, and that his theme was going to be the importance of everyone accepting the responsibilities of citizenship as well as enjoying the privileges. I consider this showed amazing foresight.

'He lived in the flat above the Admiralty during the week, and used to dash down to Bishops Waltham for the week-end, whenever he could. There, of course, he had a scrambler on his telephone. He used to love his fishing and often went off with Brooke, who was also a keen fisherman, as well as an ornithologist.'

Allocation of resources especially in craft and men, together with plans for future ship production, continued to weigh heavily and were closely linked with Allied strategy. Not the least problem was the question of agreeing on the necessity for and the organising of a British fleet for the Pacific, a matter which was not finally settled until late in 1944; but that is another story.

A brief account of working for ABC is provided by Admiral Sir Guy Grantham[6] who as a senior captain was a member of the Joint Planning Staff. He had already, as Captain successively of the *Phoebe*, *Naiad*, and *Cleopatra*, been in the thick of the fighting in the Mediterranean.

'Andrew, as you know, was my great hero, and I am thankful I was able to serve with him not only in the Mediterranean but later as Director of Plans, when I saw him not less than once every day. When I left that job and went to say good-bye he thanked me and then said "My goodness, you have taken some knocks!" I replied, "Yes, sir, but I have always known exactly where I stood."

'As a member of the Joint Planning Staff, Spring 1944 to Spring 1946, six days a week I took part in preparing all the military papers for the Chiefs of Staff. As a matter of principle we always produced agreed papers – no minority views – and, in working out a compromise, it was at times necessary to subordinate the purely naval view on a particular problem. There were days when he said, "What the hell do you mean by signing this paper?" and I had to stick to what I had signed and try and explain the reasons.

'The other Chiefs of Staff were Brooke and Portal: a very strong team, each with his individual character and talent, but all were firm friends. They were a strong combination and, with Pug Ismay's help, were able to avoid the potential diversions in forming strategic policy. When the Combined Chiefs of Staff met, the Joint Planners prepared all the military papers and cleared them with the British COS before they were put to the American COS. The JPS then went with the COS to the joint conferences and I was at Quebec II, Yalta, and Potsdam. At times new subjects had to be examined during the conferences and we then worked on them and produced papers. By and large the joint conferences were interesting and a fairly easy time for the staff.

'Nearly all "personal" telegrams to the First Sea Lord he handed to me to draft replies, and there were many. He nearly always accepted my drafts, and I think we well understood one another.

'I have no hesitation in saying that he was an excellent First Sea Lord and everyone loved working for him. He was very quick in decision, had a great sense of humour, and was human to a degree.'

Honours accrued in those victorious years in which Cunningham held high office. He was created Knight of the Thistle in the New Year Honours, 1 January 1945, an honour which he prized more than any other. It was moreover a particularly inspired idea of Winston Churchill's. A year later he was elevated to the rank and dignity of Viscount. Having served until victory was complete over Germany and Japan, he stepped down from his high seat in 1946, to be relieved as First Sea Lord by Admiral Sir John Cunningham. In the birthday honours of 1946 he was awarded the Order of Merit.

Perhaps it is timely to cast a brief glance at his two term-mates of nearly half a century earlier. Admiral Sir Charles Little had been given the Portsmouth Command upon relinquishing his post as Head of the British Admiralty Delegation, Washington, in 1942, and then retired at the end of the war. After commanding Force H, Admiral Sir James Somerville was appointed Commander-in-Chief Eastern Fleet, December 1945. In the summer of 1943, both Cunningham and he were in turn nominated Supremo for the new unified Command proposed for South-East Asia, an involved appointment complicated in the beginning not only by national susceptibilities but by uncertainties about areas of responsibility and limitation of command. From the retired list, on which he had served since being invalided from the Navy before the war, Somerville was, in August 1944, restored to the active list. In October 1944 he was appointed Head of the British Admiralty Delegation,

Washington, in succession to Admiral Sir Percy Noble. He was promoted Admiral of the Fleet on 8 May 1945, and died on 19 March 1949.

The Bishop of Portsmouth,[7] who had served as a naval chaplain in the *Queen Elizabeth*, saw much of ABC after the latter's retirement from office, and remarks upon his continued activity and his great interest in the young. 'He understood them and what was needed for the development of their manhood, and they held him in respect and affection.' He also describes how happy and proud ABC was to have been appointed High Commissioner of the General Assembly of the Church of Scotland, and specially remarks on the great support given by his wife, Lady Cunningham, at all times during a life in which, despite its fullness, time could always be found for hospitality and welcome for others. In his later years Cunningham began to suffer from heart trouble, obviously due to those many years of concentrated activity and stress. He died suddenly, in a taxi in London, on 12 June 1963, at the age of 80.

'There seemed to be something,' continues the Bishop (by that time Bishop of Norwich), 'in keeping with his character, that he should have died in a taxi rather than at home in bed.'

Cunningham was buried at sea off Portsmouth in wet weather and a rising gale. Admiral Sir Wilfrid Woods,[8] once his Staff Officer Operations, who had never been allowed to forget his report of the 'hostile dog' heard from a submarine lying offshore at night, was as Commander-in-Chief Portsmouth one of the pall bearers who embarked in H.M.S. *Hampshire* at the South Railway Jetty for the burial at sea.

'The procession through the streets of Portsmouth,' writes Woods, 'was profoundly moving. The pavements were lined with people, and the number of ex-sailors who had turned out wearing their medals was very striking.

'The mood changed markedly on board the *Hampshire*. Lady Cunningham's calm, dignified presence, ABC's many distinguished contemporaries and colleagues, and the immaculate bearing and conduct of the ship's company as we steamed out towards the Nab Tower dispelled the heavily charged atmosphere of the procession through the streets.

'After the committal, during the return passage, people began to exchange reminiscences of ABC, and at once our spirits rose. By the time we reached Spithead it was blowing too hard for the ship to enter harbour, and the guests, including numerous ladies, had to be landed by tug. This was no mean performance, involving the negotiation of a very steep brow from ship to tug. It was a scene which everyone felt ABC would have savoured, and there was much speculation as to what his comments would have been.

'Nobody,' concludes Woods, 'who ever met ABC would have failed to have been impressed by his electric personality. He was without question the finest leader I have ever met. He led by sheer force of personal example, and it was this above all that made his hard driving easy to accept, while his ebullient sense of fun and his warm humanity inspired affection as well as respect. During the war the Mediterranean Fleet would have gone through Hell for him, and often did.'

It is pertinent to consider in retrospect what would have happened without the presence of Cunningham in command in the Mediterranean. There was always the risk of his early death in action, especially during 1940 and 1941, and even a chance of his supersession or resignation. It would be generally agreed that the provision of a relief of the same calibre was not possible. It was Cunningham who, on more than one occasion, stuck out for holding the Mediterranean at all cost. Had we abandoned the Mediterranean we should, in Wavell's view, have lost Egypt. If Hitler had then brought Russia quickly to her knees with his blitzkrieg, unrestrained by the fierce struggle to retain Crete, could Britain have long survived? For America was not to enter the war until she was forced into action by Japan's attack on Pearl Harbor at the end of 1941. It may be salutary for those with pacifist tendencies, who disparagingly refer to the glorification of war as if it were an end in itself, to consider for a while whether there would be any sort of freedom now without leaders of the calibre of Cunningham. Apart from his determined struggle in the Mediterranean 1940–42 it is well to remember the fear, as well as the honour and respect, in which he was held by his adversaries. It is also right to emphasise his great contribution to victory by virtue of his acceptability to the American leaders, and the mutual regard and confidence which soon became established.

In a beautiful sermon at the memorial service to Admiral of the Fleet Viscount Cunningham of Hyndhope, KT, GCB, OM, DSO, in St. Paul's Cathedral on Friday 12 July 1963, the Bishop of Norwich (formerly Bishop of Portsmouth) said:

'He was a godly man. . . . I find it entirely fitting to interpret his qualities and gifts as the outcome of a disciplined and thoughtful integrity of response to the will and guidance of God. . . . Thank God for giving our people and nation such a man at such a time.'

In an assessment of Cunningham as Commander it is interesting to analyse him under headings used by Wavell in his Lees-Knowles lectures on 'Generals and Generalship' given at Cambridge in 1939. This seems particularly appropriate in view of the great regard in which Cunningham held Wavell. Briefly the headings are as follows:

Qualities Required by a Commander

1. *Imagination to use New Forces*

ABC had great success in the full employment of the FAA, as at Taranto; radar, as at the Matapan night action; and, in spite of initial difficulties, air reconnaissance and fighter cover at sea, as in operations TORCH, HUSKY and AVALANCHE.

2. *Robustness to Withstand the Shock of War*

ABC excelled in this quality, as revealed at Crete and during the following year of adversity, particularly in the loss of all his battleships late in 1941. In spite of the gloomy outlook he was defiant and resilient in adversity. In victory he was magnanimous but always prepared for reverses. Included under this heading should be his quick decision (19 December 1941) to make appearances normal, with a show of ceremony at the hoisting of 'colours' in battleships which had been seriously damaged during the night.

3. *Robustness to Stand up to Pressure from Political Masters*

He had the self-assurance and independence of mind to be resolute concerning well-considered strategy and bold tactics. His verbal capacity was sufficient to respond in an articulate and convincing manner to the prodding interference from home. He shone particularly in his sensitive handling first of the defeated French and later of the defeated Italian naval forces in spite of advice from home contrary to his own views. His evident integrity and firmness of purpose helped him to excel in establishing confidence in others.

4. *Humanity*

This was one of ABC's great assets and at the root of the confidence which he inspired in those under his command. 'It's going to be all right' was the feeling he inspired; 'the Old Man's with us'. He expected the utmost from everyone, just as he demanded the utmost from himself.

5. *Survival*

ABC had the constitution to continue to drive himself, and by example to keep others going. He had the good luck (and the optimism) to survive where many others failed through ill health or fatigue. He survived despite ignoring his own rules about wearing a steel helmet or falling prostrate before a bomb. To many he seemed to be indestructible.

6. *Flexibility of Mind*

ABC loathed accepted slogans or fixed principles, and refused to be limited by them or by staff advice that savoured of orthodoxy. It is probable that his concern that other commanders should have flexibility of mind was the reason for his repudiating any attempt at interference with another command. 'Leave it to the commander on the spot,' he would say, 'unless you are aware of something important of which he is ignorant.' His tactics throughout the battle of Matapan were the result of quick decisions, not necessarily conforming to staff opinion. 'I paid respectful attention . . .', he says, 'and told them I would have my evening meal and would see how I felt afterwards.' In the event he decided to attack, despite the advice that it would be unwise to charge blindly after the retreating enemy in the dark.

It is fortunate that Cunningham was esteemed and suitably honoured as a great sailor during his lifetime. Reputations sometimes tend to fade after death. How appropriate, therefore, that less than four years after his death a bust should be unveiled by H.R.H. Prince Philip, the Duke of Edinburgh, and dedicated to his memory on Sunday 2 April 1967, in Trafalgar Square. As at his burial at sea in 1963, the rain lashed down driven by a fitful wind. Buglers of the Royal Marines sounded the alert, as the Duke arrived wearing the uniform of an Admiral of the Fleet. The Duke was received by the Lieutenant of Greater London, Field-Marshal Earl Alexander of Tunis.

Those who were there to honour the great warrior were so impressed by the solemnity of the occasion as scarcely to notice the squalls and the heavy rain. Cunningham had come to join three other great sailors, Nelson, Jellicoe, and Beatty, in the Square which commemorated Britain's greatest naval victory. How fitting the words Tennyson attributes to Nelson on an earlier occasion:

> *Who is he that cometh, like an honour'd guest,*
> *With banner and with music, with soldier and with priest,*
> *With a nation weeping, and breaking on my rest?*

The Viscountess Cunningham of Hyndhope received many heart-warming letters from those who had attended this impressive ceremony. In all there is a note of affection or gratitude: 'We count ourselves so fortunate that we have been able to see first hand yours and Uncle Ned's fine example, which the world so much needs to-day.' In one there is jocularity at the thought of ABC himself witnessing the scene: 'I suspect the Admiral was delighted to see the gentlemen from Whitehall getting a thoroughly good soaking in the rain.' In another there is reference to 'strong feelings of loyalty and regard for the greatest seaman of the century'. It is relevant to quote three further statements because of the allusion to Nelson.

The first[9] stated simply: 'When we were home we raised our glasses to his memory, with the Baltic toast to Nelson, "May he who is no longer our Commander, be our example".'

The second[10] said: 'Greatness lies in Courage, Energy, and Honesty. Anyone who excelled in all three, as Andrew did, was destined to become one of the stars of history. In this he stands with Nelson. I think that no great man was ever loved so much, certainly not more. The love and confidence of his fleet was the same as that reposed in Nelson.'

The third,[11] from Field-Marshal the Earl Alexander of Tunis, remarked with simple grace:

'I cannot refrain from saying how moved and impressed I was at the unveiling ceremony this morning. . . . Everything was just right for the memorial to a great Sailor. . . . And what a terrific, honoured privilege to have one's personal memorial in perpetuity there in Trafalgar Square beneath the shadow of Nelson's Column. He has earned his place there amongst the great Sea Commanders of our island race. We soldiers who owed so much to the Royal Navy during the last World War feel deeply privileged to-day in having our opportunity to pay our respects and homage to your husband and our Wartime Comrade.

Yours sincerely,
Alexander'

Few of those who really knew Cunningham would disagree seriously with the view that Cunningham was of the same company as Nelson. Eisenhower himself, that great judge of competence and character, described Cunningham as 'the Nelsonian Type who believed that ships went to sea in order to find and destroy the enemy. The degree of affection in which he was held by all, both British and American, was nothing short of remarkable.' I put the question to his term-mate of *Britannia* days, Admiral Sir Charles Little, who was kind enough to send me the following reply:

' "Comparisons are odious" and given equal capabilities, success comes with opportunity. Jellicoe was robbed of a second "1st June" by the fact of meeting the High Seas Fleet very late in the day. Beatty was robbed at the Dogger Bank of a great and possibly far-reaching success, by a lucky shot in the *Lion*'s feed water system! Why should not all these we are considering have done as well as Nelson if they had had the conditions and opportunities. I can't see Beatty holding back at Aboukir Bay! All would have adhered to Nelson's saying, "Close with a Frenchman". The Germans were completely demoralised by the Grand Fleet, as we witnessed at the Surrender, our leaders must have credit for this, a situation unique in History.'

It seems appropriate then that all four, Nelson, Jellicoe, Beatty, and Cunningham, are represented in Trafalgar Square, and with them we should remember all those other sailors who had the welfare of their country at heart. This is in keeping with Cunningham's final phrase in *A Sailor's Odyssey*, in which he says: 'To the end of my life, I shall remain convinced that there is no Service or profession to compare with the Royal Navy.'

Finally let us have an assessment of ABC from the two officers who probably knew him best.

The first, a brief one, is from Vice-Admiral Sir H. Geoffrey Norman, KCVO, CB, CBE, who first served with him in the 8th DF at Port Edgar in 1924, and on later occasions. 'He greeted me with "Better the fool you know" when he had me flown out to Cairo as his Additional COS there in the autumn of 1940. I was there for 2½ years and served in Middle East GHQ under 12 Commanders-in-Chief from the three Services, and two Ministers of State – to make the baker's dozen; and in that time met a great number of service and political leaders of course as well, and of them all two stand out – ABC as a sea commander and Archie Wavell as the greatest man I've ever met.

'The Bible refers to "men under authority" but it was a revelation to me to see the mutual trust and understanding between ABC, 'Archie' Wavell, and 'Arthur' Longmore who were the three Cs-in-C to begin with.

'It was at the time of Greece and Crete that ABC and Wavell showed true greatness in adversity, and I saw it closely as I was very much their line of communication. ABC was often criticised for not leaving Alexandria but this period showed the rightness of his decision not to leave the Fleet and move to Cairo.'

The second is from Rear-Admiral Royer Dick, CB, CBE, DSC, who was with him as staff officer, Deputy COS, and finally COS over a period of many years:

'In reading of a man's life and works it is useful if one can visualise the individual. Andrew Cunningham was slightly below medium height, one would not think of him as short, perhaps because of his personality. He had piercing light coloured eyes which gave the impression of boring into you and which were often a barometer of mood for they tended to look red veined in moments of anger or stress. His complexion was highly coloured at all times giving an impression of rude health which was indeed the case. He always moved fast and would take stairs in bounds even late in life when perhaps he should not have been doing so.

'But the enduring impression he gave was of force, of a man intensely alive and brimming with energy and intention. I think however most people will remember that he was smiling and indeed laughing a great deal of the time. I say "a great deal" because no one could look, or be, more formidable and on many occasions at that. He dearly enjoyed what in an old-fashioned term I can only call "ribbing" people. In his homes in Malta and Alexandria he was a splendid host and an evening there was a tonic of gaiety and laughter and he took a childlike pleasure in all sorts of games, push football (to see him playing this in Algiers with men like Eisenhower and Tedder and whatever Admiral happened to be in harbour in the middle of the war was a sight that had to be seen to be believed), table tennis, and many another game. In the out-door world he played a lot of golf and tennis, which he played with the single-hearted determination to win which he showed in his professional life, and was not above foxing his opponents if he could. I never saw him take any interest in bathing. He was fond of and skilful at sailing of course. He was very fond of dogs and whenever possible had them with him. He was also a keen fisherman.

'Although meticulous about uniform he was not at all dressy, indeed rather the opposite and most conservative in what he wore. Entirely decisive in manner and quick in repartee he was apt to be less at home in conference partly because he always said precisely what he meant and was not normally good at discussion. He was also essentially modest and though one hears of his being overbearing this sprang from conviction not arrogance. I never heard him boast at all. He would say so often, "Do you remember when *we* did so and so" or "Why didn't *we* do so and so before", though I have to admit that in the latter case it was often something one had been urging for weeks!

'His method was to raise every possible objection to propositions put forward by his staff in order to make quite sure they really had thought them through and were not just having bright ideas. Once convinced he would take the scheme up with whole-hearted enthusiasm.

'Similarly the first few weeks under his command or on his staff were pretty tricky. Everything you did was apt to be queried and it was quite essential to fight back and show him *why* you had taken some action or other. When satisfied he would nod with no sign of approbation but when you knew him better you knew that meant that all was well. Once however you had passed this baptism of fire his trust became almost embarrassingly complete.

'A remarkable facet was his almost feminine concern if anyone was ill or injured (or of course wounded). So healthy himself he was immensely concerned about others and contrary to what one might expect there was never a glimmer of thought that anyone was taking it easy or making too much of their condition. He was also very tender-hearted, not only in his concern if ships were in trouble when he would sit up much of the night trying to work out further ways of helping them: but also when people did fail he tended to give them much more rope than might be expected and that despite being told that all was not well. You have only to read his book to see this aspect for you will find no word of criticism of those who served him.

'Again he had a strong sense of the beautiful things in nature and a considerable feeling for poetry. He read a lot of books latterly and though through many years did the minimum of writing, produced his autobiography basically on his own, writing daily in longhand; and it was only in the shaping and so forth that he took help. Of his analytical mind and mathematical background one is aware and it was a very big factor in his success.'

Let Tennyson have the last word with his response to Nelson's question, as applicable to-day as it was more than a century ago:

> *Such was he : his work is done*
> *But while the races of mankind endure,*
> *Let his great example stand*
> *Colossal, seen of every land.*
> *And keep the soldier firm, the statesman pure :*
> *Till in all lands and thro' all human story*
> *The path of duty be the way to glory.*

Appendix I. Summary of Events in Cunningham's Life

1883   Andrew Browne Cunningham born in Dublin, 7 January

1897   *Britannia* as NAVAL CADET, 15 January

1898   *Fox* as MIDSHIPMAN, 15 June; and various ships later

1900   With the Naval Brigade (Boer War), February–September

1901   Channel Squadron, 7 January

1902   Training courses ashore

1903   Promoted SUB-LIEUTENANT, 14 March

1904   Promoted LIEUTENANT, 31 March

1908   FIRST COMMAND *TB No. 14*

1911   *Scorpion*, in command, and until January 1918; with service in Home Fleet (1911–13), and Mediterranean (1913–18)

1915   Promoted COMMANDER, 30 June. Awarded DSO for service in the Dardanelles

1918   *Ophelia, Termagant, Swiftsure*

1919   *Seafire*. Awarded Bar to DSO for services in the Dover Patrol

1920   Promoted CAPTAIN, 1 June. Awarded Second Bar to DSO, for services in the Baltic

1922   SOTC. Captain D 6 in *Shakespeare*. Captain D 1 in *Wallace*

1924   Captain in Charge, Port Edgar, October

1926   Flag Captain and CSO to C-in-C AWI in *Calcutta*, May; and in *Despatch* later

1929   IDC. *Rodney*, in command, December. Married to Miss Nona Byatt, 22 December

1931   COMMODORE RNB, Chatham, July

1932   Promoted REAR-ADMIRAL, 24 September

1934   CB. RAD (Med) in *Coventry*; later *Despatch*, and finally *Galatea*

1936   Promoted VICE-ADMIRAL, 22 July

1937   In command BCS (flag in *Hood*), July. Second in command, Med. Fleet

1938   DCNS, September

1939   KCB. C-in-C Mediterranean (as acting ADMIRAL with flag in *Warspite*), June

1940   French Squadron at Alexandria immobilised, 5 July. CALABRIA 9 July, TARANTO 11 November

1941   GCB. Promoted ADMIRAL, 3 January. MATAPAN, 28 March. CRETE, 20 May–1 June. *Barham* sunk 24 November. *Queen Elizabeth* and *Valiant* mined 19 December

1942   BAD Washington (June–October). Created BARONET, June. Appointed ANCXF, November

1943   Promoted ADMIRAL OF THE FLEET, 21 January. RETRIBUTION,

May. HUSKY, July. AVALANCHE, September. Italian surrender, September. Appointed FIRST SEA LORD, October

1945   KT.   PEER OF THE REALM

1946   Raised to the dignity of VISCOUNT. OM. Retires from post of First Sea Lord

1963   Death in London, 12 June, aged 80. Buried at sea

1967   Unveiling and dedication of bust in Trafalgar Square, and plaque in the crypt of St. Paul's Cathedral, London, 2 April

Appendix II. Operation and Conference Code Names

(a) *Britain and Commonwealth Alone* (1940–41)

HATS	Med. Fleet reinforcements	August–September 1940
COAT	Reinforcements prior to Taranto	November 1940
JUDGMENT	FAA attack on Taranto	November 1940
COLLAR	Complex passage of three eastbound fast merchant ships and reinforcements	November 1940
COMPASS	Operation in Western Desert	December 1940
EXCESS	Complex convoy: *Illustrious* badly damaged	January 1941
LUSTRE	British and Commonwealth forces to Greece	March 1941
DEMON	Evacuation from Greece	April 1941
TIGER	Fast convoy with tanks and aircraft for Egypt	May 1941
BATTLEAXE	British counter-offensive in Western Desert	June 1941
SUBSTANCE	Convoy from the west for Malta	July 1941
CRUSADER	British offensive in the desert	November 1941

(b) *Anglo-American* (1941–43)

ARCADIA	Washington Conference	December 1941
BOLERO	Build-up of US forces in United Kingdom	1942 onward
SLEDGE-HAMMER	Proposed cross-Channel emergency landing	1942
ROUNDUP	Proposed large-scale cross-Channel invasion for 1943; (later became OVERLORD in 1944)	1943
GYMNAST	British plan to occupy French North Africa, which developed into Anglo-American SUPER-GYMNAST, and was renamed TORCH	
TORCH	Allied landing in N.W. Africa	November 1942
RETRI-BUTION	'SINK, BURN, DESTROY: let nothing pass'	May 1943
TRIDENT	Washington Conference	May 1943
BRIMSTONE	Allied plan to capture Sardinia	1943
HUSKY	Invasion of Sicily	July 1943
QUADRANT	Quebec Conference	August 1943
BAYTOWN	Invasion of Italy across Messina Straits	3 September 1943
AVALANCHE	Invasion of Italy at Salerno	9 September 1943

GIBBON   Italian Fleet surrender   11 September 1943

(c) *German* (1940–42)

MERKUR   The capture of Crete   May 1941
BARBAROSSA The attack on Russia   June 1941
ATTILA   1940 plan to invade unoccupied France to
           secure French Fleet at Toulon:
                          implemented 27 November 1942

Appendix III. Abbreviations

AA	Anti-aircraft
ACNS	Assistant Chief of the Naval Staff
AOC	Air Officer Commanding
A/S	Anti-submarine
BAD	British Admiralty Delegation
BCS	Battle Cruiser Squadron
BJSM	British Joint Staff Mission
CAS	Chief of the Air Staff
CCO	Chief of Combined Operations
CCS	Combined Chiefs of Staff
CIGS	Chief of the Imperial General Staff
CNS	Chief of the Naval Staff
COS	Chief of Staff; Chiefs of Staff
C-in-C	Commander-in-Chief
COs	Commanding Officers
CSO	Chief Staff Officer
DCNS	Deputy Chief of the Naval Staff
DF	Destroyer Flotilla
DUKW	Amphibious Truck
FAA	Fleet Air Arm
FGO	Fleet Gunnery Officer
FNO	Fleet Navigation Officer
FNC	Fleet Naval Constructor
FTO	Fleet Torpedo Officer
IDC	Imperial Defence College
JIC	Joint Intelligence Committee
JPS	Joint Planning Staff
LCA	Landing Craft Assault
LCP	Landing Craft Personnel
LCM	Landing Craft Mechanical
LCT	Landing Craft Tank
LSH	Landing Ship Headquarters
LSI	Landing Ship Infantry
LST	Landing Ship Tank
MGB	Motor Gun Boat

MTB	Motor Torpedo Boat
MOF	Master of the Fleet
NOIC	Naval Officer in Charge
OOW	Officer of the Watch
RA(D)	Rear-Admiral (Destroyers)
SOIS	Senior Officer Inshore Squadron
SOO	Staff Officer Operations
SOTC	Senior Officers Technical Courses
SOP	Staff Officer Plans
STO	Squadron Torpedo Officer
TB	Torpedo Boat
TBD	Torpedo Boat Destroyer
TSR	Torpedo Spotter Reconnaissance
USAF	US Air Force (originally USAAF: signifying US Army Air Force)
VALF	Vice-Admiral Light Forces
VA(M)	Vice-Admiral (Malta)
VCNS	Vice Chief of the Naval Staff
W/T	Wireless Telegraphy

Chapter References

Chapter 1. A Glimpse of Cunningham

1. Eisenhower speaking to Lieutenant-Commander C. R. Rowe, Secretary to Admiral Sir Gerald Dickens (Flag Officer Tunisia), Naval HQ, Bizerta, 8 June 1943.
2. Letter from Captain R. W. Ravenhill, CBE, DSC, April 1972; i/c H.M.S. *Nubian* at Crete 1941.
3. Letter from Admiral Sir Irvine Glennie, KCB, May 1972; RA(D) Mediterranean at time of Crete.
4. Letter (quoting Tovey) from Admiral Sir Henry McCall, KCVO, KBE, CB, DSO; June 1972; i/c H.M.S. *Dido* at Crete.
5. *The Forgotten Fleet*, J. Winton, p. 58.
6. Letter from Rear-Admiral R. L. Fisher, CB, DSO, OBE, DSC, May 1972.
7. Now C.P.O. Amos West.
8. Letter from Captain J. S. S. Smith, OBE, May 1972; assistant secretary ABC, 1937.
9. As for 4.
10. Letter from Commander H. T. Isaac, OBE, May 1972; Secretary RA(D) Mediterranean, 1934–36.
11. Macmillan, Harold, *The Blast of War*, p. 416.
12. Pack, S. W. C., *Admiral Lord Anson*, p. 159.
13. Letter from Commander J. M. Wilkinson, June 1972; served as Lieutenant (Observer) with ABC in H.M.S. *Galatea*, 1935.
14. Letter from Admiral Angelo Iachino, February 1972; Commander-in-Chief Italian Fleet, 1941–43.
15. Letter from Lord Cunningham, 27 June 1960.
16. Fleet Gunnery Officer in the *Warspite*, 1940–41; later Vice-Admiral Sir Geoffrey Barnard, KCB, CBE, DSO.
17. Letter from Rear-Admiral W. J. Yendell, CB, May 1972.
18. Letter from Admiral Sir Frederick-Dalrymple Hamilton, KCB, June 1972.
19. Letter from General Sir Richard O'Connor, KT, GCB, DSO, June 1972.
20. Letter from Admiral Sir William James, GCB, April 1972.

Chapter 2. Fight You on Sunday: Formative Years (1883–98)

1. Smith, H., *An Admiral Never Forgets*.
2. Pack, S. W. C., *'Britannia' at Dartmouth*, p. 102.
3. Letter from Admiral Sir Charles Little, GCB, GBE, June 1972.
4. Pack, S. W. C., *'Britannia' at Dartmouth*, p. 126.
5. Cork and Orrery, Admiral of the Fleet the Earl of, *My Naval Life*.

Chapter 3. A Taste for Action (1898–1917)

1. Letter from Admiral Sir Charles Little, GCB, June 1972.
2. Pack, S. W. C., *The Battle of Matapan*, p. 35.
3. Cunningham, Lord, *A Sailor's Odyssey*, p. 48.
4. Letter from Admiral Sir Robert Ross Turner, KBE, CB, DSO, April 1972.
5. Pack, S. W. C., *Sea Power in the Mediterranean*, p. 159.
6. Letter from Writer W. Gravenhall, July 1972.
7. Letter from Commander W. M. Phipps-Hornby, RN, April 1972.
8. Letter from Captain F. C. Flynn, RN, June 1972.
9. Cunningham, Lord, *A Sailor's Odyssey*, p. 87.

Chapter 4. Impressionable Days with Keyes and Cowan (1918–19)

1. Letter from Engineer Lieutenant-Commander J. L. Quine, RN.
2. Letter from Admiral Sir Frederick Dalrymple-Hamilton, KCB, April 1972.
3. Letter from ABC to Captain Casper Swinley, DSO, DSC, RN, 11 May 1941.
4. Cunningham, Lord, *A Sailor's Odyssey*, p. 122.
5. Letter from Admiral Sir Charles Little, GCB, GBE, June 1972.
6. Cunningham, Lord, *A Sailor's Odyssey*, p. 101.
7. Letter from Captain F. C. Flynn, RN, June 1972.

Chapter 5. Post Captain (1920–31)

1. Letter from Commander H. T. Isaac, OBE, RN, May 1972; secretary to RA(D) Mediterranean, 1934–36.
2. Letter from Rear-Admiral A. S. Bolt, DSO, DSC*, April 1972; observer in *Warspite*, 1941.
3. Letter from Captain C. L. Keighly-Peach, DSO, OBE, RN, April 1972; SOO to RA(D) Mediterranean, 1935; Commander (F) in *Eagle*, 1939–41.
4. Cunningham, *A Sailor's Odyssey*, p. 115.
5. Letter from Mr. E. J. Freestone, DSM, June 1972; signalman in *Wallace*, 1922–23; Chief Yeoman of Signals in *Warspite*, 1941.
6. Cunningham, *A Sailor's Odyssey*, p. 117.
7. Letter from Commander W. M. Phipps-Hornby, RN, April 1972; S.T.O. to D1 Atlantic Fleet, 1922–23.
8. Letter from Vice-Admiral Sir W. Geoffrey Robson, KBE, CB, DSO*, DSC, 28 March 1973.
9. Appraisal of ABC by Vice-Admiral Sir James Troup, KBE, CB, after ABC's death in 1963.
10. Cunningham, *A Sailor's Odyssey*, pp. 133–6.
11. Cunningham, *A Sailor's Odyssey*, p. 137.
12. Letter from Vice-Admiral Sir Dymock Watson, KCB, CBE, June 1972.
13. Letter from Admiral Sir Geoffrey N. Oliver, GBE, KCB, DSO**, June 1972.
14. Note from Captain F. P. Baker, DSC, RN, December 1972.

Chapter 6. Flag Rank (1932–36)

1. Cunningham, *A Sailor's Odyssey*, p. 151.
2. Letter from Captain the Rev. Geoffrey Gowlland, RN, 15 May 1972.
3. Letter from Admiral Sir Frederick Dalrymple-Hamilton, KCB, 12 April 1972.
4. James, *Admiral Sir William Fisher*, p. 157.
5. James, *Admiral Sir William Fisher*, p. 128.
6. Later Admiral of the Fleet Sir Charles Lambe, GCB, CVO; First Sea Lord 1959–60; see Warner's *Life of Lambe*, p. 53.
7. Letter from Admiral Sir Geoffrey Oliver, GBE, KCB, DSO**, 11 June 1972.
8. Letter from Captain Renfrew Gotto, CBE, DSO*, RN, 14 November 1972.
9. Letter from Commander H. T. Isaac, OBE, RN, 13 May 1972.
10. Letter from Captain C. L. Keighly-Peach, DSO, OBE, RN, 29 April 1972.
11. Letter from Rear-Admiral C. R. L. Parry, CB, DSO, 22 June 1972.
12. Letter from Captain C. S. B. Swinley, DSO, DSC, 24 April 1972.
13. Letter from Commander J. H. Wilkinson, RN, 2 June 1972.
14. Letter from Vice-Admiral J. S. C. Salter, CB, DSO**, OBE, 2 July 1972.
15. Pack, S. W. C., *Sea Power in the Mediterranean*, p. 174.
16. Cunningham, *A Sailor's Odyssey*, p. 651.

Chapter 7. Command of the Battle Cruisers and an Unexpected Spell at Admiralty (1937–39)

1. Letter from Captain J. S. S. Smith, OBE, RN, 5 May 1972.
2. Letter from Vice-Admiral Sir Dymock Watson, KCB, CBE, 20 June 1972.
3. Cunningham, *A Sailor's Odyssey*, p. 190.
4. Letter from Admiral Sir Charles Little, GCB, GBE, 4 June 1972.
5. Cunningham, *A Sailor's Odyssey*, p. 197.
6. Cunningham *A Sailor's Odyssey*, p. 194.
7. Letter from Admiral Sir William James, GCB, 1 March 1968.

Chapter 8. In Command in the Mediterranean (1939–40)

1. Later Captain W. P. Carne, CBE, RN.
2. Cunningham, *A Sailor's Odyssey*, p. 227.
3. Cunningham, *A Sailor's Odyssey*, p. 242.
4. Cunningham, *A Sailor's Odyssey*, pp. 244–56.
5. Letter from Captain W. P. Carne, CBE, RN, April 1972.
6. Cunningham, *A Sailor's Odyssey*, p. 253.
7. Letter from Captain J. S. S. Smith, OBE, RN, 5 May 1972.
8. Cunningham, *A Sailor's Odyssey*, p. 240.

Chapter 9. Seek Out and Destroy (1940)

1. de Belot, R., *The Struggle for the Mediterranean 1939–1945*, p. 68.
2. Letter from Captain C. L. Keighly-Peach, DSO, OBE, 29 April 1972.

3. Cunningham, *A Sailor's Odyssey*, p. 260.
4. Cunningham, *A Sailor's Odyssey*, p. 262.
5. *Italian Navy in World War II*, p. 29.
6. *Italian Navy in World War II*, p. 31.
7. Letter from Captain W. P. Carne, CBE, RN, April 1972.
8. *Italian Navy in World War II*, p. 33.
9. Letter from Rear-Admiral D. M. Lees, CB, DSO, April 1972.
10. Cunningham, Add. MS. 52565.
11. Cunningham, Add. MS. 52560.
12. Marder, A., *Winston is Back*, p. 5.
13. Cunningham, *A Sailor's Odyssey*, p. 279.
14. de Belot, *Struggle for the Mediterranean*, p. 20.
15. Letter from Captain J. S. S. Smith, OBE, RN, 5 May 1972.
16. Cunningham, *A Sailor's Odyssey*, p. 294.
17. Cunningham, Add. MS. 52561.
18. Letter from Dudley Pound to Cunningham, 25 November 1941; Cunningham Add. MS. 52561.
19. Butler, J. R. M., *Grand Strategy*, Vol. III, p. 514.
20. Letter from General Sir Richard O'Connor, KT, GCB, DSO, 14 June 1972.
21. Cunningham, *A Sailor's Odyssey*, p. 300.

Chapter 10. The Luftwaffe Intervenes (January 1941–March 1941)

1. Cunningham, *A Sailor's Odyssey*, p. 305.
2. Roskill, S. W., *Naval Policy between the Wars*, p. 322.
3. Cunningham, Add. MS. 52565.
4. Letter from Commander A. J. McHattie, OBE, DSC, RD, JP, RNR, 12 June 1972.
5. Cunningham, *A Sailor's Odyssey*, p. 359.
6. Ismay, Memoirs, p. 273.
7. Tedder, *With Prejudice*, p. 146.
8. Cunningham, Add. MS. 52561.
9. Letter from Captain J. S. S. Smith, OBE, RN; assistant secretary to C-in-C Mediterranean 1940 to 1942; later secretary to Admiral Sir John Edelsten.
10. Letter from General Sir Richard O'Connor, KT, GCB, DSO, 14 June 1972.
11. Cunningham, *A Sailor's Odyssey*, p. 364.
12. Tedder, *With Prejudice*, p. 47.
13. Tedder, *With Prejudice*, p. 216.
14. Letter from Admiral Sir Wilfrid Woods, GBE, KCB, DSO*, 29 July 1972.
15. Letter from Admiral Sir Guy Grantham, GCB, CBE, DSO, 14 January 1973.

Chapter 11. Matapan (March 1941)

1. Letter from Captain T. M. Brownrigg, CBE, DSO, RN, June 1960.
2. Pack, S. W. C., *The Battle of Matapan*, Appendix IV.

3. Cunningham, *A Sailor's Odyssey*, p. 330.
4. Later Vice-Admiral Sir Geoffrey Barnard, KCB, CBE, DSO*.
5. Lieutenant-Commander J. Lee-Barber (later Rear-Admiral, CB, DSO*).
6. Letter from Admiral Iachino to the author, 5 February 1972.
7. Pack, S. W. C., *The Battle of Matapan* (with five appendices).
8. Pack, S. W. C., *Night Action off Cape Matapan* (with statistical and technical appendices).
9. de Belot, *The Struggle for the Mediterranean*, p. 110.
10. Cunningham, Add. MS. 52569.

Chapter 12. Withdrawal from Greece and Crete (April 1941–May 1941)

1. Tedder, *With Prejudice*, p. 76.
2. Cunningham, *A Sailor's Odyssey*, p. 344.
3. Cunningham, *A Sailor's Odyssey*, p. 347.
4. Warner, Oliver, *Admiral of the Fleet Sir Charles Lambe*, p. 100.
5. Playfair, *Mediterranean and Middle East*, Vol. 2, p. 95.
6. Letter from Rear-Admiral R. L. Fisher, CB, DSO, OBE, DSC, May 1972.
7. Cunningham, Add. MS. 52561.
8. Letter from Captain W. P. Carne, CBE, RN, April 1972.
9. Cunningham, *A Sailor's Odyssey*, p. 363.
10. For fuller naval details see S. W. C. Pack, *The Battle for Crete*, Ian Allan 1973.
11. Cunningham, *A Sailor's Odyssey*, p. 375.
12. Pack, S. W. C., *The Battle for Crete*, p. 52.
13. Hodgkinson, *Turn of the Tide*, p. 141.
14. Hodgkinson, *Turn of the Tide*, p. 142.
15. Cunningham, *A Sailor's Odyssey*, p. 384.
16. Letter from Major Ian Manson, 23rd Battalion, 5 New Zealand Brigade, 27 July 1941.

Chapter 13. The Mediterranean Fleet in Adversity (June 1941–December 1941)

1. Pack, S. W. C., *The Battle for Crete*, p. 65.
2. Letter from Admiral Sir Guy Grantham, GCB, CBE, DSO, 16 January 1973.
3. Letter from Rear-Admiral D. M. Lees, CB, DSO, May 1972.
4. Letter from Admiral Sir Henry McCall, KCVO, KBE, CB, DSO, June 1972.
5. Warner, *Admiral of the Fleet Sir Charles Lambe*, p. 101.
6. Cunningham, Add. MS. 52561.
7. Tedder, *With Prejudice*, p. 113.
8. Cunningham, *A Sailor's Odyssey*, p. 391.
9. Letter from Colonel R. B. Moseley, May 1972.
10. Cunningham, *A Sailor's Odyssey*, p. 402.
11. Cunningham, *A Sailor's Odyssey*, p. 402; and Tedder, p. 116.
12. Cunningham, *A Sailor's Odyssey*, p. 424.

13. Letter from Rear-Admiral W. J. Yendell, CB, May 1972.
14. Letter from the Right Rev. Launcelot Fleming, DD, 18 January 1973.
15. Letter from Rear-Admiral H. M. Creswell, CB, DSO, DSC, to Oliver Warner, 1967.
16. Letter from Admiral Sir Wilfrid Woods, GBE, KCB, DSO*, July 1972.
17. Letter from Rear-Admiral W. J. Munn, CB, DSO, OBE, 17 December 1972.

Chapter 14. In Adversity: Defiance (January 1942–March 1942)

1. Letter from Admiral Sir Guy Grantham, GCB, CBE, DSO, 16 January 1973.
2. Cunningham, *A Sailor's Odyssey*, p. 452.
3. Moseley, Lieutenant-Colonel R. B. (liaison officer at Alexandria N.H.Q.).
4. Pack, S. W. C., *'Britannia' at Dartmouth*, pp. 163–4.
5. Woods, Commander W. J. W., then SOO (later Admiral Sir Wilfred, GBE, KCB, DSO*).
6. McCall, Captain H. (now Admiral Sir Henry, KCVO, KBE, CB, DSO).

Chapter 15. The Combined Chiefs of State, Washington (June 1942–October 1942)

1. Bryant, *Turn of the Tide*, p. 316.
2. Leahy, Fleet Admiral William D., *I Was There*, p. 106.
3. Written by Rear-Admiral R. M. Dick, CB, CBE, DSC, who served ABC closely for several years
4. Letter from Rear-Admiral G. A. Thring, CB, DSO*, April 1972.
5. Ismay, p. 255.
6. Letter from Rear-Admiral R. M. Dick, CB, CBE, DSC, April 1972.
7. Eisenhower, *Crusade in Europe*, p. 99.
8. Letter from Captain J. A. Grindle, CBE, RN, 3 October 1972.
9. Cunningham, Add. MS. 52561.
10. Roskill, Stephen, *The War at Sea*, Vol. I, p. 513.

Chapter 16. Allies Naval Commander North Africa Landings (November 1942–February 1943)

1. For fuller detail see Howard, Michael: *Grand Strategy*, Vol. IV, chapter VII.
2. Letter from Admiral Sir G. N. Oliver, GBE, KCB, DSO**, 11 June 1972.
3. Cunningham, Add. MS. 52570.
4. Cunningham, *A Sailor's Odyssey*, p. 482.
5. Contributed by Mr. J. C. Purser who served throughout the war in the S.S. *Orion*.
6. Liddell Hart, B.H., *History of Second World War*, p. 466.
7. de Belot, R., *The Struggle for the Mediterranean 1939–1945*, p. 191.
8. Cunningham, *A Sailor's Odyssey*, p. 501.
9. As for 2 above.
10. Letter from Surgeon Captain C. B. Nicholson, CBE, RN, 26 July 1972.

11. Letter from Mr. W. Humphries, 8 July 1972.
12. Letter from Constructor Captain I. E. King, CB, CBE, RCNC, 8 November 1972.
13. Howard, Michael: *Grand Strategy*, Vol. IV, pp. 265–6.
14. Tedder, *With Prejudice*, pp. 216, 363–4, 370.
15. Ambrose, *The Supreme Commander*, p. 188.

Chapter 17. Prelude to Victory in the Mediterranean (March 1943–August 1943)

1. Playfair, *The Mediterranean and Middle East*, Vol. IV, pp. 255–7.
2. Pack, S. W. C., *Sea Power in the Mediterranean*, pp. 230–3.
3. Macmillan, *The Blast of War*, pp. 272–3.
4. Letter from Captain J. A. Grindle, CBE, 3 October 1972.
5. Letter from Rear-Admiral Royer Dick, CB, CBE, DSC, 11 October 1972.
6. Roskill, *War at Sea*, Vol. III, Part 1, pp. 107–8.
7. Cunningham, *A Sailor's Odyssey*, p. 529.
8. Liddell Hart, *Second World War*, p. 435.
9. Cunningham, *A Sailor's Odyssey*, p. 536.
10. Morison, *Two-Ocean War*, p. 247.
11. Liddell Hart, *History of Second World War*, p. 445.
12. Roskill, *War at Sea*, Vol. III, Part 1, chapter VI.
13. Letter from Admiral Sir Geoffrey Oliver, GBE, KCB, DSO**, 11 June 1972.
14. Ambrose, *Supreme Commander*, p. 242.

Chapter 18. In Victory: Magnanimity (September 1943)

1. Cunningham, *A Sailor's Odyssey*, p. 562.
2. Letter from Admiral Sir Geoffrey Oliver, GBE, KCB, DSO**, 11 June 1972.
3. Howard, Michael, *Grand Strategy*, Vol. IV, chapter xxvii.
4. Cunningham, *A Sailor's Odyssey*, p. 569.
5. Roskill, *War at Sea*, Vol. III, Part 1, pp. 177–9.
6. de Belot, *Struggle for the Mediterranean*, pp. 227–8.
7. Bragadin, *Italian Navy in World War II*, p. 319.
8. Cunningham, *A Sailor's Odyssey*, p. 563.
9. I am assured by Admiral Royer Dick, who wrote the original signal, that this is the correct version, despite a slightly different version quoted both by Cunningham in *A Sailor's Odyssey* and by Roskill in *The War at Sea*.
10. Letter from Commander J. N. N. Synnott, DSC, RN, 10 July 1972. Navigating officer of *Nelson*, Force H, 1943.
11. Letter from Lieutenant-Colonel F. Palmer Cook, OBE, TD, RE, 12 May 1972.
12. Howard, Michael, *Grand Strategy*, Vol. IV, p. 570.
13. Howard, Michael, *Grand Strategy*, Vol. IV, p. 578.
14. Ismay, *Memoirs*, pp. 316–17.

15. Roskill, *War at Sea*, Vol. III, Part 1, p. 60.
16. Cunningham, *A Sailor's Odyssey*, p. 574.

Chapter 19. Great Sailor

1. Cunningham, Add. MS. 52560.
2. Letter from Admiral Sir Manley Power, KCB, CBE, DSO*, 30 April 1972.
3. Cunningham, *A Sailor's Odyssey*, p. 578.
4. Bryant, A., *Triumph in the West*, p. 56.
5. Letter from Rear-Admiral G. K. Collett, CB, DSC, 21 February 1972.
6. Letter from Admiral Sir Guy Grantham, GCB, CBE, DSO, 16 January 1973.
7. Letter from the Right Reverend Launcelot Fleming, DD, MS, 18 January 1973.
8. Letter from Admiral Sir Wilfrid Woods, GBE, KCB, DSO*, 29 July 1972.
9. Letter to Viscountess Cunningham from Captain Eric Bush, DSO**, DSC, RN, April 1967.
10. Letter to Viscountess Cunningham from Rear-Admiral G. Hector Cresswell, CB, DSO, DSC, April 1967.
11. Letter to Viscountess Cunningham from Field-Marshal the Earl Alexander of Tunis, April 1967.

Bibliography

Official Histories of the Second World War

Butler, J. R. M., *Grand Strategy*, Vol. II, HMSO.
Butler, J. R. M. and Gwyer, J. M. A., *Grand Strategy*, Vol. III, HMSO.
Howard, M., *Grand Strategy*, Vol. IV, HMSO.
Morison, Rear-Admiral S. E., *History of US Naval Operations*, Vol. IX, Little, Brown.
Playfair, I. S. O., *The Mediterranean and Middle East*, Vols I, II, III, IV, HMSO.
Roskill, Captain S. W., *The War at Sea*, Vols I, II, III, HMSO.

Other Published Works

Ambrose, S. E., *The Supreme Commander*, Cassell.
Bennett, G., *Naval Battles of the First World War*, Batsford.
Bradley, General O. N., *A Soldier's Story*, Eyre & Spottiswoode.
Bragadin, Commander Marc, *The Italian Navy in World War II*, United States Naval Institute.
Bryant, A., *The Turn of the Tide*, Collins.
Bryant, A., *Triumph in the West*, Collins.
Cunningham, Admiral of the Fleet Viscount, *A Sailor's Odyssey*, Hutchinson.
de Belot, Rear-Admiral R., *The Struggle for the Mediterranean*, Princeton University Press.
Eisenhower, General D. D., *Crusade in Europe*, Heinemann.
Fraccaroli, A., *Italian Warships of World War II*, Ian Allan.
Hart, Captain B. H. Liddell, *History of the Second World War*, Cassell.
Hodgkinson, Lieutenant-Commander H., *Before the Tide Turned*, Harrap.
Ismay, Lord, *Memories*, Heinemann.
James, Admiral Sir William, *Admiral Sir William Fisher*, Macmillan.
Jackson, W. G. F., *Alexander of Tunis as Military Commander*, Batsford.
Kemp, Lieutenant-Commander P. K., *H.M. Destroyers*, Herbert Jenkins.
King, Ernest and Whitehill, W. M., *Fleet Admiral King*, Eyre & Spottiswoode.
Langmaid, Commander K., *The Blind Eye*, Jarrold.
Leahy, Fleet Admiral William D., *I Was There*.
Lenton, H. T. and Colledge, J. J., *Warships of World War II*, Ian Allan.
Lewin, R., *Montgomery as Military Commander*, Batsford.
Lewin, R., *Rommel as Military Commander*, Batsford.
Macmillan, H., *The Blast of War*, Macmillan.
Marder, A. J., *From the Dreadnought to Scapa Flow*, O.U.P.
Marder, A. J., *Winston is Back. Churchill at the Admiralty* 1939–40, Longmans.
Morison, Rear-Admiral S. E., *The Two Ocean War*, Little, Brown.

Macintyre, Donald, *The Battle for the Mediterranean*, Batsford.
Macintyre, Donald, *The Naval War against Hitler*, Batsford.
Macintyre, Donald, *Fighting Admiral (Life of Somerville)*, Evans.
Pack, S. W. C., *Admiral Lord Anson*, Cassell.
Pack, S. W. C., *Britannia at Dartmouth*, Redman.
Pack, S. W. C., *The Battle of Matapan*, Batsford.
Pack, S. W. C., *The Battle for Crete*, Ian Allan.
Pack, S. W. C., *Sea Power in the Mediterranean*, Arthur Barker.
Roskill, S. W., *The Navy at War*, Collins.
Roskill, S. W., *Naval Policy between the Wars*, Vol. I, Collins.
Schofield, B. B., *British Sea Power* (Naval Policy in the Twentieth Century), Batsford.
Sixsmith, E. K. G., *Eisenhower as Military Commander*, Batsford.
Tedder, Lord, *With Prejudice*, Cassell.
Vian, Admiral of the Fleet Sir Philip, *Action This Day*, Muller.
Warner, Oliver, *Cunningham of Hyndhope*, John Murray.
Warner, Oliver, *Admiral of the Fleet Sir Charles Lambe*, Sidgwick & Jackson.
Winton, J., *The Forgotten Fleet*, Michael Joseph.

Index